THE EYES OF FAITH

THE EYES OF FAITH

The Sense of the Faithful & the Church's Reception of Revelation

ORMOND RUSH

The Catholic University of America Press ❧ *Washington, D.C.*

LIBRARY OF CONGRESS CATALOGING-IN-PUBLICATION DATA

Rush, Ormond, 1950–

The eyes of faith : the sense of the faithful and the church's reception of
revelation / Ormond Rush.

p. cm.

Includes bibliographical references (p.   ) and index.

ISBN 978-0-8132-1571-6 (cloth : alk. paper)   1. Sensus fidelium.

2. Catholic Church—Doctrines.   I. Title.

BX1746.R87 2009

231'.042—dc22   2008045952

How will it be when none more saith, "I saw"?

Robert Browning, "A Death in the Desert"

Contents

Acknowledgments

I began research for this book during a six-month sabbatical in 2004. In that time, and over the following two years, I had the opportunity to dialogue about the *sensus fidelium* with biblical scholars and theologians, some of whom have read part or all of this text in various stages of development. Their conversations and written feedback have been invaluable.

My heartfelt gratitude is therefore due to Wolfgang Beinert, François Bovon, Brendan Byrne, Mary Coloe, Francis Schüssler Fiorenza, Tony Kelly, Francis Moloney, Gerald O'Collins, Salvador Pié-Ninot, Michael Putney, David Rankin, Tom Ryan, John Thornhill, Dario Vitali, Jared Wicks, and in particular Richard Lennan, who has read and commented on the manuscript at all stages. Their academic hospitality, support, and critique have deepened my appreciation of the dialogic nature of ecclesial theological scholarship. Any remaining weaknesses in the book, of course, are mine, but any strengths are due in no small measure to the honest critique I have received. My gratitude also goes out to the faculty and staff of my home academic institution, St. Paul's Theological College within the Brisbane College of Theology, for their friendship and support.

I am grateful to the editor of *Theological Studies* for permission to reproduce as chapter 8 a revised version of an article, "*Sensus Fidei:* Faith 'Making Sense' of Revelation," published in that journal in 2001. For that article, I was greatly helped by several readers whose comments on the draft helped refine and clarify my argument—in addition to some of the above, Bradford Hinze and Richard Gaillardetz. The comments and suggestions of the two reviewers for the Catholic University of America

Press have been invaluable, as have been the encouragement and professional assistance of Jim Kruggel, Theresa Walker, and Ellen Coughlin.

During my sabbatical, I was offered generous hospitality and the opportunity to research and write. I would like to mention in particular Fr. Bill Williams of the parish of Hull, Massachusetts; Msgr. Dennis Sheehan and the priests of the St. Paul Rectory, Cambridge, Massachusetts; and, for a sabbatical place of rest to write by the sea, Paula and Jim Gardiner.

I would like to express gratitude to my family for their love and support always. I dedicate this book to my parents, John and Bernadette Rush, who passed on to me the faith of the church and who, in their own way, taught me to see with the eyes of faith.

Feast of Pentecost, 2007

Abbreviations

Documents of the Second Vatican Council

AA   *Apostolicam Actuositatem:* Decree on the Apostolate of the Laity

AG   *Ad Gentes:* Decree on the Missionary Activity of the Church

DV   *Dei Verbum:* Dogmatic Constitution on Divine Revelation

GS   *Gaudium et Spes:* Pastoral Constitution on the Church in the World of Today

LG   *Lumen Gentium:* Dogmatic Constitution on the Church

PO   *Presbyterorum Ordinis:* Decree on the Ministry and Life of Priests

SC   *Sacrosanctum Concilium:* Constitution on the Sacred Liturgy

UR   *Unitatis Redintegratio:* Decree on Ecumenism

Other Sources

AAS   *Acta Apostolicae Sedis*

DS   Henry Denzinger and Adolf Schönmetzer, eds. *Enchiridion Symbolorum: Definitionum et Declarationum de Rebus Fidei et Morum,* 37th edition

PL   J. B. Migne, ed. *Patrologiae Cursus Completus, Series Latina*

ST   Thomas Aquinas, *Summa Theologica*

THE EYES OF FAITH

Introduction

The origins of the *sensus fidelium* lie in the origins of the church. The first disciples' encounters with Jesus begin a process of interpreting his teaching, his actions, and his identity, but there is nevertheless a certain misunderstanding of him during his pre-Easter ministry. However, after his death and resurrection, and with the coming of the Holy Spirit, full Christian faith in him begins. Now, from the new perspective of Easter, and with a sense of being guided in their understanding and interpretation by a special gift from the Holy Spirit, the believing disciples of the Crucified and Risen One continue to "make sense" of their faith in him, not only for their own sake, but especially for the sake of inviting others to experience the salvation they have known through him, for this is their mission. The writings of the New Testament are a product of this interpretative process.

In later ecclesial reflection, the Spirit's gift for understanding and interpreting revelation, given to the whole church at Pentecost, comes to be named retrospectively as "the faithful's sense of the faith" *(sensus fidei fidelium)*.[1] Without using the actual term, the New Testament witnesses

1. "Unfortunately there is no historical monograph which would describe the evolution of the concept of *sensus fidei*. The reality of that *sensus fidei* was already present in the consciousness of the Church before the expression of it was forged." Hervé Legrand, "Reception, *Sensus Fidelium*, and Synodal Life: An Effort at Articulation," in *Reception and Communion Among Churches,* eds. Legrand, Julio Manzanares, and Antonio García y García (Washington: The Catholic University of America Press, 1997), 417. For surveys of the history of the notion, see William M. Thompson, "Sensus Fidelium and Infallibility," *American Ecclesiastical Review* 167 (1973): 450–86; Josef Steinruck, "Was die Gläubigen in der Geschichte der Kirche zu vermelden hatten," in *Mitsprache im Glauben? Vom Glaubenssinn der Gläubigen,* ed. Günther Koch (Würzburg: Echter, 1993), 25–50; Wolfgang Beinert, "Der Glaubenssinn der Gläubigen in Theologie- und Dogmengeschichte: Ein Überblick,"

to this ecclesial gift in which all individual believers participate and which enables the whole church to receive and to transmit the faith effectively and faithfully into new cultures and contexts.[2] Fundamentally, this *sensus fidelium* is "a basic means of understanding the faith and as such exercises a truth-finding and truth-attesting function that has as its special characteristic that it takes into account the faithful's experience in the world."[3] The ecclesial activity of interpreting the Christ event thus goes to the very heart of the church's nature and mission. The *sensus fidelium* is an ecclesiological reality, because it assures epistemological continuity in the church's reception of revelation throughout history.[4] It enables the church to proclaim the Gospel in new times and cultures throughout history.

After the New Testament period, various synonyms soon come to be used to name this ecclesial capacity for faithfully interpreting revelation.[5] In line with similar biblical expressions, one finds in the patristic writings reference to an organ for perceiving the faith, with expressions such as "the eyes of the heart," "the eyes of the spirit," and "the eyes of faith."[6] Augustine asserts: "After all, faith has its eyes."[7] Aquinas later talks of "the

---

in *Der Glaubenssinn des Gottesvolkes: Konkurrent oder Partner des Lehramts?* ed. Dietrich Wiederkehr, Questiones Disputatae 151 (Freiburg: Herder, 1994), 66–131; Daniel J. Finucane, *Sensus Fidelium: The Use of a Concept in the Post–Vatican II Era* (San Francisco: International Scholars, 1996), 66–131.

2. For an overview of the New Testament witness to this reality in the individual and community specifically in terms of *sensus fidei*, see Walter Kirchschläger, "Was das Neue Testament über den Glaubenssinn der Gläubigen sagt," in Koch, ed., *Mitsprache im Glauben? Vom Glaubenssinn der Gläubigen*, 7–24.

3. Wolfgang Beinert, "Sensus Fidelium," in *Handbook of Catholic Theology,* ed. Wolfgang Beinert and Francis Schüssler Fiorenza (New York: Crossroad, 1995), 655–57, at 656.

4. I deliberately employ the phrase "ecclesiological reality" in imitation of the title in Yves Congar, "Reception as an Ecclesiological Reality," *Concilium* 77 (1972): 43–68. The original article is to be found in Yves Congar, "La 'Réception' comme réalité ecclésiologique," *Revue des Sciences Philosophiques et Théologiques* 56 (1972): 369–402. Both the notion of "*ecclesial* reality" (a real factor at work in the life of the church) and the notion of "*ecclesiological* reality" (a real factor needing to be made explicit in any systematic ecclesiology) are intended by Congar. I too intend both senses of the term. Congar's article highlights the ecclesial reality in terms of a dynamic of reception or exchange between local churches in the early centuries of the church, such as exchange of scriptural works, liturgical practices, synodal letters, etc.

5. A range of similar phrases can be found, e.g., *universus ecclesiae sensus, sensus christianus, catholicus intellectus, communis fidei conscientia.* For an overview, see Beinert, "Der Glaubenssinn der Gläubigen in Theologie- und Dogmengeschichte," 71.

6. For these and the references below, I am dependent on the survey in Salvador Pié-Ninot, "*Sensus Fidei,*" in *Dictionary of Fundamental Theology,* ed. René Latourelle and Rino Fisichella (Middlegreen, Slough, England: St. Paul, 1994), 992–95, at 993.

7. "Habet namque fides oculos suos." *Epist.* 120.2.8 [PL 33:458].

light of faith"[8] and of "a faith endowed with eyes."[9] In the sixteenth century, Melchior Cano lists "the common consent of the faithful" as a source of theological knowing.[10] In the nineteenth century, discussion of the notion of the *sensus fidelium* becomes more explicit in the writings of theologians and canon lawyers.[11] These studies are in part stimulated by the process leading up to and after the promulgation in 1854 of the Marian dogma of the Immaculate Conception, during which the importance of the sense of the faithful is cited as a warrant for the promulgations.[12] In 1910, retrieving and developing Aquinas's notion of "the light of faith" and "a faith endowed with eyes," Pierre Rousselot publishes a seminal article, "The Eyes of Faith," without however speaking specifically of the *sensus fidei*.[13] Reflection on the theme continues up till the eve of Vatican II, particularly in the light of the Marian dogma promulgated in 1950.[14]

Vatican II retrieves this long-held belief regarding the reality of the

---

8. "Through the light of faith, they see that these things are to be believed." *ST,* 2-2, q. 1, a. 5, ad 1.

9. *ST,* 3, q. 55, a. 2, ad 1.

10. *De locis theologicis* 3.3.

11. For detailed discussion of the approaches of thinkers such as Johann Adam Möhler, Ferdinand Walter, George Phillips, Matthias Scheeben, John Henry Newman, Giovanni Perrone, Carlo Passaglia, Johannes Baptist Franzelin, and others, see Robert W. Schmucker, *Sensus Fidei: Der Glaubenssinn in seiner vorkonziliaren Entwicklungsgeschichte und in den Dokumenten des Zweiten Vatikanischen Konzils* (Regensburg: Roderer Verlag, 1998), 19–76; Christoph Ohly, *Sensus Fidei Fidelium: Zur Einordung des Glaubenssinnes aller Gläubigen in die Communio-struktur der Kirche im geschichtlichen Spiegel dogmatisch-kanonistischer Erkenntnisse und der Aussagen des II. Vaticanum* (St. Ottilien: EOS Verlag, 1999), 42–172; Marko Miserda, *Subjektivität im Glauben: Eine theologisch-methodologische Untersuchung zur Diskussion über den "Glaubens-Sinn" in der katholischen Theologie des 19. Jahrhunderts* (Frankfurt am Main: P. Lang, 1996).

12. For one survey of the discussion, see James L. Heft, "'Sensus Fidelium' and the Marian Dogmas," *One in Christ* 28 (1992): 106–25.

13. The article is published in English as Pierre Rousselot, *The Eyes of Faith,* ed. John M. McDermott and Avery Dulles (New York: Fordham University Press, 1990). Commenting on the significance of Rousselot for contemporary theologies of faith, Dulles writes: "For Rousselot the light of faith is something by which we see, not something seen. It is, in Scholastic terminology, an *obiectum quo,* not an *obiectum quod.* It gives us the 'eyes of faith.' . . . He deserves credit for reviving the doctrine of Thomas Aquinas that the grace of faith is a light—an active power of discernment—given to the mind by God, and that it instills in the soul a vital connaturality with the things of God. Rousselot's theory, better than most others, gives intelligibility to the strong affirmations of Orange II regarding the impossibility of advancing toward faith without the help of grace. It also brings into Scholastic theology the insights of Newman regarding the logic of convergence." Avery Dulles, *The Assurance of Things Hoped For: A Theology of Christian Faith* (New York: Oxford University Press, 1994), 111.

14. For a general survey of literature treating the period from Vatican I to the eve of Vatican II, see Finucane, *Sensus Fidelium,* 173–209.

sensus fidei in the faithful, but recontextualizes the teaching by treating it within its discussion of the whole People of God's participation in the "prophetic office" of the church.[15] In *Lumen Gentium* 12, the council teaches that the whole People of God possesses, as a gift which is "aroused and sustained by the Spirit of truth," a capacity for faithfully receiving the Word of God.[16] This capacity ensures infallibility "in believing" and enables the People of God, with the guidance of the magisterium, to adhere to, penetrate, and apply the faith in daily life. The council calls this capacity "the supernatural sense of the faith of the whole people," *supernaturalis sensus fidei totius populi* (often referred to as *sensus fidei fidelium,* or simply *sensus fidelium*). It is of a different order to the diverse charisms or gifts which the Spirit bestows freely, and which *Lumen Gentium* 12b goes on to address in the paragraph after its treatment of the *sensus fidei*. The *sensus fidei* is given to all baptized believers within the gift of faith itself; special charisms are given diversely to different individuals.

Since Vatican II, there has been significant reflection by theologians on Vatican II's teaching. In a series of survey articles, John Burkhard has summarized the major international literature where theologians continue to develop the notion.[17] Some of these writers narrowly focus on particular aspects of the *sensus fidelium;* others provide more systematic, comprehensive, and integrative proposals in order to advance the debate.

15. For details of the conciliar drafting and debate regarding *LG,* 12a, specifically in reference to the *sensus fidei,* see Schmucker, *Sensus Fidei,* 120–219; Ohly, *Sensus Fidei Fidelium,* 173–272.

16. *LG,* 12a: "The holy people of God has a share, too, in the prophetic office of Christ, when it renders him a living witness, especially through a life of faith and charity, and when it offers to God a sacrifice of praise, the tribute of lips that honour his name. The universal body of the faithful who have received the anointing of the holy one, cannot be mistaken in belief. It displays this particular quality through a supernatural sense of the faith in the whole people when 'from the bishops to the last of the faithful laity,' it expresses the consent of all in matters of faith and morals. Through this sense of the faith which is aroused and sustained by the Spirit of truth, the people of God, under the guidance of the sacred magisterium to which it is faithfully obedient, receives no longer the words of human beings but truly the word of God; it adheres indefectibly to 'the faith which was once for all delivered to the saints'; it penetrates more deeply into that same faith through right judgment and applies it more fully to life." Tanner translation.

17. See John Burkhard, "*Sensus Fidei:* Theological Reflection Since Vatican II. Part I: 1965–1984," *Heythrop Journal* 34 (1993): 41–59; John Burkhard, "*Sensus Fidei:* Theological Reflection Since Vatican II. Part II: 1985–1989," *Heythrop Journal* 34 (1993): 123–36; John J. Burkhard, "*Sensus Fidei:* Recent Theological Reflection (1990–2001). Part I," *Heythrop Journal* 46 (2005): 450–75; John J. Burkhard, "*Sensus Fidei:* Recent Theological Reflection (1990–2001). Part II," *Heythrop Journal* 47 (2006): 38–54. See also the extensive survey and evaluation of post–Vatican II scholarship up to 1996 in Finucane, *Sensus Fidelium,* 253–491.

Among the latter, one writer in particular, Wolfgang Beinert, integrates his notion of the *sensus fidelium* into a wider theological epistemology and ecclesiology.[18]

In what follows, I attempt to build on and advance the work of those theologians by proposing a hermeneutical approach to a systematic theology of the *sensus fidelium,* grounded on explicitly interrelated theologies of the Trinity, revelation, faith, the church, and the teaching office of the church. In particular, this proposal highlights the operation of the Holy Spirit in the *sensus fidelium* and presents a coherent way of conceiving the interrelationship between the *sensus fidelium,* tradition, Scripture, theology, and the magisterium in the church's ongoing reception of revelation through faith.

I will use the terms *sensus fidei* and *sensus fidelium* in particular ways. *Lumen Gentium* 12 uses the term *supernaturalis sensus fidei totius populi,* "the supernatural sense of the faith of the whole people." I will refer to that corporate ecclesial sense as the *sensus fidei fidelium,* "the sense of the faith of the faithful," or more briefly the *sensus fidelium,* "the sense of the faithful." For the sense of the faith of an individual believer, I will use the term *sensus fidei fidelis.* When I use the term *sensus fidei,* context will determine its reference either to the individual or to the community, or to both.

In my proposal, I employ the category of "reception" both for enunciating an integrating (or structuring) principle for a comprehensive systematic theology of the *sensus fidelium,* and for enunciating an investigative principle used in the interpretation of sources and the methodological procedures of that theology.

The *integrating* or *structuring principle* for any systematic theology is the overarching category that a theologian might choose in order to give systematic unity and coherence to his or her treatment of the whole range of theological doctrines such as revelation, faith, creation, theological anthropology, Christology, pneumatology, Trinity, grace, church, sacraments, eschatology, etc.[19] Another way of describing an integrating

18. For example, see Wolfgang Beinert, "Theologische Erkenntnislehre," in *Glaubenszugänge: Lehrbuch der Katholischen Dogmatik,* vol. 1, ed. Wolfgang Beinert, (Paderborn: Ferdinand Schöningh, 1995), 47–197; Wolfgang Beinert, *Kann man dem Glauben trauen? Grundlagen theologischer Erkenntnis* (Regensburg: Verlag Friedrich Pustet, 2004). For some of his other works on the *sensus fidelium,* see the surveys by Burkhard above.

19. On the notions of integrating and investigative principles, see John Thornhill, *Christian*

principle is to see it as a "root metaphor" for the systematic theological task.[20] A systematic theology, of course, need not necessarily employ such an overarching metaphor or category. Indeed, the choice of a single integrating principle can be limiting of the full reality of Christian faith, and force a systematic presentation of that faith into the fixed category of the selected principle. However, despite that danger, an integrating principle may also prove to be *a heuristic principle that opens up new ways of understanding the Christian faith not previously appreciated.*

The category of "reception," I believe, provides such a root metaphor which could be consistently employed as the overarching principle for enunciating a whole range of theological themes, and which, I hope to show, proves to be a heuristic principle that does open up new ways of understanding the Christian faith not previously appreciated. Since, as we shall see in chapter 1, the dynamic of reception is so fundamental to Christian revelation, "reception" can be legitimately employed as an "architectonic principle" with which all themes of theology can be approached. From theological anthropology to eschatology, the category of "reception" can provide a framework that is consonant with the structure of the revelatory process itself. For example, Joseph Komonchak, in writing of the need for a theological anthropology based on the notion of reception, claims that "what is needed is a *theological* anthropology, not one elaborated on the basis of *a priori* philosophical or scientific criteria. It must be an anthropology of the reception of the Christian gospel."[21] Closely related to such a revised theological anthropology is a corresponding theological epistemology (a theology of how we come to know and understand God), itself related to theologies of revelation and

---

Mystery in the Secular Age: The Foundation and Task of Theology (Westminster, Md.: Christian Classics, 1991), 139–42. Thornhill is here employing the framework of Battista Mondin, "Legitimacy and Limits of Theological Pluralism," *L'Osservatore Romano* (April 6, 1978): 6.

20. See John McIntyre, *Faith, Theology and Imagination* (Edinburgh: The Handsel Press, 1987), 129, where he writes on root metaphors and models: "A person selects one area of his life and tries to comprehend the rest of his life by reference to it." He later speaks of such a model/ root metaphor as an "integrating principle." Ibid., 147. According to McIntyre, "most, if not all, theologians of stature employ models in theological construction; and their brilliance lies in the choice of the most comprehensive, comprehensible and extensible model, as well as in the illumination which the employment of the model and the doctrines consequent upon it throw upon the major themes of theology." Ibid., 147–48.

21. Joseph A. Komonchak, "Defending Our Hope: On the Fundamental Tasks of Theology," in *Faithful Witness: Foundations of Theology for Today's Church,* ed. Leo J. O'Donovan and T. Howland Sanks (New York: Crossroad, 1989), 14–26, at 20.

faith. John Burkhard, in lamenting the lack of integration into church life of Vatican II's teaching on *sensus fidelium,* has rightly warned that such an integration will not take place until there is a coherent theology of revelation and faith, according to the teaching of Vatican II:

> Many in the Church still see [the categories of revelation and faith] in highly intel-lectualised and propositional terms. Theologians will need to continue to dedicate their efforts at expressing an epistemology which responds far better to the richness of truth and to the mutuality of basic human acts of knowing, willing, loving and feeling. It will not be easy to regain a unified understanding of the person, but until we do we will not have a satisfactory understanding of revelation and faith either.[22]

In this book I propose, not only a theology of revelation and of faith, but in particular a theology of a "sense of the faith."

The *investigative principle* employed by a systematic theologian guides the particular hermeneutics and method that the theologian employs in the interpretation of revelation. An investigative principle is at work not only in the theologian's interpretation of events, texts, symbols, and prac-tices from the past, but in his or her interpretation of all dimensions of Christian experience in the present. A theology's investigative principle should provide an interpretative theory and a methodological approach which is the most appropriate for its subject matter, ultimately the Tri-une God. As Paul Tillich stated with regard to his own method of "cor-relation," so too one could say with regard to "reception": "the method is an element of the reality itself."[23] Tillich in his own work moves from the affirmation that "the divine-human relation is a correlation,"[24] to the proposal that a method of correlation is the most appropriate method for Christian theology. Use in theology of a hermeneutics and a method ar-ticulated from the perspective of reception finds its theological justifica-tion in the reality of God as three persons in mutual *communio* and *recep-tio,* as will be shown in chapter 1. Employing the investigative principle of "reception," this book will therefore propose that the most appropriate hermeneutics for the interpretation of revelation is a reception herme-neutics, and the most appropriate theological methodology is a reception methodology, as will be progressively outlined in chapters 3, 7, and 9.

22. John Burkhard, "*Sensus fidei:* Meaning, Role and Future of a Teaching of Vatican II," *Lou-vain Studies* 17 (1992): 18–34, at 32.

23. Paul Tillich, *Systematic Theology,* Vol. 1: *Reason and Revelation; Being and God* (Chicago: University of Chicago Press, 1951), 1:60.

24. Ibid., 1:61.

Throughout the book I use the word "reception" in at least nine senses, emerging from its employment as both an integrating and an investigative principle, with its consequent reception hermeneutics and reception methodology. These different usages at times parallel the variety of ways in which the term "reception" is used in the current philosophical, aesthetic, literary, biblical, theological, historical, canonical, and ecumenical literature. These nine uses name different aspects of "the reception of revelation."

Firstly, "reception" is used as a root metaphor which captures a fundamental dimension of human relationships, communication, interaction, and learning. Love is not a relationship unless the gift of love is mutually received; a gift offered is not truly given until it is received. Likewise, communication is realized only in its reception; a message sent is not truly communicated until it is received, at least through being understood. Genuine human interaction, likewise, requires mutuality of encounter and engagement; the language of reception here highlights human attitudes of openness to the other in dialogue and the spirit of hospitality in reception of the other as guest. Human learning, similarly, occurs when one's horizons of understanding are widened through encounter with something new or unfamiliar; the language of reception here captures the growth and learning that takes place when one makes one's own another reality, such as a new viewpoint. In this general sense, in all these aspects of human experience, we could say with St. Paul: what do we have that we have not first received.[25] All is gift; all is grace.

Secondly, there is "spiritual reception."[26] When the above broad sense of reception (as a dynamic in human relationships, communication, interaction, and learning) is used of religious experience and the divine-human relationship, "reception of revelation" is equivalent to "faith," in the sense of both a personal response to and appropriation of God's salvific self-communication through Jesus Christ in the Spirit (*fides qua*

---

25. 1 Cor 4:7.

26. In this and the following two senses, I am employing Alois Grillmeier's three categories of "spiritual," "legal/kerygmatic," and "theological" reception. See Alois Grillmeier, "The Reception of Church Councils," in *Foundations of Theology*, ed. Philip McShane (Dublin: Gill and Macmillan, 1971), 102–14; Alois Grillmeier, "The Reception of Chalcedon in the Roman Catholic Church," *Ecumenical Review* 22 (1970): 383–411; Alois Grillmeier, *Christ in Christian Tradition. Volume Two: From the Council of Chalcedon (451) to Gregory the Great (590–604). Part One: Reception and Contradiction: The Development of the Discussion about Chalcedon from 451 to the Beginning of the Reign of Justinian* (Atlanta: John Knox Press, 1987), esp. 6–10.

creditur), and the believer's assent to the content communicated within God's personal self-revelation, proposed by the church as beliefs *(fides quae creditur).* Accordingly, therefore, the term "spiritual reception" in this book will refer to both the personal appropriation of revelation and the assent to the content of "the faith" by believers, as they attempt to adhere to, penetrate, and apply it in their daily lives *(LG,* 12).

Thirdly, there is "juridical reception," understood as the canonically required assent to a teaching by the magisterium.[27] This element overlaps with spiritual reception, but needs to be distinguished. It relates to the different grades of authoritative teaching by the magisterium, and the consequent grades in response required of the individual believer. Deliberate lack of juridical reception is dissent.

Fourthly, the term "theological reception" will refer to the way theologians and scholars in related disciplines help their ecclesial communities to deepen their understanding of what has been handed down in Scripture and tradition, in the light of the particular contexts and experience of their local communities. A theologian's attention to contemporary context and experience includes attention to the many "spiritual receptions" and "juridical receptions" (or otherwise) of individuals within those communities. It is the task of theology to present the Christian vision and its implications in the light of contemporary Christians' experience of salvific revelation, i.e., their spiritual receptions. In chapters 7 and 9, we will examine this ecclesial role of "theological reception."

Fifthly, the term "approbative reception" will refer to the process of evaluation by the whole church in judging whether particular spiritual, juridical, or theological receptions are faithful to revelation. This will be especially relevant when we examine the dynamic between the individual and the community, between a *sensus fidei fidelis* and the *sensus fidei fidelium,* between charism and institution, and between the *sensus fidelium,* theology, and the magisterium. When the ecclesial approbative reception process arrives at a formal judgment by the hierarchical teaching authority, the magisterium, in dialogue with theologians and the *sensus fidelium,* I will refer to that approbative reception as a *consensus fidelium.*

Sixthly, the appropriation by a writer of another literary work into their own new work will be termed "literary reception." The history of

---

27. According to Grillmeier, "legal" or "kerygmatic" reception refers to the appropriate response to teachings which are "officially promulgated by ecclesiastical authority." Grillmeier, "The Reception of Chalcedon," 386.

literature displays the phenomenon of writers incorporating past genres, themes, types, and particular texts into their new works as they address new questions and experiences in new social and cultural contexts. This phenomenon of literary reception will be relevant when we examine phenomena such as the literary reception by New Testament writers of the Septuagint, the literary reception of Mark's Gospel by Luke and Matthew, or the literary reception of theological and spiritual "classics" throughout the tradition of the church.

Seventhly, the term "intra-ecclesial reception" will refer to the exchange dynamic between Christian communities, and the acceptance (or non-acceptance) from other churches in communion of documents, conciliar decisions, creeds, or practices relevant to the life of faith in the early church (so-called "classical reception"),[28] and throughout the history of the church. When referring to this dynamic after the division between the East and the West and after the Reformation, the term "intra-ecclesial reception" will refer specifically to such exchanges between local churches in the Roman Catholic communion. That includes not only reception among the local churches of the Latin Rite, but also between the churches of the other rites and the Latin Rite.

Eighthly, the synonymous terms "ecumenical reception" and "inter-ecclesial reception" will refer to exchange between separated churches and ecclesial communities in the present situation of a divided Christianity. This dynamic of learning between separated churches and ecclesial communities has come to be termed "receptive ecumenism." After hundreds of years of separation those churches are coming to recognize that some of the ways of being Christian which have developed independently during those centuries can now be judged to have been authentic receptions of the apostolic tradition. The process and final documents of ecumenical dialogue are the fruit of such receptive ecumenism. The terms "ecumenical reception" or "inter-ecclesial reception" are, however, sometimes used in two narrower senses, referring either to a formal endorsement of and ecclesial

28. The strict definition of Yves Congar here applies: "the process by means of which a church (body) truly takes over as its own a resolution that it did not originate in regard to itself, and acknowledges the measure it promulgates as a rule applicable to its own life . . . it includes a degree of consent, and possibly of judgment, in which the life of a body is expressed which brings into play its own original resources." Congar, "Reception as an Ecclesiological Reality," 45. Common usage of the phrase "classical reception" to refer to this early church dynamic seemingly can be attributed to its first use by John Zizioulas, "The Theological Problem of 'Reception,'" *Centro Pro Unione Bulletin* 26 (1984): 3–6.

appropriation by a church of a document resulting from ecumenical dialogue with another or other churches (itself a form of approbative reception), or to the act of formally entering into full communion with a previously separated church. In fact, it has been research into "intra-ecclesial reception" in the first millennium, before the divisions between East and West and the Reformation, that has brought to the fore the significance of the whole category of reception for "inter-ecclesial reception."

Finally, the word "reception" will be used more often in a general hermeneutical sense, as a synonym for the interrelated moments of "understanding," "interpretation," "application." In this sense, "hermeneutical reception" refers to the interpretative process at the heart of revelatory experience, and the expressions of faith that emerge within that experience. The medieval scholastic axiom captures this notion of reception: *quidquid recipitur ad modum recipientis recipitur* (that which is received is received in the mode of the receiver). Hermeneutical reception, we will see, is the process of faith seeking understanding, interpretation, and application. Thus, there is a hermeneutical dimension to all of the previous notions of reception.

The book is structured in three parts, each with three chapters. Part 1, *The Principle,* proposes that the Holy Spirit is the principle which enables reception of revelation, who animates the church, and who gifts baptized individuals and the whole community with a *sensus fidei,* a sense for the faith, enabling them to make sense of the faith. Part 2, *The Norm,* traces the early disciples' interpretation of the life, death, and resurrection of Jesus Christ both before Easter and after Pentecost, proposing the hypothesis that it is through the *sensus fidei* in individuals and the *sensus fidelium* of the community that the normative New Testament writings are produced as individual works and then gradually recognized and selected as a canon. This traditioning work of the Holy Spirit through the *sensus fidelium,* it is proposed, constitutes the inspiration of Scripture, which comes to realization in its reception. Part 3, *The Task,* explores the ecclesiological implications of the process outlined in part 2. Both the process and product of canon formation are normative for the ongoing mission of the church—to receive and tradition the Gospel. It proposes a synthesis of Vatican II on the teaching office of the church, examines the operation of the *sensus fidei* in the lives of individual believers, and proposes a dialogic approach to interrelating the *sensus fidelium,* theology, and the magisterium in the contemporary Catholic Church.

PART ONE

The Principle

The Holy Spirit, Faith, and *Sensus Fidei*

CHAPTER I

The Holy Spirit and Revelation

Lumen Gentium 12 teaches that all believers possess "a supernatural sense of the faith" which enables an infallibility in believing. This supernatural sense of the faith is "aroused and sustained by the Spirit of truth." A theology of the *sensus fidelium* must begin by attending to the role of the Holy Spirit in divine revelation. It is central to the belief of Christians that God is fully encountered in Jesus Christ, the Crucified and Risen One; that salvation from God is mediated through him; and that, within that salvific encounter, God is revealed to humanity. What is the role of the Holy Spirit in that process of revelation? How might a trinitarian theology of revelation be constructed that gives appropriate emphasis to that role?

In this chapter, we begin our exploration of the *sensus fidelium* by firstly highlighting the witness of Scripture to the enlightening role of the Holy Spirit, as but one of the many interrelated dimensions of the Spirit's assistance in empowering Christians to appropriate the salvation Jesus Christ offers. This chapter therefore does not attempt a comprehensive exploration of the role of the Holy Spirit in the Christian life. After examining the scriptural witness to this Christian experience of enlightenment by the Spirit in the economy of salvation, this chapter then proposes a trinitarian theology of revelation in which the Holy Spirit is seen to be "the principle of reception" in the process of divine revelation.

THE EXPERIENCE OF THE HOLY SPIRIT

Jesus was being interpreted from the moment his public ministry began, yet being misinterpreted. The four Gospels consistently preserve the memory that, during his ministry, the earliest disciples misunderstand Jesus.[1] This misunderstanding is later corrected by three decisive "events": Jesus' death on the cross, his resurrection from the dead, and the early disciples' experience, after the resurrection, of being given an ability to understand aright the meaning of Jesus' teaching and ministry, of his death and resurrection, and of his identity as God's bearer of salvation. In this section, it is this gift of an ability to understand Jesus that I particularly wish to focus on, without wanting to reduce the Spirit's work to a purely cognitive dimension.

For the early Christian community, after Easter something dramatic happens. They are given a power beyond them not only to understand Jesus' teaching, his actions, the significance of his death and resurrection, and his identity, but also a power to live out the divine salvation he offers. The nature of the God of Jesus Christ and its implications for human living are now comprehended in a new light; the way of life Jesus taught is now able to be put into practice; how Jesus acted now becomes a way of life that can be imitated; the reign of God that Jesus preached and embodied is now able to be made real for them and by them in diverse ways in diverse contexts. This dramatic change is experienced in the coming of the Holy Spirit. The Crucified and Risen One gives them the power of the Spirit who empowered him. The whole of the New Testament witnesses to a rich variety of metaphors for expressing the difference Jesus Christ brings, through and because of the coming of the Spirit. It is the Holy Spirit who now makes possible the living out and the understanding of the salvific revelation that Jesus Christ has incarnated. Life in Christ *is* life lived in the power of the Spirit.

Chronologically, the gift and reception of that enabling and enlightening Spirit is narrated in different time frames by the New Testament writers. Luke's narrative places that dramatic event fifty days after the resurrection, on the feast of Pentecost;[2] John narrates how Jesus hands over the Holy Spirit to his disciples from the cross and during his appearance immediately after the resurrection.[3] But, according to the salvation histo-

---

1. The theme of the pre-Easter disciples' lack of full comprehension will be explored in chapter 4.

2. Acts 2:1–41.

3. Jn 20:19–23. Through this book I will use the Lukan "Pentecost" to refer to the event of the Spirit's coming witnessed to by the whole of the New Testament.

ry narrated across the whole Bible, the history of the Spirit does not begin with "Pentecost." Throughout the Old Testament, the Spirit of God is depicted as a personification of God's activity from the time of creation and throughout the history of God's relating with the chosen people. In the New Testament, the Spirit is depicted as being involved in the life, ministry, death, and resurrection of Jesus Christ. As Walter Kasper asserts:

[A]ccording to the scriptures, the Spirit of God is present and effective as the breath of life in the whole of creation and history, which it leads towards their eschatological goal. It reaches this goal by enabling the incarnation of the Son of God (cf. Luke 1.35), in his anointing (Luke 4.18) and, finally, in the cross and resurrection (Rom. 1.4). *The entire life and work of Jesus is brought about and accompanied by the Spirit.*[4]

The Spirit is involved in the conception of Jesus, comes upon him at his baptism, and anoints him as he begins his teaching and ministry. Jesus is the *Christos,* the Anointed One, because of this anointing by the Spirit. After the resurrection, it is this Spirit which the Risen One sends upon the community of his disciples, anointing them.

Not only are there different time frames, but there are different emphases discernible in the New Testament's presentation of the Holy Spirit.[5] There is a common thread within these different approaches. All witness to the empowering role of the Spirit in the appropriation of the salvation mediated through Jesus Christ. Rich metaphorical language is used of the saving work of Jesus Christ and of the Spirit's role in that salvation process (justification, adoption, sanctification, enlightenment, etc).[6] In this first section, without wanting to reduce the manifold activ-

4. Walter Kasper, "The Renewal of Pneumatology in Contemporary Catholic Life and Theology: Towards a Rapprochement between East and West," in *That They May All Be One: The Call to Unity* (New York: Burns & Oates, 2004), 96–121, at 101. My italics.

5. See the range of articles in Graham Stanton, Bruce W. Longenecker, and Stephen C. Barton, eds., *The Holy Spirit and Christian Origins: Essays in Honor of James D. G. Dunn* (Grand Rapids, Mich.: W. B. Eerdmans, 2004). For surveys, see Raymond E. Brown, "Diverse Views of the Spirit in the New Testament: A Preliminary Contribution of Exegesis to Doctrinal Reflection," in *Biblical Exegesis and Church Doctrine* (New York: Paulist Press, 1985), 101–13; George T. Montague, "The Fire in the Word: The Holy Spirit in Scripture," in *Advents of the Spirit: An Introduction to the Current Study of Pneumatology,* ed. Bradford E. Hinze and D. Lyle Dabney (Milwaukee, Wis.: Marquette University Press, 2001), 35–65.

6. On the many metaphors for "grace," for example, in the New Testament, see Edward Schillebeeckx, *Christ: The Christian Experience in the Modern World* (London: SCM Press, 1980), 463–538. See also Piet F. Fransen, *The New Life of Grace* (London: Geoffrey Chapman, 1971), 55: "All these various conceptions—divine love, presence, indwelling, image and likeness, sanctification

ity of the Holy Spirit to only a cognitive dimension (that of enlightenment and inspiration), my narrower focus will be on the enlightening
and revelatory role affirmed of the Spirit by the early Christian communities. I will limit my examination to the three main witnesses to this
conviction of the early church—Paul, Luke, and John. I will give greater
attention to the Johannine pneumatology because of its distinctive emphasis on the revelatory and interpretative role of the Spirit.

For Paul, "both the understanding of the gospel and the event of
preaching, including the hearing that leads to faith, are the work of the
Spirit."[7] For example, throughout his first letter to the Corinthians, Paul
affirms the revelatory role of the Spirit who knows the depths of God,
and because believers are taught by the Spirit, they now have the mind
of Christ, enabling them to understand the gifts of God.[8] While affirming that the Holy Spirit graces particular individuals with particular
charisms, Paul also affirms that communal discernment of the experience
of charismatic individuals is necessary; an individual perspective has no
independent authority. His image of the community as a body emphasizes both the diverse contribution individuals make, and also that individual charisms are given by the Spirit for the sake of the whole community.

Paul also witnesses to the graced quality of his re-reading of the Jewish Scriptures; it is the Holy Spirit who enables him to properly interpret

---

and justification—are simply different approaches, through different symbolisms, to one identical
reality: that through grace we share in the divine life."

7. Gordon D. Fee, *God's Empowering Presence: The Holy Spirit in the Letters of Paul* (Peabody,
Mass.: Hendrickson Publishers, 1994), 853. For a summary of this work, see Gordon D. Fee, *Paul,
the Spirit, and the People of God* (Peabody, Mass.: Hendrickson Publishers, 1996). On the experience of the Spirit in the Pauline communities, see James D. G. Dunn, *Jesus and the Spirit: A Study
of the Religious and Charismatic Experience of Jesus and the First Christians as Reflected in the New
Testament* (London: SCM Press, 1975), 199–342.

8. 1 Cor 2:9–16: "But, as it is written, 'What no eye has seen, nor ear heard, nor the human
heart conceived, what God has prepared for those who love him'—*these things God has revealed
to us through the Spirit; for the Spirit searches everything, even the depths of God.* For what human
being knows what is truly human except the human spirit that is within? So also *no one compre-
hends what is truly God's except the Spirit of God.* Now we have received not the spirit of the world,
but the Spirit that is from God, *so that we may understand the gifts bestowed on us by God.* And we
speak of these things in words not taught by human wisdom but *taught by the Spirit, interpreting
spiritual things to those who are spiritual.* Those who are unspiritual do not receive *the gifts of God's
Spirit,* for they are foolishness to them, and they are unable to understand them because they are
spiritually discerned. Those who are spiritual discern all things, and they are themselves subject
to no one else's scrutiny. 'For who has known the mind of the Lord so as to instruct him?' But *we
have the mind of Christ.*"

them. He believes that his proclamation of the Gospel is a divinely assisted interpretation of the tradition. For example, in 2 Corinthians 3:12–18, he writes of understanding the reading of Scripture in the light of Christ, and of the Spirit's role in removing the veil that would prevent proper interpretation. Paul is here naming the Christian experience of the Holy Spirit as the source of the capacity to interpret the new in terms of the old, and the old in terms of the new.

In the letters of the later Deutero-Pauline communities, Paul urges Timothy to "guard the good treasure [the Gospel] entrusted to you, with the help of the Holy Spirit living in us."[9] In Colossians and Ephesians, without mentioning the Holy Spirit specifically, there are prayers for enlightenment in the understanding of Christ.[10] This divine enlightenment is elsewhere named explicitly as the work of the Holy Spirit.[11]

The Holy Spirit appears prominently in Luke's portrayal both of Jesus in his Gospel and of the life and mission of the early church after Pentecost.[12] His narrative account of the Pentecost event in Acts 2 evokes the wind of the creational Spirit in the paradigmatic creation story.[13] This

---

9. 2 Tm 1:13–14.

10. Col 1:9–10: "For this reason, since the day we heard it, we have not ceased praying for you and asking *that you may be filled with the knowledge of God's will in all spiritual wisdom and understanding,* so that you may lead lives worthy of the Lord, fully pleasing to him, as you bear fruit in every good work and *as you grow in the knowledge of God.*" Col 2:2–3: "I want their hearts to be encouraged and united in love, so that they may have *all the riches of assured understanding and have the knowledge of God's mystery, that is, Christ himself, in whom are hidden all the treasures of wisdom and knowledge.*" Eph 1:17–19: "I pray that the God of our Lord Jesus Christ, the Father of glory, may give you *a spirit of wisdom and revelation as you come to know him,* so that, with the eyes of your heart enlightened, you may know what is the hope to which he has called you, what are the riches of his glorious inheritance among the saints, and what is the immeasurable greatness of his power for us who believe, according to the working of his great power."

11. Eph 3:5: "In former generations this mystery was not made known to humankind, as *it has now been revealed to his holy apostles and prophets by the Spirit.*" Eph 3:16–19: "I pray that, according to the riches of his glory, he may grant that you may be *strengthened in your inner being with power through his Spirit,* and *that Christ may dwell in your hearts through faith,* as you are being rooted and grounded in love. I pray that you may have *the power to comprehend,* with all the saints, what is the breadth and length and height and depth, and to know the love of Christ that surpasses knowledge, so that you may be filled with all the fullness of God."

12. For studies on the Holy Spirit in Luke, see Ju Hur, *A Dynamic Reading of the Holy Spirit in Luke-Acts* (Sheffield, England: Sheffield Academic Press, 2001); William H. Shepherd, *The Narrative Function of the Holy Spirit as a Character in Luke-Acts* (Atlanta, Ga.: Scholars Press, 1994); Roger Stronstad, *The Prophethood of All Believers: A Study in Luke's Charismatic Theology* (Sheffield: England: Sheffield Academic Press, 1999); Matthias Wenk, *Community-Forming Power: The Socio-Ethical Role of the Spirit in Luke-Acts* (Sheffield, England: Sheffield Academic Press, 2000).

13. Gn 1:2.

experience of the whole Christian community, not just select individuals, being gifted with the Spirit gives them a boldness *(parrhesia)* for proclaiming the Gospel: "When they had prayed, the place in which they were gathered together was shaken; and they were all filled with the Holy Spirit and spoke the word of God with boldness."[14] Luke later depicts this boldness as characterizing their preaching the Gospel in new situations.[15] The words "boldness" and "witness" appear regularly throughout the Lukan narrative: the boldness is founded on an assurance that their witness will be faithful to what they have received, an assurance that they have the capacity to address the Gospel to new situations as the church expands, and an assurance that they will indeed be effective in opening their hearers to the Gospel they witness to, according to Jesus' promise: "you will receive power when the Holy Spirit has come upon you; and you will be my witnesses in Jerusalem, in all Judea and Samaria, and to the ends of the earth."[16] After Pentecost, it is baptismal initiation into the *koinonia* of the community which assures them that they continue to be gifted with the Spirit of Pentecost.[17]

Throughout Acts, the revelatory/interpretative role of the Holy Spirit is depicted in several ways. The disciples experience guidance from the Spirit when having to make choices[18] and when taking new direction in their missionary work.[19] The Holy Spirit, for example, influences the decisions of Paul regarding a certain course of action;[20] the Holy Spirit guides the community in the appointment of leaders.[21] The paradigmatic event for receiving guidance from the Spirit in Luke's pneumatology is the so-called council of Jerusalem,[22] where the final decision is founded on the experience that "it seemed good to the Holy Spirit and to us."[23]

---

14. Acts 4:31. Acts 2:1 states: "When the day of Pentecost had come, they were *all* together in one place."

15. On the notion of "boldness," see Stanley B. Marrow, "*Parrhesia* and the New Testament," *Catholic Biblical Quarterly* 44 (1982): 431–46.

16. Acts 1:8. On the pervasive notion of "witness" in the New Testament, see Allison A. Trites, *The New Testament Concept of Witness* (New York: Cambridge University Press, 1977).

17. Acts 2:38; 8:15–17; 9:17; 15:8; 19:5–6.

18. Acts 1:15–26; 6:1–7; 15:1–35.

19. Acts 8:29, 39; 10:38, 44–47; 11:12, 15; 13:2, 4.

20. For example, Paul redirects his plans according to the Spirit's guidance to go into Europe (Acts 16:6–7) and later decides to go to Rome (Acts 19:21).

21. Acts 20:28.   22. Acts 15:1–35.

23. Acts 15:28.

Thus, every essential step in the Acts story of how witness was borne to Christ from Jerusalem to the end of the earth is guided by the Spirit, whose presence becomes obvious at the great moments where human agents would otherwise be hesitant or choose wrongly.[24]

Thus Luke's vision of the Holy Spirit is that of a director and guide for the community in its mission. However, there is a mechanism that is recognized as necessary for interpreting the direction and guidance of the Spirit, that of community discernment. Just as the Pauline letters highlight the need for the community to discriminate and come to a judgment when there are conflicting interpretations of the Spirit, so too Luke narrates how the community would come together in council in order to discern the assistance of the Spirit. "It seemed good to the Holy Spirit and to us"[25] sums up the three-way Lukan vision of the working and interpretation of the Holy Spirit: individual interpretation, the community's judgment, and the Holy Spirit working through both.

According to Johannine pneumatology, Jesus promises another Paraclete, the Spirit of Truth who will enable the community to understand the meaning of Jesus.[26] Helmut Gabel neatly summarizes the Johannine vision:

In the view of the Gospel of John, the word of the eye-witnesses of Jesus and that of the future disciples is work of the Spirit. The entire tradition process is a process enabled by the Spirit. The Spirit is, as it were, the "interpreter" of Jesus, who leads to the true understanding of the Christ event and reveals the event in its deepest sense.[27]

---

24. Raymond E. Brown, Carolyn Osiek, and Pheme Perkins, "Early Church," in *The New Jerome Biblical Commentary*, ed. Raymond E. Brown, Joseph A. Fitzmyer, and Roland E. Murphy (Englewood Cliffs, N.J.: Prentice-Hall, 1990), 1338–53, at 1345. Elsewhere, Brown notes that this Lukan confidence concerning the guidance of the Holy Spirit in major turning points of the church's history persists throughout history; he gives the example of the bishops at Vatican II daily praying for the Spirit's guidance, alongside the parallel belief, true to the tradition of the Pastoral epistles, that the bishops have been given the Spirit at ordination. See Brown, "Diverse Views of the Spirit," 109.

25. Acts 15:28.

26. 1 Jn 2:20–21, 27: "But you have been anointed by the Holy One, and all of you have knowledge. I write to you, not because you do not know the truth, but because you know it, and you know that no lie comes from the truth. . . . As for you, the anointing that you received from him abides in you, and so you do not need anyone to teach you. But as his anointing teaches you about all things, and is true and is not a lie, and just as it has taught you, abide in him."

27. Helmut Gabel, *Inspirationsverständnis im Wandel: Theologische Neuorientierung im Umfeld des Zweiten Vatikanischen Konzils* (Mainz: Matthias-Grünewald-Verlag, 1991), 321.

The Johannine vision can be outlined in four points. Firstly, the Johannine literature emphasizes that the Spirit/Paraclete is given to all individuals in the community. Secondly, Jesus promises another Paraclete who will take the place of Jesus; nevertheless, although the Spirit/Paraclete takes the place of Jesus, the Spirit/Paraclete does not supplant or negate Jesus. The "secessionists," according to the author of 1 John, are wanting to give independent authority to the Spirit over against Jesus, thereby severing the necessary element of continuity with Jesus. The Johannine literature emphasizes that it is the role of this Spirit/Paraclete to ensure continuity with Jesus. A phrase recurs: "from the beginning." The Spirit ensures continuity with the pre-Easter Jesus. Thirdly, the Johannine literature emphasizes that it is the role of this Spirit/Paraclete, not only to ensure continuity with Jesus, but also to enable the community to *interpret* the word of Jesus for a new context, ensuring faithful adaptation and innovation. Fourthly, the Johannine literature emphasizes that it is the role of this Spirit/Paraclete to indeed *further* the teaching of Jesus beyond what Jesus was able to teach, speaking a new word of *the glorified Jesus.*[28]

Several issues need to be highlighted before we continue our investigation of the Johannine literature. The first is the relationship between the Spirit and the Paraclete.[29] The word *parakletos* appears only in the Farewell Discourse of the Gospel (chapters 13–17) and is not used in the later Johannine epistles. The title *parakletos* can be interpreted as a synonym for the *pneuma* title in the rest of the Gospel and the later epistles. The role of the Spirit/Paraclete should be interpreted within a courtroom forensic model and its notion of witness.[30] Here the two parties on trial

28. For an interpretation of the Johannine Spirit of Truth/Paraclete as a hermeneutical assistant, see Felix Porsch, *Pneuma und Wort: Ein exegetischer Beitrag zur Pneumatologie des Johannesevangeliums* (Frankfurt: Knecht, 1974); Gary M. Burge, *The Anointed Community: The Holy Spirit in the Johannine Tradition* (Grand Rapids, Mich.: W. B. Eerdmans, 1986).

29. See Raymond E. Brown, "The Paraclete in the Fourth Gospel," *New Testament Studies* 13 (1966–67): 113–32.

30. One author who rejects a predominantly forensic setting for interpreting the role of the Paraclete is Tricia Gates Brown, *Spirit in the Writings of John: Johannine Pneumatology in Social-Scientific Perspective* (New York: T&T Clark International, 2003). Gates Brown's social-scientific thesis that the model of "brokerage" best names the Johannine worldview regarding the Paraclete at times forces the evidence to fit the interpretative methodology. Nevertheless, her model of a chain of brokerage (Jesus as broker, the Spirit as broker for Jesus, the disciples as brokers for Jesus, helped by the Spirit-broker) is a useful perspective for enriching our understanding of the Paraclete's role in the Johannine understanding of the Spirit's assistance in new situations. However, the model does not do justice to the courtroom setting evoked by the notion of "witness," pervasive not only throughout the Johannine literature, but throughout the Old and New Testaments.

are God (the Father) and the world. Jesus is a witness giving testimony for the side of God; the Spirit takes Jesus' place in his witness role when he is gone. Historically, two factors are at play in the desire of the author to assure the Johannine communities of the Spirit/Paraclete's continuing role as witness: the apostles who were the original eyewitnesses are now dead, and the coming of the parousia has been delayed. Jesus, however, the author assures them, is still present; the Spirit has taken his place. Continuing access to Jesus is assured.

The Fourth Gospel portrays Jesus giving his disciples the assurance that the Spirit/Paraclete will, in the future, be the teaching voice of Jesus himself.

I have said these things to you while I am still with you. But the Advocate, the Holy Spirit, whom the Father will send in my name, will teach you everything, and remind you of all that I have said to you.[31]

The Spirit/Paraclete will bring the *past* to memory, but the Spirit/Paraclete will be the voice of the glorified Jesus teaching in new situations in the *present*. However, this new teaching will be anchored in the Jesus of the past, because the Spirit/Paraclete will be speaking anew on behalf of the glorified Jesus.

It is this claim of access to new teaching that becomes problematic within the Johannine communities. The controversy lurking behind the themes of the first epistle is the divergent reception of the Fourth Gospel. The author claims that the group emphasizing its pneumatic authority and an access to the new teaching of the glorified Jesus is losing its grounding in the tradition and the teaching of the pre-Easter Jesus. Thus there is a tension within the communities between those emphasizing the tradition *(anamnesis)* and those emphasizing the creative voice of the glorified Jesus going beyond the teaching he had given before the resurrection (inspiration).[32] The writer of the epistle claims that both *anamnesis* and inspiration are demanded. It is a tension that will mark the history of the Spirit not only throughout the Johannine communities, but

---

See Trites, *The New Testament Concept of Witness.* Furthermore, Gates Brown's broker model precludes her giving sufficient weight to the *revelatory/interpretative* role of the Paraclete in the Johannine vision.

31. Jn 14:25–26.

32. On the *anamnesis*/inspiration (tradition/prophecy) schema to describe the Spirit's role, see Burge, *The Anointed Community,* 216.

throughout the history of the church.[33] In summarizing the Johannine vision, Felix Porsch speaks of the Spirit/Paraclete as the one who brings to realization the revelation of Jesus:

Behind the presentation of the Fourth Gospel stands simply the experience of the church. The Spirit had introduced it to the revelation of Jesus and this Spirit was even the "Spirit of Jesus" (cf. 2 Cor. 3:17; 1 Cor. 12.3) whose work entirely referred to the person and work of Jesus. Consequently he appeared as the one who continues the revelation of Jesus. Or better still, *he is the one who realizes Jesus' revelation.*[34]

This survey of the three major New Testament witnesses to the enlightening role of the Holy Spirit reveals that there is an intertextual unity-in-diversity in the New Testament writings when read together as a fixed collection of diverse texts. While the distinctive pneumatologies of each emphasize different aspects of the early church's experience, there is a common witness to the Holy Spirit as the one who enables future generations, after the resurrection and ascension, to appropriate and interpret the salvation and revelation Jesus Christ mediates.

Our examination of New Testament pneumatologies so far has been mainly a synchronic one, looking at the final texts intertextually. It is important now to note the diachronic development of this scriptural witness to the experience of the Holy Spirit. The pneumatological development evident within the New Testament is a development which runs parallel to, and is intertwined with, the *christological* reflection within the early churches. Raymond Brown sees the christologies of the New Testa-

---

33. Raymond Brown gives an important reminder regarding the benefits and the burdens of being guided by the Spirit: "The Spirit is not confined to charismatics, whether they be apostles or prophets or teachers or administrators, but is the possession of every believing Christian. The ultimate teacher of the church is not the property of any office. The church was not crippled when the apostles died; for, indeed, it was the Paraclete/Spirit that enabled the first generation to bear witness. This same Paraclete/Spirit enables the ordinary believer to bear witness just as effectively as the first generation bore witness. This is not the sweeping Spirit of Acts, coming at an awesome moment; rather, the Paraclete is always there. Ultimately such an understanding of the Spirit means that there are no such things as a second-class Christian either in position or in time because every Christian has the Spirit of God in his or her heart. And yet, this understanding too has its difficulties. If the Spirit is in the heart of every Christian, what happens when two Christians disagree? How do people know which is the voice of the Spirit? Later on in this same Johannine tradition that gave us the Paraclete, another writer has to warn complainingly, 'Do not believe every Spirit; rather put these Spirits to the test . . . so we can know the Spirit of Truth from the Spirit of Deceit' (1 John 4:1,6)." Brown, "Diverse Views of the Spirit," 110.

34. Porsch, *Pneuma und Wort*, 323–24. Quoted in Burge, *The Anointed Community,* 38. My italics.

ment developing according to a certain logic of questioning which pushes back in time the issue of Jesus' identity:

If one begins with the reconstructed pre-50 material and then moves through the extant NT writings in the likely order of their composition, one can trace a peculiar pattern of christological moments that seems to move "backwards" in terms of Jesus' career. The earlier evidence interpreted christologically scenes at the end of Jesus' life; the later evidence interpreted christologically scenes at the beginning of his life.[35]

There is, according to Brown, a certain logic in the questioning of the early communities, and their attempt to answer new questions through the development of their christologies. For example, if Jesus is affirmed as "Lord" by virtue of his resurrection (as Paul does), what then is his identity during his pre-Easter ministry? Matthew and Luke's theological reply is to portray characters in their narrative addressing Jesus with the title "Lord" during scenes throughout his ministry. Their infancy narratives are an attempt to answer the further question of Jesus' identity before his baptism. John will push even further the logic of the questioning: what then of Jesus' identity before his conception and birth? The prologue of his Gospel proclaims the creational pre-existence of the Word.

Similarly, Brown sees this "backwards pattern" of questioning at work throughout the New Testament with regard to relating Jesus and the Spirit. Paul sees the resurrection as the significant moment in the relationship between Jesus and the Spirit. In depicting Jesus' ministry, Matthew and Luke push back the relationship of Jesus to the Spirit to the moment of his baptism and the beginning of his ministry; their infancy narratives push it back further and envisage Jesus' conception by the Spirit. John indirectly relates the Logos and the Spirit from the moment of creation.[36]

In all these stages (creation, conception, baptism, resurrection) the Spirit plays a role in what God has done in Jesus Christ, so intimate a role that one cannot separate the two. Jesus acts by the Spirit: if the Spirit creates, the Word creates; if the Spirit sanctifies, Jesus sanctifies.[37]

---

35. Raymond E. Brown, "The Christologies of New Testament Christians," in *An Introduction to New Testament Christology* (New York: Paulist Press, 1994), 103–52, at 108–9.

36. See Brown, "Diverse Views of the Spirit," 104–6.

37. Ibid., 107.

It is significant, therefore, that the very pattern of development of these pneumatologies, in which the Spirit is increasingly highlighted, is the result of *an interpretative process which itself is experienced as being guided by that very Spirit.* There is a circularity of reflection in which the one who is experienced as the hermeneutical guide in the process of interpretation is more and more inserted into the narrative of God, and made more explicit in their theological reflection regarding the Spirit's role in the reception of revelation. Thus the experience of pneumatic assistance feeds into the interpretative process, with a developing sense of the distinct identity of the Spirit and the Spirit's relationship to God and to the person and work of Jesus Christ. It is a process of articulation that reaches its high point in the creed of the Council of Constantinople in 381 and with the patristic trinitarian theologies that followed.

A TRINITARIAN THEOLOGY OF REVELATION-FAITH

The early church's experience of God's salvific revelation through Christ in the Holy Spirit becomes the foundation for the church's credal confession of God as Triune. In this section I propose a trinitarian theology of revelation which highlights the particular function of the Holy Spirit as the one who brings to realization God's revelatory and salvific purposes. If Jesus Christ is, as Walter Kasper formulates it, "the principle of our endowment with grace,"[38] then the Holy Spirit is, I propose, *the principle of its reception.*

My proposal can be briefly stated in two theses. First: within the economy of salvation, the Spirit is the principle of reception in the human appropriation of salvific revelation coming through God's Word, Jesus Christ. Second: within the inner trinitarian life, the Spirit is the *receptio* in the mutual exchange between Father and Son. I wish, therefore, to outline a coherent theology of the economic Trinity and of the immanent Trinity, which gives adequate emphasis to the distinctive and proper (not merely appropriated) role of the Holy Spirit in the process of salvific revelation.

In *Dei Verbum,* evoking images of divine hospitality and divine reception of humanity, the *missio Dei* in the economy of salvation is depicted in terms of God as a gracious host:

---

38. Walter Kasper, *Jesus the Christ* (New York: Paulist Press, 1976), 253.

It pleased God, in his goodness and wisdom, *to reveal himself* and *to make known the mystery of his will,* which was that people can draw near to the Father, through Christ, the Word made flesh, in the holy Spirit, and thus become *sharers in the divine nature.* By this revelation, then, the invisible God, from the fullness of his love, addresses men and women as his friends, and lives among them, *in order to invite and receive them into his own company.*[39]

Divine revelation, according to Vatican II, is not simply a communication of truths about God and humanity, but also, and fundamentally, God's loving *self-*communication to humanity.[40] Revelation is primarily communication of Godself through a sharing in the divine life. From the perspective of a scholastic theology of grace, this divine self-gift would be termed "uncreated grace."[41] Such divine self-communication involves both personal encounter and cognitive knowledge, with the latter being communicated through the former. Through the concrete images of Jesus' teaching and in the tangible encounters with his person, and in his death and resurrection, the whole Christ event makes God's reality known; he is "the mediator and the fullness of all revelation."[42] What is revealed is the compassionate heart of God, and ultimately the knowledge that is communicated is of the mystical kind, a knowing which comes through living within God. Revelation is thus the realization of the divine invitation to share in God's own life. It is this sharing in God's inner life which constitutes ultimate salvation for humanity. In the personalist terms of *Dei Verbum,* salvation and revelation are almost synonyms.[43] Thus "revelation" signifies salvific revelation; "salvation" signifies revelatory salvation. It is the possibility of experiencing this reality that the early church called "the Gospel": God lovingly reaching out to humanity through Christ in the Holy Spirit, enabling human beings to be received into God's inner life, for the sake of their salvation.

Reception *into* God requires human reception *of* God. While the final realization of God's self-communication is reception into God, the process

---

39. *DV,* 2. Flannery translation.

40. *DV,* 6: "By divine revelation God wished to manifest and communicate both himself and the eternal decrees of his will concerning the salvation of humankind."

41. See Karl Rahner, "Some Implications of the Scholastic Concept of Uncreated Grace," in *Theological Investigations,* vol. 1 (New York: Seabury, 1961), 1:319–46.

42. *DV,* 2. Tanner translation.

43. For example, the two notions are used together in *DV,* 7: "God in his goodness arranged that whatever he had revealed for the salvation of all nations should last for ever in its integrity and be handed on to all generations." Tanner translation.

of salvific revelation, however, needs to be conceived not only in terms of the initiating communicator (God) but also in terms of the intended receiver (humanity). Revelation requires reception for its realization.[44] Faith is the human reception of divine revelation. "Faith is answered revelation. Accepted revelation is faith. Faith is revelation arrived at its goal."[45] According to Joseph Ratzinger, "revelation always and only becomes a reality where there is faith."[46] The divine and human poles of this personal communication are so intertwined that, as Paul Tillich asserted, "revelation" should always be taken to mean *Offenbarungsglaube* [revelation-faith].[47] "Revelation is not an act which ends with the speaking of the word but with its reception and appropriation in human lives."[48] As Karl Barth affirms, that which has been objectively revealed must be subjectively manifested.[49] Thus, faith—the human reception of salvific revelation—is necessary for salvation; if the gift is not received, the gift has not yet been given.

Faith itself is a gift from God; it is a supernatural gift.[50] It is the result of the attracting love of God rather than the effort of human beings. The belief that the "supernaturality" of faith's reception of revelation is related to the Holy Spirit is a doctrine long professed by the church. The classic text is from the Second Council of Orange in 529, which teaches: "It is through the infusion and inspiration of the Holy Spirit that we believe,

44. Vorgrimler, summarizing Rahner, states: "God's revelation is only heard if his self-communication is experienced and accepted, and not as a theory, but, far more radically, in the existential mode of human life." Herbert Vorgrimler, "From *Sensus Fidei* to *Consensus Fidelium*," *Concilium* 180 (1985): 3–11, at 7. Sandra Schneiders likewise states: "[R]evelation is an interpersonal reality. It comes to actualisation only in human experience, only in the human response of reception and reciprocal self-gift." Sandra M. Schneiders, *The Revelatory Text: Interpreting the New Testament as Sacred Scripture*, 2nd ed. (Collegeville, Minn.: Liturgical Press, 1999), 53.

45. Heinrich Fries, *Fundamental Theology* (Washington, D.C.: The Catholic University of America Press, 1996), 182.

46. Joseph Ratzinger, "Revelation and Tradition," in *Revelation and Tradition,* ed. Karl Rahner and Joseph Ratzinger (New York: Herder and Herder, 1966), 26–49, at 36.

47. Paul Tillich, *Frühe Hauptwerke* (Stuttgart: 1959), 353. Quoted in Gerald O'Collins, *Foundations of Theology* (Chicago: Loyola University Press, 1971), 33.

48. Komonchak, "Defending Our Hope," 20.

49. Karl Barth distinguishes *revelation* and *manifestation* (the realization of revelation): "Becoming manifest has to be something specific, a special act of the Father or the Son or both, that is added to the givenness of the revelation of the Father and the Son. . . . This special element in revelation is undoubtedly identical with what the New Testament usually calls *the Holy Spirit as the subjective side in the event of revelation*." Karl Barth, *Church Dogmatics. Volume 1: The Doctrine of the Word of God. Part 1,* ed. G. W. Bromiley and T. F. Torrance, 2nd ed. (New York: T&T Clark International, 2004), 449. My italics.

50. On the "supernaturality" of faith, see Dulles, *The Assurance of Things Hoped For,* 224–26.

will or are able to do all these things as is required."[51] Vatican II's *Dei Verbum* recalls this Christian doctrine concerning the role of the Holy Spirit in enabling the personal response of faith, in facilitating understanding of revelation *by means of* faith, and in facilitating understanding *of* the faith.[52] As the facilitator of the gift of faith, the Holy Spirit is, therefore, the principle of the reception of revelation, since revelation requires faith for its realization.[53]

Living the life of faith is possible only through grace. As with the gift of faith, so too it is the consistent Christian belief that the gift of grace is related to the indwelling and work of the Holy Spirit. Through baptismal anointing by the Spirit, the Christian is enabled to be drawn into the trinitarian life because of the indwelling of the Holy Spirit. If, as noted above, Jesus Christ is "the principle of our endowment with grace,"[54] then the Spirit is the principle of our reception of Christ's grace. Living the life of Christ is only possible in the Spirit; life in Christ is life in the Spirit. Christ is God's self-gift; the Spirit always accompanies the gift, enabling its reception. Grace is "the real self-communication of God in and through the indwelling of the hypostasis of the Holy Spirit. Through the indwelling of the Holy Spirit, who has been given to us, we participate in the divine nature (2 Peter 1:4)."[55] This hypostatic indwelling of the Spirit not only constitutes the condition for the possibility of the reception of God's self-communication, but also brings to fulfillment the goal of that self-communication: reception of God's self-gift incarnate in Christ. The Spirit, as the principle of reception in the divine revelatory process, en-

51. Council of Orange II, canon 7 (DS 180 [377]). The translation here is from Jacques Dupuis and Josef Neuner, *The Christian Faith in the Doctrinal Documents of the Catholic Church,* 7th rev. and enl. ed. (New York: Alba House, 2001), no. 1918.

52. Vatican II's teaching on faith is to be found in *Dei Verbum,* 5: "'The obedience of faith' must be our response to God who reveals. By faith one freely commits oneself entirely to God, making 'the full submission of intellect and will to God who reveals,' and willingly assenting to the revelation given by God. For this faith to be accorded we need the grace of God, anticipating it and assisting it, as well as the interior helps of the holy Spirit, who moves the heart and converts it to God, and opens *the eyes of the mind* and 'makes it easy for all to accept and believe the truth.' The same holy Spirit constantly perfects faith by his gifts, *so that revelation may be more and more deeply understood.*" Flannery revised translation; my italics. The council is first quoting Vatican I's *Dei Filius,* chapter 3, and, secondly, the Council of Orange II, canon 7 (DS 180 [377]), also quoted in the same chapter of Vatican I's *Dei Filius.*

53. *DV,* 8c teaches: "The Holy Spirit, too, is active, making the living voice of the gospel ring out in the church, and through it in the world, leading those who believe into the whole truth, and making the message of Christ dwell in them in all its richness." Tanner translation.

54. Kasper, *Jesus the Christ,* 253.

55. Walter Kasper, *The God of Jesus Christ* (London: SCM Press, 1983), 226.

ables the realization of that process, the gift of the divine trinitarian life that transforms human lives.[56]

Like the overlapping terms "revelation" and "salvation," so too "salvation" and "grace" can be seen as somewhat synonymous. Both terms capture different nuances of the Christian experience: only God can save us; only God's grace enables human beings to respond to the offer of salvation and the possibility of new life. Grace is the Holy Spirit freeing Christians from all that impedes them from being lured into the inner life of God, that is, all that impedes the reign of God. Within the helplessness of sin, hatred, and evil, it is the Spirit who enables the Father, through Christ, to deliver us from evil and enables us to live the way of Jesus, the way of God, the way to God.[57] "Salvation is . . . participation through the Holy Spirit in the life of God revealed in Jesus Christ."[58]

These Christian beliefs regarding faith as a gift of the Holy Spirit, and of grace as an indwelling of the Holy Spirit, have implications for a coherent exposition of the doctrine of the Trinity from the perspective of salvific revelation. Such an exposition must be faithful to the overall witness of Scripture with regard to the relationships of the Spirit to the Father and to the Christ/Son/Word. The Spirit is both the Spirit of the Father[59] and the Spirit of the Son,[60] the Spirit of Jesus Christ.[61] Just as the Spirit whom the Father sends (the Spirit of God) is the Spirit whom Jesus Christ sends (the Spirit of Christ), so too the Christ whom the Father sends is the Christ whom the Spirit empowers, and therefore the Christ of the Spirit.[62] Jesus is the *Christos,* the Anointed One, because of

---

56. As Kasper asserts: "Grace is . . . first of all uncreated grace, God's self-communication in the Holy Spirit. To say this is not to exclude created grace. For uncreated grace changes the human person from within; it has created effects, and it requires an acceptance by man that is possible only through grace. Therefore uncreated grace, or the indwelling of the Holy Spirit, requires created grace to prepare the way for it, just as it also has created grace for a consequence. It is impossible, therefore, to conceive of the self-communication of God in the Holy Spirit apart from the manifold gifts of the Holy Spirit that are distinct from God and therefore created." Ibid., 227.

57. The Preface from the Second Eucharistic Prayer for Masses of Reconciliation names this Christian experience and belief: "[Father,] in the midst of conflict and division, we know it is you who turn our minds to thoughts of peace. Your Spirit changes our hearts: enemies begin to speak to one another, those who were estranged join hands in friendship, and nations seek the way of peace together. Your Spirit is at work when understanding puts an end to strife, when hatred is quenched by mercy, and vengeance gives way to forgiveness. For this we should never cease to thank and praise you."

58. Kasper, *Jesus the Christ,* 253.

59. Jn 15:26.

60. Jn 14:16, 26.

61. Gal 4:6; Rom 8:9; Phil 1:19.

62. Lk 1:35; 4:18.

his anointing by the Spirit; it is the Spirit who constitutes him as Christ. It is because he is the Christ of the Spirit that Christ can send his Spirit upon his disciples.[63]

Thus the Spirit comes from the Father, accompanying Jesus who is sent, both anointing Jesus as the Christ and anointing the community of Christ's disciples, enabling it to receive the Christ who is sent. The Spirit whom God sends enables reception of the Christ/Son/Word whom God sends. The two missions are inseparable. This inseparability is best preserved conceptually by conceiving Christ as, in Kasper's words, "the principle of our endowment with grace,"[64] and of the Spirit as the principle of reception of Christ and Christ's grace. Without the principle of endowment, the principle of reception leaves the receiver eternally longing; without the principle of reception, the principle of endowment leaves the giver eternally longing.[65]

Throughout the rest of this book, I wish to ground a theology of faith, a theology of "a sense of the faith," a theology of church, and a theology of the church's teaching office and its exercise, on an interrelated theology of the economic and immanent Trinity, with the Holy Spirit conceived as the Spirit of Reception. To that end, I now propose four analogies regarding the economic Trinity and the immanent Trinity. Each analogy attempts to safeguard the monarchy of the Father as the primordial *fons et origo,* the source of all, and attempts to highlight the receptive role of the Spirit in the relationships within the Trinity and in the Triune God's outreach to humanity. Each of the analogies evokes many of the images employed by patristic writers and theologians throughout the long history of theological reflection on the Trinity. Portrayed in this way, what the following formulations bring to the fore is the importance of reception. The four analogies are (1) the dynamic of sending and receiving a mes-

---

63. Jn 14:16, 26.

64. Kasper, *Jesus the Christ,* 253.

65. "Without the Spirit, the Son is the way, and the truth and the life, but without actualisation. . . . Without the mission of the Spirit no one can grasp the hem of the Son's garment, we never receive the eternal life extended to us, the sending of the Son is a dispatch into a void, a messenger who never arrives, a light illuminating nothing, a road to nowhere, and the resurrection is a non-event. . . . Without the mission of the Son the Spirit is a hand deprived of something to grasp, lacking a mystery to be present to, devoid of a mystery to make real in history and in our hearts, divested of a ministry to empower, bereft of children to transform into daughters and sons, wanting in offspring to gather into unity in the church and in human community." Kilian McDonnell, *The Other Hand of God: The Holy Spirit as the Universal Touch and Goal* (Collegeville, Minn.: Liturgical Press, 2003), 228–29.

sage, (2) the dynamic of giving and receiving, (3) the dynamic of a dialogue or conversation, and (4) the dynamic of lovers united in love. In all four analogies, "reception" is at the heart of the *dynamis* concerned. The first analogy refers exclusively to the economic Trinity, the other three to the immanent and economic Trinity.

The first analogy is the dynamic of communicating a message. In God's outreach to humanity, the divine message is God's vision for the full flourishing of human life, that which God desires for humanity—the divine will regarding humanity's salvation. In the communication of this salvific message to humanity, the Father is the Sender of the message. The Son is the one who is sent, the Messenger who delivers the message. The Spirit is the Interpreter who enables understanding of the message—what the message says about God and says about human life. The Sender, the Messenger, and the Interpreter constitute distinct elements in the one dynamic of communication. Without understanding, the message is not received. Once again, the Spirit, as the Interpreter, is the principle of reception. The *Verbum Dei* requires the *Spiritus Dei* to be understood.

The second analogy is the dynamic of giving and receiving. God the Father desires to give of himself to humanity through Jesus Christ. Jesus Christ, at once, gives of himself in obedience to the Father's will and is, thereby, God's self-gift to humanity. The Father is, at once, the Giver of God's self-communication and the Receiver of Christ's self-gift to the Father in return. Jesus Christ is, at once, the paradigmatic instance of humanity's reception of God and of God's reception of humanity. The Holy Spirit is the *dynamis* of mutual giving (*traditio*) and receiving (*receptio*) between Father and Son, and between the Triune God and humanity. The Holy Spirit is the Spirit of Reception, therefore, in both cases. This Holy Spirit of Reception coming upon Jesus constitutes him as both humanity's reception of God's self-gift and God's reception of humanity's self-gift to God. Within the immanent Trinity, the Father is Giver and Receiver, the Son is Receiver and Giver, the Spirit is the dynamic of mutual Reception. Within the economy of salvation, the Spirit is the dynamic of receiving and giving between God and humanity, so as to constitute the principle of humanity's reception of divine revelation.

The third analogy is the dynamic of communication in a conversation or dialogue. The Father speaks forth the Word and receives a Word in reply. The Father is the Speaker and Listener; the Son is Listener and Speaker; the Spirit is the Dialogue between the mutual Speaking and Listening of Father and Son. The word that goes forth from the Father is received (listened to) so totally by the Son that he becomes that Word; the (perfectly echoed) word of response by the Son is received (fully accepted) by the Father as the validated Word of God. The Son is, at once, the Word Spoken and the Word Received. In the process of divine self-communication within God, the Spirit is the Dialogue between Father and Son. In the process of divine self-communication between the Triune God and humanity, the Spirit is the Dialogue who enables response to God's Word of Address to humanity.

The fourth analogy is the dynamic of lovers united in a communion of love. In the communion of love within God, the Father is both Lover and Beloved, and the Son is both Beloved and Lover in return. The Father's love for the Son is not unrequited; the Son's love for the Father is not unrequited. Their love is mutual, and so constitutes a communion of love. In that loving *communio,* the Spirit is the mutual *receptio* of love between them, the *vinculum amoris*—the bond of love. There is no communion if the love given is not received and is not reciprocated. Communion is constituted by mutual reception and reciprocity. *Communio* in the Trinity therefore involves an active process of *receptio* within the Trinity. Humanity's invitation into loving *communio* with God is an invitation to participate in the dynamic of loving *receptio* within God. It is the Holy Spirit who facilitates this active "participation" *(koinonia, communio)* in the divine life, what St. Paul called "the *koinonia* of the Holy Spirit."[66]

These four analogies are intended to be complementary. Each one captures one way of speaking about the intra-trinitarian relationships and the relationship between God and humanity. In each, the Spirit is the dynamic of reception, and therefore within the economy of salvation constitutes the principle of reception of God's outreach, ensuring, in turn, the realization of divine revelation through ultimate reception into the divine life.

This receptive role of the Spirit suggests a way of reconceiving the generation of the Son/Word and the procession of the Spirit within the immanent Trinity. As Congar asserts:

[T]he Word proceeds *a Patre Spirituque,* from the Father and the Spirit, since the latter intervenes in all the acts or moments in the history of the Word incarnate. If

---

66. 2 Cor 13:13.

all the *acta et passa* of the divine economy are traced back to the eternal begetting of the Word, then the Spirit has to be situated at that point.[67]

Both Son and Spirit derive from the Father. In the Father's begetting the Son, in his uttering the Word, the Spirit is implied; in his breathing the Spirit, the Son/Word is implied. It seems to me that the formula *ex Patre cum Spiritu* (from the Father *with* the Spirit) best captures the character of the generation of the Son in relationship to the Spirit. Similarly, the formula *ex Patre cum Filio* (from the Father *with* the Son) best names the procession of the Holy Spirit in relationship to the Son.

When the divine processions are formulated in that way, the missions of the Word and of the Spirit to humanity will not be seen to be independent. Both "a constricted and one-sided Christocentricism" and "the opposite extreme of pure pneumatocentricism"[68] will be thereby excluded. The Word operates *with* the Spirit; and the Spirit operates *with* the Son. The mission of the Word and the mission of the Spirit are mutually dependent.

This suggests that the role of the Spirit as the principle of reception of the Word is best conceived as a role that is proper and distinctive to the Spirit, and not merely to be conceived in an "appropriated" manner.[69] Although the process of God's self-communication to humanity has the life of the Triune God as its origin and goal, it is the distinctive role of the Spirit to open the hearts and minds of the human addressees of that loving outreach, so that they may freely respond through faith, be transformed by grace in order to live the Christ life, come to understand its concrete meaning for all that they say about God and human existence, and ultimately be drawn into God's life and so experience divine hospitality.[70]

67. Yves Congar, *The Word and the Spirit,* trans. David Smith (London: Geoffrey Chapman, 1986), 93. Congar's formula uses the Latin preposition "a"; I will use the preposition "ex," as found in Tanner's Latin version of the Nicene-Constantinopolitan creed of 381 *(ex patre procedentem).* See Norman P. Tanner, *Decrees of the Ecumenical Councils,* 2 vols. (Washington, D.C.: Georgetown University Press, 1990), 1:24.

68. Kasper, "The Renewal of Pneumatology," 100.

69. For a discussion of contemporary approaches to appropriated and proper roles for the persons of the Trinity in the events of salvation history, and his own proposal regarding the distinctive and proper role of the Spirit in creation, see Denis Edwards, *Breath of Life: A Theology of the Creator Spirit* (Maryknoll, N.Y.: Orbis Books, 2004), 117–29.

70. "The function of the Spirit is to bring what happened in Jesus Christ once and for all to fulfilment in the Church and in world history. He does this by enabling those who believe in Christ to participate in the anointing of Jesus through the Spirit. He makes present the work of Christ, not in a legalistic but in a spiritual way." Kasper, "The Renewal of Pneumatology," 101–2.

Asserting that the proper mission of the Spirit is to facilitate reception of the Son is not to subordinate the role of the Spirit to that of a servant of the Son.[71] The mission of the Son is dependent on the Spirit for its reception, just as the mission of the Spirit is unintelligible except in relation to the Son. Nor does such a formulation necessarily cloud the personal character or *hypostasis* of the Spirit. The freedom of the Spirit, much attested to in Scripture, is preserved. That freedom is demonstrated precisely in the diversity of receptions of the Word from a multitude of contexts and situations, not only in Scripture, but also throughout the history of the church. It is in this plurality of receptions, facilitated by the Spirit, that the universality of the salvation mediated through the Word is demonstrated. Because of the Spirit of Reception, the Word is salvific for the world at all times and in all places.

If the Spirit is seen in this way as the principle of the reception of the Son, which the Father and the Son hand over to the disciples, the formula *ex Patre cum Filio* safeguards, I suggest, the perspectives of the complementary and non-contradictory formulas of the West *(ex Patre Filioque)* and the East *(ex Patre per Filium)* regarding the procession of the Holy Spirit within the immanent Trinity. The Spirit proceeds from the Father *and the Son,* because, as experienced within the economy of salvation, the Father sends the Spirit upon the disciples, the very Spirit sent by the Father who has constituted Jesus as the *Christos,* and whom the Risen Christ then likewise shares with his disciples. The Spirit proceeds *through the Son* because, as experienced within the economy of salvation, the mission of the Spirit is not independent and unrelated to the mission of the Son; the principle of reception is inextricably linked to the principle of endowment.

Through the four analogies outlined above, and the concept of the Spirit's procession *ex Patre cum Filio,* the trinitarian theology of revelation I have proposed attempts to be faithful to the early church's experience of the process of revelation: *within* the encounter with Jesus Christ, the Crucified and Risen One, is experienced a power to follow him and

---

71. "[T]he Spirit does not simply follow the work of Christ; he goes before it, supporting and enabling it. He is the Spirit of the Son but not (as stated by the Pneumatomachi) his servant. He is not a slavish administrator of the word and work of Christ; he is a sovereign and life-giving Spirit [*"Dominum et vivificantem"*] who interprets spiritually the person, word and work of Christ with relative freedom, in the freedom of the Spirit. 'Where the Spirit of the Lord is, there is freedom' (2 Cor 3:17). Thus the Holy Spirit is always good for a surprise." Ibid., 102.

an ability to understand him. This power and this ability is a gift resulting from the indwelling of the Holy Spirit in baptized believers. In the
cognitive apprehension of salvific revelation (as in all dimensions of the
transformation effected when Christ is received in faith), the Spirit is
the principle of its reception. Any coherent theology of revelation and
faith, and especially a theology of a "sense of the faith," needs to highlight adequately this principle of reception which is given within God's
revelation in Christ; otherwise it falls into the danger of either "a constricted and one-sided Christocentricism" or "the opposite extreme of
pure pneumatocentricism."[72] Both extremes lead to unbalanced theologies of the ecclesial traditioning of revelation in the church and lead to
unbalanced accounts of the teaching office of the church.

We therefore now need to explore the implications for a theology of
church of the trinitarian theology of revelation which we have just outlined.

72. Ibid., 100.

CHAPTER 2

The Holy Spirit and the Church

In the previous chapter, we discussed the early church's experience of the Word as the principle of the endowment of grace, and of the Spirit as the principle of its reception. We then reflected on the Spirit within the triune life of God, and proposed analogies for understanding the Spirit as the Spirit of Reception. The nature and mission of God determines the nature and mission of the church. The church is called to be an icon of the Trinity.[1] In this chapter we move to a more specific discussion of the role of the Spirit in the economy of salvation, and in particular, the role of the Spirit in co-instituting the church as "the universal sacrament of salvation."[2]

THE SPIRIT AS CO-INSTITUTING PRINCIPLE

Since the gift of faith comes from the Spirit's activity, the community of faith, the church, exists through the power of the Spirit. The church is the community of Christ's disciples who live by the faith and the grace of the Spirit.

The Spirit from the Father, with whom Jesus the *Christos* was anoint-

1. See Bruno Forte, *The Church: Icon of the Trinity. A Brief Study* (Boston: St. Paul Books and Media, 1991).
2. *LG,* 48; *GS,* 45; *AG,* 1.

ed, is the same Spirit whom the Father sends upon, and whom the Risen One shares with, the community of Christ's disciples at Pentecost. If Christ is the principle of endowment of grace in the history of salvific revelation, and the Spirit is the principle of its reception, the church is the place where the mission of the Word and the mission of the Spirit find their clearest point of conjuncture in human history. In this sense, the Spirit is the "co-instituting principle" of the church, along with the principle of the Word.[3] Both Word and Spirit bring the church of the Triune God into being. This "instituting" is not to be seen simply in the chronological sense of a one-off "beginning"; the Word and Spirit continuously enable the church to be church throughout its history.

As the co-instituting principle of the church, the Holy Spirit is the principle not only of the church's beginning but also of the church's continuing existence, i.e., the guarantee of the church's indefectibility, the belief "that Christ's Church would never succumb either to external hostility or to internal corruption."[4] Vatican II affirms this inability of the church to fail as due to the action of the Holy Spirit.[5] Christ's promises, that the gates of hell shall not prevail against the church,[6] and that he, Christ, would be with his disciples till the end of time,[7] are promises guaranteed fulfillment through the work of the Holy Spirit. The indefectibility of Christ's church fundamentally means that its continuing existence is assured by the Holy Spirit.[8]

Included in this general assurance is the more specific conviction that

---

3. On the two missions of Word and Spirit, and the Spirit as the co-instituting principle of the church, see Yves Congar, *I Believe in the Holy Spirit* (New York: Crossroad, 1997), 2:5–14.

4. Francis A. Sullivan, *Magisterium: Teaching Authority in the Catholic Church* (New York: Paulist Press, 1983), 4. Also on the indefectibility of the church, see Yves Congar, "Indefectibility and Infallibility," *Compass* 5 (1971): 43–45; Sullivan, *Magisterium*, 4–23.

5. *LG*, 9 states: "As the church journeys through temptations and tribulations, it is strengthened by the power of the grace of God that was promised it by the Lord, so that it does not fall away from perfect fidelity through the weakness of the flesh, but remains the worthy spouse of its Lord, and so that, under the action of the holy Spirit, it does not cease from renewing itself until, through the cross, it arrives at the light which knows no setting." Tanner translation.

6. Mt 16:18.

7. Mt 28:20.

8. "The Church's confidence that she will 'remain a bride worthy of the Lord' is not a matter of human pride. It is a matter of humble faith in the power of God's grace and the abiding assistance of the Holy Spirit. It is only by the power of grace and the work of the Holy Spirit that she will be able to overcome the weakness of the flesh and never cease to renew herself. But she knows that her Lord has promised her this grace and this abiding presence of the Holy Spirit, and that his promises will never fail of their fulfilment." Sullivan, *Magisterium*, 5.

the church's mission to proclaim the truth of the Gospel faithfully will also be guaranteed. The Holy Spirit likewise is here the guarantor that the church will always be "the pillar and bulwark of the truth."[9] This narrower aspect of the church's indefectibility in the truth relates to the church's conviction regarding its infallibility, both in believing and in teaching. According to *Lumen Gentium* 12, the church's infallibility in believing is rooted in the *sensus fidei* of the whole People of God, and becomes manifest when that *sensus fidei* brings forth a *consensus* in matters of faith and morals. In this way, the church "adheres indefectibly *(indefectibiliter)* to 'the faith which was once for all delivered to the saints' (Jude 3)."[10] This paragraph had earlier affirmed:

> The universal body of the faithful who have received the anointing of the holy one (see 1 Jn 2:20 and 27) cannot err in matters of belief [*in credendo falli nequit*]. It displays this particular quality through a supernatural sense of the faith in the whole people when "from the bishops to the last of the faithful laity," it expresses the consent of all in matters of faith and morals.[11]

The paragraph then moves on to address the issue of the relationship between the whole People of God and the magisterium, introducing implicitly the interrelationship between the whole People of God and its *infallibilitas in credendo* (infallibility in believing) and the magisterium and its *infallibilitas in docendo* (infallibility in teaching), the latter theme being addressed in greater detail in *Lumen Gentium* 25. Part 3 of this book will examine the interrelationship of these aspects of the church's indefectibility. Here, at this stage of our enquiry regarding the Holy Spirit and the church, the point to be highlighted is that, in all aspects of the church's indefectibility, and more particularly its infallibility, it is the Holy Spirit who, as the co-instituting principle of the church, remains the guarantor of the church's ongoing faithful reception of Christ.

As the place where the mission of the Word receives human reception through the mission of the Spirit, the church's mission is the *missio Dei*. "The pilgrim church is of its very nature missionary, since it draws its ori-

---

9. 1 Tm 3:15. Sullivan summarizes this belief when he speaks of "the quite general agreement among Christians that the Holy Spirit is promised to abide with the Church, as the Spirit of truth, who will guide the Church into all the truth. It is faith in this abiding presence and assistance of the Spirit of truth to the Church which founds the Christian conviction of the Church's indefectibility in the truth." *Magisterium*, 6.

10. *LG*, 12. Tanner translation.

11. Ibid.

gin from the mission of the Son and the mission of the holy Spirit, in accordance with the plan of God the Father."[12] The church's mission is to
always "hand on" *(tradere)* to the world that which it has received: God's
offer of salvific revelation through being drawn into the very inner life of
the Triune God. Thus, in this sense, the mission of the church is to receive and to tradition God's offer of salvific revelation.[13] The Spirit and
the Word continuously co-institute the church in that mission.

In order to explore further the particular role of the Spirit in the co-
instituting of the church, we need to examine the relationship between
reception and tradition. Reception and tradition are two correlative aspects of the one continuous mission of the church: what is received must
be handed on, and what is handed on must then be received anew if it is
to be effectively traditioned to new generations in new cultures and contexts.[14] The church does this by its very life: "in this way the church, in
its teaching, life and worship, perpetuates and hands on to every generation all that it is and all that it believes."[15] In this sense, reception and
tradition are co-extensive with the life and mission of the church.

This reception and ongoing traditioning by the church in the present looks both to the past and to the future; the Spirit is the bridge to
both. Firstly, the church seeks to be faithful to the "content" of revelation revealed definitively in the past, that which has been revealed in the
concrete teaching and imagery, behavior and commitment to the reign
of God in the life and ministry of Jesus of Nazareth, and in his manner
of death and the reality of his resurrection. It is through the experience of
this whole Christ event that Christians can give content to the revelation
of God, and through no other means. The Christ event, as witnessed to
in Scripture and tradition, is thus normative for all that Christians proclaim and teach about God. God, for Christians, is the God of Jesus
Christ. The Spirit anchors the church in that normative content.

Secondly, the church's faith in the God of the Crucified and Risen One

12. *AG,* 2. Tanner translation.

13. Throughout this book, I will sometimes use the word "tradition" as a verb. I do so deliberately in order to avoid a static notion of tradition and to use it to refer not only to the products of
an ecclesial process of transmission, but also to the active nature of that historical process.

14. "The transmission of the tradition is the act of reception, and it is the act of reception that
renders the content of tradition concretely effective or formative of the life of the church." Michael J. Scanlon, "Catholicism and Living Tradition: The Church as a Community of Reception,"
in *Empowering Authority: The Charisms of Episcopacy and Primacy in the Church Today,* ed. Patrick
J. Howell and Gary Chamberlain (Kansas City: Sheed and Ward, 1990), 1–16, at 3.

15. *DV,* 8. Tanner translation.

not only looks to the past, but is an eschatological faith. The church's believing and that which it believes will achieve their fulfillment at the end of time when God's purposes are finally achieved, when the reign of God is accomplished. It is the mission of the Spirit, as the principle of reception of the Word, to enable the church to be a servant of that reign, as it moves toward its eschatological fulfillment. "When the Spirit of truth comes, he will guide you into all the truth" (Jn 16:13).

But to speak of the eschatological nature of faith does not mean that the Spirit brings forth new revelation beyond that which is revealed in Jesus Christ, the Word, "both the mediator and the fullness of all revelation,"[16] as witnessed to in Scripture and tradition. There is no "development," beyond that which is revealed in Jesus Christ; what *is* new are the manifold ways in which the original reality, the Word, is received throughout human history.[17] The proper mission of the Spirit is always orientated to the reception of God's revelation through Jesus Christ, crucified and risen. The Spirit enables reception of that reality in new contexts within human history into the future. The meaning and truth of God's revelation through Christ for a particular time and place is revealed only in the Spirit; the necessary particularity of any meaningful and true appropriation of God's self-gift through Christ is possible only through the Holy Spirit. There is one Word, but many receptions.

The theologies of the New Testament testify to the early church's experience of and reflection on the freedom of the Spirit in their lives. Scripture witnesses to a diversity of receptions of the meaning and truth of Jesus Christ. The early church communities encountered situations and questions for which the teachings and traditions concerning Jesus were unable to provide specific solutions and answers. However, we find exhibited over and over the firm belief that the Spirit's gift for understanding, which had been given at Pentecost and which they believed continued to abide in their communities, was a gift that enabled them to effectively proclaim the salvific Word as the early churches expanded into new cultures and contexts. There was a belief that the fundamental truth of what they had received through Christ, the saving Gospel, would be found to be universally "true," in all situations. With the sense of the ever-present Spirit who accompanied their mission, they boldly and cre-

16. *DV,* 2. Tanner translation.

17. On the inadequacies of the "development" metaphor, see Ormond Rush, "Reception Hermeneutics and the 'Development' of Doctrine," *Pacifica* 6 (1993): 125–40.

atively interpreted and applied the meaning and truth of Jesus Christ for this or that new situation. This experience of the freedom of the Spirit in the reception of revelation is likewise manifested throughout later church history, in the rich variety of spiritualities through which communities of faith lived and expressed the salvation they found in Jesus Christ.

THE CHURCH AS A COMMUNITY OF RECEPTION

The church is "a community of reception."[18] Reception marks the very nature and mission of the church, and reaches to all levels of its life. As Komonchak states: "The apostolic faith comes with the power of the Spirit and is received by faith. . . . The whole ontology of the Church— the real 'objective' existence of the Church—consists in the reception by faith of the Gospel. Reception is constitutive of the Church."[19]

The church is a community of reception in at least five ways. (1) It receives the Holy Spirit, the principle of reception of God's self-communication. (2) Because of that principle, the church receives God's self-gift in Jesus Christ. (3) It receives in trust as normative for its life the witness to that divine self-giving in Scripture and tradition. (4) It receives a mission, to proclaim and inaugurate God's reign in the world, by offering the possibility of salvation through Christ in the power of the Spirit. And (5), it receives and initiates into its community individuals who freely accept in faith this divine offer of salvation.

Firstly, the church receives the Holy Spirit. All believers together con-

---

18. Wolfgang Beinert, "The Subjects of Reception," in Legrand, Manzanares, and García y García, eds., *Reception and Communion Among Churches,* 324–46, at 325. Gilles Routhier writes: "One can speak of reception . . . as a fundamental, original, and originating structure of Christian activity. The Christian faith is essentially an act of reception of what has been transmitted. The Church is constituted in this act of exchange; i.e., the gift of God and its reception, the proclamation of the Word and the response to that proclamation. It is only at this depth that we can understand what is reception in its fullness in the Christian dispensation. The other facts of reception participate in this much broader and fundamental paradigmatic fact of reception, which is described in the New Testament." Gilles Routhier, "Reception in Current Theological Debate," in Legrand, Manzanares, and García y García, eds., *Reception and Communion Among Churches,* 17–52, at 33. For similar uses of the phrase "a community of reception," see Giuseppe Alberigo, "The Christian Situation after Vatican II," in *The Reception of Vatican II,* ed. Giuseppe Alberigo, Jean Pierre Jossua, and Joseph A. Komonchak (Washington, D.C.: The Catholic University of America Press, 1987), 1–24, at 3, and Scanlon, "Catholicism and Living Tradition," with its subtitle, "The Church as a Community of Reception."

19. Joseph A. Komonchak, "The Epistemology of Reception," in Legrand, Manzanares, and García y García, eds., *Reception and Communion Among Churches,* 180–203, at 193.

stitute the community of reception in this sense. "Do you not know that you are God's temple and that God's Spirit dwells in you?"[20] Luke's account of Pentecost emphasizes that "all of them were filled with the Holy Spirit."[21] It is significant that this original ecclesial experience of the Spirit occurred "when they were all together in one place."[22] It is at a meeting of the community that the coming and reception of the Holy Spirit is manifested. The New Testament does not record that individuals separately experienced the Spirit, and then shared their own experiences; individual experiences are later recounted in terms of the Holy Spirit who has been first given to the whole community.[23]

Secondly, the church receives Jesus Christ. As a community of faith (of believing, in the sense of *fides qua creditur*), the church is a community of reception, since it is the community of those who have received God's self-gift in Jesus Christ. It is because it has received the Spirit, the principle of reception, that it is enabled to receive that gift. The church is the place where God's proffered gift is received in faith, the place where the Father's self-gift through Christ is received in the Spirit, the place where divine salvation coming through Christ finds its realization in human lives.

This divine self-giving in Christ is *Emmanuel,* God with us. "The Church [is] a place of welcome or reception of the visit of God."[24] But in offering hospitality to God among us, believers are only responding to God's prior offer of hospitality. The church receives the divine invitation to live in communion with God and enjoy divine hospitality. It is the mission of the church to pass on ("tradition") that divine self-communication, reiterating the invitation to divine hospitality to all of humanity. It is the Spirit of Reception who will enable the church to fulfill that mission, because it is only when the divine gift is received that the divine Giving achieves its goal. Because the church is called to be a sacrament of communion with God and of communion among all humanity,[25] the church

---

20. 1 Cor 3:16.   21. Acts 2:4.

22. Acts 2:1.

23. "[I]f the Spirit is received when believers are *together,* it is not because there is one body that there is only one Spirit—it is rather because there is only one Spirit of Christ that there is only one body, which is the Body of Christ. The Spirit *acts* in order to enable men to enter that Body, but he is *given* to the Body and it is in that Body that we receive the gift of the Spirit." Congar, *I Believe in the Holy Spirit,* 2:15. Original italics.

24. Routhier, "Reception in Current Theological Debate," 31.

25. *LG,* 1.

is called to be *a sacrament of reception* into that communion with God and among all humanity.

Just as the Holy Spirit at Pentecost was given to and received by the whole community, so too it is the whole community of believers, and not just certain individuals within it, who are entrusted with God's salvific and revelatory outreach through Christ in the Spirit. Vatican II firmly teaches this truth in the very structure of *Lumen Gentium,* where the chapter on the People of God comes before the chapter on the hierarchy. Thus, it is the entire church which is the recipient of Christ; it is the entire church which is anointed by the Holy Spirit to enable its reception of Christ; it is the entire church which is the trustee of the *missio*—to tradition the reality of salvation, "the integral and living Gospel *(evangelium integrum et vivum)."*[26] It is the entire community which is the community of reception.

Thirdly, the church receives the Word of God, as witnessed to in Scripture and tradition. As a community of faith (in the sense of *fides quae creditur*), the church is a community of reception of a sacred treasure. "Tradition and scripture together form a single sacred deposit of the word of God, entrusted to the church."[27] That sacred deposit is "the faith that was once for all entrusted to the saints."[28] Scripture and tradition witness to the "integral and living Gospel"[29]—the reality of God's loving and salvific outreach to humanity through Jesus Christ in the Holy Spirit—which is the "divine wellspring" from which Scripture and tradition flow.[30] This living Gospel, testified in Scripture and tradition, constitutes "the principle of all of the Church's life for all time."[31] And the principle of the Gospel's reception is the Holy Spirit: "The holy Spirit . . . is active, making the living voice of the gospel ring out in the church, and through it in the world, leading those who believe into the whole truth, and making

---

26. *DV,* 7. Tanner translation.

27. *DV,* 10. Tanner translation. "The 'deposit' [of faith] is the inclusive term for this faith and way of life bequeathed by the apostles and their coworkers to the churches founded by their proclamation of the good news about Jesus Christ. The apostles left as their legacy a coherent pattern of faith, teaching, and modes of biblical interpretation, of worship and community structures of service, and of life in the world according to the word and example of the Lord Jesus." Jared Wicks, "Deposit of Faith," in *Dictionary of Fundamental Theology,* ed. René Latourelle and Rino Fisichella (Middlegreen, Slough, England: St. Paul, 1994), 229–39, at 229.

28. Jude 3.   29. *DV,* 7. Tanner translation.

30. *DV,* 9.

31. *LG,* 20. See also John Thornhill, "The Gospel: The Ultimate Authority in the Life of the Church," *Australasian Catholic Record* 72 (1995): 131–42.

the message of Christ dwell in them in all its richness."[32] Significantly, *Dei Verbum* teaches that tradition and Scripture are entrusted to "the church . . . the entire holy people," and not solely to the magisterium.[33]

Fourthly, the church receives a mission. As a sacrament of salvation, the church is a community of reception, since it has received a mission: to proclaim the reign of God begun through Jesus Christ. "When . . . the church . . . receives the mission of announcing the kingdom of Christ and of God and of inaugurating it among all peoples, it has formed the seed and the beginning of the kingdom on earth."[34] *Gaudium et Spes* later teaches:

While it helps the world and receives much from the world, the church has only one goal, namely the coming of God's kingdom and the accomplishment of salvation for the whole human race. Whatever good God's people can contribute to the human family, in the period of its earthly pilgrimage, derives from the church's being "the universal sacrament of salvation," which shows forth and at the same time brings into effect the mystery of God's love for humanity.[35]

This reign of God is none other than the economy of salvation: God reaching out to humanity through Christ in the power of the Spirit. The church receives a mission to tradition this salvific offer.

Fifthly, the church receives into its midst all who respond to the Gospel of Jesus Christ and wish to become his disciples in the community of faith. Reception *into* the divine life, and reception *of* the divine life, is offered through reception into the church. The three sacraments of initiation into the community of faith (Baptism, Confirmation, Eucharist) together mark the Christian as not only a member of a community which is anointed by the Spirit, but also as an individual who is personally anointed by the Spirit. None of these three sacraments of initiation should be seen in isolation in any ecclesiology, as if one sacrament alone can carry the weight of being the locus for the confluence of the mission of the Word and the mission of the Spirit. All three sacraments of reception into the community continue to mark the identity of the Christian throughout the stages of their lifelong journey of faith.

Although there is a chronological sequence to the original celebration of these sacraments, individuals' relationship to the Spirit with whom

32. *DV,* 8. Tanner translation.   33. *DV,* 10. Tanner translation.
34. *LG,* 5. Tanner translation.
35. *GS,* 45. The council is here quoting its earlier document *LG,* 48.

they are sealed is not a static one. Through Baptism and Confirmation, by being sealed with the Spirit, the Christian individual is incorporated into the Body of Christ; the baptized's first reception of Eucharist is the high point of that initiation, and regular reception of the Eucharist sustains that communal identity of the individual as a *Christos,* an anointed one, a "Christian." To be initiated into the Eucharistic community is the endpoint, yet only the beginning, of full membership in the Body of Christ, united in the Spirit. Ongoing participation "in Christ" is only possible through ongoing participation *(koinonia)* in the Spirit, hence the need for the ongoing *epiclesis* (invocation) for the Spirit. The individual's relationship to the Holy Spirit is a relationship that requires nurturing and nourishment. Baptismal identity is therefore not a static status; it is a relational identity in which the Spirit, as the principle of reception, enables ongoing daily conversion to Christ and fidelity to his way.

Thus the church is a community of reception because it has received the Holy Spirit as the principle of reception; it has received Jesus Christ as God's self-gift; it has received the witnesses to that divine revelation, Scripture and tradition, as normative for its life; it has received a mission to hand on the offer of that salvific revelation; it receives into its midst those who respond in faith to that offer. Although individual members are anointed with the Spirit, it is fundamentally the community as a whole who is the primary recipient of the Holy Spirit and therefore the community of reception.

MARKS OF THE SPIRIT

The significance of the Spirit's freedom as the principle of the reception of revelation is evident when we examine the traditional framework of the four marks or attributes of the church as one, holy, catholic, and apostolic, as listed in the Nicene-Constantinopolitan Creed.[36] It is the Spirit who preserves the unity, holiness, catholicity, and apostolicity of the church as it seeks to fulfill its mission of traditioning revelation. Each of these marks

---

36. On the marks of the church, see Francis A. Sullivan, *The Church We Believe In: One, Holy, Catholic, and Apostolic* (New York: Paulist Press, 1988). On the Spirit and the marks of the church, see Richard Lennan, *Risking the Church: The Challenges of Catholic Faith* (New York: Oxford University Press, 2004), 105–16. On the "classic" four and other more contemporary attempts at naming the marks of the church, see William Madges and Michael J. Daley, eds., *The Many Marks of the Church* (New London, Conn.: Twenty-Third Publications, 2006).

is a mark of the Spirit, since it is a mark of the Spirit's work of effecting reception for the sake of effective traditioning of revelation.

The unity of the church is a unity in the Holy Spirit.[37] According to *Lumen Gentium,* the Spirit is "the principle of union and unity *(principium congregationis et unitatis)* in the teaching of the apostles, in communion, in the breaking of bread and in prayers."[38] The oneness created by the Spirit is manifested in various overlapping aspects. Using spatial and temporal metaphors, we could say that the Spirit creates unity in three dimensions: "vertical" unity (between the church and the Triune God), "horizontal" unity (among believers), and "temporal" unity with the church of the past and into the future (among believers).

In terms of "vertical" unity, the Spirit draws believers into communion with the Triune God. In the first chapter we discussed this primary notion of *communio* within God and *communio* of humanity with God. Communion with the Triune God is the ultimate goal of God's salvific and revelatory outreach to humanity through Christ in the Spirit. It is the Spirit of Reception who opens human hearts to this divine outreach through the gift of faith, the human response to God's offer, and thus is the source of unity of faith (as believing, *fides qua creditur).* The highest expression of that communion or unity in believing, responding to God's offer, is communal liturgical worship, especially the Eucharist. The community's acknowledgment that only the Spirit enables such unity is its prayer for the Holy Spirit to come upon them, the *epiclesis.*

In terms of "horizontal" unity, the Spirit is the bond of unity in all things regarding "the one and the many" in the church. It is because it is the same Spirit who is given both to the whole body of the faithful *(universitas fidelium)* and to the individuals within that community that the church can be a communion of persons *(communio fidelium* or *congregatio fidelium).* It is because it is the same Spirit who animates each local church that the church is a communion of churches *(communio ecclesiarum).* It is because it is the same Spirit who is involved in the sacramental ordination of each individual bishop in each local church that the church universal is a communion of local churches under its bishop, in communion with the bishop of Rome *(communio hierarchica).* Vatican

---

37. On the unity of faith, see William Henn, *One Faith: Biblical and Patristic Contributions Toward Understanding Unity in Faith* (New York: Paulist Press, 1995). The literature on church unity in contemporary ecumenical discussion is too extensive to be listed here.

38. *LG,* 13. Tanner translation.

II's notions of *communio fidelium* (unity in the *universitas fidelium*),[39] *communio ecclesiarum* (the universal church concretized fully in each local church),[40] and *communio hierarchica* (unity of collegiality among the bishops with and under the bishop of Rome)[41] capture different nuances of the way the one Spirit maintains oneness or communion among "the many." This threefold "horizontal" unity is founded on its "vertical" unity, the oneness created by the church's *receptio* into *communio* with God, made possible through the Spirit of Reception. Furthermore, on all these levels, the church is united because it shares a common mission: to proclaim the one faith, the living Gospel, the possibility and reality of *communio* with God. The source and summit of that unity is *communio* with Christ and with one another in the Eucharist, a unity invoked in the *epiclesis* and made possible by the Spirit.

The Spirit also effects a *communio* through time. The *communio fidelium* extends not only synchronically to believers throughout the world at one time, but also diachronically with all believers in the past, extending into the future to the *eschaton,* beyond human time. Eucharistic communion of believers with Christ and among themselves, and between Eucharistic communities throughout the world, extends both backwards in time, in unity with that great cloud of witnesses in the past and, beyond human time, to the *communio sanctorum,* the communion of saints in heaven.[42] Temporal unity throughout the history of the church is expressed in its common mission to be the sacrament of salvation and its common confession through time of the one faith, the common creed of the beliefs it professes. The church is one and the same throughout history because it continues to profess "the faith that was once for all entrusted to the saints."[43]

In all of these dimensions, the Spirit creates *koinonia (communio).* The Spirit is "the principle of unity,"[44] "the principle of communion."[45] The

---

39. On the church as a *communio fidelium,* see *LG,* 13; *UR,* 2; *AA,* 18. For example, *UR,* 2 states: "It is the holy Spirit, dwelling in those who believe and filling and ruling over the church as a whole, who brings about that wonderful communion of the faithful *(communionem fidelium).* He brings them all into intimate union with Christ, so that he is *the principle of the church's unity.*"

40. On the church as a *communio ecclesiarum,* see *LG,* 23.

41. On the church as a *communio hierarchica,* see *LG,* 21–22; *PO,* 15.

42. See *LG,* 49–50.   43. Jude 3.

44. *UR,* 2.

45. On the Holy Spirit as the principle of communion, see Congar, *I Believe in the Holy Spirit,* 2:15–23.

forging of bonds of communion on all these levels, however, presumes a dynamic of reception on all these levels. There is no *communio* without mutual *receptio.* If the church is called to be the icon of the Trinity, and *receptio* is at the heart of the trinitarian *communio,* as we have seen, then *receptio* must be at the heart of, and indeed constitute, ecclesial *communio* in all aspects of oneness in the church—vertical, horizontal, and temporal. Furthermore, if the church is called to be the icon of the Trinity, and dialogue is at the heart of trinitarian *communio,* as we have seen, then dialogue must be at the heart of, and indeed constitute, ecclesial *communio* on all levels—vertical, horizontal, and temporal. In the economy of salvation, it is the Spirit who is the principle of *receptio* in all dimensions of the church's *communio*—vertical, horizontal, and temporal. In maintaining the unity of faith, the church learned early in its history that the Spirit was best discerned when individuals were together, in community, in council, in synod, just as the coming of the Spirit at Pentecost was experienced when they were "all together."[46] Thus the principle of synodality or conciliarity was experienced as the way of the Holy Spirit, the principle of reception, who is the Spirit of Dialogue within God and between God and humanity.[47]

Discussion of the church's unity necessarily merges with discussion of the church's catholicity; all the aspects of unity and communion discussed above achieve richer formulation when the catholicity of communion is examined.[48] Catholicity marks both the inner life and the missionary thrust of the church. The church's inner unity is a catholic unity. Here too, precisely because the Spirit is the principle of unity, the Spirit is also "the principle of catholicity."[49] Because it is the proper mission of the Spirit to enable Christ to be received throughout history and throughout the world, the Holy Spirit can be truly called "the principal agent of mission."[50] Thus the Spirit maintains the catholicity of the church not

---

46. Acts 2:1.

47. See Yves Congar, "The Conciliar Structure or Regime of the Church," *Concilium* 167 (1983): 3–9; Yves Congar, "The Council as an Assembly and the Church as Essentially Conciliar," in *One, Holy, Catholic, and Apostolic: Studies in the Nature and Role of the Church in the Modern World,* ed. Herbert Vorgrimler (London: Sheed and Ward, 1968), 44–88.

48. On catholicity, see Avery Dulles, *The Catholicity of the Church* (Oxford: Clarendon Press, 1985); Robert J. Schreiter, *The New Catholicity: Theology between the Global and the Local* (Maryknoll, N.Y.: Orbis Books, 1997).

49. See Congar, *I Believe in the Holy Spirit,* 2:24–38.

50. See John Paul II, *Redemptoris Missio,* chapter 3.

only in its life *ad intra* but also in its mission *ad extra*. It is to the whole world that the church is sent on mission. The one church is sent as a servant of the *missio Dei* to bring "the integral and living Gospel" (salvific revelation) to the ends of the earth, to all peoples and cultures.

Just as the notions of *communio fidelium, communio ecclesiarum,* and *communio hierarchica* name aspects of the "horizontal" unity of the church, so do they name aspects of the "horizontal" catholicity of the church. Vatican II's teaching on collegiality among the bishops and the pope, and its teaching on the local church as the fullness of the church catholic gathered around its bishop in that place, all highlight Vatican II's shift to a notion of the church catholic as a truly "world-church." Indeed, Karl Rahner has claimed that Vatican II is to be interpreted in its most fundamental sense as an epochal shift in the church's self-understanding, from a Hellenistic phase lasting one and a half millennia, to a sense of being a truly "world-church," a truly "catholic" church.[51] With a greater appreciation of "history" and "historical consciousness," culture and context have been recognized as highly significant factors needing to be addressed if the church is to be effective in fulfilling its mission—traditioning the Gospel to the ends of the earth. According to the approach taken in this book, the catholicity of the church is best appreciated in terms of the reception of revelation (the Gospel) from different cultures and contexts. Thus local churches constitute diverse *loci receptionis* (places of reception) where the one Spirit enables those churches to appropriate divine salvation coming through the one Jesus Christ in their particular *locus,* and where the one Spirit enables those churches to understand and interpret their experience of salvation from the perspective of that particular *locus.*[52] In enabling reception of the salvific power of Jesus Christ in local contexts, the Spirit reveals Jesus Christ as *universal* Savior. Just as the Spirit preserves unity in all things related to "the one and the many" in the church, so too it is the Spirit who stimulates the manifold ways in which the saving Gospel is inculturated and contextualized throughout the world.

This catholic diversity is also apparent when we examine the tempo-

---

51. Karl Rahner, "Basic Theological Interpretation of the Second Vatican Council," in *Theological Investigations,* vol. 20 (London: Darton, Longman & Todd, 1981), 20:77–89.

52. On the notion of diverse *loci receptionis* of revelation, see Ormond Rush, *The Reception of Doctrine: An Appropriation of Hans Robert Jauss' Reception Aesthetics and Literary Hermeneutics* (Rome: Gregorian University Press, 1997), 206–11, 331–58.

ral dimension of catholicity. Despite the correctness of Rahner's thesis regarding Vatican II's conscious shift to being a world-church, the history of the church does reveal, nevertheless, how the church to a certain degree in the past engaged with the culture and context of its times. The source of this creative diversity is the creativity of the Spirit of Reception. Genuine diversity is revealed in the ways of expressing the faith in "doctrine, life and worship"[53] in different times, circumstances, and cultures. This engagement is demonstrated in the painting, music, architecture, sculpture, spirituality, and organizational structures of each age of the church's mission through time. The history of theology, moreover, reveals great diversity in the theological receptions of revelation throughout the church's history. This pluralism of theologies witnesses to the way theology has always appropriately employed different "background theories" in order to express the faith in the intellectual frameworks accepted at a certain time.[54] A Catholic *fides* has always promoted a dynamic relationship between *fides* and *ratio*. The importance of theological scholarship in the mission of the church's traditioning of the faith is an ecclesial activity recognized by Vatican II as assisted by the Holy Spirit.[55] Ultimately, this temporal catholicity is grounded in the vertical dimension. The temporal reception of Scripture and tradition takes place within the horizon of contemporary experience of the same God witnessed to in Scripture and tradition. In each age of the church's history, God is reaching out to humanity through Christ in the power of the Spirit. From that contemporary horizon of salvific experience, the church receives Scripture and tradition, bringing forth new interpretations of salvific revelation, in a rich catholicity of understanding the one faith.

Just as discussion of the church's unity merges with discussion of its catholicity, so too discussion of catholicity leads to and overlaps with that of apostolicity.[56] The word "apostolic" refers more to the foundational period in the early church than exclusively to the twelve individuals whom Christ chose to play a symbolic role in the group he gathered around

---

53. *DV,* 8.

54. On "background theories" in theology, see Francis Schüssler Fiorenza, "Systematic Theology: Task and Methods," in *Systematic Theology: Roman Catholic Perspectives,* ed. Francis Schüssler Fiorenza and John P. Galvin (Minneapolis: Fortress Press, 1991), 3–87.

55. *DV,* 8.

56. On apostolicity, see John J. Burkhard, *Apostolicity Then and Now: An Ecumenical Church in a Postmodern World* (Collegeville, Minn.: Liturgical Press, 2004).

him.[57] *Dei Verbum* 7 speaks of a wider group than the Twelve, of the apostles "with others in the apostolic age." In chapter 5 we will examine more closely the notions of "apostle," "apostolic faith," "apostolic tradition," and "apostolic succession," as well as issues of authority in the transmission of the apostolic faith. But at this stage it is important to emphasize that foundational revelation was given not just to the Twelve, who then handed it to the whole community, but rather foundational revelation was given to the whole community of witnesses in that foundational "apostolic" period of the church, which ends with the formation of Scripture.[58]

The notion of "witness" or "testimony" so pervades the New Testament that it could be said that the original apostolic mission was to witness to Christ in word and deed.[59] The catholic faith is one throughout time because it is always that original apostolic witness to Christ which continues to be received over and over, albeit from new horizons of understanding. Because this process necessarily involves interpretation of the apostolic witness, the mark of apostolicity is guaranteed because it is the Spirit who will be the Interpreter enabling faithful interpretation of the apostolic tradition. "Since it is the Spirit who inspired that original witness, it is also the Spirit who keeps it alive through the history of the church."[60]

The mark of apostolicity highlights the elements of continuity and identity through time. Apostolicity marks authenticity in the church's witness by virtue of the manifest link with the foundational period of the church and its foundational witnesses. The church is the one church of Jesus Christ through time if it remains true to that foundational witness to Christ in the apostolic era. Just as then it was the Holy Spirit who gifted those first witnesses with an ability to understand and interpret God's revelation through Christ, so too throughout the church's history that same Spirit enables the church to faithfully and freshly proclaim the original apostolic faith. As the *Catechism of the Catholic Church* teaches, "the Holy Spirit is the Church's living memory."[61] Here the mark of apostolicity overlaps with that of unity. In terms of "temporal unity," the church is one throughout time because it is in continuity with the apos-

---

57. For a discussion on the notions of "apostle," "the Twelve," and "apostolicity," see ibid., 1–70.

58. See Karl Rahner, *Inspiration in the Bible,* 2nd rev. ed. (London: Burns & Oates, 1964), 45.

59. See Trites, *The New Testament Concept of Witness.*

60. Lennan, *Risking the Church,* 113.

61. *Catechism of the Catholic Church* (London: Geoffrey Chapman, 1994), para 1099.

tolic church, that first group of believers whose witness to Christ, conveyed in Scripture and tradition, becomes the norm for the church's later life and mission. Under this "temporal" aspect, the Holy Spirit is "the transcendent subject of tradition,"[62] enabling the one apostolic faith to be proclaimed and transmitted through time (diachronically) and in the diverse cultures and situations of local churches at one time (synchronically). The principle of reception enables effective traditioning.

Apostolicity is not to be understood in terms of a static notion of continuity. Failure in transmitting the apostolic faith can come from misunderstanding its meaning and truth in cultures and times different from its original formulation. Genuine continuity demands ongoing reinterpretation. Strikingly, within the very apostolic tradition itself, as witnessed to in the New Testament, we indeed see a process of reception and traditioning within the apostolic era that shows creative and innovative adaptation of the Gospel as the early church expanded into new cultures and contexts. In part 2, "The Norm," we will focus particularly on the apostolic era and the formation of the New Testament, which becomes the primary norm for judging fidelity to the apostolic faith. The normativity of the New Testament, we shall see, relates not just to the *content* of its writings. What is also normative is the witness those writings give to the *hermeneutical process* by which the apostolic church maintained continuity in the proclamation of the faith, precisely through creative adaptation. It is this pattern of creative adaptation which is also normative for all future traditioning in the church. Thus the twin aspects of continuity and creativity in the tradition and reception process are significant criteria in judging the mark of apostolicity throughout history. A static traditioning of the faith endangers the apostolicity of the church. It is in this sense that Yves Congar highlights the eschatological orientation of apostolicity, as well as its orientation to the past.

Apostolicity is the mark that for the Church is both a gift of grace and a task. It makes the Church fill the space between the Alpha and the Omega by ensuring that there is a continuity between the two and a substantial identity between the end and the beginning. . . . [T]he part played by the Holy Spirit in bringing about and maintaining the continuity and even the identity between the Alpha and the Omega [is best understood through] the category of testimony.[63]

---

62. Yves Congar, *The Meaning of Tradition* (New York: Hawthorn Books, 1964), 51–58.
63. Congar, *I Believe in the Holy Spirit*, 2:39, 41.

We have already seen how the category of "witness" or "testimony" names an essential element in the apostolic mission. It now leads us to the fourth mark of the church, the fourth mark of the Spirit.

With the mark of holiness, we come to that quality of the church which above all enables it to be a *lumen gentium,* a light to the nations. It is above all in holiness of life that the power of the integral and living Gospel shines forth, that the faith is transmitted. It is above all in the witness of lives transformed by grace that the reality of divine salvation is realized and manifested. Here apostolicity and holiness merge, since as we saw, the apostolic mission was to witness to the power of the Gospel in word and deed. According to Barth, as we have seen, revelation requires manifestation for its realization.[64] As the principle of reception of salvific revelation, the Holy Spirit is the Sanctifier, the one who "makes holy," the one who brings about holiness of life, who transforms sinful human beings into holy human beings. Through the waters of baptismal initiation, the Spirit washes clean and renews.[65] Life in Christ and life in the Spirit are the one reality, a human being living the life of grace. All baptized believers are not just called to such holiness; they are *enabled* to become holy, through the indwelling of the Holy Spirit.

The call to holiness is ultimately the call to become like God. "Be holy, as I the Lord your God am holy."[66] To become holy is to be "separated" from all that is not of God, from all that would impede the reign of God, from all that prevents God's purposes for human life from becoming a reality. The power to be like God can only come from God. The Spirit's "making holy" (sanctification) is all God's work, pure grace. The human response to such a gift is to give thanks, praise, and glory to God. Thus, the holiness of the church is the mark of the church which highlights its nature as a community of worship. Gathered in communal liturgy for celebration of the sacraments, the church comes to the source of its holiness as the holy People of God, and expresses most clearly its utter dependence on the principle of reception, the Holy Spirit

---

64. Barth, *The Doctrine of the Word of God. Part 1,* 449.

65. Ti 3:5–7: "He saved us, not because of any works of righteousness that we had done, but according to his mercy, through the water of rebirth and renewal by the Holy Spirit. This Spirit he poured out on us richly through Jesus Christ our Savior, so that, having been justified by his grace, we might become heirs according to the hope of eternal life." Acts 1:5 associates the coming of the Holy Spirit with baptism: "for John baptized with water, but you will be baptized with the Holy Spirit not many days from now."

66. Lv 19:2; 1 Pt 1:15–16.

who unites them as the People of God, the Body of Christ, the Temple of the Holy Spirit. In liturgy, the holy People of God comes to "worship in the Spirit of God."[67]

In the New Testament, while it does not use the adjective "holy" to directly describe the church, believers are regularly called "holy ones," saints.[68] The word "holy" is also used in the context of images of the church. The church is "the bride of Christ"[69] and "God's holy temple."[70] The church is "a spiritual house," "a holy priesthood," "a holy nation."[71] Parallel to metaphors of "temple" and "household" are those of "dwelling" and "habitation," particularly "indwelling" by the Holy Spirit. Paul and John speak of this indwelling of the Holy Spirit.[72] Likewise, they both speak of the anointing in the Spirit.[73]

But this anointing is "a first installment."[74] Because of the sinfulness of its members, the church is "marked with a genuine though imperfect holiness."[75] Because of the "eschatological nature of the pilgrim church,"[76] the church is both "indefectibly holy"[77] and "imperfectly holy."[78] Both in the lives of its individual members and in the community as a whole,

67. Phil 3:3: "For it is we who are the circumcision, who worship in the Spirit of God and boast in Christ Jesus and have no confidence in the flesh."

68. For example, Col 1:12.

69. Eph 5:25–27: "Husbands, love your wives, just as Christ loved the church and gave himself up for her, in order to make her holy by cleansing her with the washing of water by the word, so as to present the church to himself in splendor, without a spot or wrinkle or anything of the kind—yes, so that she may be holy and without blemish."

70. 1 Cor 3:16ff.

71. 1 Pt 2:5, 9: "Like living stones, let yourselves be built into a spiritual house, to be a holy priesthood, to offer spiritual sacrifices acceptable to God through Jesus Christ. . . . You are a chosen race, a royal priesthood, a holy nation, God's own people, in order that you may proclaim the mighty acts of him who called you out of darkness into his marvelous light." In Rom. 15:16, Paul speaks of himself as "a minister of Christ Jesus to the Gentiles in the priestly service of the gospel of God, so that the offering of the Gentiles may be acceptable, sanctified by the Holy Spirit."

72. 1 Cor 3:16–17; 6:19; Jn 14:15–17; 1 Jn 4:12–13.

73. 2 Cor 1:21–22: "But it is God who establishes us with you in Christ and has anointed us, by putting his seal on us and giving us his Spirit in our hearts as a first installment." See also 1 Jn 2:20, 27.

74. 2 Cor 1:22.

75. *LG*, 48. This is the title of the chapter on the mark of holiness in Sullivan, *The Church We Believe In*, 66–83.

76. *LG*, 48. Tanner translation.

77. *LG*, 39. Tanner translation.

78. *LG*, 8: "[T]he church, containing sinners in its own bosom, is at one and the same time holy and always in need of purification and it pursues unceasingly penance and renewal." Tanner translation. This tension, and the notion of "imperfectly holy," is discussed in Sullivan, *The Church We Believe In*, 66–83.

the Holy Spirit enables the church to respond to Christ's call to constant conversion: "In its pilgrimage on earth Christ summons the church to continual reformation *(perennem reformationem),* of which it is always in need, in so far as it is an institution of human beings here on earth."[79] But, on that pilgrim journey, it is above all through the holiness of the saints that the renewing power of the Holy Spirit shines forth most effectively. They are those who have truly received Christ in the Spirit.

All four of these marks of the church are marks of the Spirit's activity. Because they are marks of the one Spirit, they are to be always interrelated.[80] Throughout the rest of this book, we will go on to claim that the *sensus fidelium* has a unique role to play in the Spirit's work of maintaining the unity, catholicity, apostolicity, and holiness of the church.

OFFICES, INSTITUTION, CHARISMS

We have already examined how Vatican II teaches that the whole People of God is the primary receiver of revelation which is entrusted with the mission of the church and that the Holy Spirit is given to the whole community, and all individuals within it, to enable it to fulfill that mission. A significant rubric with which *Lumen Gentium* presents the nature and mission of the entire church is that of the threefold office *(triplex munus)* or the three offices *(tria munera)* of Christ as Priest, Prophet, and King. This rubric is not only an interpretative framework for its theological presentation of the church, but is also used to structure chapters 2, 3, and 4 of the document. In the final version, after a deliberate reordering of chapters from a previous draft, chapter 2 on the People of God first states how the whole church participates in the three offices; chapter 3 then goes on to discuss how the hierarchy specifically participates in them; and chapter 4 how the laity specifically participates in them.

The notion of "office" *(munus* or *officium)* in theological and canonical literature is somewhat problematic, being translated and used in a va-

---

79. *UR,* 6. Tanner translation.

80. Congar writes: "[T]here is a close relationship between apostolicity and catholicity, just as there is between catholicity and unity. Rather like the functions of Christ himself, the marks of the Church exist one within the other. Christ's priesthood is royal and prophetic, his prophetism is priestly and royal, and his royalty is prophetic and priestly. In the same way, the unity of the Church is apostolic, holy and catholic, its catholicity is holy, one and apostolic, its apostolicity is catholic, one and holy, and its holiness is apostolic, catholic and one." Congar, *I Believe in the Holy Spirit,* 2:27.

riety of senses.[81] "Office," in a general sense, is used to speak of leadership and authority structures in the church, and in this sense "office" connotes "institution." In the history of the Catholic Church, it has generally been held that only the ordained could be "office bearers" and that they alone have ecclesiastical "authority" or "power" *(potestas)*. Vatican II's innovation, that all in the church, ordained and laity, together participate in the "offices" *(munera)* of Christ, presents an understanding of the church which theologians and canonists are still attempting to resolve conceptually. However, that innovation is to be found juxtaposed with other, more classical, understandings of the church, leaving the interpreter of Vatican II to propose new syntheses which the council did not itself attempt, but left to theologians and canonists.

In part 3, we shall return to a fuller examination of these issues, particularly with regard to the relationship between the authoritative, institutional function of the magisterium, theologians, and the *sensus fidelium* in the teaching activity of the church. Our concern at this stage is the use of the *tria munera* only in chapter 2 of *Lumen Gentium,* leaving to later an examination of the specific and distinctive ways in which the hierarchy (chapter 3) and the laity (chapter 4) participate in the three offices of Christ. Chapter 2 teaches that the *universitas fidelium* (the whole body of the faithful) participates in (1) the *munus sacerdotalis* (the priestly office), which is the *munus sanctificandi* (the office of sanctifying); (2) the *munus propheticum* (the prophetic office), which is the *munus docendi* (the office of teaching); and (3) the *munus regalis* (the kingly or pastoral office), which is the *munus regendi* (the office of governing).

Throughout this chapter we have been examining the relationship between the church and the Holy Spirit as the principle of the reception of Christ. I now wish to outline briefly a pneumatological approach to the three offices of Christ, an approach which will be developed more fully in part 3. A pneumatological approach to the three offices of Christ enables us to avoid a false dichotomy between a purely christological approach that grounds "ecclesiastical office," "ordination," and "institution" in the intention of Christ, and a purely pneumatological approach that sees charisms coming directly from the Pentecostal Spirit, and pit-

---

81. For overviews of the usage, see Klaus Mörsdorf, "Ecclesiastical Authority," in *Sacramentum Mundi: An Encyclopedia of Theology,* ed. Karl Rahner (New York: Herder and Herder, 1968), 2:133–39; Klaus Mörsdorf, "Ecclesiastical Office: I. In Canon Law," in Rahner, ed., *Sacramentum Mundi: An Encyclopedia of Theology,* 2:167–70.

ting them over against the institutional elements coming directly from Christ. Only an approach grounded in the dual missions of Christ and the Spirit, as outlined in the previous chapter, enables us to avoid such a false dichotomy. If the Spirit is the principle of reception of Christ, how might a pneumatology of the three offices of Christ be conceived?

Lumen Gentium implicitly links the three offices of Christ to the mission of the Holy Spirit:

> For this God sent his Son, whom he appointed heir of all things, that he might be teacher, king and priest [*magister, rex et sacerdos*] of all, head of the new and universal people of the children of God. For this finally God sent the Spirit of his Son, the Lord and giver of life, who is for the whole church and for each and every one of the faithful the principle of union and of unity in the teaching of the apostles, in communion, in the breaking of bread and in prayers.[82]

Although this passage does not explicitly link the role of the Spirit to the fulfillment of the offices of Christ in the church, I believe, given all that has been said earlier in this and the previous chapter, it is legitimate to see the Spirit as the principle of reception of the threefold office of Christ in the church. The Holy Spirit enables the church to be a prophetic, priestly, and kingly people. As the principle of the reception of Christ, it is the Holy Spirit who enables the church to participate fully in, and effectively exercise, the three offices of Christ. In a pneumatological approach to the threefold office, we can see how the rubric of the four marks of the church overlaps significantly with the rubric of the three offices of Christ.

Discussion of the priestly office, the *munus sacerdotalis,* which is the *munus sanctificandi* (the office of sanctifying), overlaps significantly with our discussion above regarding the Spirit's distinguishing mark of "holiness" in the church. It is the Spirit who is the Sanctifier. As *Lumen Gentium* makes clear, there is a distinction between the common priesthood, in which all the baptized participate, and the ministerial priesthood, in which those ordained to holy orders participate, but it is the one Spirit who works through both. The church is a priestly people because of the Holy Spirit.

The kingly or pastoral office, the *munus regalis,* is the *munus regendi*

---

82. *LG,* 13. Tanner translation corrected. Tanner confusingly translates *magister* as "master." *Lumen Gentium* clearly aligns the prophetic office with the office of teaching, the *munus docendi.* In contemporary English, the word "master" is rarely used in its sense of "teacher."

(the office of governing). *Lumen Gentium* generally replaces the notion of "king" with that of "pastor" or "shepherd."[83] In our discussion above, issues of governance were implicitly raised in our discussion of the four marks of the church. Maintaining unity, catholicity, apostolicity, and holiness involves an ordered church life in which authorities, ministries, institutions, and structures are necessary. We have already noted the necessary tension in the church regarding any issues related to "the one and the many." This is true in many of the relationships related to governance in the church: the relationship between institution and charisms, the relationship between the individual and the community, the relationship between the local church and the church universal, the collegial relationship among the bishops and the bishop of Rome (and, by extension, with his administrative organization, the Roman Curia). At all levels, the office of governance necessarily involves the Holy Spirit as the principle of reception of Christ, the one who came not to be served, but to serve.[84] This relationship between the Spirit and the office of governance requires clearer recognition in the canon law of the church.[85]

In turning to the prophetic office of Christ we turn to the primary focus of this book. It is the task of the prophetic office (the *munus propheticum*), which is the *munus docendi* (the office of teaching), to maintain the unity of the faith throughout the church catholic, to ensure the apostolicity of the faith, and to promote living witness to the Gospel by ensuring the vibrant link between doctrinal beliefs and the demands of a life of holiness in the contemporary world. Since, as we have seen, it is the Spirit who is the principle of unity, catholicity, apostolicity, and holiness, then the Spirit is the ultimate Teacher in the teaching office of the church. Moreover, safeguarding the deposit of faith is the task of the whole People of God, a preservation guaranteed through the assistance

---

83. For example, *LG,* 21, where "shepherd" replaces "king."

84. See Mk 10:45.

85. On the lack of recognition of the Holy Spirit in the Code of Canon Law, the canonist James Coriden writes: "The exclusion of the Holy Spirit and charisms from the code was not due to ignorance or casual neglect; it seems to have been a conscious choice. It is difficult to detect the real reasons for this deliberate exclusion. It may have been motivated by a fear of a mysterious charismatic element that might be difficult to verify or control, and that might prove disruptive or dangerous. Or the revisers of the code may have been reluctant to acknowledge any source of authority in the Church other than the exclusively Christocentric and hierarchic sources recognized for centuries. They may have been unwilling to recognize the Spirit who dwells within each one of the Christian faithful and gives them gifts for the building of the Church." James A. Coriden, "The Holy Spirit and Church Governance," *The Jurist* 66 (2006): 339–73, at 372.

of the Holy Spirit. Within the participation by the *universitas fidelium* in the prophetic office, however, the magisterium has a special role, as bearer of the "charism of truth,"[86] in safeguarding the faithful transmission of revelation. Nevertheless, faithful traditioning of the faith is not the magisterium's exclusive preserve. It is the preserve of the whole church. *Dei Verbum* 8 speaks of the progress of the apostolic tradition by means of the Spirit's assistance to the *sensus fidelium,* theologians, and the magisterium. Part 3 will explore the function and interrelationship of these three, as three *authorities* within the one teaching *office* of the whole church.

The reception of Vatican II's teaching regarding the participation of the entire church in the offices of governing, sanctifying, and teaching is an ongoing task. I do not wish to explore so much the implications of that teaching regarding the offices of sanctification and governance, although the three offices overlap in many ways. My primary focus is the *sensus fidelium* and the teaching office. Oftentimes, the *sensus fidelium* is confusingly appealed to in calls for greater participation of the laity in the *governance* of the church. Technically, at least in terms of *Lumen Gentium* 12a, the *sensus fidelium* relates to the teaching office of the church. Certainly, issues of governance will arise in our discussion, particularly in the issue of structures of participation and the role of the Roman Curia in the discipline of ensuring orthodoxy in the church. But the issue of participation of the laity in church governance would perhaps benefit from the use of categories other than the *sensus fidelium,* although the faithful's perceptions on matters of faith and morals do have application for issues of governance and the way it is exercised.

In part 3, with particular reference to the teaching office in the church, we shall treat in greater detail another aspect of the Spirit's relationship to the church, the relationship between "institution" and "charisms." Each of the three offices of Christ in the church incorporates both institutional and charismatic elements, and roles which involve the ordained and the non-ordained. In the priestly office, some specific ministries fall only to the ordained; but that does not preclude "fully conscious and active participation" in the liturgy of all involved.[87] In the kingly office, governance involves ecclesiastical offices held by both ordained and laity. In the teaching office, the hierarchical magisterium has an official function

86. *DV,* 8.
87. *SC,* 14.

of "authoritatively" *(authentice)* interpreting revelation, of which, however, the *universitas fidelium* are the primary receivers. At the heart of all three offices is the relationship between institution and charism.

A balanced pneumatological approach to the church will not pit these two dimensions of institution and charism against each other, as if the Spirit were at work only in one or the other. When the church is seen in terms of the rubric of institution and charism, it is the same Spirit who unites all dimensions. "[T]he institution must be understood as a function of the Spirit, and ecclesiology as a function of pneumatology."[88]

In all dimensions of the church discussed above, a dynamic relationship is at work, a *dynamis* that the witness of Scripture and tradition attributes to one and the same Spirit. The *dynamis* can be rightly called a tension, if the notion of "tension" is conceived in a positive and productive way. In the maintenance of unity, catholicity, apostolicity, and holiness, in the participation in and exercise of the three offices of teaching, sanctifying, and governing, in the relationship between institution and charism, between the individual and the structured communion of the church, there is necessarily a "tension." It is one and the same Holy Spirit with whom all are baptized and with whom ministers are ordained, with whom the individual and the whole community are anointed, by whom one individual receives a charism for a particular service and another receives a charism for some other service.

The history of the church gives abundant evidence of problems with charismatic individuals and individual charisms. Paul's Corinth and the Montanist crisis are but two examples among many. However, at Vatican II, we find a positive approach to the ecclesial significance of the Spirit's "charisms" *(charismata),* or what it variously calls "gifts" *(dona)* or "graces" *(gratiae).* Immediately after its teaching on the *sensus fidei totius populi* as a gift of the Holy Spirit, the second section of *Lumen Gentium* 12 goes on to teach how the Holy Spirit

apportions his gifts "to each individually as he wills" (1 Cor 12:11), and among the faithful of every rank he distributes special graces by which he renders them fit and ready to undertake the various tasks and offices which help the renewal and the building up of the church, according to that word: "To each is given the manifes-

---

88. Walter Kasper, "The Apostolic Succession: An Ecumenical Problem," in *Leadership in the Church: How Traditional Roles Can Serve the Christian Community Today* (New York: Crossroad, 2003), 114–43, at 142.

tation of the Spirit for the common good" (1 Cor 12:7). . . . The judgment about their genuineness and their ordered use belongs to those who preside over the church, to whom it belongs especially not to extinguish the Spirit but to test everything and hold fast to what is good (see 1 Thes 5:12 and 19–21).

In retrieving a positive appreciation of charisms, the council teaches that the tension between institution and charism, between formal authority and individual freedom, demands careful discernment, lest the Spirit be extinguished. It is a tension that we will frequently revisit throughout the rest of this book.

In the chapters which follow, just as we will go on to claim that the *sensus fidelium* has a unique role to play in the Spirit's work of maintaining the unity, catholicity, apostolicity, and holiness of the church, so too the *sensus fidelium* will be shown to play a unique role in the Spirit's work as Teacher within the teaching office of the church, operating through a dynamic relationship between the *sensus fidelium,* theology, and the institutional teaching authority (the magisterium).

CHAPTER 3

The Holy Spirit and a Sense for the Faith

Since faith is the reception of revelation, at the heart of the nature of the church as a community of reception is its nature as a community *of faith*. Faith is a gift of the Holy Spirit which has two fundamental dimensions: faith as believing, i.e., as a personal response to God's loving initiative *(fides qua creditur)*, and faith as beliefs and assent to beliefs, i.e., as an affirmative response to the content of what has been revealed *(fides quae creditur)*. As the principle of reception, the Holy Spirit is at work in both these dimensions of faith's reception of revelation. Without wishing to reduce faith to intellectual knowledge, in this chapter we will begin to examine more closely the cognitive dimension of faith in terms of understanding, interpreting, and applying to daily life one's relationship to God and the beliefs one professes. Here we begin to address more specifically the Spirit's activity through the *sensus fidei*, by proposing a pneumatological approach to faith's understanding of revelation which is consistent with the trinitarian theology of revelation and consequent ecclesiology outlined in the previous two chapters.

FAITH'S ORGANON FOR UNDERSTANDING

In the first chapter, we examined the early church's experience of the Holy Spirit as the one who enabled them to appropriate Jesus Christ and the salvific revelation he offered. Within that empowerment to live the Christ-life was experienced an ability to understand the sense of what was being given. As the texts cited in the first chapter demonstrate, the New Testament, without using the actual phrase *sensus fidei,* alludes to a capacity for perceiving the faith that comes from the Holy Spirit. "An effort to base the *sensus fidei* theologically finds in the New Testament clear testimonials to the reality of *an organ of faith and its understanding,* the work of the Spirit, in each of the baptized, as well as in the entire church."[1] Through this "organ of faith and its understanding," the Holy Spirit enables believers to comprehend and make their own God's salvific offer. We have seen how the fourth evangelist, for example, speaks of another Advocate who would anoint the disciples and lead them to the fullness of truth.[2] Indeed, because of that anointing, they have no need of any other teacher.[3] In Colossians, we read of the gift of "spiritual insight."[4] The writer of the letter to the Ephesians prays that his community may have a capacity to perceive revelation.[5]

Herbert Vorgrimler notes that the New Testament witness regarding access to knowledge of the faith nowhere envisages any gradation in the knowledge received:

The biblical witness to faith's post-Easter reflection, put briefly, is this: the Spirit of God creates faith, vitalises it in diverse ways and produces tangible "fruits of the Spirit." There is no mention of any privileges in the knowledge of faith, as if some receive a special, personal source of knowledge, or a better, greater or deeper knowledge than others. They do not, because of their positions or functions in and for the community, have at their disposal a kind of secret lore. Early Christianity resisted the temptation (from Gnosticism) towards the elite and the esoteric. But

---

1. Pié-Ninot, *"Sensus Fidei,"* 923. My italics.

2. See Jn 14:26: "But the Advocate, the Holy Spirit, whom the Father will send in my name, will teach you everything, and remind you of all that I have said to you." See also Jn 16:12–14: "I still have many things to say to you, but you cannot bear them now. When the Spirit of truth comes, he will guide you into all the truth; for he will not speak on his own, but will speak whatever he hears, and he will declare to you the things that are to come. He will glorify me, because he will take what is mine and declare it to you. All that the Father has is mine. For this reason I said that he will take what is mine and declare it to you."

3. 1 Jn 2:27.

4. Col 1:9.

5. Eph 1:17–19: "May the God of our Lord Jesus Christ, the Father of glory, give you a spirit of wisdom and perception *(apokalypsis)* of what is revealed, to bring you to full knowledge *(epignosis)* of him. May he enlighten *the eyes of your mind* so that you can see what hope his call holds for you, what rich glories he has promised the saints will inherit and how infinitely great is the power he has exercised for us believers."

the problem of the growth of "false teaching" led, as the later NT writings show, to the view that office-bearers were necessary to guarantee the purity of the apostolic tradition of faith.[6]

Therefore, the New Testament, while witnessing to the need for figures in the community whose function it is to ensure continuity in the faith, gives clear testimony to the belief that, through the Holy Spirit, all believers fully participate in the revelatory knowledge that believing brings.[7]

In a cluster of articles, Karl Rahner discusses a problem closely connected to discussion of the *sensus fidei:* the relationship between this "inner knowledge" of the faith and the church's official teachings regarding the content of the faith.[8] Most Catholics, Rahner claims, wouldn't know a fraction of what is in a full collection of official church teachings such as Denzinger-Schönmetzer, let alone explicitly assent to all those beliefs formulated by the church. In practice, he asserts, there is often a discrepancy between "what the church officially teaches and what the people actually believe."[9] Nevertheless, despite this, he says, Christians' reception of revelation (my phrasing) can still be "a faith which leads them to sal-

---

6. Vorgrimler, "From *Sensus Fidei* to *Consensus Fidelium,*" 3–4.

7. A neat summary of Catholic belief on these matters is given by Pope John Paul II, at the conclusion of his apostolic exhortation *Catechesi Tradendae:* "The Spirit is . . . promised to the Church and to each Christian as a Teacher within, who, in the secret of the conscience and the heart, makes one understand what one has heard but was not capable of grasping: 'Even now the Holy Spirit teaches the faithful,' said Saint Augustine in this regard, 'in accordance with each one's spiritual capacity. And he sets their hearts aflame with greater desire according as each one progresses in the charity that makes him love what he already knows and desire what he has yet to know.'" *Catechesi Tradendae,* 72. Quoting Augustine, *In Ioannis Evangelium Tractatus,* 97, 1: PL, 35, 1877.

8. For example, see Karl Rahner, "Pluralism in Theology and the Unity of the Creed in the Church," in *Theological Investigations,* vol. 11 (London: Darton, Longman & Todd, 1974), 11:3–23; "Heresies in the Church Today?" in *Theological Investigations,* vol. 12 (London: Darton, Longman & Todd, 1974), 12:117–41; "The Faith of the Christian and the Doctrine of the Church," in *Theological Investigations,* vol. 14 (London: Darton, Longman & Todd, 1976), 14:24–46; "A Hierarchy of Truths," in *Theological Investigations,* vol. 21 (London: Darton, Longman & Todd, 1988), 21:162–67; "The Act of Faith and the Content of Faith," in *Theological Investigations,* vol. 21 (London: Darton, Longman & Todd, 1988), 21:151–61; "What the Church Officially Teaches and What the People Actually Believe," in *Theological Investigations,* vol. 22 (London: Darton, Longman & Todd, 1991), 22:165–75; "The Relation Between Theology and Popular Religion," in *Theological Investigations,* vol. 22 (London: Darton, Longman & Todd, 1991), 22:140–47.

9. See Rahner, "What the Church Officially Teaches." Regarding the central doctrine of the Trinity, Rahner states: "[D]espite their orthodox confession of the Trinity, Christians are, in their practical life, almost mere 'monotheists.' We must be willing to admit that, should the doctrine of the Trinity have to be dropped as false, the major part of religious literature could well remain unchanged. . . . One has the feeling that, for the catechism of the head and heart (as contrasted with

vation and (given the further assumptions) justification, even though the contents of their faith, their *fides quae,* are of the most diverse and often contradictory kind."[10] Rahner provocatively writes:

Today's Christians face the problems of synthesizing their faith with all they know and experience as individuals. To this end, they must differentiate between more and less binding church teachings. . . . The formed Christian must be aware of the "hierarchy of truths," must know the effectively central and existentially meaningful roots of the faith so as to deepen this understanding and, while not denying, pay less attention to what is secondary. Formed Christians must find their own idea of God and of eternal salvation in Jesus Christ. Not knowing exactly how many sacraments there are needn't be all that bad, for despite such dearth of information we are still quite capable of correctly resolving our burdened consciences.[11]

Is this what a "sense of the faith" is? A sense *for* the faith? A Spirit-given capacity that all baptized Christians possess, which enables them, within the struggle of their daily lives, to "synthesize their faith with all they know and experience as individuals," and to "find their own idea of God and of eternal salvation in Jesus Christ"? *Sensus fidei,* I will propose, is such an imaginative capacity which, within their daily reception of God's self-communication, Christians, in some relatively adequate way (at least adequate in terms of salvation), "make sense of" their lives and "make sense of" the God reaching out to them in their lives through Christ in the Spirit.

I have already defined in the Introduction my usage of the terms *sensus fidei* and *sensus fidelium,* but it perhaps needs repeating here. Although *Lumen Gentium* 12 uses the term *sensus fidei totius populi,* "the sense of the faith of the whole people," I will refer to that corporate ecclesial sense as the *sensus fidei fidelium,* "the sense of the faith of the faithful," or more briefly the *sensus fidelium,* "the sense of the faithful." For the sense of the faith of an individual believer, I will use the term *sensus fidei fidelis,* or just *sensus fidei.* When I use the term *sensus fidei* context will determine its reference either to the individual or to the community, or to both.

There is a double meaning to the word *sensus* that I wish to retain. I use the above cognates of *sensus fidei,* at different times, to name two distinct

---

the printed catechism), the Christian's idea of the incarnation would not have to change at all if there were no Trinity." Karl Rahner, *The Trinity* (New York: Herder and Herder, 1970), 10–11.

10. Rahner, "The Act of Faith and the Content of Faith," 152.

11. Karl Rahner, "Reflections on the Adult Christian," *Theology Digest* 31 (1984): 123–26, at 125.

aspects of the interpretative dynamic at the heart of not only *fides quae creditur,* but also *fides qua creditur.* The *sensus fidei* is both (1) the ecclesial *sensus* for the understanding, interpretation, and application of revelation, and (2) the interpretation that results from the exercise of that interpretative *sensus.* In the first meaning, it is a *sensus for* the faith;[12] in the second meaning, it is a *sensus of* the faith.[13] In the first meaning, it is an ability to interpret the faith; in the second meaning, it is a particular interpretation of the faith.[14] In the first meaning, it is more (but not exclusively) a dimension of faith as *fides qua creditur;* in the second meaning, it is more (but not exclusively) a dimension of faith as *fides quae creditur.*

With regard to the first usage, the Latin word *sensus* can be translated in various ways.[15] Salvador Pié-Ninot, as we have seen, refers to the *sensus fidei* as an "organ of faith and its understanding."[16] I will oftentimes refer to that *sensus,* analogously, as an *organon* of faith, an interpretative "instrument" which is given with the gift of faith. Following John Hen-

---

12. Here Salvador Pié-Ninot's definition captures the nuance: "a quality of the subject, upon whom the grace of faith, love and the gifts of the Holy Spirit confers a capacity to perceive the truth of faith and to discern what is contrary to the same." Pié-Ninot, *"Sensus Fidei,"* 992.

13. Herbert Vorgrimler"s definition captures this second nuance: "The term *'sensus fidei'* designates a special kind of knowledge, springing from faith and embracing its fundamental features. . . . As the New Testament and a long tradition testify, *everyone* who believes in God's revelation has this sense of faith. First of all therefore, it is the individual consciousness, 'illuminated' by faith and hence by God himself." Vorgrimler, "From *Sensus Fidei* to *Consensus Fidelium,"* 3. Vorgrimler goes on to state that *sensus fidei,* "in a wider sense, refers to the collective faith-consciousness and so is also called *sensus fidelium,* the 'sense of the faithful.'"

14. The deeply personal act of faith, of course, involves much more than cognitive and interpretative elements. I focus more narrowly on the cognitive and interpretative elements of faith because *Lumen Gentium*'s discussion of the *sensus fidei* takes place within its discussion of the teaching office of the church, the office which necessarily focuses on the cognitive and interpretative aspects of faith.

15. Throughout the theological literature, the Latin word *sensus* is translated variously as a "capacity," a "faculty," an "instinct," a "sixth sense," a "spiritual sense," an "appreciation," or a "flair" for the faith. For the wide range of meanings of the Latin word *sensus,* see "Sensus," in *Oxford Latin Dictionary,* ed. P. G. W. Glare (Oxford: Clarendon, 1980), 7:1735–36. Ten meanings are listed: (1) a capacity to perceive by the senses, sensation; (2) any one of the five physical senses; (3) an impression consequent on perception by the senses, sensation; (4) the faculties of perception (mental and physical); an impression on the mind, experience; (5) self-awareness, consciousness; awareness, consciousness (of situations, conditions); (6) the faculty of making distinctions, judgment, understanding; perception of what is appropriate, sensibility; the faculty of feeling emotions, heart; an undefined faculty, instinct; (7) a mental feeling, emotion; (8) one's feeling in regard to someone or something; character, disposition; (9) that which occurs to the mind, an idea, thought; the thought underlying an action, intention, purpose; an epigrammatic notion, conceit; the sense, meaning (of a word or words; also of a writer); (10) a self-contained expression, a sentence or period.

16. Pié-Ninot, *"Sensus Fidei,"* 923.

ry Newman's usage of the word to describe the "illative sense" as a "living *organon*,"[17] I use the Aristotelian notion of *organon* in a general (not necessarily Aristotelian) sense, to refer to "an instrument of thought or knowledge; a means by which some process of reasoning, discovery, etc., is carried on."[18]

I use the term analogously, similar to common linguistic usage of terms such as the "imagination" or the five "senses." Just as we might speak of "imagination" as a faculty for giving meaningful shape to past and present experience by integrating and organizing it and envisaging future possibilities, so too we might speak of *sensus fidei* as a faculty or organon for interpreting the past, giving shape to Christian identity in the present, and envisaging future possibilities. Similarly, just as the five physical "senses" mediate experience in our embodied existence and enable us to negotiate our way through a world that is physical, so too the *sensus fidei* can be spoken of as a "sixth sense," an organon of faith-knowing for interpreting the data of salvific revelation, past and present.

Thus, the *sensus fidei* can be spoken of variously and analogously as an organon, a faculty, a capacity, a capability, with which one is gifted. Such a "gift" is as ineffable and intangible, but as real, as many other human capacities, such as a musician's "gift for music" and "musical sense"; in the case of the *sensus fidei,* however, the gift is given to all. These cognates of *sensus* attempt to name, in the believer, *a spiritual sensibility for understanding, interpreting, and applying salvific revelation in a meaningful way, and for discerning what interpretations of salvific revelation are true to that revelation and what are not.*[19]

Although the notion of "faculty" continues to provide the dominant metaphor for depicting aspects of the human person (e.g., the mind, the will, the imagination), care must be taken when employing such "faculty psychology" for a theological epistemology, lest it become reduction-

17. John Henry Newman, *An Essay in Aid of a Grammar of Assent* (Notre Dame, Ind.: University of Notre Dame Press, 1979), 250.

18. "Organon," in *The Oxford English Dictionary,* ed. J. A. Simpson and E. S. C. Weiner (New York: Clarendon Press, 1989), 10:925.

19. I deliberately avoid using the term "charism" to characterize the *sensus fidei,* in order to prevent confusion with *Lumen Gentium* 12's treatment of the various charisms which the Spirit bestows differently on individuals. The *sensus fidei* is not a charism *in that sense;* such *charismata* are given to different believers in different ways, and are not equal, such that we can speak of an ordering among the charisms of the church. The *sensus fidei,* on the other hand, is a capacity given to all baptized believers and is a dimension of the gift of faith itself. There is, however, a sense in which the *sensus fidei* is a charism, in the generic sense of a "gift" of the Holy Spirit.

istic.[20] The psychology of the individual or the communal consciousness of embodied human believers cannot be adequately described in terms of separate "faculties." Just as "conscience" is not so much a "faculty" but a process of discernment involving the whole person,[21] and just as "the imagination" is not so much a "faculty" but rather "the whole mind working in certain ways,"[22] so too *sensus fidei* is the whole ecclesial process of faith seeking understanding, interpretation, and application of salvific revelation—on the communal and individual level. Nevertheless, the language of faculty psychology remains useful heuristically, as a way of analogously naming and explaining factors in an interpretative process. Just as Paul can speak of Christians having "the mind of Christ,"[23] or of "the renewal of your mind,"[24] or of God enlightening "the eyes of your heart,"[25] so too a systematic theology of faith, and in particular a systematic theology of a "sense of the faith" (faith's *sensus* for understanding), can appropriately speak of such a *sensus* as an organon of faith seeking understanding, interpretation, and application of revelation.

This organon of *sensus fidei* is the gift for understanding revelation which is given at Pentecost, and which, "aroused and sustained by the Spirit of truth,"[26] is continuously the possession of baptized believers and the community anointed with the Spirit. *If the Spirit is the principle of revelation's reception, then the* sensus fidei *is faith's organon bestowed by the Spirit for revelation's reception.* It is a capacity which the Spirit gives with the gift of faith, enabling the understanding, interpretation, and application of the faith.[27] Its activity in the believer is the activity of the in-

---

20. For a summary and critique of "faculty psychology" and notions of a "disembodied mind," see George Lakoff and Mark Johnson, *Philosophy in the Flesh: The Embodied Mind and Its Challenge to Western Thought* (New York: Basic Books, 1999), esp. 409–14.

21. Seán Fagan writes: "More and more christian writers are coming to see that it is a misleading metaphor to speak of a person 'having a conscience.' The reality is that one *is* a conscience. In this sense it is not a special faculty or power, or indeed, a specific act. . . . It is rather the whole human person characterized by a drive towards and a demand for the realization of value." Seán Fagan, "Conscience," in *The New Dictionary of Theology*, ed. Joseph A. Komonchak, Mary Collins, and Dermot A. Lane (Dublin: Gill and Macmillan, 1987), 226–30, at 227.

22. McIntyre, *Faith, Theology and Imagination*, 159.

23. 1 Cor 2:16; cf. Phil 2:5.

24. Rom 12:2. "'Mind' [*nous*] for Paul denotes the thinking, discerning aspect of the human person. . . . [the] inner faculty of discernment." Brendan Byrne, *Romans* (Collegeville, Minn.: Liturgical Press, 1996), 369.

25. Eph 1:18.

26. *LG*, 12. Tanner translation.

27. In the language of scholastic theology, if, as we have seen in chapter 1, revelation as God's

dwelling Spirit. In the words of Karl Barth: "When Scripture speaks of the Holy Spirit as an element of revelation we are dealing with an ability or capacity or capability which is given to man as the addressee of revelation and which makes him a real recipient of revelation."[28] It is this ability, or capacity, or capability which I refer to as the organon of *sensus fidei.* With it, faith has "eyes" to perceive the meaning and truth of revelation. The organon of *sensus fidei* constitutes "the eyes of faith."[29]

There is a second way in which I will be using the term *sensus fidei* and its cognates to name a distinct aspect of the interpretative dynamic at the heart of faith. *Sensus fidei* is not only the organon for interpretation, but the term can also refer to the resulting sense or meaning or interpretation which individual Christians or the community as a whole make of the faith, consciously or unconsciously, explicitly or implicitly. As an interpretation of the faith, it is a dimension of *fides quae creditur* (faith as assent to beliefs), because, in assenting, the believer is understanding a particular belief in his or her own way. When referring to an interpretation of the faith by an individual, it is termed a *sensus fidei fidelis.* For example, "St. Paul's *sensus fidei*" would refer to what the Paul of Ephesians calls "my understanding of the mystery of Christ."[30] Since the nominative plural of the Latin *sensus fidei* is also *sensus fidei,* I will sometimes use English expressions throughout this book for the plural, such as "senses of the faith" or "interpretations of the faith." Any common ecclesial formulation of the faith approved by the community, which attempts to bring together multiple senses of the faith *(sensus fidei fidelium),* will be termed a *consensus fidelium.*[31]

---

self-communication can be spoken of in terms of "uncreated grace," then the organon of *sensus fidei,* as the capacity for a graced human understanding of that encounter, can be spoken of in terms of "created grace."

28. Barth, *The Doctrine of the Word of God. Part 1,* 456. Elsewhere, Barth states: "[T]he Spirit is the great and only possibility in virtue of which men can speak of Christ in such a way that what they say is witness and that God's revelation in Christ thus achieves new actuality through it. . . . The Holy Spirit is the authorisation to speak about Christ; He is the equipment of the prophet and apostle; He is the summons to the Church to minister the Word." Ibid., 454–55.

29. In speaking of that organon for understanding in terms of the ocular metaphors of "eyes" and "sight," I do not wish to exclude dimensions of the human experience of God that might be more appropriately captured by metaphors related to the other four senses of hearing, smell, taste, and touch.

30. Eph 3:4.

31. The nominative plural of the Latin *consensus* is also *consensus.*

CIRCLES OF UNDERSTANDING

In order to develop a systematic theology of this phenomenon of graced human understanding of God's revelation and the interpretative process at the heart of revelatory experience, I will be critically appropriating several background theories and presupposing them throughout the chapters which follow.[32] One such background theory is philosophical hermeneutics, which sees human knowing in terms of a differentiated notion of "understanding." Furthermore, I will also be drawing upon a particular theory of art (reception aesthetics) and a particular theory of the interpretation of art that follows on from such a reception aesthetics (reception hermeneutics). The theory of interpreting literary works of art (literary hermeneutics) that will be appropriated here will therefore be a literary hermeneutics conceived in terms of reception. Thus, throughout this book the particular hermeneutics I will employ, through critical appropriation of these various background theories, will be conceived as a "reception hermeneutics." From these background theories, the notions of "horizon," "the hermeneutical triad," and "the hermeneutical circle" will be particularly important.

Hermeneutics employs the ocular metaphor of "horizon" in its discussion of the interpretative dimension of all experience. It is an "ocular" metaphor because it refers to one's viewpoint or visual perspective on a particular object. Individuals always experience from a particular horizon. One's horizon is the limit of one's view. It is the particular perspective I have. Therefore, an individual's perspective is always partial; no one "sees" a reality from every possible viewpoint. Metaphorically, however, if I move forward or sideways or higher or lower, how I see things will change. While one's perspective is always conditioned by and limited to the place where one is "standing," such location enables understanding to take place; it makes understanding possible. There is no perspective-free way of understanding anything. The multiple elements that determine one's horizon of understanding include one's personality, language, culture, moment in history, family upbringing, education, gender, religious tradition, personal life history, perceived social status, perceived economic status. We could call all this "baggage" of who we are "the tra-

---

32. On relevant background theories and theological method, see Francis Schüssler Fiorenza, *Foundational Theology: Jesus and the Church* (New York: Crossroad, 1984), esp. 310–11.

dition" of our past, which shapes us and determines our present experiences and perspectives, for good or bad. All of these variables can be analyzed by the human sciences in anthropological, psychological, gender, social, cultural, economic, political categories. Such analyses might highlight ways in which distortion and domination have played a role in conditioning the horizon of present understanding. All these diverse factors make up "the context" within which one experiences reality and comes to understanding.

Related to the insight that all understanding is perspectival and contextual is "the basis of hermeneutics":[33] the hermeneutical triad of "understanding," "interpretation," and "application." This triad has its origins in Pietist hermeneutics, and is developed further within the philosophy of Hans Georg Gadamer.[34] Gadamer's development of the notion can be criticized for its "ultimately passive notion of understanding."[35] However, a critically reconceived notion of the triad, I believe, can continue to provide a helpful *general rubric* for capturing the active role of "the receiver" in the act of understanding, especially for highlighting the importance of present context as the horizon out of which one understands, and the transformative goal of "application" in addressing that context.

The three moments of the hermeneutical triad, while they can be distinguished, constitute "one unified process."[36] *Understanding* within experience is already an *interpretation* out of a familiar framework from the past which enables an *application* of meaning to and consequent action within one's present context. To come to *understanding* means that I have made sense of an experience or text by means of the *interpreta-*

33. Hans Robert Jauss, "Limits and Tasks of Literary Hermeneutics," *Diogenes* 109 (1980): 92–119, at 97. On the unity of the hermeneutical triad and its appropriation for a hermeneutical theology, see Rush, *The Reception of Doctrine*, 98–100, 315–25.

34. The origins of the triad lie in the classical distinction between *subtilitas intelligendi* (understanding) and *subtilitas explicandi* (interpretation), to which Pietism added the third element of *subtilitas applicandi* (application). See Hans Georg Gadamer, *Truth and Method*, 2nd rev. ed. (New York: Crossroad, 1989), 307–10.

35. For a critique of Gadamer's "ultimately passive notion of understanding" with his notion of understanding as a "fusion of horizons," see Hans Robert Jauss, *Question and Answer: Forms of Dialogic Understanding* (Minneapolis: University of Minnesota Press, 1989), 197–231, at 205.

36. Gadamer, *Truth and Method*, 308. In highlighting the entwinement of the hermeneutical triad, Gadamer certainly wishes to reject any naïve notion of application as a simple translation of a text's meaning onto a particular context: "This is not to return to the pietist tradition of the three separate 'subtleties,' for, on the contrary, we consider application to be just as integral a part of the hermeneutical process as are understanding and interpretation." Ibid.

tive framework provided by the categories of my previous experience and knowledge; that I understand and have made sense of something, furthermore, means that I have already found meaningful *application* to my present context, its categories of thinking and its ethical demands. Thus, according to a critical philosophical hermeneutics, understanding, interpretation, and application are hermeneutical moments that can be distinguished but not separated.

This general rubric of the hermeneutical triad, I believe, can continue to be useful for theology, if the triad is understood to incorporate also insights from theories of ideological critique which highlight the impact of distortion and domination in the process of understanding, and to incorporate concerns from praxis-oriented theories which highlight a critical relationship between theory and praxis.[37] A reception hermeneutical theology therefore critically appropriates insights from such background theories, and explores their relevance, within a particular context, for the questing and questioning dynamic of "*faith* seeking understanding" (Anselm), or, as I would prefer, "faith seeking understanding, interpretation, and application."[38]

Such questing and questioning in the discipline of theology is a process no less at work in the individual's life of believing, no matter how unsophisticated his or her theological framework of interpretation.[39]

37. For a comprehensive approach to such issues and their implications for conceiving theological understanding, see the work of Francis Schüssler Fiorenza, who proposes that hermeneutical reconstruction of the tradition proceed in wide reflective equilibrium with relevant background theories, attention to praxis as a reproductive warrant, and the discourse of faith among the various voices within the Christian community. See especially Schüssler Fiorenza, "Systematic Theology: Task and Methods," 70–84; Schüssler Fiorenza, *Foundational Theology,* 285–321.

38. The entwinement of the hermeneutical triad as outlined here parallels elements of the dynamic highlighted in Schillebeeckx's notion that all revelatory experience is "interpretative experience." See Schillebeeckx, *Christ,* 29–64; Edward Schillebeeckx, *Interim Report on the Books "Jesus" & "Christ"* (New York: Crossroad, 1981), 10–19. Schillebeeckx highlights the importance of conceiving "application" in an active, praxis-oriented sense, entwined with interpretation: "Updating (i.e., contemporary application) . . . amounts therefore to interpretation; but because the old utterance is itself already an interpretation, we might also speak of 're-interpretation' or 'modernizing interpretation'. In it there appears what the past has to say to us here and now. On the other hand 'updating' can also and equally mean putting the gospel message into operation in the present day, having regard to completely new experiences which are in themselves foreign to the Bible. What such updating demands therefore is an interpretation which is *creative* and yet *true to Jesus.*" Edward Schillebeeckx, *Jesus: An Experiment in Christology* (London: Collins, 1979), 753. Original italics.

39. Karl Rahner writes: "Since the analysis by the hearer of what he is told is an inevitable moment in the process of hearing itself, and since utter non-understanding destroys even the hearing

There is perhaps no more succinct definition of the quest of the organon of *sensus fidei* than this: *sensus fidei* is faith seeking understanding, interpretation, and application of salvific revelation. The sense of faith which emerges from that quest is an understanding, interpretation, and application of the faith within a specific context and from the particular perspective of individuals within that context.[40] Throughout this book, the phrase "hermeneutical reception" will be used to name the active process, generated by the organon of *sensus fidei,* of faith's understanding, interpretation, and application of any authoritative text, practice, person, or event in the light of a specific context in the present. Moreover, any reference throughout the book to a single moment of the hermeneutical triad (e.g., "understanding," "interpretation," or "application") always presumes hermeneutical entwinement of that moment with the other two moments.

This unified yet differentiated process of understanding is further captured in the notion of "the hermeneutical circle." A dialectic exists between our understanding of "the whole" of a subject matter and our understanding of "a part." Understanding is a movement back and forth between a sense of the whole and a sense of the part. What we are already familiar with (tradition, the past) gives us a framework (albeit limited) for understanding the unfamiliar (the new, the present). In turn, one's understanding of the new in terms of the old leads to a different understanding of the old.

The hermeneutical circle can be described as an ongoing enquiry that proceeds according to "the logic of question and answer."[41] The dynamic

---

itself, *a certain degree of theology belongs as an inner moment to hearing itself,* and the mere hearing in faith is already a human activity in which man's own subjectivity, together with its logic, its experience, native concepts and perspectives, already enters into play. What we call theology and hence dogmatic statement in the strict sense is therefore merely a further development, an unfolding, of that basic subjective reflection which already takes place in the obedient listening to the Word of God, i.e. in faith as such. From this it follows, however, that dogmatic reflection and its statement can and must never separate themselves completely from the source from which they spring, i.e., from faith itself. This refers always, as has been said, not merely to the object of faith but also to its exercise. The latter remains the basis and support of the dogmatic statement as such itself." Karl Rahner, "What Is a Dogmatic Statement?" in *Theological Investigations,* vol. 5 (New York: Seabury, 1975), 5:42–66, at 49. Italics mine.

40. On the contextual and perspectival nature of Christian truth and meaning, see Janet Martin Soskice, "The Truth Looks Different from Here: On Seeking the Unity of Truth from a Diversity of Perspectives," in *Christ and Context: The Confrontation between Gospel and Culture,* ed. Hilary D. Regan and Allan J. Torrance (Edinburgh: T&T Clark, 1993), 43–62.

41. On "the logic of question and answer," see R. G. Collingwood, *An Autobiography* (New

of understanding is here conceived according to the metaphor of "conversation" or "dialogue." Furthermore, the notions of "question" and "answer" are used analogously. For example, the issue of contemporary suffering or injustice can constitute for the enquirer a "question" demanding an "answer." Moreover, an "answer" to such a question would need to go beyond a purely propositional statement of intellectual meaning, but include transformative praxis which directly responds to the "question," thereby constituting an effective "answer."

The dialogic circle of enquiry between question and answer typically begins with a question; the circle of enquiry therefore has its starting point in a present context and the questions that arise from that context. Understanding comes about if an answer is discovered to "my question." My present question might be posed to an authoritative text, practice, person, or event of the past, and an answer sought; the very seeking of an answer is an expression of a not-knowing, of not understanding fully, or of a possible misunderstanding seeking correction. Any answer that may be found in this circle of enquiry may however raise new questions that demand further answers, in an ongoing circle of question and answer. Thus the hermeneutical circle displays an ongoing dialectic between whole and part, the familiar and the unfamiliar, the old and the new, the past and the present, question and answer. All human understanding, according to philosophical hermeneutics, proceeds in this way.

Faith too comes to understanding through a dialogue involving question and answer.[42] Whether it be dialogue with the past or dialogue in the present, a helpful way of understanding the search for the meaning and truth of revelation is to see it as an ongoing conversation generated by *questions*. A dogmatic statement emerging from an ecumenical council, for example, is an answer to a particular question posed to the tra-

---

York: Oxford University Press, 1939), 29–43. The notion receives hermeneutical development in Gadamer, *Truth and Method,* 362–79.

42. With regard to the pertinence of the logic of question and answer for biblical hermeneutics, and the necessary starting point of the dialogue with contemporary questions, Paul Ricoeur writes: "[H]ow could the subject matter of the text be identified, if not with the help of the *logic of question and answer?* (Who is the God of Israel? Who is Jesus Christ?) And how could such questions be raised, if they were not also *our* questions, although in a cultural context different from that of the text? In other words, is it possible to start and to pursue an inquiry into the hermeneutical process going on *within* the text, without any interest in the theological concerns *of the present?*" Paul Ricoeur, "Response to Josef Blank," in *Paradigm Change in Theology: A Symposium for the Future,* ed. Hans Küng and David Tracy (Edinburgh: T& T Clark, 1989), 283–86, at 284. Original italics.

dition in a particular way, within a particular horizon of understanding the subject matter under discussion. A truth defined by that council, and promulgated as binding on believers, is to be considered true in the sense that it is a true answer to that particular question posed at that time, given the conditions for what constitutes a valid truth claim in that context.[43] However, its meaning and validity as a truth claim is not confined to that original context. It can be a meaningful and a true statement also for now and can have continuing validity.[44] But such a statement is limited to a certain degree; both its *meaning* and its *truth claim* for now must be reinterpreted.[45] Its meaning and truth endures only through its reinterpretation (its hermeneutical reception), which ultimately includes its application—its being lived out within a specific context and its transformative truth manifested.

Christian faith proclaims that the same God witnessed to in the authoritative texts of the Christian tradition is likewise revealing to and saving human beings in the present. Consequently, attention to present salvific and revelatory experience of God can enable faithful interpretation of the past foundational texts witnessing to the same God's salvific and revelatory activity in the past. The present becomes a hermeneutical lens for interpreting the past foundational and normative texts; those normative texts can then, in turn, become a lens for interpreting and discerning present experience.

Therefore, questions arising out of present Christian experience can become the appropriate entry into the hermeneutical circle of theologi-

43. On the complex issues that need to be addressed in any discussion of meaning and truth claims, see Schüssler Fiorenza, *Foundational Theology,* 289–96.

44. For an appropriation of Bernard Lonergan's notion of "critical realism" for understanding the ongoing validity of doctrinal statements, see Thornhill, *Christian Mystery,* 97–112. See Bernard Lonergan, "The Origins of Christian Realism," in *A Second Collection: Papers,* ed. William F. Ryan and Bernard Tyrrell (Toronto: University of Toronto Press, 1996), 239–61.

45. Thornhill writes: "Properly defined questions, 'intending' reality, and the answers given to them constitute the procedure which must be used by all inquirers after truth; it is a procedure which is limited by its very nature, pretending to answer only the questions which have been asked. This is the procedure which critical realism must employ to reaffirm the revealed truth. When this realism claims that doctrinal assertions can have a lasting validity, therefore, this claim is very modest indeed. These assertions do no more than answer particular questions which have been faced by the believing community. . . . Lonergan's critical realism, therefore, in contrast to a naïve realism, recognizes the severe limitations which are inherent to doctrinal statements. As answers to questions concerning the truth embodied in the Christ-event, these statements are capable of a realism which has an enduring validity. But their capacity to mediate the reality of the Christ-event is severely limited on several scores." See Thornhill, *Christian Mystery,* 109, 111.

cal enquiry. The enquiry is initiated by a question arising in the present context, which seeks an answer for the present. That answer is to be sought in dialogue with normative texts and practices of Scripture and tradition relevant to the contemporary question. This requires reengaging the question-and-answer dynamic which first generated any relevant biblical text or official teaching. Correctly interpreting the meaning and truth claim of a past text includes hermeneutical reconstruction of the intended meaning of the original authors in terms of the question they set out to answer, and then hermeneutical reconstruction of the answer they proposed. This reconstructed answer is not "the eternal meaning" of the text or teaching; rather, the reconstructed answer for the past question becomes the answer for the present context out of which the initiating question arose. We have no direct access into the minds of those in the past; their expression of the truth must be constantly reinterpreted and applied in the light of our questions so that we can discover our answers. In this way, implications for contemporary praxis of a particular past belief may indeed change from generation to generation, from one context to another, each with their own new questions.

Present understanding, interpretation, and application of the faith on a particular issue, therefore, is arrived at by setting in dialogue the present reception context, with its question requiring an answer, and past reception contexts, with their question-and-answer dynamic. Consequently, it is hermeneutically naïve to see the meaning of a past teaching of the church, for example, as some eternal essence that can simply "change its clothes" and be re-expressed differently in different horizons.[46] Rather, "the meaning" *is* its reinterpretation and application. *Retrospectively,* we can certainly make a distinction between "the content" of a past teaching and "the way it is expressed."[47] However, *we cannot do that with our own formulations.* We cannot stand outside our own historical situation

46. Schillebeeckx asserts that, in the history of the church, the gospel "can only be found in the forms of *particular cultures* (the Jewish, Judaic-hellenistic, Hellenistic, Carolingian, Celtic, Roman, African, Asian cultures), never above or outside them; one never comes across a 'peeled substance' of faith; there is no way of stripping off the skin and getting down to the essence of the gospel." Edward Schillebeeckx, "The Role of History in What Is Called the New Paradigm," in *Paradigm Change in Theology: A Symposium for the Future,* ed. Hans Küng and David Tracy (Edinburgh: T&T Clark, 1989), 307–19, at 311. Original italics.

47. On the problematic nature of the content/form schema, see Edward Schillebeeckx, "The Problem of the Infallibility of the Church's Teaching Office: A Theological Reflection," *Concilium* 3 (1977): 77–94; Schillebeeckx, "The Role of History"; Ricoeur, "Response to Josef Blank."

of understanding. Only future generations will be able to stand back and see the way our reinterpretation of the past has or has not maintained continuity with that past. In that sense, "orthodoxy lies always in the future."[48] As Maurice Blondel stated concerning the historical process of tradition, "with the help of the past [the church] liberates the future from the unconscious limitations and illusions of the present."[49]

Therefore, according to a reception hermeneutics, interpretation is not simply a matter of reinterpreting a past answer and "applying it" to the present. Application has its starting point in a contemporary question arising from a particular context and, through hermeneutical reconstruction, entering into the reception context of a relevant past authoritative formulation, with its own question-and-answer dynamic. Faithful interpretation requires bringing into dialogue not simply past answers and present questions, but rather the present reception context with its particular question-and-answer dynamic, and the past reception context with its particular question-and-answer dynamic.[50]

48. The phrase comes from the audio recording of a talk Rowan Williams gave in Melbourne, Australia, in 1998 in a series of lectures on the Holy Spirit. Williams goes on to say: "When one looks at any major moment of Christian self-understanding and self-discovery in history, the moments when classical formulations and credal formulations come to concretion, as in the fourth century, one realises how, at any given moment in that process, nobody yet knew what it would mean to be orthodox. And it is worth putting ourselves in analogy to that position. The church's divisions and uncertainties over a whole range of issues at the moment are not wholly unlike the situation of the church in the middle of the fourth century. The average bishop, struggling in a small market town in Asia Minor in about 350, did not know (I mean, really, did not know) what it would mean to accept the Nicene creed; did not know what it would mean to be orthodox by the definitions of even a few decades later on. It doesn't mean that fidelity was not important to him; it doesn't mean that the formulations that emerged were somehow accidental or marginal or unnecessary. Far from it. But that imaginary, rural bishop in 350, is a figure I return to constantly in my own imagining. I feel for him. I suspect he feels for me. And for all of us. For him, orthodoxy, in the sense I now mean it, lay in the future."

49. Maurice Blondel, "History and Dogma," in *The Letter on Apologetics and History and Dogma* (New York: Holt, 1965), 219–87, at 282. Blondel goes on to state: "After having fought for so long against various forms of a dissolving *latitudinarianism,* [the church] will realize, in the plenitude of her power, and in her need for self-expansion, that to be too broadminded and to minimize Revelation is not the only way of departing from orthodoxy, that it is equally possible to be too narrow-minded and to restrict the Redemption: that is also a heresy, and one which has been the least effective in breaking up Christian society." Ibid.

50. Similarly, Paul Ricoeur writes, with regard to biblical hermeneutics: "The hermeneutical rule which I see as the only operable one would be: *our* answers should be to *our* problems what the answers of the biblical writers were to the problems of their time, as we perceive them by means of biblical exegesis. This relation of *analogy* between the question-answer relationship of today and the question-answer relationship of the primitive church seems to me the best approximation of the kind of truthfulness that we can expect from a Christian hermeneutical

This approach of bringing present and past dialogic reception contexts into dialogue with each other (rather than simply correlating a past answer with a present question) has similarities with the "correspondence of relationships model" proposed by Clodovis Boff.[51] Boff rejects both a simplistic "gospel/politics model" (which follows the model of deductive application of "a rule" to "a context"), and a "correspondence of terms model" (which, although more hermeneutically sophisticated, attempts to correlate the original message and its context with the contemporary situation and the contemporary meaning of the message).[52] Both of these approaches, according to Boff, fail to concede the hermeneutical complexity of the original context out of which the normative texts of the tradition arose, the hermeneutical complexity of the present context, and the complexity of bringing past and present contexts into dialogue. He proposes what he calls a "correspondence of relationships model," which seeks to relate the circle of enquiry within and between the original formulation and its context, and the contemporary context and its demand for fresh response.[53] In his hermeneutical model, Boff says, "we are dealing with a relationship of relationships."[54] Edward Schillebeeckx and Hermann Pottmeyer both propose models with similarities to Boff's correspondence of relationships model.[55]

---

theology. But because this truthfulness relies on an analogical relationship to the interpretation of questions and answers which constitute the hermeneutical process at work in the text, it does not exclude, but rather requires, imagination, boldness and coherence." Ricoeur, "Response to Josef Blank," 286.

51. For his discussion of hermeneutics and the "constitution of theological pertinency," see the chapter in Clodovis Boff, *Theology and Praxis: Epistemological Foundations* (Maryknoll, N.Y.: Orbis Books, 1987), 132–53.

52. See Ibid., 142–46. A similar typology of hermeneutical approaches is outlined by Bradford E. Hinze, *Practices of Dialogue in the Roman Catholic Church: Aims and Obstacles, Lessons and Laments* (New York: Continuum, 2006), 13. Appropriating the work of Matthias Scharer and Jochen Hilberath, Hinze criticizes both a "hermeneutics of application" and a "hermeneutics of correlation," and advances the "hermeneutics of difference" exemplified in the work of Gustavo Gutiérrez. Like Boff's definition of the word "application" in regard to the "gospel/politics model," Hinze's understanding of a "hermeneutics of application" (as a quasi-biblical fundamentalism) differs significantly from the active and transformative sense of "application" in my proposal. Boff, despite his initial use of "application" in reference to the "gospel/politics model," does go on to use the notion of "application" in its praxis-oriented sense throughout his delineation of the "correspondence of relationships model."

53. Boff, *Theology and Praxis,* 146–50. For a summary of Boff's "correspondence of relationships model" as generally paradigmatic of a liberation theology approach, see Peter C. Phan, "Method in Liberation Theologies," *Theological Studies* 61 (2000): 40–63, at 54–57.

54. Boff, *Theology and Praxis,* 149.

55. "[Christian] identity of meaning can only be found *on the level of the corresponding relation*

In a similar way, reception hermeneutical theology, as proposed in this book, attempts to set in dialogical relationship the whole question-answer reception context of contemporary believers, and the whole original question-answer reception context of any relevant past authoritative formulation (e.g., of Scripture and the context of its production and reception, or of a teaching from a council and the context of its production and reception). The model could well be named a "dialogue of reception contexts model." According to such a model, the interrelated triad of understanding, interpretation, and application proceeds according to the logic of question and answer, a process generated initially by questions from the present context. The circle of further understanding requires a dialogue, not simply between a present question and a pre-set past answer from tradition requiring simple application, but between a contemporary dialogic reception context with its particular questions seeking answers, and the authoritative texts of the past, with their answers likewise generated in response to unique particular questions in another particular context. In this way, questions put to the old answers generate a dialogue between dialogues, in which that old answer is eventually reformulated as a new answer, meaningful in and transformative of a contemporary context.

In that process, it may be that new questions arise in the present, which have never been raised or answered by the church in the past; Scripture or tradition has simply not considered them or could not even have conceived them. If the question has never been posed in a particular way, then the tradition has not yet given a specific answer whose original question-answer dynamic can be re-engaged. As we will discuss in part 3, "The Task," contemporary answers to such new questions can indeed be constructed from interpretation of Scripture and tradition, but only through a dialogue between the present reception context and a

---

between the original message (tradition) and *the always different situation,* both in the past and in the present. The fundamental identity of meaning between subsequent periods of Christian understanding of the tradition of faith does not concern the corresponding terms; it concerns the corresponding relations between the terms (message and situation, then and now). . . . The Christian *perception* of meaning takes place *in* a creative process of *giving* meaning: a re-reading of the tradition from within new situations. Interpretation produces new traditions, in creative faithfulness. This is what it means to hand on the tradition of faith in a living way to future generations." Schillebeeckx, "The Role of History," 313. Original italics. For Pottmeyer's appropriation of Boff's model, see Hermann J. Pottmeyer, "Theologische Erkenntnislehre als kritische Hermeneutik," in *Philosophisch-theologische Grenzfragen,* ed. Julie Kirchberg and Johannes Müther (Essen: Ludgerus, 1986), 205–10.

hermeneutical reconstruction of the "spirit" of the whole of the scriptural witness and the whole of the church's tradition, in the light of the new question. The new answer that results from the dialogue of dialogic contexts will be the result of an ecclesial judgment of the whole church in the present as to what is "true to Jesus,"[56] "the mediator and the fullness of all revelation."[57]

As a way of describing the process of arriving at such "answers," Gadamer's notion, "fusion of horizons" *(Horizontverschmelzung),* is inadequate.[58] More often, understanding takes place through a *"differentiation* of horizons" *(Horizontabhebung).*[59] Whether it be dialogue between persons or dialogue with a text, the logic of question and answer requires attentiveness to "the other" and openness to the perspective of the other. Oftentimes the strangeness or "alterity" of the other, rather than being a block to communication of meaning, becomes the opportunity for a broadening of one's own partial horizon of understanding. Likewise, a naïve expectation of arriving at understanding through some "fusion" of horizons can be precluded by attention to "difference" and "otherness" (alterity). A reception hermeneutics that brings to the fore this differentiation of horizons is "a hermeneutics of alterity."[60] We will later see that, for a hermeneutics of the reception of revelation, this focus on "difference" and "alterity" has implications for discussion of issues such as a contemporary sense of the strangeness of Scripture, the claim on the present of such authoritative texts from the past, resolution of the conflict of interpretations in contemporary ecclesial dialogue, the need to highlight the otherness of God, and the consequent eschatological nature of human reception of divine truth, faith.

Throughout this book, the notion of the hermeneutical circle will be helpful for outlining several dynamic relationships: the relationship between revelation and faith, between revelation and a sense of the faith, between revelation and tradition, between revelation and Scripture, between Scripture and tradition, between tradition and present experience, between each of the four marks of the church, between each of the three offices of Christ in the church, between the church's infallibility in be-

---

56. Schillebeeckx, *Jesus,* 753.

57. *DV,* 2. Tanner translation.

58. See Gadamer, *Truth and Method,* 300–307.

59. Jauss, *Question and Answer,* 205.

60. Hans Robert Jauss, "Rückschau auf die Begriffsgeschichte von Verstehen," in *Wege des Verstehens* (Munich: Wilhelm Fink, 1994), 11–29, at 22.

lieving and its infallibility in teaching, between the *sensus fidelium* and theology, between theology and the magisterium, and between the magisterium and the *sensus fidelium*.[61] Each of these relationships names different aspects of ecclesial reception of revelation that mutually inform each other; some highlight different groups in the church whose receptions of revelation are to be conceived in terms of active circles of ongoing ecclesial understanding, interpretation, and application of the faith, according to the logic of question and answer and the productive differentiation of horizons of understanding within the world-church.

At this stage of our enquiry, however, this circularity in understanding is particularly relevant for our discussion of *sensus fidei* with regard to two relationships which we will now briefly examine more closely: (1) the dynamic relationship between the faith of the individual Christian and the faith of the ecclesial community; and (2) the dynamic relationship between *fides qua creditur* and *fides quae creditur*.

Firstly, while the faith of the Christian is always a received ecclesial faith, its reception by the individual is hermeneutically unique. In chapter 8 we will examine in greater detail the individual's sense of the faith, the *sensus fidei fidelis*. Here it is important to highlight the ecclesial nature of Christian faith, and the importance of not isolating individual faith from ecclesial faith, and vice versa. An individual Christian's reception of the faith generally takes place within a Christian community which hands on "the faith" and enables the experience of Christian salvation to be recognized and named.[62] St. Paul reminds the Corinthians: "What do you have that you did not receive? And if you received it, why

61. For one theologian's use of the notion of "the hermeneutical circle," see Boff, *Theology and Praxis,* 135–39, where he applies the notion to the relationship between (1) Scripture and the word of God, (2) the creation and the perception of meaning, (3) structure and meaning, (4) present and past, and (5) *techne hermeneutike* and *hermeneia*.

62. See Richard R. Gaillardetz, *Teaching with Authority: A Theology of the Magisterium in the Church* (Collegeville, Minn.: Liturgical Press, 1997), 256, who writes: "[A]s Christians, we do not profess a private faith. The act of faith, while certainly personal in character, is also communal. Just as it is a mistake to isolate discrete teaching acts of the magisterium from the life of the Church, so too is it misguided to isolate the response of the individual believer to Church teaching from the corporate reception of Church doctrine by the whole people of God. The character and significance of an individual's response to church teaching both influences and is influenced by the ecclesial community. The response of the active Christian committed to an ecclesial community cannot be the same as the response of a Christian who lives on the periphery of an ecclesial community. This is the important point made by many who resent the presentation of Gallup polls as if their findings constituted the *sensus fidelium*. Such polls fail to acknowledge the importance of ecclesial context."

do you boast as if it were not a gift?"[63] These individual and communal dimensions of faith exist in a relationship that can be best described as a hermeneutical circle of ecclesial understanding.

Secondly, the hermeneutical circle is helpful for avoiding any sharp separation between faith as relationship and faith as assent. *Fides qua creditur* is faith seen as a personal response by the individual and the community to God's loving self-communication. It is the act or activity of faith; it is faith as believing. *Fides quae creditur* names the dimension of faith as an assent to the content of beliefs taught by the church, that which is to be believed, "the faith." These two dimensions of faith may be distinguished but not separated. Given the circularity of understanding outlined above between whole and part, past and present, the old and the new, tradition and present experience, a Christian individual's believing in God is already informed and fashioned by received symbols, doctrines, metaphors, pictorial images, narratives, rituals, liturgical texts, hymns, categories, concepts, and experiences. These elements form the framework out of which an individual Christian is able to recognize and interpret "the religious dimension of human experience."[64] How one experiences faith as a personal relationship of trust in and intimacy with God will be conditioned to a significant degree by particular beliefs already held about God. New experiences of God, shaped by already held beliefs, in turn will "correct" one's previous interpretation of those beliefs and thereby enrich future possible experiences. On both the individual and the communal level, a *sensus fidei,* understood as an interpretation of the faith, arises out of this hermeneutical circle of understanding between *fides qua creditur* (faith seen as a response by the individual person to God's self-communication) and *fides quae creditur* (faith as an assent to the content of beliefs taught by the church).[65]

We have so far examined mainly the theological appropriateness of

63. 1 Cor 4:7.

64. See the approach taken throughout John E. Smith, *Experience and God* (New York: Fordham University Press, 1995).

65. Avery Dulles writes of the dialectic between understanding and assent to beliefs: "Faith and understanding, therefore, enter into a dialectical unity. Understanding and believing are not identical, but it is when I believe that I best understand, and it is when I understand that I believe most fully as I should. The Christian is convinced that the beliefs of his own tradition are capable of leading to the fullest and highest understanding available to man." Avery Dulles, *The Survival of Dogma: Faith, Authority and Dogma in a Changing World* (New York: Crossroad, 1987), 43. I am grateful for the helpful comments of Bradford Hinze on this section concerning the importance of a "thick description" of faith as believing and as beliefs.

insights from philosophical hermeneutics, such as the hermeneutical triad and the hermeneutical circle. Other background theories have been
mentioned, such as reception aesthetics and a literary hermeneutics,
which presupposes the nature of literary art according to a reception aesthetics.[66]

The appropriateness of reception aesthetics requires some exploration.
Reception aesthetics sees a work of art communicating meaning on three
"levels": (1) the producer, (2) the work of art itself, and (3) the receiver of
the work of art. All three are involved in the communicative event that
is "art." Indeed, the receiver can legitimately be seen as a "co-producer"
with the original producer, in the sense that it is in the act of reception
that the work communicates its meaning. The receiver (the hearer of the
music, the reader of the novel, the viewer of the sculpture or painting)
brings to the work of art a horizon of meaning in which the work is realized in the hearing, the reading, the viewing. Thus, for the work to have
an effect, active involvement of the receiver is required; there is no effect
(Wirkung) without reception *(Rezeption).*

For a literary work of art, a text is dead until it is read. The reader
brings a particular horizon of expectation to the act of reading which enables understanding to take place. The act of reading is therefore an act
of the imagination through which the work is brought to life anew. This
is not to downplay the importance of the author's intention when originally creating the work of art; nor is it to downplay the importance of
literary genre or structure or rhetoric in the communication of meaning through the work of art. But it is to highlight the importance of the
long-forgotten third in the full communicative process of author-text-
reader. A reception aesthetics seeks to highlight the importance of the receiver, without downplaying the other two factors.[67]

From such an aesthetics of reception can be developed an appropriate hermeneutics for the interpretation of works of art so understood.
A literary work of art requires a literary reception hermeneutics. Since
all three factors of author, work, and reader are involved in the com-

66. In theology's own appropriation of these background theories in the light of faith and contemporary experience, we could say there is a circle of understanding between these background
theories and the procedures of theology. For a sophisticated theory regarding this ongoing circle
of theological enquiry, see Francis Schüssler Fiorenza's notion of "wide reflective equilibrium." See
Schüssler Fiorenza, *Foundational Theology,* 301–4.

67. For a more extended exploration of reception aesthetics, see Rush, *The Reception of Doctrine,* 11–124.

munication of a text's meaning, the interpretation of a literary work of art requires a threefold hermeneutical reconstruction: (1) of the meaning discovered by the reader, (2) of the meaning emerging from the literary elements of the text itself, and (3) of the meaning of the author's original intention. These three enquiries seek to reconstruct three worlds: the world in front of the text, the world of the text, and the world behind the text.[68] These three enquiries are to be related to each other in an ongoing circle of enquiry. Whether for interpreting biblical, liturgical, doctrinal, or other classic texts, symbols, or practices, interpretation proceeds through the same circles of ongoing enquiry.

THE PROPOSED MODEL

I have proposed that the analogous notion of the epistemological organon of *sensus fidei* is helpful heuristically for conceiving the hermeneutical process of interpreting revelation as a process that is guided by the Holy Spirit. In part 2, which follows, I propose a hypothesis in which the formation and canonization of the New Testament is retrospectively modeled as a process generated by the hermeneutical organon of *sensus fidei,* the Spirit's instrument within believers for interpretation of revelation. The gift of a hermeneutical organon, given by the Holy Spirit after Easter, accounts for the bridging of the gap between the disciples' inability to understand Jesus aright before Easter and their ability to understand him after Easter. It accounts for the newfound post-Easter confidence that they could now make sense of him and therefore preach him effectively. The wide diversity of theologies throughout the New Testament writings can only be explained by such a confidence and such a freedom.

In part 2, "The Norm," I propose that the development of the oral and written traditions which eventually come to make up the Gospels of the canonical New Testament are generated by the organon of *sensus fidei* in individuals and the community. The activity of the same *sensus fidei* is evident in the perspective of the other writers of the New Testament. It is this organon which is the "engine" generating the early Christian tradi-

---

68. The writings of Paul Ricoeur make use of this terminology of "three worlds." See especially Paul Ricoeur, "Time and Narrative: Threefold Mimesis," in *Time and Narrative, 1* (Chicago: University of Chicago Press, 1984), 52–87. For an appropriation of Ricoeur's hermeneutics for a biblical hermeneutics, see Schneiders, *The Revelatory Text.*

tion process, of which the New Testament is a product, hence the order in the subtitle of part 2: *sensus fidelium,* tradition, and Scripture. Within this process, there is a dynamic interplay between the *sensus fidei* of individuals and that of the community, a dynamic in which the approbation of individuals by the whole community is constantly seen to be highly significant. If the model is appropriate, it must cohere with recent biblical scholarship regarding the formation of these individual writings and their selection and collection as a canon. If the model is appropriate, it must explain as legitimate the diversity within the unifying norm of the canon. If the model is appropriate, it must offer a way of conceiving the long-held Christian belief that somehow this emergent canon is inspired by the Holy Spirit. I propose that the model outlined in part 2 answers those demands.

Before we proceed, one point requires noting. Although the gift of this organon comes only with the gift of full Easter faith, its activity post-Easter of making sense of Jesus lies on a continuum with the pre-Easter remembering of those disciples who do not fully comprehend Jesus, but who would nevertheless play a vital role post-Easter in assuring faithful remembering of the pre-Easter "Jesus tradition."[69] It is they who, despite their initial misunderstanding, provide the details which will make up the stories and sayings of the Jesus tradition as it is consolidated post-Easter. The disciples' faith pre-Easter is an Israelite faith, which attempts to make sense of Jesus in the light of the tradition of that faith. While their misunderstanding of Jesus will be corrected by the further events of Calvary and the resurrection, and by the ability to interpret these events through enlightenment by the Holy Spirit at Pentecost, their faith lies along a continuum of believing in "the God of Jesus Christ." After Easter, their faith is in the God of the Jesus Christ who is now recognized as the Crucified and Risen One and as the mediator of God's salvific revelation. For such insight the light of the Holy Spirit is needed. However, the post-Easter "eyes of the faith" of the disciples are able to recognize the Risen One only with a memory of his actions and teachings that had been forming during his ministry, and fashioned according to the inter-

---

69. I use the phrase in the sense of James D. G. Dunn, "Jesus in Oral Memory: The Initial Stages of the Jesus Tradition," in *Jesus: A Colloquium in the Holy Land,* ed. Doris Donnelly (New York: Continuum, 2001), 84–145, at 84. "'Jesus tradition' is shorthand for the material used by the Gospel writers, particularly . . . the Synoptic Gospels—that is, stories about Jesus, teachings attributed to Jesus."

pretative frameworks of their Jewish faith. Despite their misunderstanding of him, there has been a consolidation of a core impression of Jesus and his faith-vision. It is this consolidating communal memory that provides the horizon out of which the disciples interpret the total newness of the events of Easter. There is, then, on the one hand, a continuity regarding the revelatory events experienced in Jesus pre-Easter and post-Easter. On the other hand, there is discontinuity, experienced in the disjuncture of the cross and the newness of the resurrection. The events of Easter become a hermeneutical lens for interpreting his pre-Easter ministry, and his pre-Easter ministry becomes a hermeneutical lens for interpreting his resurrection as an action of the God of Jesus Christ.

I am not claiming that this hermeneutical account of faith and its interpretative capacity is what is explicitly meant in the New Testament writings by the term *pistis* (faith).[70] Nor am I attempting a full systematic theology of faith, of which a systematic theology of the *sensus fidelium* would constitute only a part. What I am claiming is that the interpretative dynamics of faith which later Christian experience articulates more finely in theology and doctrine can be retrospectively attributed to the interpretative dynamics of faith at work in the reception of Jesus by his first followers before and after Easter, and in all stages of the canon's formation, as presented in recent biblical scholarship. I believe that the particular model proposed is mutually illuminative both for understanding the nature and function of *sensus fidei,* and for understanding the formation, canonization, and inspiration of Scripture.

70. See Dieter Lührmann, "Faith: New Testament," in *The Anchor Bible Dictionary,* vol. 2, ed. David Noel Freedman (New York: Doubleday, 1992), 2:749–58; Carroll Stuhlmueller, "The Biblical View of Faith: A Catholic Perspective," in *Handbook of Faith,* ed. James Michael Lee (Birmingham, Ala.: Religious Education Press, 1990), 99–122. For an extensive examination of Old and New Testament understandings of "faith," see Henn, *One Faith,* 5–85.

PART TWO

The Norm

Sensus Fidelium, Tradition,
and Scripture

CHAPTER 4

Receiving Jesus Christ in the Spirit

The production of the bipartite Christian Bible is the result of a process of reception and tradition involving the interpretative organon of the *sensus fidei*. This organon is at work from the very start of the Jesus tradition till the written expression par excellence of that tradition in the canon of New Testament writings, with its constant theological presupposition—the Jewish Scriptures. With the Gospel written onto their hearts, the believing disciples remembered, retold, and applied their faith in Jesus Christ out of their shared experience of that Gospel. This hermeneutical process involves the understanding, interpretation, and application of Jesus pre-Easter and post-Easter in the light of their (Jewish) faith; it involves the application of the Jesus tradition post-Easter as they understand and interpret his meaning and identity in new contexts; and it involves ongoing approbation of such application through communal discernment and control.

In what follows, we will be focusing mainly on the *process* of interpretation; a survey of the emerging *content* of Christian belief expressed in the diverse theologies in the New Testament will not be attempted. Such a survey would need to propose a historical reconstruction of the possible interpretative frameworks that may have been at work in those who first encountered Jesus.[1] Furthermore, it would need to both highlight

---

1. For one such historical reconstruction by a systematic theologian, see Schillebeeckx, *Jesus.*

the diachronic development in belief that takes place post-Easter during the first century,[2] as well as address the issue of unity and diversity in the theologies to be found in the final canonical and known non-canonical works.[3] We will give attention in the next chapter to the significance of that diversity in the formation of the canon as a unifying standard. However, our more narrow focus in this chapter is the hermeneutical process of interpreting Jesus by the pre-Easter disciples and the post-Easter church, and the role of the *sensus fidei* within that process.

RECEIVING AND TRADITIONING JESUS

This section highlights a twofold and interrelated continuum operating in the reception of Jesus pre-Easter and post-Easter: (1) the continuum of "faith" in the disciples pre-Easter and post-Easter, and (2) a continuum in the pre-Easter and post-Easter oral traditioning of stories and perceptions about Jesus, i.e., a continuum in their "sense of the faith" regarding Jesus.

The Jesus tradition has its beginnings with the disciples' earliest encounters with Jesus, pre-Easter.[4] He attracts disciples who respond positively to him and his message. From their first encounters, these disciples would have been understanding and interpreting him in particular ways,

2. On the pattern discernible in the diachronic development of the diverse New Testament christologies, see Brown, "The Christologies of New Testament Christians."

3. For example, on unity and diversity across the Bible, see A. Andrew Das and Frank J. Matera, *The Forgotten God: Perspectives in Biblical Theology. Essays in Honor of Paul J. Achtemeier on the Occasion of his Seventy-fifth Birthday* (Louisville, Ky.: Westminster John Knox Press, 2002). On the issue of unity and diversity in the New Testament, see James D. G. Dunn, *Unity and Diversity in the New Testament: An Inquiry into the Character of Earliest Christianity,* 2nd ed. (London: SCM Press, 1990); John Henry Paul Reumann, *Variety and Unity in New Testament Thought* (New York: Oxford University Press, 1991); Frank J. Matera, *New Testament Christology* (Louisville, Ky.: Westminster John Knox Press, 1999).

4. Throughout this book, I use the somewhat awkward word "traditioning" to name the oral and scribal process of transmitting traditions about Jesus and interpretations of Jesus from generation to generation, from context to new context. As noted earlier, my intention is to avoid a static notion of tradition and to highlight the active nature of ecclesial transmission of revelation. The word "traditioning" is regularly used, for example, by Walter Brueggemann, who refers to "the traditioning process of telling and retelling in order to make faith possible for the next generation." Walter Brueggemann, *An Introduction to the Old Testament: The Canon and Christian Imagination* (Louisville, Ky.: Westminster John Knox Press, 2003), 9. See also Orlando O. Espín, "Traditioning: Culture, Daily Life and Popular Religion and Their Impact on Christian Tradition," in *Futuring Our Past: Explorations in the Theology of Tradition,* ed. Orlando O. Espín and Gary Macy (Maryknoll, N.Y.: Orbis Books, 2006), 1–22.

trying to make sense of him.[5] The framework out of which they try to make sense of him is no doubt the framework of their Jewish faith in the God of Abraham, Isaac, and Jacob.[6] Whatever of the diversity of Second Temple Judaisms at the time of Jesus' ministry, those whom Jesus attracted as disciples would have interpreted him from the framework of their particular tradition of Judaism. With imaginations fashioned by that tradition and particularly by the world of their common Scriptures, the pre-Easter disciples interpret Jesus out of their "biblical imagination." These interpretations can be called, analogously, "senses of the faith."

In this way, we can speak of the disciples, pre-Easter, having "faith," if not at this stage faith "in Jesus Christ," the Crucified and Risen One. And we can speak of their having a "sense of the faith" which comes to bear on the way they see and interpret Jesus with the eyes of faith and their biblical imagination: "Who is this Jesus? How is he to be understood in the light of the God of Abraham, Isaac, and Jacob, witnessed to in our Scriptures?" This faith-interpretation is not yet full "Easter faith," understanding Jesus in the light of the resurrection and Pentecost. But there is a continuum of believing between this pre-Easter Jewish faith and a full Christian faith in Jesus Christ post-Easter. The affirmation of this continuum will find its clearest expression in the persistent way the New Testament writers use the Jewish Scriptures in their writings, and in the bipartite shape of the final Christian Bible, with the Old Testament inseparable from the New Testament. Because of that continuum, it is legitimate to speak of an incipient *sensus fidei* at work in the formation of the Jesus tradition, pre-Easter.

Much of biblical scholarship of the last few centuries has been devoted

5. For one reconstruction of the possible expectation horizons and "ready-to-hand Jewish models" out of which the disciples, pre-Easter, may have been interpreting Jesus in the light of their faith, see Schillebeeckx, *Jesus,* 439–515.

6. On "faith" in the Old Testament, see Joseph P. Healey, "Faith: Old Testament," in *The Anchor Bible Dictionary,* vol. 2, ed. David Noel Freedman (New York: Doubleday, 1992), 2:744–49; Stuhlmueller, "The Biblical View of Faith: A Catholic Perspective," esp. 101–4. In speaking of Jesus' Jewish disciples' "faith," I do so in terms of a Christian theology of faith. As Avery Dulles points out: "Like the term 'Old Testament' itself, the Christian concept of faith in the Old Testament is constructed by reading the Hebrew Scriptures backwards, so to speak, in the light of the 'New' Testament. Christians usually form their concept of faith from the New Testament and from the tradition of the Church, and then look to the Old Testament to find words or incidents that can ground or illustrate what they understand by faith. The Old Testament has no single term exactly corresponding to the New Testament term *pistis* [faith] and its cognates." Dulles, *The Assurance of Things Hoped For,* 7. Likewise, my own application of the hermeneutical notion "sense of the faith" to the pre-Easter disciples' "faith" is a "reading backwards" from the perspective of Christian faith.

to retrieving historical traditions about Jesus that have not been colored by post-Easter faith. That some scholars are now acknowledging the significance of the disciples' pre-Easter "faith" interpretation is seen by James Dunn as a new stage in historical Jesus research.[7] This enables a new way of conceiving the formation of the Jesus tradition. According to Dunn,

> The traditions which lie behind the Gospels . . . began from the various encounters between Jesus and those who by virtue of these encounters became disciples. The earliest traditions are the product of *disciple-response*. There is not an objectified meaning to be uncovered by stripping away the accretions of disciple faith. The tradition itself in its earliest form is in a crucially important sense the creation of faith; or to be more precise, it is the product of the encounters between Jesus and the ones who became his disciples. *The hearing and witnessing of the first disciples was already a hermeneutical act, already caught in the hermeneutical circle.*[8]

We can therefore say, albeit analogously, that "faith goes back to the very origins of the Jesus tradition . . . the Jesus tradition emerged from the very first as the expression of faith."[9] Even during his ministry, the impact of Jesus' teachings and activities is being interpreted, remembered, and re-narrated by his followers in a process that consolidates the essential features of the impact/reception of Jesus in their memories and interprets them in the light of Jewish faith.

This distinction between "impact" and "reception" is significant here, and will be throughout the remaining chapters of this book.[10] There is no

---

7. See James D. G. Dunn, *A New Perspective on Jesus: What the Quest for the Historical Jesus Missed* (Grand Rapids, Mich.: Baker Academic, 2005). See also Terrence W. Tilley, "Remembering the Historic Jesus: A New Research Program?" *Theological Studies* 68 (2007): 3–35.

8. James D. G. Dunn, *Jesus Remembered* (Grand Rapids, Mich.: W. B. Eerdmans, 2003), 129. My italics. Dunn makes a distinction between the pre-Easter disciples' "initial faith" and their "Easter faith." Dunn elsewhere states: "[F]aith among the disciples of Jesus did not first arise with Easter. Of course, that earlier faith was illuminated and transformed by what happened on the first Good Friday and Easter day. . . . But the disciples of Jesus did not first become disciples at the cross or on Easter day. They were already believers in Jesus prior to that; the faith was no doubt inadequate in the light of its subsequent fuller version, but it was still faith." Dunn, *A New Perspective on Jesus,* 23. Unfortunately, Dunn does not make explicit the implication that such faith was a Jewish faith, nor does he highlight the hermeneutical significance of the Jewish frameworks for interpreting Jesus pre-Easter. In terms of a systematic theology of Christian faith, the pre-Easter disciples' "initial faith" could be seen to be analogous to the "initial faith" attributed to enquirers for initiation into the church. On "initial faith," see the Introduction to International Committee on English in the Liturgy, *Rite of Christian Initiation of Adults,* study ed. (Washington, D.C.: United States Catholic Conference, 1988).

9. Dunn, *Jesus Remembered,* 132.

10. Dunn does not give sufficient attention to this hermeneutical nuance. On the interrelationship between "effect" and "reception," see Rush, *The Reception of Doctrine,* 68–70.

impact or effect *(Wirkung)* of a person, teaching, or event without a reception *(Rezeption)* of that person, teaching, or event. Jesus makes an impact only where active reception takes place; and such reception always involves interpretation. Thus the Jesus *tradition* is the disciples' *reception* of Jesus.[11] Reception enables tradition; that reception is always an interpretation. The disciples' "remembering Jesus" is not a mere repetition of "pure facts"; at the heart of their remembering is an interpretation of the salvific meaning for the disciples of what he has said and done, and of his identity as the bearer of that salvation. The interpretative reception and consequent memory of an individual disciple is his or her *sensus fidei,* their faith-reception of Jesus' meaning. It is thus through the *sensus fidei's* reception of Jesus that the Jesus tradition is perpetuated.

The canonical Gospels will later come to record communal memories of Jesus during his pre-Easter ministry explicitly attempting to consolidate his schooling of his disciples and to correct their understanding, because of their constant misinterpretation of him during that time.[12] However, even during the pre-Easter stage of reception, there is a further corrective process at work. The disciples begin to form a self-correcting *communal* memory of Jesus. The continuum of pre-Easter and post-Easter faith-interpretation, generated by the *sensus fidei,* operates within a culture that is primarily oral. This oral dimension highlights two important features of the Jesus tradition process both before and after Easter: the interrelationship between the individual and the community, and the authority of certain individuals within the community.

Almost simultaneously with the original events, it would have been an immediate response to being with Jesus for the disciples to share their initial impressions among themselves regarding the "salvific impact" he had made on them personally, recalling events involving Jesus that had

11. On the notion of tradition *as* reception, Hans Hübner remarks, "For where there is historicity, there is reception. For there to be no reception [*Rezeptionslosigkeit*] is an ontological impossibility." Hans Hübner, *Biblische Theologie des Neuen Testaments* (Göttingen: Vandenhoeck & Ruprecht, 1990), 3:244. Quoted in Mogens Müller, "The Theological Interpretation of the Figure of Jesus in the Gospel of Matthew: Some Principal Features in Matthean Christology," *New Testament Studies* 45 (1999): 157–73.

12. On the perduring memory in the early church regarding the failure of the historical disciples in fully understanding Jesus pre-Easter, as witnessed to in Mark's Gospel, see Bertram L. Melbourne, *Slow to Understand: The Disciples in Synoptic Perspective* (Lanham, Md.: University Press of America, 1988); Francis J. Moloney, *Mark: Storyteller, Interpreter, Evangelist* (Peabody, Mass.: Hendrickson Publishers, 2004). On the significance for this issue of Peter's denials of Jesus in the Fourth Gospel, see Francis J. Moloney, "John 18:15–27: A Johannine View of the Church," in *A Hard Saying: The Gospel and Culture* (Collegeville, Minn.: Liturgical Press, 2001), 131–47.

happened, stories and sayings Jesus had taught, as well as interpreting the significance, meaning, and application of those events, actions, and teachings. As James Dunn suggests:

> In the beginning, already during Jesus' own ministry, as soon as disciples began to gather around him, we can envisage initial impressions and memories being shared among the group. "Do you remember what he did/said when he . . . ?" must have been a question often asked as the embryonic community began to feel and express its distinctiveness. . . . We can assume, of course, that Jesus was giving fresh teaching (as well as repeat teaching) all the while. But in more reflective gatherings, or when Jesus was absent, the impulse to tell again what had made the greatest impact on them would presumably reassert itself.[13]

Although biblical studies have long acknowledged the role of oral traditioning before the Jesus tradition achieved written form, studies of oral cultures give a fresh insight into the oral traditioning among Jesus' disciples.[14] A characteristic of the "oral thinking" within such cultures is an ability to maintain the thrust of a story, while adapting and varying it in the retelling for a particular audience; the performance of a tradition maintains the "same" within "difference," displaying both *fixity* and *flexibility*.[15] This pattern of movement toward and maintenance of fixity in the tradition, while maintaining necessary flexibility in applying the meaning of the Jesus tradition to new contexts, is a pattern that marks the process of oral remembering.

13. Dunn, *Jesus Remembered*, 239.

14. There is extensive literature on the nature and significance of oral tradition. For a typology of three major models appropriated by biblical scholars regarding oral tradition and the Jesus tradition, see Richard Bauckham, *Jesus and the Eyewitnesses: The Gospels as Eyewitness Testimony* (Grand Rapids, Mich.: W. B. Eerdmans, 2006), 240–63. For debate on the approach of James Dunn and his use of Kenneth Bailey, see Bengt Holmberg, "Questions of Method in James Dunn's *Jesus Remembered*," *Journal for the Study of the New Testament* 26 (2004): 445–57; Samuel Byrskog, "A New Perspective on the Jesus Tradition: Reflections on James Dunn's *Jesus Remembered*," *Journal for the Study of the New Testament* 26 (2004): 459–71. For Dunn's response to their critique, see James D. G. Dunn, "On History, Memory and Eyewitnesses: In Response to Bengt Holmberg and Samuel Byrskog," *Journal for the Study of the New Testament* 26 (2004): 473–87. For a summary (and critique) of some influential works on oral tradition, see Dunn, *Jesus Remembered*, 193–210.

15. Dunn, summarizing and quoting Werner Kelber, writes: "'Oral thinking consists in formal patterns from the start'; 'formulaic stability' and 'compositional variability' go hand in hand— 'this mid-state between fixed and free'. Oral transmission 'exhibits "an insistent conservative urge for preservation" of essential information, while it borders on carelessness in its predisposition to abandon features that are not met with social approval'. 'Variability and stability, conservatism and creativity, evanescence and unpredictability all mark the pattern of oral transmission'—the 'oral principle of "variation within the same."'" Dunn, *Jesus Remembered*, 199–200.

The work of Kenneth Bailey proposes that gatherings of Jesus' disciples, with or without Jesus, would have been similar to the present-day Middle Eastern nightly village gathering (called *haflat samar*), when poems, proverbs, and stories judged significant for communal identity are retold, along with other less significant stories.[16] It is a pattern that would have likewise marked post-Easter communal remembering among Christian communities. Bailey particularly notes the significance of the element of communal control at work in such present-day gatherings.

In the *haflat samar* the community exercises control over the recitation. These poems, proverbs and stories form their identity. The right telling of these stories is critical for that identity. If someone tells the story "wrong," the reciter is corrected by a chorus of voices. Some stories may be new. But the stories that matter are the accounts known by all. The occasion is *informal* but the recitation is *controlled*.[17]

Bailey formulates this dynamic as "informal controlled tradition."[18] A similar dynamic, he proposes, is at work in the fashioning of the Jesus tradition, as the particular interpretations of individual disciples is "controlled" in an informal way by the corporate memory of the group.

Richard Bauckham's critique of Bailey's model advances the discussion regarding the mechanisms of communal discernment by noting the element of formality as well as informality in the control by the community.[19] Bailey, he claims, does not give sufficient explicit attention to the role of actual eyewitnesses in the traditioning process. These eyewitnesses are not to be seen simply as the originators of the Jesus tradition, who then drop out of the picture, as envisaged by some models. Bauckham highlights the vital significance of three groups of eyewitnesses who would have been active till their death in the communal remember-

16. Kenneth E. Bailey, "Informal Controlled Oral Tradition and the Synoptic Gospels," *Asia Journal of Theology* 5 (1991): 34–54; Kenneth E. Bailey, "Middle Eastern Oral Tradition and the Synoptic Tradition," *Expository Times* (1995): 363–67. I note here in particular aspects highlighted in Dunn's appropriation of Bailey. For Tom Wright's use of Bailey's work, see N. T. Wright, *Jesus and the Victory of God* (London: SPCK, 1996), 133–37. For a more recent summary of Bailey's proposal, see Kenneth E. Bailey, *Jacob and the Prodigal: How Jesus Retold Israel's Story* (Downers Grove, Ill.: InterVarsity Press, 2003).

17. Bailey, "Middle Eastern Oral Tradition." Quoted in Dunn, *Jesus Remembered*, 207. My italics.

18. Dunn summarizes the notion: "In informal controlled tradition the story can be retold in the setting of a gathering of the village by any member of the village present, but usually the elders, and the community itself exercises the 'control.'" Dunn, *Jesus Remembered*, 206.

19. See Bauckham, *Jesus and the Eyewitnesses*, 252–63.

ings envisaged by Bailey.[20] Firstly, there would have been "minor" eye-witnesses: the actual individuals named in the stories of the Jesus tradi-tion, people like Jairus and Bartimaeus, who would have told their own version of the original event over and over. Secondly, there would have been those eyewitnesses who experienced firsthand much of Jesus' minis-try, and could give "comprehensive witness" regarding Jesus and his min-istry; this group would have potentially been a large group. And finally, there were the Twelve, who, having been in Jesus' inner group of follow-ers, would have had special authority as witnesses to a comprehensive memory of Jesus. These eyewitnesses would have been active transmit-ters of the Jesus tradition well into the second generation of the early church.

When these eyewitnesses were gone from the scene, their function within the community would have been taken over by those who had directly heard and could verify the comprehensive memory of these actual eyewitnesses. Bauckham's refinement of Bailey's proposal there-fore gives us a more refined model of the Jesus tradition in which both formal and informal elements control the communal remembering of Jesus. Among Jesus' disciples, control would be exercised by actual eye-witnesses during their lifetime, or those who have heard the "compre-hensive witness" from actual eyewitnesses; for the next generation, au-thority passes to those who have heard such secondhand witnesses speak, and so on.

Similar to Bauckham's notion of "comprehensive witness" to Jesus is Dunn's reference to "the characteristic Jesus."[21] Within the Jesus tradi-tion, the controlling factor among the controllers is conformity to the group memory of Jesus and conformity to previous agreed impressions regarding core elements of some parable or saying of Jesus, or some story about Jesus. As Dunn suggests:

We can imagine a group of disciples meeting and requesting, for example, to hear again about the centurion of Capernaum, or about the widow and the treasury, or what it was that Jesus said about the tunic and the cloak, or about who is greater, or about the brother who sins. In response to which a senior disciple would tell again the appropriate story or teaching in whatever variant words and detail he or

---

20. For his treatment of these three groups, see ibid., 262.

21. On "the characteristic Jesus," see Dunn, *A New Perspective on Jesus*, 57–78. Dunn takes over the phrase from Leander E. Keck, *A Future for the Historical Jesus: The Place of Jesus in Preaching and Theology* (Philadelphia: Fortress Press, 1981), 33.

she judged appropriate for the occasion, with sufficient corporate memory ready to protest if one of the key elements was missed out or varied too much.[22]

Variability in the retelling of a particular story and adaptation to a different contemporary context is permitted to the degree that it coheres with the communal memory regarding "the characteristic Jesus." Is this particular rendition of an element in the Jesus tradition characteristic of the comprehensive witness to Jesus demanded by the communal memory? From that communal sharing and mutual critique, a shared memory of "the characteristic Jesus" provides the stable element over against which any flexible renditions of a story would have been judged.

In terms of the rubric of *sensus fidei,* we can reformulate these proposals for understanding communal approbation within the Jesus tradition. The memory and retelling of an individual disciple, pre-Easter or post-Easter, is his or her *sensus fidei,* which is shared with the wider group. However, the *sensus fidei* of an individual comes under the critique and approbation of the communal organon for interpretation, the *sensus fidelium,* which constitutes the communal memory of "the characteristic Jesus."

The oral traditioning process, with its balancing elements of free adaptation and communal control, does not cease when the Jesus tradition begins to be fixed in written form, which may have already been in process within thirty years after the death of Jesus.[23] This fact is important for explaining the variations in the Jesus tradition to be found in later written forms of the tradition, such as the four canonical Gospels. Biblical scholarship over the last few hundred years, in making sense of these variations and discrepancies, has predominantly worked out of a model of *literary* transmission; such discrepancies were more often attributed to departure from original written versions, either through mistake or for deliberate theological purposes on the part of the redactors along the way.[24]

---

22. Dunn, *Jesus Remembered,* 240.

23. "There is considerable evidence that oral and written cultures existed side by side in the ancient world, particularly since writing tended to be used as a help to memory rather than as an autonomous and independent mode of communication." Walter J. Ong, *Orality and Literacy: The Technologizing of the Word* (London: Routledge, 1982, 2002), 40.

24. On the need for a wider notion of the traditioning process, Werner Kelber writes: "If we can wean ourselves from the notion that texts constitute the center of gravity in tradition, we may be able to imagine and work with a vastly broader concept of tradition and assign texts their proper place within it." Werner H. Kelber, "Jesus and Tradition: Words in Time, Words in Space,"

While acknowledging that this literary redaction is certainly an aspect of the wider process, a model that gives greater attention to the predominantly *oral* nature of the traditioning process, even after the Jesus tradition finds a certain written fixity, enables us to give a more plausible account of the continuing elements of *fixity* and *flexibility* in the Jesus tradition.[25] Differences in the use of Mark by Matthew and Luke, for example, are not only to be attributed to departures from a literary version, but may also be the result of the evangelists' appropriation into the narrative of the perspective of the ongoing oral tradition within their communities at the time of redaction.

Furthermore, these Gospels are marked by the same elements of "formal" and "informal controlled tradition." The fixed Gospels we now have are possibly only one "performance" of what were living oral works, whose live performances were marked by creativity and stability.[26] It is the communal memory of "the characteristic Jesus," the *sensus fidelium*, which is the criterion for control over the elements of adaptation in the new performance. It is the benchmark over against which earlier performances of the Gospel would have been tested, and no doubt refashioned in the light of that testing. But significantly it might be the limitation of a particular community's memory of Jesus which is also under critique by the work's creative adaptation in this particular performance. In this way, an individual *sensus fidei* can challenge the *sensus fidelium* of the community. Through this individual-communal dynamic, the received

---

Semeia 65 (1994): 139–67. According to Dunn, there is a need to change "the default setting" among most scholars who continue to envisage the traditioning process according to "the literary paradigm," that of literary texts being edited and redacted. See James D. G. Dunn, "Altering the Default Setting: Re-envisaging the Early Transmission of the Jesus Tradition," *New Testament Studies* 49 (2003): 139–75, and the development of this thesis throughout Dunn, *A New Perspective on Jesus.*

25. Such a model, Dunn proposes, "asks whether it is not more realistic in historical terms, in reference to groups/churches functioning initially in a highly oral society, to conceive of these groups/churches all having quite extensive repertoires of the Jesus tradition, overlapping with that of other groups/churches and regularly shared by those (apostles, prophets and teachers) who moved among these groups/churches. And it asks for a reconceptualization of the use made of the Jesus tradition, including its transmission to new converts and other groups/churches, in terms of oral performances rather than of written traditions." Dunn, *Jesus Remembered,* 883.

26. For a survey of this recent trend in biblical studies, see David Rhoads, "Performance Criticism: An Emerging Methodology in Second Testament Studies. Part I," *Biblical Theology Bulletin* 36 (2006): 118–33; David Rhoads, "Performance Criticism: An Emerging Methodology in Second Testament Studies. Part II," *Biblical Theology Bulletin* 36 (2006): 164–84. See also Richard A. Horsley, Jonathan A. Draper, and John Miles Foley, eds., *Performing the Gospel: Orality, Memory, and Mark* (Minneapolis: Fortress, 2006).

tradition is being tested and adapted in order to make it challenging and meaningful for *this* group. The ongoing reception of the Jesus tradition, itself the result of previous receptions, therefore exhibits both fixity and flexibility, stability and adaptability, application and approbation, conservatism and creativity, for the sake of more effective ongoing transmission of the Jesus tradition.

The above discussion highlights two essential features of the *sensus fidelium* at work in the formation of the Jesus tradition, one *adaptive* or *applicative,* and the other *evaluative* or *approbative.* Firstly, the *sensus fidelium* is the community's ability to remember the basic elements of the tradition and to creatively retell the basic elements in a new performance for a different audience. Secondly, the *sensus fidelium* is the ability to critically measure and evaluate those adaptations according to the norm of "the characteristic Jesus" of communal memory. What is exhibited by the transmitters of the Jesus tradition, then, is a twofold confidence: a confidence for instinctively adapting the tradition and applying it to new contexts, and a confidence for instinctively evaluating whether a particular reception is true to the communal memory of Jesus and what does not fit its measure or standard. Therefore, characteristic of the activity of the organon of the *sensus fidelium* is (1) a creative, adaptive instinct for expressing the old (tradition) in terms of the new (context); and (2) a critical, evaluative instinct for discerning what reinterpretations are true or false to the communal memory. In that process, the *sensus fidei* of individuals in the community comes under constant testing by the rest in the group. Both individuals and the community as a whole are active transmitters of the tradition. In this way, the early Christian communities continually refashion their sense of the faith within new situations.

RECEPTIONS OF THE "OLD TESTAMENT"

The writings of the New Testament, particularly the Gospels, are hermeneutical receptions of Jesus Christ on two levels. Firstly, they are literary hermeneutical receptions which weave lines of continuity and newness between the received pre-Easter Jesus tradition and the post-Easter perspectives of the early Christian communities. Secondly, they are literary hermeneutical receptions of the Jewish Scriptures, weaving lines of continuity and newness between those Jewish Scriptures and the new event of Jesus Christ. Both levels of reception have the same goal:

the delineation of the meaning of Jesus and of Christian identities in the post-Easter context of each author. I am proposing that, on both levels, it is the ecclesial capacity of *sensus fidei/fidelium* which facilitates such reception. *Sensus fidei/fidelium* is the community's epistemological organon or instrument for hermeneutical reception. In this section we will examine the literary (and thus hermeneutical) reception of the Jewish Scriptures within the New Testament writings. In the following section, we will focus more narrowly on the nature of the Gospels as receptions of the Jesus tradition addressed to new post-Easter contexts.

The Christian writings that were eventually included in the canon are, in different ways, literary receptions of the Jewish Scriptures.[27] How do the disciples, after the resurrection, make sense of what they have experienced in Jesus Christ? We have already highlighted the significance of the Jewish faith and biblical imagination of the pre-Easter disciples for the way they would have initially understood and interpreted Jesus. There is a faith-continuum between that "initial faith" and the faith reflection of the post-Easter disciples. This is evident from the fact that a highly significant hermeneutical lens in that post-Easter interpretative process remains the imaginative world of the Jewish Scriptures and the imaginative world of the inter-testamental literature.[28] If the disciples' experience of the Christ event (captured in the already-interpreted data of the emerg-

27. For general works on the reception of the Old Testament in the New, see Steve Moyise, *The Old Testament in the New: An Introduction* (New York, London: Continuum, 2001); Steve Moyise, ed., *The Old Testament in the New Testament: Essays in Honour of J. L. North* (Sheffield, England: Sheffield Academic Press, 2000); D. A. Carson and H. G. M. Williamson, eds., *It is Written: Scripture Citing Scripture. Essays in Honour of Barnabas Lindars, SSF* (New York: Cambridge University Press, 1988); John M. Court, *New Testament Writers and the Old Testament: An Introduction* (London: SPCK, 2002); Fredrick Carlson Holmgren, *The Old Testament and the Significance of Jesus: Embracing Change—Maintaining Christian Identity. The Emerging Center in Biblical Scholarship* (Grand Rapids, Mich.: W. B. Eerdmans, 1999).

28. It is not necessary for us to examine in detail the complex issue of when the Jewish canon was fixed, and what translations and versions were available to and were quoted by New Testament writers. The following passage from the Pontifical Biblical Commission succinctly summarizes a certain consensus in biblical scholarship today: "Generally, the authors of the New Testament manifest knowledge of the deuterocanonical books and other non-canonical ones since the number of books cited in the New Testament exceeds not only the Hebrew canon, but also the so-called Alexandrian canon. When Christianity spread into the Greek world, it continued to use sacred books received from Hellenistic Judaism. Although Hellenistic Christians received their Scriptures from the Jews in the form of the Septuagint, we do not know the precise form, because the Septuagint has come down to us only in Christian writings. What the Church seems to have received was a body of Sacred Scripture which, within Judaism, was in the process of becoming canonical. When Judaism came to close its own canon, the Christian Church was sufficiently

ing Jesus tradition) constitutes the first lens through which they interpreted Jesus, what constitutes the second lens (making up their two-eyed interpretative spectacles, as it were) is the Jewish biblical imagination, or what Richard Kearney calls the "Hebraic imagination" of their Scripture.[29] It is the second lens through which their *sensus fidei* interprets Jesus' life, ministry, death, and resurrection. The story of Jesus is told as a story of the God of the covenant whose promises have now been fulfilled.

As already mentioned, the Jewish Scriptures no doubt constitute the interpretative matrix out of which the disciples' direct *pre*-Easter experiences of Jesus are formed.[30] And post-Easter, the familiar Jewish Scriptures continue to provide a literary, metaphorical, conceptual, and narrative framework for interpreting and narrating the story of the Christ event.[31] Their Scriptures shape their "pre-understanding," enabling them,

---

independent from Judaism not to be immediately affected. It was only at a later period that a closed Hebrew canon began to exert influence on how Christians viewed it." Pontifical Biblical Commission, *The Jewish People and Their Sacred Scriptures in the Christian Bible* (Vatican City: Libreria Editrice Vaticana, 2002), 38–39 [para 17]. For a thorough study of the issues, see Jennifer M. Dines, *The Septuagint* (New York: T&T Clark, 2004).

29. Richard Kearney, *The Wake of Imagination: Toward a Postmodern Culture* (London: Routledge, 1994). Richard Hays writes: "Jesus and his first followers were Jews whose symbolic world was shaped by Israel's scripture: their categories for interpreting the world and their hopes for God's saving action were fundamentally conditioned by the biblical stories of God's dealings with the people of Israel. Therefore, it is not surprising that as the earliest Christian communities began to tell and retell stories about Jesus, they interpreted his life, death and resurrection in relation to those biblical stories (i.e., the texts that Christians later came to call the Old Testament)." Richard B. Hays, "The Canonical Matrix of the Gospels," in *The Cambridge Companion to the Gospels,* ed. Stephen C. Barton (New York: Cambridge University Press, 2006), 53–75, at 53.

30. What Steve Moyise states of the post-Easter perspective of the New Testament writers must surely apply to the initial hermeneutical framework of the pre-Easter misunderstanding of Jesus' disciples: "One might argue, therefore, that Christian experience comes first and reflection on the [Jewish] scriptures follows. On the other hand, it is also true that the New Testament writers were largely 'formed' by the [Jewish] scriptures before they ever set eyes on Christ." See Moyise, *The Old Testament in the New,* 135. In philosophical hermeneutics, this insight into the enabling role of "pre-judice" ("pre-understanding") is a major insight in Gadamer, *Truth and Method,* 265–307.

31. "For the authors of the New Testament the holy writings of Judaism were a basic generator of meaning in their conceptual universe. In their eyes Jesus Christ was not just someone who appeared in his own right; his life story was believed to be deeply integrated in the revelation embodied in the collection of books later called the Old Testament. . . . The holy books of Judaism quite simply were the first Bible of the Church. Seen in its proper perspective New Testament literature can be characterized as an attempt to maintain a specific interpretation of the Old Testament." Mogens Müller, "The New Testament Reception of the Old Testament," in *The New Testament as Reception,* ed. Mogens Müller and Henrik Tronier (New York: Sheffield Academic Press, 2002), 1–14, at 1.

at least initially, to understand their experience of something new, in the light of something already familiar. There is, therefore, a hermeneutical circle of understanding between "the old" and "the new." "The old" enables them to make sense of "the new," i.e., the new and unfamiliar is interpreted in the light of the old and familiar.[32] But similarly, they read the old through the lens of the new, i.e., the old and familiar is reinterpreted in the light of new experience. In other words, although the Jewish Scriptures remain a lens for interpreting the new, their experience of Jesus Christ brings about a conversion of their biblical imagination.

There are two levels to this "newness" and the conversion of their biblical imagination. Firstly, the resurrection is a new event which now enables the disciples to understand Jesus' pre-Easter ministry and his identity in a new way, from a new perspective. Secondly, with regard to what God has been doing in the past, the whole Christ event constitutes an event in which God is doing something new, beyond what has happened in the past. The "old" is not totally sufficient to name that newness. Therefore, as the first Christians, post-Easter, "look back" to their Scriptures with the eyes of faith, the experience of salvific revelation in and through the Crucified and Risen One becomes the lens through which they refocus the Old Testament. That it is the same God who has spoken through the Jewish Scriptures and who has now raised Jesus Christ from the dead enables them, they claim, to reinterpret those Scriptures in the light of Christ.[33] Their experience of the event of Jesus Christ (his life, ministry, death, and resurrection) becomes the matrix out of which they interpret and understand anew the past tradition. In that sense, Jesus Christ becomes the lens for interpreting "the old."

---

32. On the reception of traditions shining a light on new situations, Paul Achtemeier writes: "If the traditions are the framework within which the community understands itself, its past, and on that basis its future, they are also the means whereby the community seeks to understand new situations into which it is thrust by its existence in the historical arena. It is precisely when those traditions are used to understand the new situation that the modification of tradition occurs which is so much a characteristic of the biblical literature." Paul J. Achtemeier, *Inspiration and Authority: Nature and Function of Christian Scripture* (Peabody, Mass.: Hendrickson Publishers, 1999), 111–12.

33. "The identity of the God who speaks in Israel's holy Scripture with the God who accomplished salvation in Christ for all humankind, is the theological precondition for the hermeneutical basic conviction of the New Testament authors." Hans Hübner, "New Testament Interpretation of the Old Testament," in *Hebrew Bible, Old Testament: The History of Its Interpretation. Volume 1: From the Beginnings to the Middle Ages (Until 1300). Part 1: Antiquity*, ed. Magne Sæbø (Göttingen: Vandenhoeck & Ruprecht, 1996), 332–72.

However, there is a range of ways in which the individual New Testament writers relate the new and the old, from negative to positive configurations; the New Testament writers do not use the Jewish Scriptures in the same way and do not have the same theological agendas when doing so. The threads of continuity and discontinuity are at times woven differently. This takes place on three levels: the historical, the institutional, and the prophetic.[34] This range of configurations can even be found in the thought of the same author, given different polemical contexts. Nevertheless, a common principle is at work: the various authors' theological interpretation of Jesus Christ entails a literary reception of the Old Testament. In the next chapter, when we come to examine the criteria for inclusion and exclusion in the canon, we will see that of primary concern was whether a work has or has not woven a thread of continuity between the God of Israel witnessed to in its Scripture and the God of Jesus Christ. A brief survey now of some of the canonical authors demonstrates the pervasive attempt throughout the New Testament to relate Christ to the story of God and God's promises of old.[35]

Interpreting Christ in the light of the Jewish tradition is at the heart of Paul's theological project: "In Paul we encounter a first century Jewish thinker who, while undergoing a profound disjuncture with his own religious tradition, grappled his way through to a vigorous and thoroughly generative reappropriation of Israel's Scriptures."[36] For example, in his first letter to the Corinthians, Paul's challenge to the Corinthians' "human wisdom" in the light of "divine wisdom" is Paul's call to "a conversion of the imagination"; he does this by leading his readers through his own particular re-reading of Scripture in the light of the Christ event.[37]

34. See Pierre Grelot, "Relations between the Old and New Testaments in Jesus Christ," in *Problems and Perspectives of Fundamental Theology*, ed. René Latourelle and Gerald O'Collins (New York: Paulist Press, 1982), 186–205.

35. For a summary of the distinctive ways in which each of the New Testament writings quote and allude to the Old Testament, see the individual chapters of Moyise, *The Old Testament in the New*.

36. Richard B. Hays, *Echoes of Scripture in the Letters of Paul* (New Haven, Conn.: Yale University Press, 1989), 2. For other works on Paul's use of Scripture, see Craig A. Evans and James A. Sanders, eds., *Paul and the Scriptures of Israel* (Sheffield, England: JSOT Press, 1993); Sylvia C. Keesmaat, *Paul and his Story: (Re)-interpreting the Exodus Tradition* (Sheffield, England: Sheffield Academic Press, 1999). On Paul's particular reading of Jewish Scripture as also a dialogue with other contemporary Jewish readers of those scriptures, see Francis Watson, *Paul and the Hermeneutics of Faith* (New York: T&T Clark International, 2004).

37. Richard B. Hays, "The Conversion of the Imagination: Scripture and Eschatology in 1 Corinthians," *New Testament Studies* 45 (1999): 391–412.

Mark, while not peppering his narrative commentary with direct quotations as much as the other synoptic Gospels do, nevertheless sets his whole narrative within the context of the Jewish scriptural tradition: "We cannot consider highly enough the fact that the Gospel of Mark starts with an Old Testament quotation which, as a fulfilment quotation, is the theological heading of the oldest Gospel."[38]

Matthew, while his work includes literary reception of Mark's Gospel (with its own distinctive placement of Jesus within the scriptural tradition), is even more concerned to make explicit the link between Jesus and what he believes to be the promises of Scripture: "Matthew's theological program should be viewed as an attempt to show how the Jewish tradition is best preserved in a Jewish-Christian context."[39] He does this through rich quotation of and allusion to Scripture.[40] Mogens Müller writes that, for Matthew, "Judaism and its holy books" constitute "the screen through which Jesus' life and works were filtered."[41]

Like Matthew, Luke is not only receiving (re-reading and thus reinterpreting) Mark and the oral and written traditions of his community in the light of a new context, but also re-reading the scriptural tradition of Jewish Scriptures.[42] According to James Sanders, "Luke is the most explicit of the evangelists in insisting that to understand what God was doing in Christ one had to know Scripture."[43]

38. Hübner, "New Testament Interpretation of the Old Testament," 348. Daniel Harrington notes that "at many pivotal points in his story, Mark appeals to OT texts and appears to assume that his readers know these texts and receive them as authoritative." John R. Donahue and Daniel J. Harrington, *The Gospel of Mark, Sacra Pagina Series; v. 2* (Collegeville, Minn.: Liturgical Press, 2002), 35. For an examination of the rich scriptural allusions in the Markan narrative, see Hays, "The Canonical Matrix of the Gospels."

39. Daniel J. Harrington, *The Gospel of Matthew, Sacra Pagina Series; v. 1* (Collegeville, Minn.: Liturgical Press, 1991), 17.

40. "Given Matthew's presupposition that the Christ is the fulfilment of Scripture, and his view that the Scripture as a whole (esp. the Prophets) predicted the eschatological times, which Matthew saw as dawning with the advent of Christ, it is understandable that he uses Scripture to add details to his story of Jesus." M. Eugene Boring, "Excursus: Matthew as Interpreter of Scripture," in *The New Interpreter's Bible*, Volume 8 (Nashville, Tenn.: Abingdon Press, 1994), 151–54, at 153.

41. Müller, "The Theological Interpretation of the Figure of Jesus," 159.

42. On Luke's reception of Jewish Scripture, see Craig A. Evans and James A. Sanders, eds., *Luke and Scripture: The Function of Sacred Tradition in Luke-Acts* (Minneapolis: Fortress Press, 1993); David P. Moessner, *Jesus and the Heritage of Israel: Luke's Narrative Claim upon Israel's Legacy* (Harrisburg, Pa.: Trinity Press International, 1999); François Bovon, "The Interpretation of the Scriptures of Israel," in *Luke the Theologian: Fifty-five Years of Research (1950–2005)* (Waco, Tex.: Baylor University Press, 2006), 87–121.

43. James A. Sanders, "Isaiah in Luke," in *Luke and Scripture: The Function of Sacred Tradition in Luke-Acts*, ed. Craig A. Evans (Minneapolis: Fortress Press, 1993), 14–25, at 18.

John's narrative likewise portrays Jesus in the light of the Old Testament. For Maarten Menken, John "is rooted, with all the singularity he may have possessed, in an early Christian tradition of reading and interpreting the OT. Standing within this tradition and at the same time transforming it, he and his community have interpreted their religious heritage, the Scriptures, in the service of their faith in Jesus as the Christ, the Son of God."[44]

Two points are noteworthy about this literary reception process: that the Old Testament itself displays a dynamic of re-reception within and between its own books, and that early Christian hermeneutics regarding the Jewish Scriptures was similar to hermeneutical practices within other Jewish communities in the first century. Firstly, the dynamic of reception of the tradition going on within the New Testament is a continuation of a process going on within the Old Testament itself.[45] The books of the Old Testament are themselves the products of a traditioning process in which previous oral and written traditions have been (re-)interpreted in the light of new situations, incorporated into new textual contexts, and oftentimes refashioned. Traditions are the products of a constant process of reception.[46] The Pontifical Biblical Commission notes this phenomenon of "re-reading" which is to be found at work in the Bible; already in the Old Testament we see that tradition and reception are both elements of the traditioning process.[47]

---

44. Maarten F. F. Menken, *Old Testament Quotations in the Fourth Gospel: Studies in Textual Form* (Kampen: Kok Pharos Publishing House, 1996), 212.

45. As Müller asserts: "The reception of the Old Testament into the New Testament books did not start from scratch. As the Christian congregation grew out of Judaism, the collection of holy books . . . was already an 'interpreted Bible'. The New Testament authors not only related to the text, but they were also tied to an exegetical tradition which meant constantly having to adapt the biblical text to new situations and preconditions. To both Jewish and Christian interpreters it was unquestionably God who spoke through the Holy Writ. This meant that there were never any conflicts or dissociations; it was only a question of reinterpretation." Müller, "The New Testament Reception of the Old Testament," 5.

46. Martin Hengel notes: "Tradition is human work, and human tradition is always also shaped by those who hand it on and interpret it." Martin Hengel, *The Four Gospels and the One Gospel of Jesus Christ: An Investigation of the Collection and Origin of the Canonical Gospels* (Harrisburg, Pa.: Trinity Press International, 2000), 115.

47. "The texts of the Bible are the expression of religious traditions which existed before them. The mode of their connection with those traditions is different in each case, with the creativity of the authors shown in various degrees. In the course of time, multiple traditions have flowed together little by little to form one great common tradition. . . . One thing that gives the Bible an inner unity, unique of its kind, is the fact that later biblical writings often depend upon earlier ones. These more recent writings allude to older ones [and] create 're-readings' *(relectures)*, which

The second point worth noting is that the hermeneutical practices of early Christians, as evidenced in the New Testament, were not unique at the time. Within contemporary Judaism, creative reception of the tradition was considered an important element in the traditioning process. The discovery of the Dead Sea Scrolls has provided new insight into the exegetical practices of a Jewish community around the time of the early Christian communities.[48] Both groups saw themselves living in the time of fulfillment of the promises of old, and themselves as heirs to those promises. Furthermore, many of the exegetical practices of the Qumran communities and those evidenced in the New Testament employ similar techniques in quoting and alluding to Jewish Scripture: "typology, allegory, catch-word links, quoting from variant texts, altering the quoted text, reading the text in an unorthodox manner, drawing on *haggada* legends, and using homiletic forms of argumentation."[49] An examination of the books of the New Testament shows re-reading of the Old Testament in two ways in particular: quotations and allusions.[50] Referring to the (yet-to-be-fixed) Septuagint Greek translation of the Torah, Prophets, and Writings, most works of the New Testament either quote directly from Old Testament passages or allude to specific texts or themes. Scholars hypothesize that there may have existed *testimonia,* collections of such passages, which became commonly used across the early Christian communities in their christological exegesis.[51]

Steve Moyise proposes that the use of the Old Testament in the New is best understood in terms of "intertextuality": texts refer to texts referring to

---

develop new aspects of meaning, sometimes quite different from the original sense. A text may also make explicit reference to older passages, whether it is to deepen their meaning or to make known their fulfilment." Pontifical Biblical Commission, *The Interpretation of the Bible in the Church* (Rome: Libreria Editrice Vaticana, 1993), 86–87 (sections III A, III A1).

48. Mogens Müller states that, among biblical scholars today, there is "a willingness to understand the group of people behind the Dead Sea Scrolls as a devout society whose self-understanding and use of Scripture to a great extent had formal parallels to the Christian society." Müller, "The New Testament Reception of the Old Testament," 1. See also the dynamic of re-reception noted throughout Eugene Charles Ulrich, *The Dead Sea Scrolls and the Origins of the Bible* (Grand Rapids, Mich.: W. B. Eerdmans, 1999).

49. Moyise, *The Old Testament in the New,* 128.

50. On clarification of terminology regarding this issue, see Stanley E. Porter, "The Use of the Old Testament in the New Testament: A Brief Comment on Method and Terminology," in *Early Christian Interpretation of the Scriptures of Israel: Investigations and Proposals,* ed. Craig A. Evans and James A. Sanders (Sheffield, England: Sheffield Academic Press, 1997), 79–96.

51. See Donald Juel, *Messianic Exegesis: Christological Interpretation of the Old Testament in Early Christianity* (Philadelphia: Fortress Press, 1988).

texts in a web of ongoing allusion.[52] Paul Ricoeur also sees the "productive imagination" at work in the biblical texts in terms of "intertextuality."[53] In Ricoeur's use of the term, texts *qua* texts reveal new meaning because of the text's surplus of meaning and the reader's imaginative reception of the text. The productive imagination within the text requires engagement by the productive imagination of the receiver.[54] At work on three levels of a literary work (in the author, in the text, and in the reader), this productive imagination constitutes the activity of what we have called the organon of *sensus fidei* as an imaginative capacity for interpretation. Appropriating Ricoeur's term "the productive imagination," we could say that the organon of the *sensus fidei* is the Christian productive imagination at work in the reception of the Jewish Scriptures. Understanding this dynamic at work historically and textually across the two Testaments has implications for understanding the formation of the canon and for how one understands the inspiration of Scripture, as we shall see in the next two chapters. It is the productive imagination of the *sensus fidei* which weaves threads of continuity and newness between the Old and the New.

This pervasive New Testament reality of re-reading the Old Testament in the interpretation of the Christ event is the reality of the *sensus fidei* at work in individuals like Paul and the evangelists (and all the bearers of the Jesus tradition before them). Furthermore, as individual faith-interpretations, their distinctive visions can be regarded as different "senses of the faith." Whether those senses of the faith will receive wider approbation by the *sensus fidelium* in an emerging *consensus fidelium* is an issue that we will examine in the next chapter. Presuming that they will be received as such, we could say that the reception of the Christ event

---

52. See Steve Moyise, "Intertextuality and the Study of the Old Testament in the New Testament," in *The Old Testament in the New Testament: Essays in Honour of J. L. North,* ed. Steve Moyise (Sheffield, England: Sheffield Academic Press, 2000), 14–41. See also R. W. Wall, "Biblical Intertextuality," in *Dictionary of New Testament Background,* ed. Craig A. Evans and Stanley E. Porter (Downers Grove, Ill.: InterVarsity Press, 2000), 541–51. For an introduction to the notion of intertextuality, see Graham Allen, *Intertextuality* (New York: Routledge, 2000).

53. For example, see Paul Ricoeur, "The Bible and the Imagination," in *Figuring the Sacred: Religion, Narrative, and Imagination* (Minneapolis: Fortress Press, 1995), 144–66, where he proposes "to seek *in* reading itself the key to the heuristic functioning of the productive imagination." Ibid., 145. He defines intertextuality as "the work of meaning through which one text in referring to another text both displaces this other text and receives from it an extension of meaning." Ibid., 148.

54. See ibid., 161: "The text interprets before having been interpreted. This is how it is itself a work of productive imagination before giving rise to an interpretive dynamism in the reader that is analogous to its own."

involves, therefore, an interrelated triad of (1) *sensus fidelium,* (2) tradition, and (3) Jewish Scripture. Later in the history of the early church, after some fixity in the formation of the Christian canon, this same interrelated triad will describe the major elements in the ongoing dynamic of the Christian reception/tradition process: *sensus fidelium,* tradition, and Christian Scripture (the New Testament placed alongside the Old Testament in a single work).

GOSPEL RECEPTIONS OF JESUS THE CHRIST

The Gospels, as well as being literary receptions of the Old Testament, are also, at the same time, receptions of the pre-Easter Jesus tradition, in the light of the cross and resurrection, with the post-Easter enlightenment of the Holy Spirit, *from* the perspective of a new communal context, *for* a new audience, for the sake of an effective traditioning of "the Gospel."[55] As receptions of Jesus Christ, the Gospels are narratives which "draw the lines of continuity between the earthly Jesus and the heavenly Christ, between the disciples of the earthly Jesus and the post-Easter Christian communities."[56] As products of the capacity of *sensus fidei* to make sense of the faith, the four Gospels are four distinct "senses of the faith," four distinct expressions of the meaning of Jesus Christ. "All we have in the NT Gospels is Jesus seen with the eyes of faith."[57] They are interpretations or "renditions" of who Jesus Christ is;[58] they are *sensus Christi* (senses of Christ), new ways in which individuals and communities have made sense of Jesus Christ. They link the story of Jesus with the story of God's dealing with humanity since creation.[59]

Biblical scholarship has long noted that the Gospels are post-Easter faith-interpretations which address the internal needs of church life and the external demands of the church's mission to preach the Gospel beyond

55. On early Christian usage of the term "Gospel," see Graham Stanton, "Jesus and Gospel," in *Jesus and Gospel* (New York: Cambridge University Press, 2004), 9–62.

56. Schüssler Fiorenza, *Foundational Theology,* 133. For a survey of possible genres for understanding the four canonical Gospels, see Alexander Loveday, "What is a Gospel?" in *The Cambridge Companion to the Gospels,* ed. Stephen C. Barton (New York: Cambridge University Press, 2006), 13–33.

57. Dunn, *Jesus Remembered,* 127.

58. On the Gospels as "renditions" of Jesus Christ, see Larry W. Hurtado, *Lord Jesus Christ: Devotion to Jesus in Earliest Christianity* (Grand Rapids, Mich.: W. B. Eerdmans, 2003), 262.

59. On the primarily *theological* intentions of the Gospels, see the collection of articles in Das and Matera, *The Forgotten God.*

the community. The approaches of form criticism and redaction criticism have highlighted this interpretative dynamic at work in the formation of the Gospels. Form criticism (with its narrow *literary* paradigm of tradition) sought to show how the post-Easter faith perspective and the liturgical and missionary needs of the communities impacted on the traditioning process; that process always involved selection and reapplication of the tradition. Redaction criticism brought to the fore the creative role of the redactors in the selection and reconfiguring of received traditions in a Gospel's final form, as well as highlighting the resulting distinctive theological perspective of each final redactor. Building on those enduring insights, narrative-critical approaches to Gospel interpretation focus on their nature as literary works, the work of creative theologians whose medium is story.[60] They may perhaps be the fixing in writing of one oral performance of the Gospel, and perhaps even intended to be further performed orally in what was still then a predominantly oral culture. As either oral or written works, the Gospels were addressed to hearers/readers whose active role in making meaning of the work would have been anticipated by the teller.[61]

The evangelists aim to retell the story of Jesus. This retelling aspect is important. The four Gospels are receptions, renditions, reinterpretations of Jesus from the perspective of a particular community context, intended for a particular audience. They set out to trace lines of continuity between the life of Jesus and his significance in the situation of the hearers or readers of the Gospel. Graham Stanton notes that the evangelists are concerned with both "story" and "significance."

Matthew, Mark, Luke, and John have written very different gospels. But all four evangelists are concerned to set out both the story of Jesus of Nazareth and also what they took to be the significance of his actions and teaching. Story and significance are intertwined. . . . The evangelists do intend to tell us the "story" of Jesus, but they are also addressing the needs and circumstances of their own Christian congregations. They do not do this directly, as Paul does, but they reinterpret the earlier traditions on which they have drawn in order to make them relevant for their readers.[62]

60. On the focus on the evangelist as creative theologian in redaction and narrative-critical approaches, see Moloney, *Mark: Storyteller, Interpreter, Evangelist,* 19–43.

61. For example, on hearing Mark as an oral performance, see Richard A. Horsley, *Hearing the Whole Story: The Politics of Plot in Mark's Gospel* (Louisville, Ky.: Westminster John Knox Press, 2001).

62. Graham Stanton, *The Gospels and Jesus,* 2nd ed. (New York: Oxford University Press, 2002), 5–6.

We have proposed that the early Christian community's Pentecost experience included an awareness of being endowed by the Holy Spirit with a gift for now, post-Easter, understanding Jesus aright. We have proposed that this gift, here named as the organon of *sensus fidei,* best explains the dramatic shift from the disciples' pre-Easter misunderstanding of Jesus to a post-Easter enlightened insight, in the light of the cross and resurrection, into the meaning of his teaching and ministry, and of his true salvific significance and identity as the bearer of God's salvation. Presupposing such an organon now enables us to name a further dynamic at work in the New Testament writings, as the church expands into new contexts and cultures. With a newfound confidence or "boldness" *(parrhesia),*[63] the capacity of *sensus fidei* enables them to proclaim the Gospel anew by bridging "story" and "significance" in the church's missionary outreach. This boldness is evident in the creative theological retellings of the four evangelists.

The organon of *sensus fidei* enables each evangelist to mediate the Jesus story and the salvific significance and identity of Jesus for a new context. "The Gospels are narratives about Jesus and stories of Christian identity. They do not just relate the story of Jesus, they also spell out the beginning of the Christian story of discipleship."[64] The identity of Jesus and the identities demanded of Christians in new and diverse contexts mutually interpret one another; the former is narrated in terms of the latter, and the latter are understood in terms of the former.[65] The evangelists retell the story of Jesus, bringing to the fore those elements of the received tradition which have been relevant to the evangelists' communities, or those elements which the evangelists now want to highlight in a new way, elements from the received tradition which their local community may have downplayed or forgotten. At the same time, and as a consequence, they move to the background, or do not even recall at all, elements that, within their new reception, are not deemed necessary for recall and application at this time. In other words, the Gospels are *selections* from the Jesus tradition and retellings of those selections. In this

---

63. Stanley B. Marrow, *Speaking the Word Fearlessly: Boldness in the New Testament* (New York: Paulist Press, 1982).

64. Schüssler Fiorenza, *Foundational Theology,* 133.

65. On the plurality of Christian identities, see Anne Fortin-Melkevik, "The Identity of the Christian Following Jesus Christ," in *Concilium. Who Do you Say That I Am?* ed. Werner Jeanrond and Christoph Theobald (London: SCM Press, 1997), 91–101.

way they bridge story and significance; in this way, they weave a new *sensus fidei*. What Francis Moloney writes of the Fourth Gospel could well be said of the task facing the writers of the other three:

> The Fourth Gospel records the Jesus-story of a community in transition. No longer able to live their new faith in Jesus as the Christ, the Son of God within the world in which Christianity came to birth, the Johannine Christians took their story of Jesus into a new world. . . . [They crossed] the bridge from one world into another. . . . New worlds are forever challenging the believer to tell and live the old story in a new way, and the Fourth Gospel did this paradigmatically in the early Church.[66]

While the four canonical Gospels can be described as the individual *sensus fidei* of each evangelist, they are also related to the (communal) *sensus fidelium* in two ways: they emerge out of a communal tradition process, and they are "proposed" to that ongoing tradition for approbation as faithful rejuvenations of that tradition. The Gospels are paradigmatic cases of a creative relationship between the organon of the *sensus fidei fidelis* and the organon of the *sensus fidei fidelium,* and between the individual's and community's sense of the faith. Firstly, the Gospels emerge out of a communal traditioning process. They are each the product of the capacity of *sensus fidei* at work in the whole communal transmission process leading up to the final form of each Gospel. The distinctiveness of the evangelist's interpretation cannot be fully divorced from this distinctive received tradition. While we may rightly speak of the particular *sensus fidei* of a particular evangelist, it must be remembered that his is a faith which has been conditioned by a particular *sensus fidelium* of his communal tradition. As receptions, each of the Gospels therefore cannot be separated from the prior interpretative work of a community.

The second way in which the four canonical Gospels are related to the (communal) *sensus fidelium* is that they are proposed, either explicitly or implicitly, to their community for approbative reception. It has been suggested that some of the evangelists are explicitly intending their Gospel as "scripture" for their particular community, i.e., that their story of Jesus is to be received as the continuation and completion of the story of God narrated in Jewish Scripture.[67] However, if that is the case, the question arises: will such a Gospel be *received* as scripture by the communi-

66. Francis J. Moloney, *The Gospel of John, Sacra Pagina Series; v. 4* (Collegeville, Minn.: Liturgical Press, 1998), 22.

67. See D. Moody Smith, "When Did the Gospels Become Scripture?" *Journal of Biblical*

ty? Certainly, very early on, the four canonical Gospels did come to be viewed as authoritative works, and therefore as "scripture" for some communities, and as sacred in some way.[68] If a Gospel eventually comes to be received by the author's own community circle as faithful to the communal tradition, the evangelist's particular expression of the faith (their *sensus fidei fidelis*) is then received *into the common tradition* as an expression of the faith approved by the *sensus fidelium,* albeit local.

In the next chapter we will see how, no matter how narrow the initial intended audience of each of the four canonical Gospels, they were, in fact, later received by an expanding circle of communities, in a widening circle of inter-ecclesial reception and approbation by the *sensus fidelium.* But the question has also been recently raised by some scholars: perhaps the evangelists, from the start, indeed sought such reception beyond their own community for their particular *sensus fidei?* Richard Bauckham, for example, has proposed a revision of the thesis that the intended audience of the four Gospels is exclusively the final redactors' own communities.[69] The evangelists' interpretation of Jesus may indeed reflect the received tradition of their own particular community and the evangelists' creative reinterpretation of that tradition in order to more provocatively and meaningfully tell the Jesus story to their community and its situation. However, according to Bauckham, the evangelists may well have been intending their retelling of the Jesus story *for any community* to which it may find a receptive audience along the "holy internet" that was the communication system of the Roman world, used so effectively by the early Christians.[70] Bauckham's thesis, if it gains wide acceptance,[71] may yet provide a further example of the ecclesial reception

---

Literature 119 (2000): 3–20. On the fourth Gospel, see also Francis J. Moloney, "The Gospel of John as Scripture," in *The Gospel of John: Text and Context* (Boston: Brill, 2005), 333–47, at 347: "[T]he author of the Gospel of John thought that he was writing sacred Scripture."

68. We will examine in the next chapter how, even though inspiration is attributed to a wide range of writings at the time, belief that the final canonical texts are "inspired" in a different and special way is a stage of retrospective attribution that comes *after* recognition of canonical status, and is not a criterion for initial inclusion in the canon.

69. See Richard Bauckham, "For Whom Were the Gospels Written?" in *The Gospels for All Christians: Rethinking the Gospel Audience,* ed. Richard Bauckham (Edinburgh: T&T Clark, 1998), 9–48.

70. See Michael B. Thompson, "The Holy Internet: Communication between Churches in the First Christian Generation," ibid., 49–70.

71. Bauckham's thesis could not yet be considered a consensus position among the majority of biblical scholars.

between an individual's *sensus fidei fidelis* and the wider communities of the Christian world.[72]

Nonetheless, whether a final redactor is intending his Gospel as a re-telling of the Jesus story for his own community and its received tradition, or for wider circulation beyond the community, or for both, does not alter the nature of his Gospel as a particular *sensus fidei* from a particular perspective, within the context of the communal tradition that has fashioned the evangelist's own faith, for the sake of creatively receiving, applying, and rejuvenating that tradition. Whether intending his Gospel for the local or the wider community of all Christians, an evangelist, in composing his Gospel, is, in effect, offering his particular *sensus fidei* to the *sensus fidelium* for approbative reception. Certain Gospels in the early church are in fact dispersed and positively received by other communities beyond their place of origin. Whether a particular Gospel is ultimately received by the *sensus fidelium* (local or beyond) is a question related to the issues of communal authority and criteria of approbation, and the issue of canonicity (local and beyond). It is to that story of canonical reception we now turn.

---

72. For one author who accepts Bauckham's proposal, see Dunn, *Jesus Remembered,* 251–52. Francis Moloney believes that Bauckham has conflated a second hermeneutical moment ("for any community") into the earlier hermeneutical moment of its production ("for a particular community"). (Personal correspondence with Francis Moloney.) For a similar response to Bauckham's thesis, but claiming that a Gospel could do both, see Donahue and Harrington, *The Gospel of Mark,* 46: "Still a gospel could both reflect the setting of its final composition and be used in a wider context."

CHAPTER 5

Authority and the Canon of Scripture

In addressing, in the previous chapter, the oral and literary formation of the Jesus tradition, the issue of communal authority was raised in terms of "approbative reception." We now continue our exploration of authority by examining in greater detail the issue of approbative reception within the lives of the communities of the New Testament writings. We will then go on to see how this same concern for approbative reception gives rise to the selection and delimitation of certain writings, and not others, as constituting an accepted norm for the Christian faith. Significantly, we will see that the final canon of New Testament writings is not primarily the result of a formal decision-making process by authority figures in the churches, but is the result of a much more inclusive and somewhat diffuse communal process, even though such authority figures play a significant role.

SAFEGUARDING THE TREASURE

In one of the later writings of the New Testament, the Paul of the Pastoral Letters writes to Timothy: "Guard the good treasure entrusted to you, *with the help of the Holy Spirit living in us.*"[1] The matter of teaching

---

1. 2 Tm 1:14.

authority in the early church, its exercise and criteria, is a complex scholarly issue.[2] However, one thing is clear: concern for fidelity to what the church had been given, the Gospel, is a pervasive concern throughout the New Testament. In this section, I do not wish to examine in detail the development of teaching authority in the early church. Rather, I want to highlight that, while the emergence of authority figures and "institutional structures" does not replace the abiding sense that the whole community is authorized as the bearer of revelation, conflicting interpretation of revelation, nevertheless, becomes problematic in the first generations of Christianity. The early church's response to that problem through a communal exercise of authority includes the specific role of certain authority figures. The implicit notion of "apostolic tradition" crystallizes the early church's concern for a norm for testing further traditioning of the Gospel.

Our enquiry begins with an examination of the words "apostolic" and "apostle." The word "apostolic" first of all refers to a foundational time in the church. At this stage it will be helpful to clarify terminology regarding the timeline we will be discussing. Regarding the foundational period of the early church, there are varying designations. I will follow the schematization of Raymond Brown. Presupposing, from the New Testament evidence, that the apostles who witnessed the pre-Easter Jesus had died by around the year A.D. 67 and that, apart from the seven authentic Pauline letters, "most of the [New Testament] was written after the death of the last known apostle,"[3] "the term 'Apostolic Age' should be confined to that second one-third of the first century, and that the last one-third of the century should be designated as the 'Sub-Apostolic Period.'"[4] In this latter period, attributing authorship to the historical apostles was intended as "a claim to apostolic adherence,"[5] and so the period warrants designation at least as "sub-apostolic." Brown includes in the "Post-Apostolic Period" writings of the next century, such as 1 Clement and the letters of Ignatius of Antioch; "this written work of a 'third generation' was moving away from claiming the direct mantle of the apostles."[6]

---

2. For an overview, see Joseph A. Fitzmyer, "The Office of Teaching in the Christian Church according to the New Testament," in *Teaching Authority and Infallibility in the Church: Lutherans and Catholics in Dialogue VI,* ed. Paul C. Empie et al. (Minneapolis: Augsburg Publishing House, 1980), 186–212.

3. Raymond E. Brown, *The Churches the Apostles Left Behind* (New York: Paulist Press, 1984), 14.

4. Ibid., 15.

5. Ibid., 16.

6. Ibid. As a caveat to his terminology, Brown notes: "The language of 'three generations'

Two points need affirming before any discussion of the issue of apostolic authority within the early church. Firstly, although there is a deep concern for oversight of the passing on of the Gospel, there is no sense in the New Testament that special knowledge has been given to one particular group in the church (such as the original apostles) which had not been revealed to all believers beyond that group. Even within the churches of the Pastoral Letters, where oversight of the truth of teaching is being formalized, the whole church is considered to be "the household of God . . . the church of the living God, the pillar and bulwark of the truth."[7] The centrality of this belief needs no other proof than the early church's rejection of the second-century Gnostics' claim to access some secret apostolic tradition beyond that which had been revealed to the whole community. Concerns to reject such Gnostic interpretations of the Gospel will play a part in the formation of a canon of Scripture and in the emergence of the episcopate, both as norms of the faith.

Secondly, as we have seen in the previous chapter, the Gospels retain the memory of the original historical apostles (who were to become significant authority figures after the resurrection), never fully understanding Jesus and indeed misunderstanding him during his pre-Easter ministry. The events which change them are the further events of Jesus' death and resurrection, and Pentecost. But these original apostles are not the only ones who experience the Risen Lord and these original apostles are not the only ones to receive the gift for understanding Jesus through the Holy Spirit. Revelation is given to all; the principle of its reception, the Holy Spirit, is given to all. The portrayal in the New Testament of authority figures within the community always presumes those beliefs.

Although the function of teaching in the time of the New Testament is not confined to the activity and role of those designated as "apostles," our discussion of apostolic authority must begin with an examination of

---

. . . is a convenient generalization, so long as it is not taken too literally. Nor are all writings covered by my distinction that second-generation NT works are written in the name of (or under the mantle of) apostles, while third-generation works often are not. II Peter belongs to the third or fourth generation and yet claims the mantle of Peter, and apocryphal works of the second and third centuries bear apostolic names." Ibid., 16n10.

7. 1 Tm 3:15. According to Wolfgang Beinert, within the New Testament, "the handing on of this doctrine [concerning Christ] is entrusted fundamentally to the whole community (Matt 18:15–20; Jn 14:16f; 15:26; 16:13; 1 Tm 3:15); within the community, however, it is a special task of the apostles (Matt 5:13; Mk 3:14; 16:15; Lk 10:16; 24:47f; Acts 1:8; 10:41)." Wolfgang Beinert, "Ecclesial Magisterium," in *Handbook of Catholic Theology*, ed. Wolfgang Beinert and Francis Schüssler Fiorenza (New York: Crossroad, 1995), 194–99, at 194.

the apostles' identity and their authoritative function. The term "apostle" is used throughout the New Testament in at least two different senses, the first in reference to authority figures in the apostolic age (the second third of the first century) when the seven authentic letters of Paul are being written, and secondly, to authority figures in the last third of that century, when most of the rest of the New Testament is being composed.[8]

Firstly, historically located within the apostolic age, there is a group in the early church who have an authoritative position because they have seen the Risen Lord and therefore are witnesses to the resurrection. Walter Kasper calls this group "the first apostles."[9] These fit into the period Brown calls "the apostolic age," ending with "the death of the last apostle." Within this group, there are two subgroups, those whom I will designate as the original Twelve historical apostles, and those like Paul who, although not apostles before the resurrection, came to be honored as authoritative witnesses to the resurrection.

The original Twelve chosen by Jesus come to be regarded early on as the apostles par excellence. Within the ministry of Jesus the Twelve have a particular symbolic function related to Jesus' vision of the restoration of Israel to its covenant commitment and the regathering of the twelve tribes of Israel.[10] After the resurrection, the Twelve seem not to have operated as missionary apostles outside of Jerusalem, and there is little evidence of their having functioned as leaders of particular local churches.[11] Only Peter among the Twelve seems to have played a significant individual role.

The role of the Twelve as a group in the early church is first of all symbolic. "The eschatological role of the twelve as judges of the twelve tribes of Israel in the new world [during the ministry of Jesus] was replaced

8. On the complex issues of "apostle" and "apostolicity," see Burkhard, *Apostolicity Then and Now*, 1–41.

9. Kasper, "The Apostolic Succession," 118.

10. John P. Meier, *A Marginal Jew: Rethinking the Historical Jesus*, vol. 3: *Companions and Competitors* (New York: Doubleday, 2001), 125–97. Meier sees the Twelve functioning as exemplars of discipleship, as prophetic symbols of the regathering of the twelve tribes of Israel, and as prophetic missionaries to Israel.

11. After asserting that the Twelve disciples of Jesus "were considered apostles of the Church from the beginning," Raymond Brown goes on to note: "However if we accept the historicity of the Twelve as apostles, the thesis that there were *only* Twelve is certainly a later simplification. There were many apostles in the early days, but the Twelve had a special place in the apostolate, not so much because of their missionary activities (. . . there is no evidence that most of them left the Jerusalem area) but because they had been the intimate companions of Jesus." Raymond E. Brown, *Priest and Bishop: Biblical Reflections* (London: G. Chapman, 1971), 49.

by the foundational role of the apostles in the household of God, the church."[12] Although Luke, in the later sub-apostolic period, will present the dominant narrative of the Twelve as the apostles par excellence, the other synoptic Gospels convey the same sense of the special nature of their apostolate. Only Matthew 10:2 speaks of "the Twelve apostles."[13]

Their role is also that of witness, in a twofold sense. They are witnesses to Jesus' teachings, actions, behaviors during his proclamation of the reign of God. They constitute a link with the pre-Easter Jesus and can therefore acts as judges of continuity for the post-Easter *kerygma* (proclamation of the Gospel). In this sense, the Twelve's role as apostles is unique, and one which could not be passed on to others. The second sense in which they are paradigmatic apostolic witnesses is because of their encounter with the Risen Lord.[14] Raymond Brown calls this Easter vision "an essential constituent of the apostolate."[15] Although many others experienced the Risen Lord,[16] some of whom Paul calls apostles, the Twelve are unique precisely because their witness is *twofold:* not only as a witness to the resurrection, but as a witness that the Jesus whose teachings, healings, and behavior they had witnessed pre-Easter was indeed the one who is risen. They function as the link of continuity with the pre-Easter Jesus and affirm of the Risen One: "It is the Lord!"[17]

Prominent among the second subgroup of "the first apostles," those who have seen the Lord, is Paul. His sense of having the authority of an apostle is grounded in his encounter with the Risen Lord. "For Paul, to be an apostle means to have seen the risen Lord, to have been commissioned and sent by him to found churches and to have demonstrated the genuineness of this commissioning through hard labors."[18] Paul, however, although he has encountered the Risen Lord and has been commissioned by the Lord to preach and found churches and, despite his claims of independent authority as an apostle, implicitly seems to acknowledge that he does not fulfill the requirement of being among the intimate group of Jesus' inner circle pre-Easter and of having experienced his teaching and actions firsthand. He believes it important to demon-

---

12. Schuyler Brown, "Apostleship in the New Testament as an Historical and Theological Problem," *New Testament Studies* 30 (1984): 474–80, at 474–75.

13. The only other reference to "the twelve apostles" is Rv 21:14.

14. 1 Cor 15:5.   15. Brown, *Priest and Bishop,* 49.

16. 1 Cor 15:6–7.   17. Jn 21:7.

18. Byrne, *Romans,* 42.

strate continuity with the traditions he has received. He cannot therefore fulfill the function of witnessing to the identity of the Risen One with the pre-Easter Jesus. Thus, Paul is keen to show (albeit reluctantly in Galatians) the importance of his contact and indeed deference to those who had been with Jesus before the resurrection.[19]

Paul, however, in the later sub-apostolic and post-apostolic periods, comes to be regarded as the paradigmatic apostle.[20] Since seven of the letters of Paul come from this apostolic period, we have evidence of how, within the communities which Paul has founded, Paul has co-workers and that he appoints people in positions of leadership in the communities.[21] In particular, there are individuals who are considered to have particular charisms given by the Holy Spirit. The notion of charisms seems to be of Pauline origin and is found in the New Testament almost exclusively in Paul, with only one use of the term outside the Pauline writings.[22] In 1 Corinthians 12:28 we find a list indicative of such people and charisms: "And God has appointed in the church first apostles, second prophets, third teachers; then deeds of power, then gifts of healing, forms of assistance, forms of leadership, various kinds of tongues." Moreover, in Romans 12:6–8, we read: "We have gifts *(charismata)* that differ according to the grace given to us: prophecy, in proportion to faith; ministry, in ministering; the teacher, in teaching; the exhorter, in exhortation; the giver, in generosity; the leader, in diligence; the compassionate, in cheerfulness."[23]

Of particular importance for our study is the role in the community

19. On the independent and dependent claims of Paul over against the Jerusalem apostles, as indicated in Galatians, see James D. G. Dunn, *The Theology of Paul the Apostle* (Grand Rapids, Mich.: W. B. Eerdmans, 1998), 572–73. Kasper, however, asserts that the distinction should not be overplayed, precisely because of Paul's concern to be in contact with them. "The distinction between the apostolic circle in Jerusalem and Paul was not so important here as is often suggested, for Paul himself often links his own apostolate to the Jerusalem apostles (1 Cor 15:8–11; Gal 1:17), and he attaches great importance to his fellowship with them (Acts 15; Gal 2)." Kasper, "The Apostolic Succession," 118.

20. Raymond Brown, while noting that the Twelve are the ones "sent forth" both during Jesus' ministry and after the resurrection ("the definitive sending forth that constituted apostolate"), remarks: "However, the NT is generally silent about the apostolate of the Twelve, and consequently the paradigm for the apostle is a figure who was not a disciple of Jesus during the ministry, namely, Paul, who is often simply called 'The Apostle.'" Brown, *Priest and Bishop*, 27.

21. See Bengt Holmberg, *Paul and Power: The Structure of Authority in the Primitive Church as Reflected in the Pauline Epistles* (Philadelphia: Fortress Press, 1978).

22. See Dunn, *The Theology of Paul the Apostle*, 553.

23. Cf. the later list of Eph 4:11, which states: "The gifts he gave were that some would be apostles [*apostolous*], some prophets [*prophetas*], some evangelists [*euggelistas*], some pastors [*poimenas*] and teachers [*didaskalous*]."

of the *didaskaloi,* the teachers.[24] In Paul's own mind, although he does not emphasize it, the notion of "apostle" overlaps with that of "teacher."[25] Paul speaks in several places of himself as a "teacher" and his ministry of "teaching."[26] In the Lukan Acts from the later sub-apostolic period, Paul is also depicted as a teacher;[27] in the Pastorals, he is the definitive teacher.[28] The function of the "teacher" in the Pauline communities is summarized by James Dunn as having a twofold function: to pass on the tradition of the *kerygma* (proclamation), and to interpret and develop the tradition.[29] "These [teachers] we may presume were responsible for retaining, passing on, and interpreting the congregation's foundation traditions, including interpretation of the prophetic scriptures and the Jesus tradition."[30] Therefore, the teacher seems to have played a particular role in terms of continuity with the received tradition, and the interpretation of the tradition's meaning for application in the present. "[A]n element of interpretation would inevitably be involved in much or most of the teaching, and the line between teaching (old tradition interpreted) and prophecy (new? revelation) would often be thin."[31] Nevertheless, two points need to be remembered when reconstructing the function of teaching authority in the Pauline communities. Firstly, as Francis Sullivan notes, "the few references in the New Testament to such *didaskaloi* tell us hardly anything about what or how they taught."[32] Secondly, although Paul speaks of those with the particular charism for teaching, teaching is still seen to be a responsibility of the whole community.[33]

24. It is the thesis of Hans Küng that these *didaskaloi* were the only teachers in the early church, and that their charism was usurped by the later-evolving monarchical bishops. See Hans Küng, *Infallible? An Inquiry* (Garden City, N.Y.: Doubleday, 1971). For a critique of Küng's thesis, see Sullivan, *Magisterium,* 35–51.

25. "Though Paul did not often describe himself as a teacher (perhaps because of his personal insistence and struggle to be recognized as an Apostle), he was aware of the function of teaching and of a special group of persons engaged in it. He recognized it as Spirit-guided. It is difficult to specify the content of it, and it would be wrong to identify it solely with the gospel, although it is clearly based on the gospel and stands under it. And he was aware that there was some sort of official or correct doctrine that was meeting with some opposition." Fitzmyer, "The Office of Teaching," 194. See also Sullivan, *Magisterium,* 46–47.

26. 1 Cor 4:17; Rom 6:17 and 16:17; 2 Thes 2:15; and the later Pauline Col 1:28.

27. Acts 11:26; 15:35; 18:11; 20:20; 21:21; 28:31.

28. 1 Tm 2:5–7; 2 Tm 1:1; 3:10.

29. See Dunn, *Jesus and the Spirit,* 282–84; Dunn, *The Theology of Paul the Apostle,* 582–83.

30. Dunn, *The Theology of Paul the Apostle,* 582.

31. Ibid., 583.

32. Sullivan, *Magisterium,* 46.

33. See 1 Cor 14:26: "When you come together, each one has a hymn, a lesson [*didache*], a

Conflict of interpretation becomes an issue with the group of first apostles themselves. Between the individual apostles, there is evidence of significant difference in interpretation of the Gospel. This Gospel is, for Paul, both a received tradition and one he experienced directly. However, his own sense of apostleship, and his own particular hermeneutical reception of the tradition he had received, leads to divergent interpretations over against the Jerusalem apostles, as depicted in Galatians. The classic case is the debate between the most prominent among the Twelve, Peter, and the most influential of the apostles not included in the Twelve, the apostle Paul. One could speak of a Petrine vision and a Pauline vision. In terms of the thesis of this book, one could speak of Peter's *sensus fidei* and the *sensus fidei* of Paul. Prescinding from the interpretative difficulties arising from the fact that the extant writings of that period are only those of Paul giving his interpretation of the state of affairs, Paul's letter to the Galatians can be seen to witness to a conflict of interpretation within the apostolic group. Paul certainly considers himself to be the receiver of a communal tradition. But his interpretation of the implication of the tradition is in conflict with that of Peter, the first among the Twelve. Therefore, within the *sensus fidelium* of the apostolic tradition itself, there is a diversity of *sensus fidei*. Eventually, the meeting of Paul and Peter brings consensus as to what is acceptable. The Lukan account, written from the perspective of the next generation in the sub-apostolic time, retains the memory of that conflict of interpretation and its resolution through the so-called council of Jerusalem.[34] Thus, within the apostolic age, one can speak of the dynamic between the exercisers of authority as a dynamic between the *sensus fidei* of individuals and the *sensus fidelium* of the group of apostles, at times leading to a *consensus fidelium*.[35]

Beyond the apostolic age, the dynamic of handing on functions continues. Just as Jesus shared his ministry with his chosen Twelve, so too the Twelve and the wider group called "apostles" in the next generation pass

revelation, a tongue, or an interpretation. Let all things be done for building up." This is also a tradition from a later Pauline church. See Col. 3:16: "Let the word of Christ dwell in you richly; *teach and admonish one another* in all wisdom; and with gratitude in your hearts sing psalms, hymns, and spiritual songs to God."

34. Acts 15.

35. In part 3 we will note that the *sensus fidei* of individual bishops is not insignificant in the exercise and perspective of their magisterium. Just as within the group of early apostles, one might also speak of a dynamic within the magisterium between the *sensus fidei* of the individual bishops (what I will be calling the *sensus episcoporum*) and the *sensus* of the group (what I will be calling the *sensus magisterii*).

on to others the functions they felt were necessary for the fulfillment of their mission. When we come to the sub-apostolic age, when all of those first apostles have died, we have witness to the emergence of roles in the community intended to carry on what Raymond Brown calls the "apostolic functions."[36] The major witnesses to such structures are the Pastoral Letters, Acts, and 1 Peter.[37] By the end of the sub-apostolic period, we find elders *(presbyteroi)* and overseers *(episcopoi)* who have assumed the leadership of Paul and his generation of co-workers.[38] Thus, by the end of the sub-apostolic period, there is experienced a greater need for oversight within the community in the movement toward a so-called "early catholicism."[39]

The work of David Dungan is helpful for understanding later developments in this process of handing on apostolic functions.[40] According to Dungan, Christianity emerged in a cultural environment shaped by the emerging democratic structures of the ancient Greek *polis* (city-state) in which the metaphor of *kanon* (standard, rule) captures the quest for accuracy, precision, and clarity among its philosophical schools. This philosophical milieu shapes both Second Temple Judaism and early Christianity, and is significant for understanding notions of authority in the early church. The influence of this milieu can be seen in the philosophical and theological presuppositions of writers such as Justin Martyr, Tertullian, Clement of Alexandria, and Origen. Dungan takes as paradigmatic of those early centuries the framework evident in a work by Diogenes Laertius (active around A.D. 230), *Lives and Opinions of Eminent Philosophers*. Dungan notes three recurring issues in Laertius's nar-

---

36. Brown, *Priest and Bishop*, 73.

37. On these developments see Francis A. Sullivan, *From Apostles to Bishops: The Development of the Episcopacy in the Early Church* (New York: Newman Press, 2001); Bernard J. Cooke, *Ministry to Word and Sacraments: History and Theology* (Philadelphia: Fortress Press, 1976).

38. "The common scholarly opinion [is] that, where they existed in the post-Pauline churches, presbyters and bishops were for all practical purposes the same, that as a group they were responsible for the pastoral care of those churches, and that we have in the Pastoral Epistles, I Peter, and Acts a picture of their activities in the 80's, if not earlier. From such NT works, it would seem that the presbyter-bishops took up where the Pauline apostles left off, being responsible for the continued care of churches founded by the apostles (whether the presbyter-bishops were appointed directly by the apostles or came on the scene only sometime later)." Brown, *Priest and Bishop*, 35.

39. For a recent treatment of the features of "early catholicism," see David J. Downs, "'Early Catholicism' and Apocalypticism in the Pastoral Epistles," *Catholic Biblical Quarterly* 67 (2005): 641–61.

40. For what follows, see David L. Dungan, *Constantine's Bible: Politics and the Making of the New Testament* (Minneapolis: Fortress Press, 2006), 11–53.

rative of the philosophical schools: (1) the importance of true succession of leadership going back to the school's founder, (2) the importance of having accurate copies of the school's writings, and (3) the importance of passing on the appropriate hermeneutic or tradition of interpretation of those writings.[41] All three issues are significant factors in the emergence of the Christian canon of Scripture. Connection with the apostolic tradition will be a dominant feature in that process.

Following the thesis of scholars such as Raymond Brown and Francis Sullivan, the next section on the scriptural canonization process will presuppose that by the end of the second century, a mono-episcopate model of oversight has become normative throughout the church. The *presbyteros/episcopos* leadership model of the Pastorals, Acts, and 1 Peter gives way to a threefold model of ministry: a single bishop in a local church with presbyters and deacons.[42] In the section that follows we will examine factors in the development of authority figures, just as we will examine factors in the emergence of a canon of authoritative writings, a process in which local bishops will play a certain role.

This brief survey has attempted to highlight the importance of "apostolic authority" in the early church, and the existence of and need for the continuation of apostolic functions throughout the apostolic and sub-apostolic periods. But the questions now arise: if the apostles are seen to be unique for the community, what is it that they provide to the community which is seen to be vital for its mission? Or, put another way, what is it that the later generation will be wanting to safeguard as they pass on the heritage of the apostles? What is the "apostolic tradition"?

In the Lukan vision, holding fast to the apostolic heritage included not just holding fast to "the teaching *(didache)* of the apostles" (Acts 2:42). What the apostles handed on was a whole way of life: "They devoted themselves to the apostles' teaching and fellowship, to the breaking of bread and the prayers. . . . All who believed were together and had all things in common; they would sell their possessions and goods and distribute the proceeds to all, as any had need."[43]

---

41. Dungan writes: "[L]aertius's history of the Greek philosophical schools reveals a basic three-fold structure: the over-all control mechanism was the school's *succession of heads,* who, generation after generation, handed on the scrupulously *correct texts of genuine writings* from the earliest days of the school, in order to remain true to the *correct interpretation,* i.e., the Truth as that school perceived it." Original italics. Ibid., 41.

42. See the summaries in Brown, *Priest and Bishop;* Sullivan, *From Apostles to Bishops.*

43. Acts 2:42, 44–45.

By the time of the Pastoral Letters, the author, a disciple of Paul, is referring to what the apostles had handed on as a *paratheke,* a treasure, a deposit. In his research on the notion, Jared Wicks highlights the importance of the meaning of this term in the Old Testament and the legal codes of Greece and Rome for understanding its significance in the early church.[44] The *paratheke* of the Pauline tradition was a precious treasure to be safeguarded and faithfully transmitted with great responsibility. The "deposit" included a broad range of teachings, practices, regulations on prayer, the example of an apostle's own life, the selection of ministers, avoiding certain false teachings, etc. Therefore, as Wicks emphasizes, this "deposit of faith," as the term came to be used in the post-apostolic period, was understood to comprise not just a static collection of teachings, although it includes narratives and affirmations of faith. Rather, the *paratheke,* as "the faith that was once for all entrusted to the saints,"[45] is a much richer, more comprehensive reality:

The "deposit" is the inclusive term for this faith and way of life bequeathed by the apostles and their coworkers to the churches founded by their proclamation of the good news about Jesus Christ. The apostles left as their legacy a coherent pattern of faith, teaching, and modes of biblical interpretation, of worship and community structures of service, and of life in the world according to the word and example of the Lord Jesus.[46]

It is this "coherent pattern" which is "the apostolic tradition." Within the lived memory of the early church, it includes the diverse *sensus fidei* of a Peter and a Paul. It is not just the teachings of Jesus as remembered by the apostles, but also the meaning of that teaching as they interpreted it after the resurrection in the light of Jewish Scriptures, and with a confident sense of being gifted in their understanding by the Holy Spirit. It includes not just stories about how Jesus acted in his lifetime and the patterns of his behavior, but the implications and applications of that action and behavior as they went about preaching and interpreting him.

44. "In antiquity, the legal codes of both Greece and Rome stipulated the obligations of persons receiving objects or sums of money deposited by another, e.g., when the latter was leaving on a journey. The depositary was above all bound to faithful safekeeping, which excluded any personal use of the deposit. . . . The Scriptures of Israel stipulate simple laws of deposit as part of the Mosaic ordinances of the covenant of Sinai (Exod 22:6–12). When a deposit is damaged or lost, the depositary must swear on oath that he has not misappropriated what was given for his safekeeping." Wicks, "Deposit of Faith," 229.

45. Jude 3.

46. Wicks, "Deposit of Faith," 229.

It includes not just memories of their following him around and being with him, but also the patterns of prayer and worship as they now related to him as the Risen Lord.

In other words, the apostolic tradition included, not just content, but also *a pattern of interpretation*—what could be called "the apostolic hermeneutic" or "the apostolic imagination": a paradigm for bridging story and significance in fidelity to the God of Israel, in fidelity to the life, death, and resurrection of Jesus Christ, and in fidelity to the new needs of the receiving audience. It is this "deposit," this condensation of the lived and applied reality of the Gospel, which was the norm that the early church constantly turned to in the sub-apostolic period, and the post-apostolic period. In the next section, we will see its importance for the Christian communities as they more and more honed the collection of writings which would be the primary (but not exclusive) mode of the transmission of that apostolic tradition.

The term "apostolic" is therefore *characteristic of this whole period.* Francis Sullivan, collapsing Raymond Brown's division into the one "apostolic" period, neatly summarizes the generic sense in which the term "apostolic" very quickly came to be used, and is generally understood today:

When we speak of the witness of the apostles in this context [of the church being "apostolic"] we do not restrict the meaning of this term to the original twelve disciples of Jesus. We certainly include St. Paul among the apostles, and he himself tells us that the risen Christ, after appearing to James, appeared to "all the apostles"—a term which hardly anyone nowadays takes as synonymous with "the Twelve" to whom he had already appeared (cf. 1 Cor 15:5–7). Indeed, when we speak of the "apostolic witness," we rightly include all the inspired writings of the New Testament, whether their authors were "apostles" in the strict sense or not. Or to put the matter in its broadest terms, "apostolic witness" is ultimately the witness of the apostolic Church, that is, the Christian Church of the period during which the New Testament was being written. This was the time of Christian revelation, and it is generally agreed that such revelation, which came to its definitive climax in Christ's resurrection and glorification as Lord at the right hand of the Father, was complete at the end of the apostolic period.[47]

The primary concern of the early church in this apostolic period is to link the community with Jesus Christ through the mediating witness of

<hr />

47. Sullivan, *Magisterium,* 10.

the community and its apostles. Two parallel beliefs assured them that such a link was guaranteed: that the whole community had been given the gift for understanding by the Holy Spirit, but also that authoritative oversight was needed in parallel to discern the diversity of interpretations among the whole community. What is not evident in the New Testament is that only the first apostles had been given the Holy Spirit; the Holy Spirit had been given to all. This is true also in the sub-apostolic period; the gift of the Holy Spirit was given not only to those called "apostles." However, these sub-apostolic apostles have special functions within the community: they are commissioned by Christ as "ambassadors for Christ"[48] (the Pauline view of the apostle); they take over the authoritative function of the first apostles and act as witnesses to the life and resurrection of Jesus Christ (the Lukan view of the apostle).

In this sub-apostolic period there is no evidence of the teaching authority acting apart from the whole community. As Walter Kirchschläger highlights, the emerging authority structure within New Testament communities is not seen to be in opposition to the whole community, understood to be the primary bearer of the tradition: "A pronounced opposition between the authority structure of the community and the rest of its members is nowhere to be found. Instead, a conscious effort is made to integrate them."[49] Furthermore, as Richard Gaillardetz points out with regard to Ignatius of Antioch's witness to authority in the post-apostolic period:

In both the ministry of Eucharistic presidency/pastoral leadership and the ministry of apostolic teaching, there was a consistent emphasis on both the authority of the bishop *and* the bishop's immersion in the Christian community. As Ignatius insisted in his letters, there can be no community without a bishop. But it is equally clear that neither could there be a bishop without a community that shared the apostolic faith.[50]

48. 2 Cor 5:20.

49. Kirchschläger, "Was das Neue Testament über den Glaubenssinn der Gläubigen sagt," 20. Quoted in Burkhard, "*Sensus Fidei:* Recent Theological Reflection (1990–2001). Part I," 467.

50. Gaillardetz, *Teaching with Authority,* 38–39. In the evidence of the second century, Gaillardetz notes: "As pastoral and liturgical leaders of their local Churches, the bishops were called to discern that which was and was not in conformity with the apostolic tradition in the life of their communities. They did this, however, as leaders of Churches that were themselves bearers of apostolicity. The bishop did not impart a secret knowledge with which his flock was unfamiliar. The bishop proclaimed the apostolic faith with authority, but in so doing he functioned as a custodian of the faith given to the whole church. In apostolic service to their communities, the bishops received, verified, validated, and proclaimed the truths of the faith that were prayed and lived in their communities." Ibid., 38.

In conclusion: in the sub-apostolic period, there emerges within the local communities the need for certain individuals who have the role of oversight in the community. Initially diverse roles which were fulfilled by different individuals in the community are funneled into the role of the single presbyter/*episcopos,* who becomes seen as the community leader and the primary preacher and teacher. By the end of the second century, in the post-apostolic period, a further refinement of specialization occurs as the threefold ministry of *episcopos* (bishop), presbyter (elder), and deacon (minister) emerges as normative across the communities of the early church.

It is also at this time, by the end of the second century, that there emerges, as we will see, a *de facto* consolidation of the core writings of what will become the New Testament canon. With the departure of original apostles from the scene in the first century, the need had become apparent for clearer specification of the assumed apostolic tradition. Later, groups such as the Montanists would claim direct access to new revelation, and eschew a communal authority and any recourse to a definitive past. "Apostolic writings . . . had to take the place of an apostolic presence, and so the written word became a matter of real importance."[51] Although the canon does not emerge over the following centuries as the result of "top-down" decisions of authority figures, these figures can be presumed to be playing a certain role in communal discernment regarding the canon, as the early church recognizes the need to preserve in some fixed form the deposit of faith mediated by the witnesses of the apostolic and sub-apostolic periods.

THE CANON AND RECEPTION

The whole canonization process of the bipartite Christian Bible can be modeled as an operation of the individual and communal organon of *sensus fidei* both generating and adjudicating between diverse and sometimes conflicting senses of the faith. The process can be depicted as operating

51. Bart D. Ehrman, *Lost Christianities: The Battle for Scripture and the Faiths We Never Knew* (New York: Oxford University Press, 2003), 231. "Given the nature of Christianity from the outset, as a religion that stressed proper belief and that required authorities on which to base that belief, literary texts very soon took on unusual importance for this religion. The apostles of Jesus, of course, were seen as authoritative sources of knowledge about what Jesus himself said and did. But apostles could not be present everywhere at once in the churches scattered throughout the empire." Ibid., 321.

throughout three overlapping phases. In the first phase, as we have seen, the works of the New Testament canon are each the result of the interpretative organon in individuals (as *sensus fidei*) and communities (as *sensus fidelium*) as they make sense of Jesus Christ and the salvation he effects through the Holy Spirit in new contexts. In the second phase, that same interpretative capacity is operating in the reception process in which the *sensus fidei* ("senses of the faith") of certain writers are appropriated by the *sensus fidelium* for liturgical, doctrinal, and catechetical use in various local communities. And in the third phase, that same capacity is operating in the emergence, across the churches of early Christianity, of a *consensus fidelium* regarding (1) a canon (standard) of faith, and (2) a canon (authoritative list) of writings that could constitute such a standard of faith.

In all three phases of the emergence of the New Testament, there is a permanent presence of the Jewish Scriptures, functioning as a criterion of faith alongside the Jesus tradition. It is only with Marcion that the presumption of the normativity of these Jewish writings is called into question. However, the bipartite character of the canonization process is evident from the very start of the Jesus tradition. In other words, the New Testament canon evolves alongside the (still emerging canon of) Jewish Scriptures. It is always presumed, Marcion aside, that the Jewish Scriptures are scripture for the Christian community; the Marcion crisis simply forces the explicit articulation of this belief. Therefore, in speaking of the emergence of the New Testament canon, it is always (in the Christian imagination) as part of a bipartite canon.

This canonization process, in all the three overlapping phases mentioned above, involves the operation of the organon of *sensus fidei/ fidelium* and its production of, and then approbation and appropriation of, various *sensus fidei*, senses of the faith. The previous chapter has already examined the operation of the *sensus fidei/fidelium* in the first phase of the canonization process, the production of the Gospels and the other writings of the New Testament. It now remains for us to highlight its operation during the overlapping second and third phases: the (at times implicit) approbation and continued use of particular *sensus fidei* (senses of the faith) within local communities; and, through inter-ecclesial reception, between communities of the wider church.

Before we proceed, some clarification regarding terminology is necessary. Firstly, clarification is required concerning the very word "scripture." The scriptures of the early Christians were the Jewish Scriptures.

However, there emerges a sense in which Christian writings soon began to be regarded in some way also as "scripture." As noted above, it is possible some of the evangelists were intending their works to be a continuation and completion of Jewish Scripture. However, if "scripture" refers to "texts that are revered as especially sacred and authoritative,"[52] a distinction needs to be made between a Christian work that is "written to be scripture" and a work that is "received as scripture." The *intention* of an author to write scripture does not necessarily constitute his work "as scripture." Scriptural status requires a further step, a community's *reception* of it, a communal approbation and appropriation of the work through which it comes to be revered and used "*as* scripture" by a community.[53] Then, that it *is* received and used liturgically, doctrinally, and catechetically as scripture by a local community *may* just be the beginning of its journey toward possible reception by other communities, which also may receive it and also revere it as sacred and authoritative, until it may eventually be used so universally that it is included in an official list of such writings for all communities.

Secondly, with regard to the relationship between the two terms "scripture" and "canon" in reference to Christian writings: if the former refers to "texts that are revered as especially sacred and authoritative" by a community of faith, the term "canon" refers to "the delimitation of such texts."[54] According to these definitions, local reception as "scripture" precedes any notion of a text belonging to a canon or list of such already-revered texts. "'Canon' presumes 'scripture.'"[55] Hence, as we shall see, throughout the complex canonization process questions are implicitly being raised: "scripture for whom?" and "canonical for whom?"

52. William A. Graham, "Scripture," in *The Encyclopedia of Religion*, ed. Mircea Eliade (New York: Macmillan, 1987), 13:133–45, at 133. Graham's definition is taken up by Moody Smith, "When Did the Gospels Become Scripture?" 4.

53. In considering "scripture" as "a relational concept," William Graham writes: "A text is only 'scripture' insofar as a group of persons perceives it to be sacred or holy, powerful and meaningful, possessed of an exalted authority, and in some fashion transcendent of, and hence distinct from, other speech and writing. What is scripture for one group may be a meaningless, nonsensical, or even perversely false text for another. . . . The 'scriptural' characteristics of a text belong not to the text itself but to its role in a community. 'Scripture' is not a literary genre but a religio-historical one." Graham, "Scripture," 134.

54. Moody Smith, "When Did the Gospels Become Scripture?" 4. It seems that the first to suggest this distinction between "scripture" and "canon" was Albert C. Sundberg, "Toward a Revised History of the New Testament Canon," in *Studia Evangelica IV, Texte und Untersuchungen 89* (Berlin: Akademie-Verlag, 1964), 452–61.

55. Moody Smith, "When Did the Gospels Become Scripture?" 4.

Therefore, thirdly, with regard to "community of faith" or "church," a distinction needs to be made between local communities and wider circles of communities. Part of the complexity of the New Testament canonization process concerns the issue of how broadly among local churches certain writings are revered as "scripture" and considered to be "canonical." Such "catholic" breadth is to be understood both synchronically and diachronically: synchronically, with regard to the extent of the circle of inter-ecclesial reception at one time, and diachronically, in regard to continuity with communities of the past and their reception of the works (the issues of apostolicity, antiquity, and reliable connection with the foundational events of the faith).

Fourthly, one could speak of "local scripture" (writings revered in a local community) and, at the end of the canonization process, "canonical scripture" or perhaps, too awkwardly, "biblical scripture" (writings universally revered and included as part of the final New Testament canon within the bipartite Christian Bible).[56] Such writings then take on the meaning of "Scripture" in common Christian parlance today, i.e., those canonical writings which have been agreed upon by the whole church as the *norma normans* (norming norm) of the Christian faith.

Fifthly, as highlighted by the last sentence, a further distinction needs to be made with regard to the term "canon" itself. Scholars often refer to Gerald Sheppard's helpful distinction between "canon 1" (a rule, standard, or norm of faith) and "canon 2" (a list of writings accepted as normative for a community of faith), terms which I will employ.[57] However, as we shall see, in the very formation of the Christian canon (canon 2), the application of a rule of the faith (canon 1) already begins to play a role from the earliest stages of the traditioning process.

Therefore, and finally, within the notion of "canon 1," a distinction can be made between the eventual bipartite canon (canon 2), constituting a *regula fidei* ("rule of faith"; Greek, *kánon tès písteos*) as a *norma normans,* and the short, oftentimes oral, summaries and narratives of the truths of faith, known in the early church as the *regula fidei* or *regula veritatis*

---

56. Local communities may have their own lists of scriptures, which could also be referred to as their "canonical scriptures." The history of the canon reveals the existence of such divergent lists. But I shall restrict the term "canonical scripture" to those twenty-seven New Testament scriptural works which are currently considered to be included in the canon of the Christian Bible.

57. See Gerald Sheppard, "Canon," in *The Encyclopedia of Religion,* ed. Mircea Eliade (New York: Macmillan, 1987), 3:62–69, at 64–67.

(*kánon tès aletheías,* canon of truth). The development of these summaries takes place alongside the process of canon formation; formation of the *regula fidei* and of the biblical canon are parallel and intertwined processes. As we shall see, in a hermeneutical spiral of understanding, both function as norms in the delineation of the faith, in a period of church history where oral transmission of the Jesus tradition within the churches continues alongside attempts to fix such traditions in writing.

Concerning "canon 2" (a normative list), we will see that the canonization process involves both *perception* and *selection*. Firstly, it involves perception of fidelity to the core of the faith. A particular writing is interpreted and judged to be true or otherwise with regard to the received faith of the community. This perception involves a theological judgment. Secondly, canonization is a process of selection. This selection process involves two interrelated dynamics: (1) expansion and delimitation, and (2) inclusion and exclusion.

For understanding this double perception and selection process, the notion "criteria of canonicity" has often been employed by scholars in the reconstruction of the canonization process. The application of criteria in the early church seems to vary greatly, and it is difficult to be precise about this long and complicated discernment process over four centuries. Various candidates have been named as possible criteria: "apostolicity" or "authorship," "antiquity" or "reliability," "orthodoxy" or "coherence with the *regula fidei*," "use" or "usefulness."[58] Notably, "inspiration" is generally not included as one of those explicit criteria.[59] Authorship by an actual

---

58. For a summary of the debate, see Lee Martin McDonald, "Identifying Scripture and Canon in the Early Church: The Criteria Question," in *The Canon Debate,* ed. Lee Martin McDonald and James A. Sanders (Peabody, Mass.: Hendrickson Publishers, 2002), 416–39.

59. Albert C. Sundberg, "The Bible Canon and the Christian Doctrine of Inspiration," *Interpretation* 29 (1975): 352–71, at 370: "Throughout the entire period of canonization, discussion in the fathers over the question of inspiration or non-inspiration or negative inspiration has to do, virtually without exception, with orthodoxy versus heresy. The question of inspiration, thus, does not function as a criteria of canonization; the common view of the church throughout this period is that inspiration is broadly and constantly present in the church." Likewise, Metzger remarks: "[T]he Fathers do not hesitate to refer to non-Scriptural documents as 'inspired', a circumstance showing that they did not consider inspiration to be a unique characteristic of canonical writings." Bruce M. Metzger, *The Canon of the New Testament: Its Origin, Development, and Significance* (New York: Oxford University Press, 1987), 256. For example, Athanasius makes a distinction between inspired books and canonical books. See Metzger, *The Canon of the New Testament,* 211 n.6. Sandra Schneiders also asserts: "It is important to note that the Church never considered inspiration the grounds or the criterion for including a writing in the canon but, once a book was canonized, it was regarded as inspired." Schneiders, *The Revelatory Text,* 47.

apostle seems to be less important compared with fidelity to the content of the faith and the reliability of a document for connecting communities with the apostolic reception of foundational events.[60] While Metzger might call apostolicity and orthodoxy, for example, "elusive standards,"[61] concern for continuity with the apostolic tradition and "the faith that was once for all entrusted to the saints"[62] were dominant and abiding ecclesial values in the canonization process. Similarly, actual use by the churches is a highly significant factor; as Lee McDonald affirms: "The question of whether a book should be regarded as scripture and placed within a canon seems to have been determined ultimately by early church use."[63] Metzger calls the whole process "a clear case of the survival of the fittest."[64] Some scholars, applying solely a hermeneutics of suspicion, in a continuation of the basic theses of Walter Bauer, see this survival of the fittest as simply the political triumph of fourth-century "orthodoxy";[65] what we have today, it is claimed, is simply a collection from which have been excluded equally valid interpretations of the Christian faith.[66]

Not sufficiently acknowledged in these latter discussions is the application from the earliest stages of the canonization process of a dual crite-

60. Campenhausen demonstrates persuasively that genuine apostolic authorship was not, in the end, an essential requirement; the crucial issue was whether the content of the faith proclaimed in a writing was in agreement with the received faith of the church: "It is the content of the prophetic or apostolic testimony which is decisive, not the question of direct authorship or authorisation. The opposite view, dominant today, that the principle for deciding whether a work should be admitted into the New Testament was that of its authorship by an apostle, is devoid of all foundation." Hans Campenhausen, *The Formation of the Christian Bible* (Philadelphia: Fortress Press, 1972), 330.

61. Metzger, *The Canon of the New Testament*, 272.

62. Jude 3.

63. Lee Martin McDonald, *The Formation of the Christian Biblical Canon,* rev. and expanded ed. (Peabody, Mass.: Hendrickson Publishers, 1995), 246. Campenhausen, likewise, highlights that "the regular use of a book for liturgical reading was a pre-condition of its later reception, that did not exclude an investigation in doubtful cases of its 'authenticity' and right to a place in the Canon." Campenhausen, *The Formation of the Christian Bible,* 331.

64. Metzger, *The Canon of the New Testament,* 286.

65. See Walter Bauer, *Orthodoxy and Heresy in Earliest Christianity,* ed. Robert A. Kraft and Gerhard Krodel (Philadelphia: Fortress Press, 1971). The German edition was originally published in 1934. For a summary of Bauer and different assessments of his theses, see Ehrman, *Lost Christianities,* 172–80; Darrell L. Bock, *The Missing Gospels: Unearthing the Truth Behind Alternative Christianities* (Nashville, Tenn.: Nelson Books, 2006), 44–55. For a response to Bauer's thesis regarding the implications for canon history of the diversity of early Christianity, see Dunn, *Unity and Diversity;* James D. G. Dunn, "Has the Canon a Continuing Function?" in McDonald and Sanders, eds., *The Canon Debate,* 558–79.

66. As an example, see Ehrman, *Lost Christianities,* 229–57.

rion: fidelity to the Jewish faith and fidelity to the God of Jesus Christ. As noted in chapter 4, fundamental to the early church's post-Easter interpretation of the Christ event is the function of the Jewish Scriptures as a hermeneutical lens through which the early Christians interpret the "newness" experienced in Jesus Christ. For those early communities, this newness does not mean a rejection of the old, but a new understanding of the God of Israel. Similarly, during the canonization process, at work in the judgment of true or false interpretations of Jesus Christ and of the God of Jesus Christ is fidelity to the ecclesial memory of Jesus' teaching, activity, death, and resurrection ("the characteristic Jesus" of the received Jesus tradition). Clearly at work in the delimitation-expansion and inclusion-exclusion dynamic of canon formation is the judgment of whether a particular work draws lines of continuity between the God professed to be at work in Jesus Christ the Crucified and Risen One and the God witnessed to in the Jewish Scriptures and their narrative world. It is a dual criterion that is applied from the earliest stage of the traditioning process and, more specifically, in the canonization process.

This sense of dual fidelity can helpfully be described retrospectively as "proto-orthodoxy."[67] Early in the history of the church, this "sense of the faith" consolidated into a cluster of core ideas which constituted the primary beliefs of Christians.[68] This cluster of core ideas would be later formulated in summaries of the content of the faith known as the *regula fidei,* the canon of faith. But from the early decades of the church it functions as a thread of ecclesial memory enabling judgment of diverse, hermeneutical receptions of "the legacy of Jesus."[69] It functions as a consolidated "sense of the faith."

67. The term "proto-orthodoxy" seems to have been first proposed by Bart D. Ehrman, *The Orthodox Corruption of Scripture: The Effect of Early Christological Controversies on the Text of the New Testament* (New York: Oxford University Press, 1993), 13. The term usefully avoids the retrospective designations of later "orthodoxy" and "heresy" employed in Walter Bauer's theses.

68. "The core can be viewed as this: There is one Creator God. Jesus was both human and divine; He truly suffered and was raised bodily. He also is worthy to receive worship. Salvation was about liberation from hostile forces, but it also was about sin and forgiveness—the need to fix a flaw in humanity that made each person culpable before the Creator. This salvation was the realization of promises that God made to the world and to Israel through Israel's Law and Prophets. The one person, Jesus Christ, brought this salvation not only by revealing the way to God and making reconciliation but also by providing for that way through his death for sin. Resurrection into a new exalted spiritual life involves salvation of the entire person—spirit, soul and body. Faith in this work of God through Jesus saves and brings on a spiritual life that will never end. This was the orthodoxy of the earliest tradition." Bock, *The Missing Gospels,* 207.

69. Arland J. Hultgren, *The Rise of Normative Christianity* (Minneapolis: Fortress Press, 1994),

Application of this criterion of the consolidated sense of the faith plays a significant role in both the expansion through inclusion of particular works (over against Marcionites) and the delimitation through exclusion of certain works (over against the Gnostics). The application of this *theological* criterion of a communal *sensus fidei* holds true, quite apart from the *historical* issue of whether Marcion "caused" the Christian canon to begin to be fixed in an expansion of Marcion's canon, or the *historical* issue whether the debates with the Gnostics caused it to be fixed, in an exclusion of certain works.[70] The *historical* and the *theological* issues are not to be conflated, although they are entwined.

The principle of fidelity to the Jewish faith and fidelity to "the characteristic Jesus" of the Jesus tradition first of all enables us to understand the felt need to reject Marcion's fixed canon of only a cut-down version of Luke and only ten letters of Paul, and the felt need to insist upon an "expanded" group of writings for use in the churches. Marcion's *sensus fidei* constitutes a rejection of Judaism and the writings of Jewish Scripture. It is a *sensus fidei* that is rejected by the wider *sensus fidelium* because it runs directly counter to the fundamental Christian tenet of continuity between the God witnessed to in the Jewish Scriptures and the God recognized at work in Jesus Christ and the Holy Spirit. As we have examined in chapter 4, the books that are eventually included in the canon all essentially presume the faith-world of the Jewish Scriptures and mostly

---

105–12. Jens Schröter states: "What was determinative for the church as it constituted itself, long before the extent of the accepted writings was established, was agreement with the rule of faith as the 'canon' of early Christianity, which secured continuity with the apostolic witness of the earliest time. The rejection of other Gospels, which therefore came to be seen as apocryphal, happened because they contradicted this canon and represented, for example, a docetic or Gnostic interpretation of Jesus' actions. Therefore, what is crucial in regards to the connection between Jesus and the canon is that the early Christian reception of Jesus' teaching took place within a spectrum of interpretation that demanded a distinction between accepted and rejected interpretations. That the rule of faith did not thereby lead to a standardization of the accepted Jesus tradition, but instead made possible a broad spectrum of interpretations, is evident especially from the fact that within the Christian canon, four Gospels, very different in their theological uniqueness, found acceptance." Jens Schröter, "Jesus and the Canon: The Early Jesus Traditions in the Context of the Origins of the New Testament Canon," in *Performing the Gospel: Orality, Memory, and Mark*, ed. Richard A. Horsley, Jonathan A. Draper, and John Miles Foley (Minneapolis: Fortress, 2006), 104–22, at 121–22.

70. On the role of Marcion, Gnosticism, and Montanism in the formation of the canon, see the summary of scholarship in Harry Y. Gamble, "The New Testament Canon: Recent Research and the Status Questionis," in McDonald and Sanders, eds., *The Canon Debate*, 267–94. For a more qualified assessment of Marcion's role in forcing the creation of a Christian canon, see John Barton, "Marcion Revisited," in *The Canon Debate*, 341–54.

allude to or quote directly from them. The consequence of this fundamental intuition in the controversy with Marcion is that only works that do affirm the fundamental continuity between the old and the new find reception in the church's liturgical, doctrinal, and catechetical life.

The same principle is at work in the controversies with the Gnostics. The Gnostics, like Marcion, eschewed the Jewish faith in the face of what they considered the utter newness of Jesus.[71] Although the Jewish Scriptures are quoted in their writings, the Gnostics' vision is ultimately determined by elements that come from outside the narrative world of the Jewish Scriptures. "The heterodox writings do not characteristically present Jesus with reference to the Old Testament and the narrative world of Israel and the God of these Scriptures (at least not positively)."[72] Their narrative world is shaped by "other conceptual schemes that probably derived more from philosophical and mythological traditions of the wider Greco-Roman era."[73] The identity of Jesus as divine, and hardly human, is not depicted in terms of Jewish monotheism.[74]

Therefore, within the Gnostic controversies, rather than leading to an expansion of necessary writings (as with the reaction against Marcion), there is a clear determination by their opponents for both delimitation to a fixed, acceptable core, and exclusion of certain writings from that core. Firstly, against the Gnostic expansion of writings and rejection of a fixed canon, there is a move toward a delimitation of acceptable texts and a fixed canon. Secondly, against the non-Jewish depiction of the mean-

71. According to Tom Wright, "the entire world-view of Gnosticism, to which the 'Gospel of Judas' makes such a fresh contribution, is inherently opposed to the fundamental worldview of mainline Judaism itself. Judaism, from Genesis to the rabbis and beyond, believes in the goodness of the created world, and in the special calling of Israel to be the light of that world. Gnosticism believes in the fundamental badness of the created world, the folly of those who take the Old Testament as their guide, and the special status of the Gnostics as the sparks of light who are to be rescued from that world. In particular, Judaism believes that the God of Israel is the good, wise and sovereign creator of all that is, while Gnosticism believes that the God of Israel is the incompetent and malicious *demiurge* who made this wicked world. If Gnosticism is true, Judaism is not, and vice versa." N. T. Wright, *Judas and the Gospel of Jesus: Understanding a Newly Discovered Ancient Text and Its Contemporary Significance* (London: SPCK, 2006), 56.

72. Hurtado, *Lord Jesus Christ,* 484.

73. Ibid., 485.

74. Ibid., 484–85: "Instead of the narrative world of the Old Testament, the master narrative recited or alluded to in the heterodox writings posits a precosmic drama of alienation of the elect from their divine origin. . . . Consequently, in the Jesus books written with such an outlook, there is no indication that Jesus' divinity posed any problem that required much thought. It was his humanity, more specifically the question of his bodily existence, that seems to have been somewhat more difficult."

ing of Jesus, there is a rejection and exclusion of these works as neither in continuity with the Jesus Christ of Christian memory nor the God of Jesus Christ, as witnessed to in the Jewish Scriptures. Ultimately, it was a "battle over who the Christian God was."[75]

While this battle might well be told historically as purely a political one, in which the dominant player wins out over other equally legitimate players, such a depiction of the canonization process is one-dimensional. It fails to address the issue of criteriology, ignoring or downplaying the primary hermeneutical and theological issues at the heart of the debate, especially the fundamental issue of continuity with regard to the Jewish faith and the God of Jesus Christ. At issue, therefore, is a conflict of divergent *sensus fidei;* this communal judgment of divergence from the received tradition involves the communal organon for recognition of illegitimate discontinuity, the *sensus fidelium.* The demand for continuity-in-newness over against radical discontinuity had been a characteristic feature of the earliest apostolic witness, the apostolic tradition; in the Gnostic debates, it continues to be applied now as a criterion for the delimitation of acceptable writings, as well as the exclusion of unacceptable ones.[76] However, it is important to note that not all writings which were eventually excluded from the New Testament canon would necessarily have "failed" according to this criterion (e.g., 1 Clement and the Didache). For such writings, other criteria would have come into play.

The complexity of this communal process of canon formation suggests that Morwenna Ludlow is correct to propose that, rather than attempting to reconstruct definitive "criteria of canonicity" which were explicitly applied by the early church, it is more historically and theologically ac-

---

75. In the fuller passage, Hurtado writes: "There are undeniable tensions for Christians in treating the Old Testament as their Scriptures: Israel versus church, Torah versus Christ, and the anthropomorphic pictures of God in the Old Testament, to name a few obvious ones. Those who urged a distinction between the Old Testament deity and the true God were not simply trying to be difficult; they were reacting to real issues. But the stakes were high, the issues far-reaching, and the potential consequences of the *battle over who the Christian God was* were monumental. Those who opposed the advocates of a God different from the world creator were correct, thus, to perceive that they were involved in a struggle over a core issue, and the very soul of Christianity." Ibid., 559–60.

76. Exclusion of writings which may very well contain authentic sayings of Jesus, such as the Coptic Gospel of Thomas, could be said to have been excluded according to this criterion. For example, Gos. Thom. 52 has Jesus urging his disciples to listen to him and not to "the twenty-four prophets." See Wilhelm Schneemelcher and R. McL. Wilson, eds., *New Testament Apocrypha,* vol. 1, *Gospels and Related Writings,* rev. ed. (Louisville, Ky.: Westminster John Knox Press, 1991), 125.

curate to speak of "*reasons why* canonicity was attributed."[77] According to Ludlow, a "central core"[78] of works emerges so early that no explicit application of carefully articulated criteria seems to be taking place. This central core is the four Gospels and a body of Paul's letters. These seem to impose themselves, rather than being deliberately chosen; and yet, at the same time, it is only because communities continue to choose to use them that they achieve prominence. It is only after their predominant usage that the church retrospectively reflects on the reasons why these works, and not others, seem to have emerged and were received more universally as a common heritage of writings. These "reasons," however, do then begin to function, at some point in the ongoing process, as "criteria" for the discernment of writings still disputed. For example, Eusebius of Caesarea, in his *Ecclesiastical History*, written shortly after the conversion of Constantine, retrospectively writes of three crucial issues related to inclusion or exclusion from the canon. David Dungan calls them "three distinct, make-or-break tests":[79] the test of theological orthodoxy, the test of genuine apostolic authorship, and the use test.

These three tests functioned individually and collectively as a "three-layer sieve" to screen out fraudulent, fictitious, or heretical writings. They were applied with intense determination: by the time Eusebius wrote his *Ecclesiastical History*, only twenty writings out of more than 100 candidates had made it through this rigorous screening process into the charmed circle of the New Testament.[80]

This screening and ecclesial "reasoning" as to why particular works have been and should continue to be used and why certain ones should be excluded, in the end, is an ecclesial balancing of various reasons/criteria/tests for different writings. Together the various reasons make up the intuition of an ecclesial *sensus*. Communities "sense" that some works, and not others, are *faithful* to communal memory of Jesus Christ

---

77. Morwenna Ludlow, "'Criteria of Canonicity' and the Early Church," in *Die Einheit der Schrift und die Vielfalt des Kanons = The Unity of Scripture and the Diversity of the Canon*, ed. John Barton and Michael Wolter (New York: Walter de Gruyter, 2003), 69–93, at 71. According to Ludlow, "[It] is not just that we lack documentary evidence about the early stages of the formation of the canon. In fact, the Church's self-conscious reflection on the canon of Scripture *always* began *in media res:* with regard to most books it was a question of explaining why it had what it had, rather than deciding on what it should have. . . . [W]hat seems to be happening—at least in part—is that the Church is formulating *reasons* or *explanations* for why it has what it has, not *criteria* for choosing what it should have in the future." Ibid., 70–71.

78. Ibid., 69.   79. Dungan, *Constantine's Bible*, 78.

80. Ibid., 83.

(the Jesus tradition), and at the same time they are judged to be in continuity with the narrative of salvation of the Jewish Scriptures and the
God witnessed to in those writings. Furthermore, they are judged, with
intuition and not necessarily explicit, definitive criteria, to be *effective*
in making "the Gospel" meaningful in new contexts (even beyond their
original context); they prove to be *useful* for the varying demands of the
liturgical, catechetical, doctrinal, moral, and disciplinary dimensions of
church life; they are recognized as *encapsulating* beliefs and practices of
the tradition regarded as essential; as spiritual works, they are experienced as *revelatory* of the saving God witnessed to in the documents; as
communicators of "the Gospel," they are recognized as *trustworthy* witnesses to the apostolic imagination. Many of these features are covered
by what Lee Martin McDonald, appropriating James Sanders, calls the
criterion of "adaptability."[81] Or, appropriating Graham Stanton, these
works are capable of bridging "story" and contemporary "significance,"[82]
if read with the same apostolic hermeneutic which produced them.

As a general and comprehensive category for understanding this fuzzy
perception-cum-selection and de-selection process of both the early central core and the later "outer ranges"[83] of the Christian writings in the
canon, that of *recognition* best names the ecclesial dynamic in which
some works rather than others emerge as "canonical scripture," sacred
and authoritative for norming church life and identity. Recognition includes the perceptive and approbative elements of hermeneutical reception; it is an interpretative evaluation, and therefore a judgment.[84] It is
the perception, by the organon of the *sensus fidelium,* that a particular

81. "The sacred writings that brought hope in a hopeless situation for the people of Israel told
a story that could be applied to new circumstances. This story, significantly enhanced through the
creative hermeneutics that were employed by the church, offered hope and life to the new people
of faith. This is, of course, the story of God's activity in Jesus, the proclaimed Christ. That story
continues to be adaptable to the changing circumstances of life of a variety of persons in a variety of cultures. Through it persons of faith perceive that God continues to release from bondage,
bring healing, and offer hope to the hopeless. That is what is adaptable and what continues to in-
spire persons in every generation, and that is what the church canonized." McDonald, "Identifying Scripture and Canon," 434–35. For a recent formulation of Sanders's notion of "adaptability"
in formation of the Jewish canon, see James A. Sanders, "The Issue of Closure in the Canonical
Process," in *The Canon Debate,* 252–63.

82. Stanton, *The Gospels and Jesus,* 5–6.

83. Jared Wicks, "Canon of Scripture," in *Dictionary of Fundamental Theology,* ed. René Latourelle and Rino Fisichella (Middlegreen, Slough, England: St. Paul, 1994), 94–101, at 101.

84. "The Church, filled with the Holy Spirit, recognizes something as connatural amongst the
writings which accord with her nature." Rahner, *Inspiration in the Bible,* 66.

sense of the faith is trustworthy, truthful, faithful, meaningful, useful, salvific, revelatory (or otherwise). Fundamental to that multifaceted perception is the judgment that a particular *sensus fidei* is in continuity with and faithful to the culminating event of revelation, the Christ event, as witnessed to by those who were its first receivers, the generation of "apostles." That is, it is truthful and faithful to that apostolic tradition which had, since then, been passed on in the church's living memory.

In judging that a *sensus fidei* is faithful to that apostolic witness, recognition of fidelity includes the perception that such a *sensus fidei* can be effective in mediating that original event in the present (i.e., it can be revelatory). Although the original Christ event itself was not directly available as a norm, the salvific revelation which it mediated was still being experienced, in the Spirit, as a present reality by later generations. That present salvific and revelatory experience in new contexts itself became a lens and a standard for judging fidelity to the original event of any expression of the faith. Only the perduring organon of the *sensus fidelium* can make that double judgment of (1) fidelity to past apostolic interpretations and (2) truthful interpretation of salvific experience in the present. Only the *sensus fidelium* can bridge "story" and "significance." By means of that organon, the same God is recognized as being at work in both the original event and its receptions.[85]

We have already seen that, in many of the writings of the first century, there is a cluster of ideas which is presupposed as the common heritage regarding the content of the faith.[86] This core system of beliefs comes to be formulated more synthetically in the second century in what is called the "canon of truth" (Latin, *regula veritatis;* Greek, *kánon tès aletheías*) or the "rule of faith" (Latin, *regula fidei;* Greek, *kánon tès pisteos*).[87] Various

---

85. On the relevance of this point to the Old Testament, see Gerald T. Sheppard, "Canonization: Hearing the Voice of the Same God through Historically Dissimilar Traditions," *Interpretation* 36 (1982): 21–33.

86. "[W]hat existed and emerged in the time before Irenaeus was a spectrum of beliefs. However—and this is the key point—along that spectrum existed points of demarcation, separating the views from each other. Most works of the period reflect this difference in thought. . . . [T]hese differences rotated around four areas: the view of God, the view of Jesus, the nature of salvation, and Jesus' work. Significant difference in any one of these areas (not necessarily all four of them, as some want to insist before questioning a work) provoked traditionalist reaction. . . . [T]hese ideas were the core of Christianity." Bock, *The Missing Gospels,* 206–7.

87. See L. W. Countryman, "Tertullian and the Regula Fidei," *Second Century* 2 (1982): 208–27; R. P. C. Hanson, *Tradition in the Early Church* (London: SCM Press, 1962), 75–129; Jared Wicks, "Rule of Faith," in *Dictionary of Fundamental Theology,* ed. René Latourelle and Rino

versions of the *regula fidei* are to be found in second-century writers in the form of variable summaries of the central narrative and central beliefs of the apostolic tradition.[88] A common feature of those summaries is the affirmation of the unity between the God witnessed to in the Old Testament and the God professed to be at work in Jesus Christ and the Spirit.

As both a rule (canon 1) and as short interpretative summaries of the faith, the *regula fidei* is yet another manifestation in the early church of the *sensus fidei,* in both meanings of the term: as the organon for making a ruling or judgment (approbative reception), and as a resulting interpretation or formulation of the faith which then, in turn, operates as a rule for judging other formulations of the faith. The perduring organon of *sensus fidei* maintains in the communal memory the essential features of the faith passed on in the apostolic tradition, features which come to be expressed in the form of both a narrative summary of the trinitarian story of salvation and as a summary of the major truths of the faith. Use of the varying versions of the *regula fidei* becomes significant in the baptismal initiation practice of the early church. It also receives prominent application in the disputes with Marcion and with the Gnostics in the second century.

This normative application of the *regula fidei* takes place alongside the formation of the canon, with the "candidates" for canonical status themselves playing a role in the very formulation of these summaries of the faith.[89] While acknowledging that there is at work between these two a

---

Fisichella (Middlegreen, Slough, England: St. Paul, 1994), 959–61; J. N. D. Kelly, *Early Christian Creeds,* 3rd ed. (London: Longman, 1972), esp. 62–99; Yves Congar, *Tradition and Traditions: An Historical and a Theological Essay* (London: Burns & Oates, 1966), 26–30.

88. For the texts of early Christian *regulae fidei,* see Jaroslav Pelikan and Valerie R. Hotchkiss, eds., *Creeds and Confessions of Faith in the Christian Tradition,* 4 vols. (New Haven, Conn.: Yale University Press, 2003). On the *regula fidei* as a synthesis of Christian belief, see Wicks, "Rule of Faith," 961: "The rule was, above all, a normative source of coherence through a single vision of God, creation, and human life in the historical world. Christian faith has a determinate content, and the rule shows this to have been the case even immediately following NT times. This content, however, was not a compelling list of tenets formulated as propositions. The rule of faith shows the content to have been, instead, an ordered understanding of God's dealing with humankind as creator of all, savior of his fallen creation, and present power of illumination, sanctification, and guidance. . . . [It is] a given framework and order arising from faith itself, which has already laid hold of a primordial synthesis."

89. "[The] central NT writings themselves had contributed much to solidifying these tenets of the ecclesial 'canon of truth.' It would be misleading to think that the rule of faith was applied to the canonical books from the outside. Tradition and Scripture, from the beginning, were coinherent with each other." Wicks, "Canon of Scripture," 99.

hermeneutical circle (rather than a "vicious" circle) of mutual judgment and formulation, the *regula fidei* (in its varying formulations) plays an important role as a retrospective "reason" for works having already been included in the emerging canon, and as an implicit "criterion" for judging works for future or continuing inclusion or exclusion in the canon. This hermeneutical circle of ecclesial reflection over three hundred years leads to much finer formulation of the contours and boundaries of Christian belief; recourse to the more summary *regula fidei* gradually fades to the background with the emergence in the fourth and fifth centuries of more precisely formulated creeds and definitions of the faith.[90]

This hermeneutical circularity also highlights the element of discovery in the canonization process. "Theologically speaking, the church did not create the canon so much as it came to recognize it. . . . Similarly, the church did not bestow authority on the canonical writings so much as it recognized the authority already there"[91]—canon presumes scripture. Certain works are recognized *as* the Word of God. The retrospective recognition of a collection of writings which, together, can be revelatory of the Word of God, and therefore are revered as sacred and adopted as authoritative (as a combined unifying standard of diverse *sensus fidei*) for judging all future receptions of revelation, relates to its ongoing adaptability for bridging story and significance in contexts beyond its original community and intended audience.

The ability of the works of the canon to continue to "prove themselves" in new contexts has been helpfully described in terms of the notion of the literary "classic" and the "impact" or "effect" that works make on readers throughout history. According to David Tracy (appropriating Gadamer's notions of "effect" and "history of effects" or "effective history"), the works of Scripture are timeless classics, literary works that continue to affect generations of readers beyond the context of original production.[92] However, a more dynamic notion of the classic is required

90. For a summary of that development and the function of creeds, see Luke Timothy Johnson, *The Creed: What Christians Believe and Why It Matters* (New York: Doubleday, 2003), 9–64.

91. Achtemeier, *Inspiration and Authority,* 107 n.22. See also Metzger, *The Canon of the New Testament,* 287: "The church did not create the canon, but came to recognize, accept, affirm, and confirm the self-authenticating quality of certain documents that imposed themselves as such upon the church."

92. See David Tracy, *The Analogical Imagination: Christian Theology and the Culture of Pluralism* (New York: Crossroad, 1981). For an application of Tracy's notion of the classic for understanding the formation of the canon, see Frances Young, *The Art of Performance: Towards a*

which would highlight more adequately the active and creative role of receivers in the process we have outlined above.[93] "Effect" *(Wirkung)* and "reception" *(Rezeption)* are two sides of any communicative event, including literary communication.[94] A work's "effective history" *(Wirkungsgeschichte)* is more fully told in terms of its "reception history" *(Rezeptionsgeschichte).* Literary works do not automatically affect and transform readers; it is the work's receivers who bring it alive and give it new meaning in new contexts.[95] Works are classics because receivers continue to find them meaningful and thereby be transformed by them, and that is so because they are able to make meaning of them and creatively apply them in a new context.[96] There is no *effect* without *reception.*

Such a dynamic notion of "classics" can help us understand the process at play in the ecclesial approbative reception of the works of the canon. Wider and wider circles of Christian communities are able to make sense of them, and hermeneutically adapt and apply them to local need, thereby demonstrating their universal applicability and usefulness for maintaining Christian identity in new cultures and contexts, as well as for maintaining unity in the faith throughout more and more communities of faith as the church expands geographically and culturally. The same Spirit at work in the production of the works is now op-

---

Theology of Holy Scripture (London: Darton, Longman & Todd, 1990), 31–33. On Gadamer's notion of *Wirkungsgeschichte* ("history of effects" or "effective history"), see Gadamer, *Truth and Method,* 300–307.

93. On Hans Robert Jauss's critique of Gadamer's Platonic notion of the timeless classic and the notion of *Rezeptionsgeschichte* ("history of reception" or "reception history"), see Rush, *The Reception of Doctrine,* 89–93.

94. We have already seen in chapter 4 that for Jesus to have an "impact" on his disciples presumes some "reception" of him by his disciples.

95. Highlighting reception as constitutive of a "classic," Brendan Byrne summarizes this communicative dynamic: "A text will be successful as a piece of communication to the extent to which it brings actual or real readers to identify with the implied reader generated by the reading. A text will *continue* to be influential (and in this sense become a 'classic') to the extent to which real readers of subsequent generations continue to make the same identification." Byrne, *Romans,* 4. Original italics.

96. "In confronting a classic, our present horizon is stretched and challenged. New possibilities for transformation are offered. As we interpret the classic, we find that our own lives are interpreted by it. A classic receives its status as a classic not by the fiat of authority, but only by gradually coming to be experienced and publicly recognized as a work of enduring quality and universal meaning. This . . . parallels how the canon of the Bible came to be recognized." Peter Schineller, "The Wisdom That Leads to Salvation: Revelation and Scripture," in *Faithful Witness: Foundations of Theology for Today's Church,* ed. Leo J. O'Donovan and T. Howland Sanks (New York: Crossroad, 1989), 85–98, at 95.

erative, through the organon of *sensus fidelium,* in making sense of the work, through application to new horizons of meaning. In this way, a work's (possibly) *implied* universal audience finds its correlate (whatever the original intention of the author) in *real* and diverse communities of reception which continue to *find it,* and *make it,* universally applicable and revelatory. Such works (canon 2) are therefore confidently judged by the churches to be a *universal* canon of faith (canon 1) for all future possible Christian communities.[97]

Examples of this movement toward universal reception are the early emergence and early wide approbation of the collection of the letters of Paul and the collection of the fourfold Gospel. The writings expressive of Paul's *sensus fidei* seem to receive wide circulation and approbation very quickly.[98] Certainly by the time 2 Peter 3:15–16 was written (probably around A.D. 130), some of Paul's letters have received acceptance beyond their original target audience.[99] Mark's *sensus fidei* must have achieved a certain reception beyond its place of origin, given his literary reception by Luke and Matthew within a short time. That these latter authors may be intending to replace Mark's work with their own as the universally accepted Gospel does not negate the dynamic of literary reception that is going on. Furthermore, that Matthew, Luke, and John may even be intending their works as "scripture" for their own communities, and perhaps beyond, at least implies that these evangelists compose with the intention of offering their works for reception by the *sensus fidelium* of their particular community.

97. Congar, we have seen, in his essay on reception as an ecclesiological reality, cites the adoption of the works of the canon across fifteen hundred years as an example of reception among local churches, and gives the following summary: "The canon of Scripture evolved by a process of reception. The very term is to be found in documents on the subject: the Muratori fragment (lines 66, 72, 82), the decree of the Roman synod of 382 and of Gelasius *De recipiendis et non recipiendis libris;* the decree of 4 February 1441 for the Jacobites ('suscipit et veneratur') (DS 1334), the decree of the Council of Trent on the writings and traditions that are to be received (DS 1501). This official, normative and express form of reception was preceded by a factual reception in the Churches, as described in the historical works on the subject." Congar, "Reception as an Ecclesiological Reality," 54.

98. See a summary of research in Stanley E. Porter, "When and How Was the Pauline Canon Compiled? An Assessment of Theories," in *The Pauline Canon,* ed. Stanley E. Porter (Boston: Brill, 2004), 95–127.

99. For this dating of 2 Peter, see Raymond E. Brown, *An Introduction to the New Testament* (New York: Doubleday, 1997), 767. The passage 2 Pt 3:15–16 states: "So also our beloved brother Paul wrote to you according to the wisdom given him, speaking of this as he does in all his letters. There are some things in them hard to understand, which the ignorant and unstable twist to their own destruction, as they do the other scriptures."

Certainly their works achieve wide, if not yet universal, reception within 120 years or so. Whatever the breadth of its reception at this stage, by around the year A.D. 200, more than a century before Constantine, there certainly exists in some circles the fourfold Gospel as we now know it, as a combined collection.[100] Referring to the testimony of Luke 1:1–3, Metzger notes that "the trend toward a multiplicity of Gospels existed from the very beginning."[101] What is *resisted* by the wider *sensus fidelium* is any attempt to reduce the number of Gospels to only one particular version (e.g., Marcion's Luke). What is *insisted* on by the *sensus fidelium,* despite the early (though not lasting) reception of Tatian's harmonizing *Diatesseron,* is that a diversity of *sensus fidei* be maintained, but diverse *sensus* which, nevertheless, must be maintained side-by-side in the one collection.[102] Any single "Gospel" alone is not the Word of God; only alongside and in tension with the other Gospels of the canon does it have that authority.

Despite the fact that each rendition of the Jesus story in the fourfold Gospel comes to be referred to separately as "the gospel according to (a distinct evangelist),"[103] there remains a belief that these are versions of *the one Gospel* of Jesus Christ, which continues to be proclaimed orally.[104] By

---

100. For a history of that emergence, see Hengel, *The Four Gospels and the One Gospel.* For a summary of this book's main thesis, see Martin Hengel, "The Four Gospels and the One Gospel of Jesus Christ," in *The Earliest Gospels: The Origins and Transmission of the Earliest Christian Gospels. The Contribution of the Chester Beatty Gospel Codex P45,* ed. Charles Horton, *Journal for the Study of the New Testament. Supplement series, 258* (New York: T&T Clark International, 2004), 13–26.

101. Metzger, *The Canon of the New Testament,* 263.

102. Francis Watson writes: "[T]he fourfold canonical gospel established itself in the face of a number of alternative proposals about the proper transmission of apostolic tradition relating to Jesus. It definitively rejects the claims that written texts are to be subordinated to oral tradition (Papias); that a uniquely privileged disciple was appointed to write a definitive gospel, far above the level of the others (Thomas); that the fourfold gospel has corrupted the pure original datum from which it derives, and must therefore be subjected to critical surgery (Marcion); that the fourfold gospel needs to be filled out with supplementary narrative material (apocryphal gospels); and that the four texts should be combined into a single text (Tatian)." Francis Watson, "The Fourfold Gospel," in *The Cambridge Companion to the Gospels,* ed. Stephen C. Barton (New York: Cambridge University Press, 2006), 34–52, at 46.

103. See Martin Hengel, "The Titles of the Gospels and the Gospel of Mark," in *Studies in the Gospel of Mark* (Philadelphia: Fortress Press, 1985), 64–84; Hengel, *The Four Gospels and the One Gospel,* 78–115.

104. "The codex began to be used for individual gospels soon after the turn of the century, a period when a plurality of gospels was known in many circles. During these decades the term 'Gospel' was used both for oral and for written 'Jesus traditions'. Use of the term 'Gospel' for two or more writings raised the question of their relationship to the *one* Gospel about Jesus Christ.

using the title "the gospel according to . . . ," two beliefs are being maintained: firstly, the good news about Jesus Christ is the one Gospel, and secondly, this one Gospel finds, and indeed requires, diverse versions or receptions. As Cullmann writes: "Four Gospels, that is, four books dealing with the content of faith, cannot be harmonized, but are required by their very nature to be set alongside one another. And in any case the faith cried out for manifold witness."[105]

Community authority plays an active part in this recognition and approbative reception. The need for approbative reception in the face of diverse interpretations is evident *within* the canonical writings themselves, and foreshadows an approbative reception process that continues after their production, as these works are themselves later received. We have already seen an approbative reception process at work within the very "apostolic tradition," i.e., between the two predominant apostolic figures during the apostolic age, Peter and Paul; the *sensus fidei* of each apostle undergoes scrutiny by the other, in a dynamic that nevertheless preserves a diversity of *sensus fidei* within the apostolic tradition. Also, authority and oversight are significant ecclesial factors in the hermeneutical battles within the Pauline and Johannine communities. In his own lifetime, Paul is constantly attempting to adjudicate the receptions of his own teachings. In the next generation, the Pastoral Letters attest to continuing conflict of interpretation among those Pauline communities regarding the Pauline *sensus fidei*. The reception of the Fourth Gospel too knows diverse trajectories and the question of the Gospel's diverging and at times conflicting reception is a major issue needing to be addressed by the time of the Johannine letters. However, although community leaders are directly involved in these controversies, they are examples of the *sensus fidelium* reaching consensus through a wide communal process over time, rather than examples of formal community judgment by the leaders alone.

This problem was solved by use of the title *euaggelion kata* . . . for individual gospels. The use of this title facilitated both acceptance of the fourfold Gospel and the use of the codex for four gospels. The four-gospel codex strongly encouraged acceptance of the fourfold Gospel, and vice versa: both are likely to have taken place shortly before the middle of the second century." Graham Stanton, "The Fourfold Gospel," in *Norms of Faith and Life,* ed. Everett Ferguson (New York: Garland, 1999), 1–30, at 24.

105. Oscar Cullmann, *The Early Church: Studies in Early Christian History and Theology* (Philadelphia: Westminster Press, 1956), 54. Quoted in Metzger, *The Canon of the New Testament,* 263–64.

This is likewise true of the role of later "authority figures" in the can-onization process. Although prominent protagonists such as Justin Mar-tyr (a layman), Irenaeus of Lyons (a bishop), or Origen (a layman, but ordained later in life) are significantly involved in disputes against Mar-cionites or Gnostics, their role in the canonization process was part of a much wider phenomenon.

Orthodoxy is not the product of third-century theologians. Those theologians cer-tainly developed and honed traditional teaching. They gave flesh to the bones and structure to the basic ideas. However, the core ideas they worked with and reflect-ed in their confessions can be found in the faith's earliest works. These works em-braced what the apostles passed on. The works we find in the New Testament also testify to this faith. That is why they were recognized as special sources for this teaching, even seen as being inspired by God. Irenaeus was not the creator of or-thodoxy; he was created by it.[106]

Similarly, although the emergence of the mono-episcopate is, in part, a result of the need for strong leadership during such disputes, the canon cannot be considered the result of decisions by bishops alone in those centuries. The reception of the canon is not due solely to formal deci-sions by official leaders.[107] Rather, the canon emerges through a process of communal recognition and approbation, and constitutes a *consensus* among the churches regarding the faith.

This *consensus fidelium* regarding the central core of what is the canon-ical New Testament emerges relatively quickly in the life of the church.

What is really remarkable is that, though the fringes of the New Testament canon remained unsettled for centuries, a high degree of unanimity concerning the great-er part of the New Testament was attained within the first two centuries among the very diverse and scattered congregations not only throughout the Mediterra-nean world but also over an area extending from Britain to Mesopotamia.[108]

---

106. Bock, *The Missing Gospels,* 212–13.

107. Campenhausen, who restricts his classic study to the first two centuries, states: "In the pe-riod under review official decisions by the Church are not involved. Synodal judgements and epis-copal pastoral letters concerning the contents of the Bible become usual only in the later fourth century." Campenhausen, *The Formation of the Christian Bible,* 331. Likewise, Achtemeier states: "The boundaries of the canon were simply not determined in accordance with any apostolic pro-nouncement or decree. The canon was assembled over a long period of time, with opinions differ-ing in different parts of the church, and indeed with opinions differing in the same areas at differ-ent periods of time." Achtemeier, *Inspiration and Authority,* 105.

108. Metzger, *The Canon of the New Testament,* 254.

To claim that what emerged as the canon should be described as the illegitimate imposition of a later orthodoxy ignores this historical fact. "Well before the influence of Constantine and councils of bishops in the fourth century and thereafter, it was clear that proto-orthodox Christianity was ascendant, and represented the emergent mainstream."[109] Alternatives to that mainstream were excluded primarily for theological reasons, as perceived by the *sensus fidelium.*

But what of those works on the "fringes" (Metzger) or "outer ranges" (Wicks)[110] or "periphery" (Ludlow)[111] of the canon which took a long time to determine? The issue of inclusion and exclusion is complicated by the fact that there were included in some "local canons" works that were eventually excluded in the final canon (e.g., 1 Clement, Gospel of Thomas, Shepherd of Hermas, the Didache), and by the fact that there were excluded in many local official lists writings that were eventually included in the final canon (e.g., Hebrews, James, 2 Peter, Revelation, 2 and 3 John, Jude). All were *sensus fidei* which found significant reception by a number of churches, and most would have been considered faithful to the "rule of faith," despite their diversity. The Gospel of Thomas may have eventually been excluded because it does not have a passion and resurrection narrative.[112] Moreover, its rendition of Jesus lacks any attempt to locate Jesus within a specific time in history, geographical location, or cultural setting; and therefore, it could not function like the fourfold Gospel to link the God of Israel with a particular person within concrete human history.[113] Indeed, it seems to portray a Jesus who rejects any link with the prophets of old.[114] The Shepherd of Hermas may not have achieved universal reception because the author fails to ground his

---

109. Hurtado, *Lord Jesus Christ,* 561.   110. Wicks, "Canon of Scripture," 101.

111. Ludlow, "'Criteria of Canonicity,'" 88.

112. I am indebted to Jared Wicks for this insight.

113. "The comparative lack of concern in the *Gospel of Thomas* to locate Jesus historically makes the wealth of historical setting in the canonical Gospels much more noticeable." Hurtado, *Lord Jesus Christ,* 267.

114. See Gospel of Thomas, 52. With regard to the spectrum of approaches to the four core elements of (1) view of God, (2) view of Jesus, (3) nature of salvation, and (4) Jesus' work, Darrell Bock writes: "A few works sit in between the ends of the spectrum, trying to reflect the alternative view but in a less contrastive way than some of its counterparts. This is where I would place [the Gospel of] Thomas and some of the works by the Valentinian school. They worked in the middle of this spectrum between orthodoxy and alternatives but in ways that show leanings to the alternative approach. This leaning, especially when it came to revelatory questions, explains why eventually they were associated with this side of the spectrum." Bock, *The Missing Gospels,* 211.

writing in Jewish Scripture,[115] and because of the perception that Hermas himself lacked connection with the apostolic age.[116]

Ultimately, the eventual exclusion or inclusion of these works on the fringes of the canon is to be attributed to reception or non-reception through use by the wider church, and the recognition that, although some of these works might well deserve inclusion, the twenty-seven works of the final canon (canon 2) were sufficient to constitute a canon of faith (canon 1) for the church's ongoing liturgical, doctrinal, and catechetical needs in new contexts.

Two points therefore can be made. First, it seems that those which received approbation relatively late were eventually received because they too proved to be "adaptable" or seemed to have maintained elements of the tradition, either formulations or practices, which were judged to have ongoing significance for church life and Christian identity. That works such as 2 Peter, Revelation, or Hebrews had *some value* for *some communities* at *some time* seemed to ensure their *universal* acceptance.

Secondly, it seems that the twenty-seven books that were included were found to be, as a collection, *sufficient* for church life in the preservation of ecclesial memory regarding the apostolic faith;[117] others might well have been worthy of inclusion, but such inclusion was determined, in the end, to be unnecessary. Books such as the Didache and the Shepherd of Hermas would continue to be used in the churches as devotional literature; however, it was deemed by usage not necessary to have them included as part of the *regula fidei* (canon 1) and the definitive list of the church's books (canon 2).

Eventually, the bipartite Christian Bible, both the Old Testament and the New Testament together, comes to constitute (in the Christian imagination at least, if not yet as a physical entity) one single "work" or "classic," more so than a collection of "works," which begins to function with

115. "Hermas . . . , in the whole of his voluminous book, nowhere cites a passage of canonical Scripture." Campenhausen, *The Formation of the Christian Bible,* 218.

116. "Hermas no longer lives in the 'apostolic age', he is no longer a representative of the classical era, and therefore he does not belong in a canon which collects and gives binding force to the documents of this primitive period. 'Primitive Christianity' finally belongs to the past, and may not be extended. This is the determining and delimiting principle behind the new Canon." Ibid., 259.

117. I am not using the notion of "sufficiency" here in the sense intended in the Reformation debates over the "material or formal sufficiency" of Scripture. I use "sufficient" in the sense of "adequacy for achieving a certain purpose or goal."

all its remaining diversity as a single norm of the faith.[118] Its emergence from diverse *sensus fidei* approved by the communal *sensus fidelium* constitutes a *consensus fidelium*. The *consensus fidelium,* and therefore, *regula fidei,* which is the final canon of Scripture, in effect, is a common recognition that these select number of diverse *sensus fidei* (senses of the faith), and not others, are capable of constituting, on the one hand, a *single* standard *sufficient* for both expressing the unity of the faith and for judging legitimate diversity in the ongoing interpretation of the Christ event. On the other hand, this *consensus fidelium* expresses the common conviction that a *plurality* of diverse senses or interpretations is *necessary* for such a unifying standard (hence, it is a combined, multifaceted standard).

Ultimately, what are used in arriving at this consensus are "prudential criteria."[119] Bruce Metzger likens this tacit recognition of the canon to the discernment of musical value in the great works of composers such as Bach or Beethoven.[120] An analogous "spiritual discernment,"[121] Metzger claims, is at work in the recognition of canonical value; correlative to the self-authenticating works of the New Testament is what John Calvin would later call the *testimonium Spiritus Sancti internum.*[122] In terms of the proposal offered in this chapter, this "interior witness of the Holy Spirit" is the Spirit's organon of the *sensus fidei* at work in all believers. To highlight the involvement of the Holy Spirit in this process, and to link Calvin's *testimonium Spiritus Sancti internum* with the *sensus fidei,* is

---

118. See Nicholas Wolterstorff, "The Unity Behind the Canon," in *One Scripture or Many? Canon from Biblical, Theological, and Philosophical Perspectives,* ed. Christine Helmer and Christof Landmesser (New York: Oxford University Press, 2004), 217–32. For the history of reception of the New Testament canon from the fourth century to the present, see Hermann von Lips, *Der neutestamentliche Kanon: Seine Geschichte und Bedeutung, Zürcher Grundrisse zur Bibel* (Zürich: Theologischer Verlag, 2004), 119–81.

119. Francis Schüssler Fiorenza, in conversation. For one example of the application of prudential criteria and the notion of *phronesis,* see Newman, *An Essay in Aid of a Grammar of Assent,* 276–81.

120. "If, for example, all the academies of music in the world were to unite in declaring Bach and Beethoven to be great musicians, we should reply, 'Thank you for nothing; we knew that already.'" Metzger, *The Canon of the New Testament,* 287.

121. Ibid.

122. John Calvin, *The Institutes of Christian Religion,* trans. A. N. S. Lane and Hilary Osborne (Grand Rapids, Mich.: Baker Book House, 1987). Bk. 1, ch. vii, § 4. Quoted in Metzger, *The Canon of the New Testament,* 288. Further on "the internal testimony of the Holy Spirit," according to the Reformed tradition, see G. C. Berkouwer, *Holy Scripture* (Grand Rapids, Mich.: W. B. Eerdmans, 1975), 39–66.

already to begin to address the matter of the inspiration of Scripture, to which we now turn in the next chapter.

In conclusion, we have seen how the production and the selection of the canonical New Testament and, simultaneously, the bipartite Christian Bible, reveals a close relationship between the *sensus fidelium,* tradition, and Scripture. Within this triad, the *sensus fidelium* has been seen to have priority, since it is the generator of tradition and Scripture, and maintains the living continuum of the faith. The sacred character of Scripture is fundamentally related to its nature as a product of the Spirit's capacity of *sensus fidei/fidelium.* It is this which constitutes the motor and guide of the tradition process, and which both produces and selects the canonical writings.

CHAPTER 6

The Inspiration of Scripture

In this chapter, I propose, as an explanatory model, that the continuous interpretative and evaluative activity of the *sensus fidei/fidelium* throughout the production, canonical selection, and ongoing reception/traditioning of the set canonical text constitutes its inspiration by the Holy Spirit. We have already seen how "inspiration" was not necessarily an explicit reason/criterion for inclusion of works in the canon, and that, in patristic times, there was a presumption regarding the inspiration of many writings circulating in local communities. Once works achieve canonical status, it is then that the notion of inspiration emerges, later in church history, as one way of retrospectively naming the *canonical* texts' uniqueness, sacredness, and authoritativeness, qualities of the texts which, thereafter, ground their normativity as a collection for traditioning the faith.[1]

Therefore, just as we have made a distinction between "local scripture" and "canonical scripture," a distinction should here be made regarding two "degrees" of inspiration: (1) broad, general inspiration, and (2) specific, canonical inspiration. In a general sense, many works in the first century may well have been regarded as inspired; in this broad sense,

---

1. On the unique sacred character of the Bible, see Thomas A. Hoffman, "Inspiration, Normativeness, Canonicity, and the Unique Sacred Character of the Bible," *Catholic Biblical Quarterly* 44 (1982): 447–69.

one could speak of 1 Clement, the Didache, or the Shepherd of Hermas as "inspired" *sensus fidei.* These works too are the product of the Spirit's organon of *sensus fidei;* they too can be regarded as *sensus fidei,* offered to the *sensus fidelium* for approbation.[2]

However, in a more specific sense, the inspiration of the works of the final canon comes to be regarded as special in some way. This specialness relates to the approbative reception by the *sensus fidelium* of these particular *sensus fidei* and to the consequent ecclesial confidence that this, albeit limited, number of works is sufficient for functioning as a norm for future receptions of revelation: through *them* (the church is claiming) the Holy Spirit links us to the definitive revelatory event, and through *them* the Holy Spirit will guide us to interpret their witness to that event in new contexts. The profession of the Bible's inspiration is thus a retrospective faith affirmation regarding *sensus fidei* which are judged capable of nourishing and norming church life into the future.[3] The doctrine of inspiration declares: God's Spirit has been at work in the authoring and selecting of these writings, and continues to be at work *through* these texts and *in* their proper reception.

The New Testament says little explicitly about the sacred character of Jewish Scripture (the yet-to-be-stabilized Septuagint),[4] but there is a pervasive biblical view "that God is the ultimate source of Scripture."[5] Vatican II's teaching echoes this biblical view when it states that the writings of the Old and New Testament "have God as their author."[6] Nevertheless, in *Dei Verbum,* "no particular theory of inspiration (dictation, prophetic, or ecclesial charism) is canonized and the theological debate on the *how* of inspiration remains open."[7]

The explanatory model of inspiration that has dominated in the history of the church has been that of the isolated and directly inspired individual prophet-like figure, communicating directly God's words.[8] How-

2. In this sense, we could speak of classics of the Christian tradition, such as the writings of an Augustine or a Teresa of Avila, as "inspired" *sensus fidei*—faithful receptions of the tradition, produced through the work of the Holy Spirit's organon for reception.

3. On the doctrine of Scripture's inspiration as a faith affirmation regarding what is a fully human process and production, see Schneiders, *The Revelatory Text,* 49–51.

4. See the classic texts: Rom 1:2; 2 Tm 3:16; 2 Pt 1:20–21; Jn 10:35.

5. Achtemeier, *Inspiration and Authority,* 98.

6. *DV,* 11.

7. John R. Donahue, "Scripture: A Roman Catholic Perspective," *Review & Expositor* 79 (1982): 231–44, at 237.

8. For a survey of historical and contemporary positions, see Raymond F. Collins, "Inspira-

ever, critical biblical scholarship over the last few centuries has gradually eroded the dominance of this individual-prophetic model.[9] In a significant shift by biblical scholars and theologians to an appreciation of the historically conditioned nature of the Bible's formation, inspiration by the Holy Spirit comes to be attributed not just to individual human authors, but to the whole social process involved in the genesis of the individual biblical writings, as well as the whole process of the formation of the Bible as a canon.[10] In further developments, other scholars, rather than focusing on inspiration in the genesis of the canon, have placed the emphasis on the final form of the text and have proposed linguistic and canonical approaches to inspiration.[11] The emphasis is varyingly placed on the text in its final form or on the reader of the final text, while highlighting in different ways the necessary interaction between text and readers.[12] However, apart from general assertions that the Holy Spirit is at work in this whole process or dynamic, and assertions that one's theology of inspiration must cohere with the nature of Scripture as proposed by critical biblical studies, there is still lacking, I believe, a coherent theology of the Holy Spirit's inspiration of Scripture that comprehensively covers all aspects of the nature of the Bible as a historical and ecclesial text, and comprehensively names theologically the specific operation of the Spirit.[13]

---

tion," in *The New Jerome Biblical Commentary,* ed. Raymond E. Brown, Joseph A. Fitzmyer, and Roland E. Murphy (Englewood Cliffs, N.J.: Prentice-Hall, 1990), 1023–33.

9. For a summary of the consensus position regarding the inadequacies of the prophetic model, see Achtemeier, *Inspiration and Authority,* 85–90.

10. On the social model of inspiration, most authors cite as seminal Rahner, *Inspiration in the Bible;* John L. McKenzie, "The Social Character of Inspiration," *Catholic Biblical Quarterly* 24 (1962): 115–24; Bruce Vawter, *Biblical Inspiration* (Philadelphia: Westminster Press, 1972).

11. An example of a linguistic approach to inspiration (but with a significant emphasis on the need for imaginative reception of the text) is Luis Alonso Schökel, *The Inspired Word: Scripture in the Light of Language and Literature* (New York: Herder and Herder, 1965). For a focus on the final form of the text, see the canonical criticism of Brevard S. Childs, *The New Testament as Canon: An Introduction* (Philadelphia: Fortress Press, 1985).

12. For example, see David R. Law, *Inspiration* (London: Continuum, 2001). However, Law's proposal is not comprehensive enough. Although his appropriation of Karl Jaspers's philosophy laudably allows him to focus on the work itself and the role of the reader, he fails to do justice to the historical formation of the individual works and the formation of the canon.

13. James Sanders names the parameters of such an approach, without offering a detailed theory as to the Spirit's activity: "the Holy Spirit [is] at work all along the path of the canonical process: from original speaker, through what was understood by hearers; to what disciples believed was said; to how later editors reshaped the record, oral or written, of what was said; on down to modern hearings and understandings of the texts in current believing communities."

An adequate theology of inspiration needs to give attention to three dimensions of the nature of Scripture: (1) the historical process of its production and canonization, (2) its ecclesial function as a fixed authoritative text, and (3) its reception in history. It must account for the Spirit's activity in each of those dimensions. The following proposal does not claim to be such a full systematic undertaking, but it does claim to propose a model that names more specifically, in the light of recent biblical studies, the way in which we can comprehensively speak of the inspiration of Scripture. The model of inspiration proposed here sees the Holy Spirit to be active through the *sensus fidei* of individuals and the *sensus fidelium* of communities in each of the above three dimensions: (1) as a generator of the reception and traditioning process that produces the writings and the canon; (2) as a "quality" of the canonical texts, as agreed upon *through* a *consensus fidelium,* and functioning *as a consensus fidelium*—a normative ecclesial collection of diverse "senses of the faith"; and (3) as a generator of the ongoing reception of canonical Scripture into the future. The *sensus fidei/fidelium* at work throughout or captured in all three dimensions constitutes Scripture's inspiration; affirming the work of the Spirit in only one of the dimensions is inadequate for a comprehensive theology of the inspiration of Scripture.

INSPIRATION OF THE PRODUCTION

Firstly, the scriptural texts can be said to be inspired because they are approved products of the ecclesial organon of the *sensus fidei,* the Spirit's gift for understanding revelation given at Pentecost.

The process outlined in the previous two chapters can now be theologically described as a process of inspiration. A brief review of that process will suffice. We have seen above that the reception/traditioning of the Christ event involves, first of all, individuals, such as original eyewitnesses (especially "the apostles"), other witnesses, storytellers, compilers of written collections, and the final redactors of the four Gospels, as well as letter writers like Paul.[14] The position of such individuals in their

---

James A. Sanders, *Canon and Community: A Guide to Canonical Criticism* (Philadelphia: Fortress Press, 1984), xvii.

14. "Inspiration is at work down the whole process as respondent after respondent carried on the task of preserving and adapting traditions upon which alone the life of the community of faith can responsibly be formed." Achtemeier, *Inspiration and Authority,* 118. Achtemeier sees inspiration

communities seemingly would have had similarities to those figures whom New Testament writers call the authoritative teacher in a local community *(didaskalos).* Furthermore, the reception/traditioning process involves, by means of the interpretative capacity of the *sensus fidei,* the reception of Jewish Scripture, already acknowledged as inspired by the Spirit. Some Gospel writers may even have seen their own works as a continuation and even completion of inspired Scripture for their communities. The *sensus fidei* is the organon by means of which the Holy Spirit enables these individuals to adapt the Gospel to new contexts and cultures.[15] Their work is the Spirit's work.

Very early on, the apostles themselves played a particularly significant role as paradigmatic models for adapting what they had received to new situations. Such adaptation takes place within a community of whose tradition the individual transmitter has been a recipient. In these transmitters of the tradition, we can speak of a *sensus fidei/fidelium* at work, at once, in both individuals and their communities. Of significance is the element of discernment by the communal capacity of the *sensus fidelium* in this process. Finally, this element of communal judgment is at work in the perception-cum-selection and de-selection of the canon, when, through a process of recognition and approbative reception by the *sensus fidelium,* certain works come to the fore and others are moved to the background, and then rejected, for a variety of reasons.

Therefore, in this first dimension, the *sensus fidei fidelis/fidelium* constitutes the Holy Spirit's inspiration of Scripture because the whole reception-tradition-reception process, from the first encounters with Jesus to the reception of certain works as canonical, is one continual process of ecclesial interpretation and evaluation enabled by the Holy Spirit. The ecclesial organon of the *sensus fidelium* is the principle of continuity throughout that process. The inspiration of Scripture is, therefore, the

---

located in the interaction of three components: traditions, situation, and respondent. See ibid., 109–21. In a similar model, James Sanders names the three elements of (1) hermeneutics, (2) text/traditions, and (3) context/situation. See James A. Sanders, *From Sacred Story to Sacred Text: Canon as Paradigm* (Philadelphia: Fortress Press, 1987). For a proposal to extend the work of Achtemeier and Sanders by means of a reception hermeneutics, see Francis Schüssler Fiorenza, "The Crisis of Scriptural Authority: Interpretation and Reception," *Interpretation* 44 (1990): 353–68.

15. As Achtemeier states it: "It was . . . from the interrelationship of *tradition, situation,* and *respondent* that the Holy Spirit summoned forth the words of Scripture. It is in such a dynamic way that inspiration is to be understood, and, we would urge, that best allows us to account for the way in which Scripture was in fact produced." Achtemeier, *Inspiration and Authority,* 120–21. My italics.

Holy Spirit enabling the *sensus fidelium*'s work of reception of the Christ event.

INSPIRATION OF THE TEXT

Secondly, inspiration is to be attributed to the canonical texts *qua* texts. They are regarded as authoritative texts, sacred to the wider faith community and reverenced by them. In referring to such "texts," the focus here is the final canonical works as inspired.[16] Whereas above it is the organon of *sensus fidei* which is the locus of the Spirit's inspiration, here on the second level it is a work's nature as a *sensus fidei* (a particular expression of the faith), approved by the *sensus fidelium,* that is the locus of inspiration. These works have not only emerged out of an inspired *process;* these are inspired *texts.* This affirmation regarding the inspired nature of the text is a retrospective faith-perception, made in the light of canonical inclusion.[17] This recognition, we have seen above, brings to a new and unique level any previous recognition regarding inspiration that may (or may not) have been presumed of a text. The Spirit works through *these* texts in a unique way, once they have been canonized.

16. However, such an acknowledgment does not necessitate referring to the final redactor of that canonical text as solely "the inspired author," in a historical-critical version of the prophetic model of inspiration. Our examination of the communal nature of the reception-traditioning process shows such a model to be simplistic. An individual "sense of the faith" is considered inspired not only because of its intrinsic worth and fidelity to revelation, but also because the community of faith has judged it to be so. Moreover, the problem would remain for any theory of "the inspired final redactor" of the existence throughout church history of slightly different textual versions of the biblical writings. Which version is the final, inspired version? A helpful distinction is made by Eugene Ulrich, who asserts that it is *the literary opus* which is the inspired "text," which nevertheless may exist in various textual versions: "Canon concerns biblical books, not the specific textual form of the books. One must distinguish two senses of the word 'text': a literary opus and the particular wording of that opus. It is the literary opus, and not the particular wording of that opus, with which canon is concerned." Ulrich, *The Dead Sea Scrolls,* 57.

17. Sundberg's comment, noted earlier, regarding the common view of the church in patristic times that inspiration was broadly and constantly present in the church, is not negated by Schneiders's point: "Indeed, if it had been possible to identify inspiration and/or distinguish it from other factors, the early Church would surely have used it as a criterion for the establishment of the canon. If those closest to the origins of the New Testament writings could not discern either the presence or the distinctive character of biblical inspiration, we can safely assume that it is not possible to do so. It would seem more to the point to start from the other end. The Bible is unique, not because it is inspired or inspired in a way that other works are not, but because of a combination of notes (of which inspiration is one) that makes this book the Church's primary sacrament of the Word of God. *Biblical inspiration is unique because the Bible is special; the Bible is not special because its inspiration is unique.*" Schneiders, *The Revelatory Text,* 52. My italics.

That uniqueness relates not only to the intrinsic worth of each work, but also to their intrinsic worth *as a collection*. For example, the four Gospels, as we have seen above, are four receptions of the Christ event; once included together in the canon, they become four normative *sensus fidei,* normative interpretations of Jesus Christ and of the God of Jesus Christ. We have spoken, for example, of the distinctive perspective of Matthew's Gospel as an expression of Matthew's *sensus fidei.* Likewise, Paul's letters express his distinctive *sensus fidei.* As we have seen, inspiration, in the general sense, may well have been presumed of such texts before their canonical inclusion. Canonical inclusion, however, leads to a retrospective ecclesial reverence for such texts on a much deeper level, which in turn leads to the affirmation that the Spirit is at work in such texts in a qualitatively different way.

It is approbative reception which demarcates the two "degrees" of inspiration. Moreover, that qualitatively different inspiration relates to the new "canonical" status of the work. Because it is the final canonical work which is the inspired text (in the specific sense), so too such individual works are considered to be inspired *only as part of the whole collection.* In other words, John's Gospel is considered inspired because its approved *sensus fidei* is itself normed by that of Matthew, Mark, and Luke (and similarly for the other three). The church judges that all four, together, are required as a canon of the faith. Similarly, for example, the Johannine ecclesiological vision ("you have no need of any other teacher") stands with that of the Pastoral Epistles and their concern regarding "false teachers" of the faith, as the Pauline vision stands alongside that of James in his letter, and so on.[18] Thus, the twenty-seven works of the New Testament, itself alongside those of the Old Testament, all mutually norm one another. In this way, the Bible, as a whole, is self-correcting; *only as part of that whole is an individual work to be considered uniquely inspired.*

This raises the importance of intertextuality for understanding the Bible as an inspired text *qua* text. As we saw in our examination of the relationship of the New to the Old Testament, so too within the New Testament itself: texts refer to texts referring to texts in a web of ongoing allusion. The broad range of literary critical approaches examining this dynamic of intertextuality, including narrative and rhetorical approach-

---

18. For an overview of the theologies and ecclesiologies of the communities "behind" the New Testament writings, see Brown, *The Churches the Apostles Left Behind.*

es, all highlight the endless capacity for this set text (the Bible) to mediate meaning for endless communities of faith, as their "worlds," "in front of the text," are normed by "the world that Scripture imagines."[19] Accordingly, Walter Vogels outlines a "linguistic text model" of inspiration.[20] Likewise, David Law understands inspiration in terms of the biblical texts' function as ciphers of transcendence which the reader appropriates and brings to realization.[21] If divine revelation is to be modeled as symbolically mediated, then Scripture functions within the church as a linguistic/symbolic mediator of revelation.[22]

In summary, it is these literary works which have been retrospectively recognized, alongside each other, to be inspired senses of the faith, because they have been recognized and approved as faithful witnesses to revelation, as revelatory in the present, as sufficient for the church's liturgical and catechetical life, and as sufficient for norming moral and doctrinal teaching. In this way, these *sensus fidei,* as a canon (canon 2), function as a *consensus fidelium* for norming the faith (canon 1). Once canonical, the collection becomes for the church the *norma normans* in the future traditioning of the faith. "This is the Word of the Lord!" It is because of this high regard for the texts as uniquely inspired that the Bible as a book is sacred to Christians, is incensed in the liturgy, and stands in a position of prominence before the bishops at an ecumenical council. "The church has always venerated the divine scriptures as it has venerated the Body of the Lord."[23]

But this sacred book is a book that is to be read "in context," a context wider than its linguistic context, that ever-widening concentric circle of words, sentences, works, and the Bible as a whole. The Bible is the church's book. It is to that ecclesial context we now turn: the reception of the Bible in faith, by individuals and communities of faith, in diverse contexts throughout history, and in diverse contexts throughout the contemporary world-church.

19. See Luke Timothy Johnson, "Imagining the World Scripture Imagines," *Modern Theology* 14 (1998): 165–80.

20. Walter Vogels, "Three Possible Models of Inspiration," in *Scrittura ispirata: Atti del Simposio internazionale sull'ispirazione promosso dall'Ateneo pontificio Regina Apostolorum,* ed. Antonio Izquierdo (Vatican City: Libreria Editrice Vaticana, 2002), 61–79.

21. See Law, *Inspiration.*

22. On the symbolic mediation of revelation and the consequently symbolic understanding of Scripture as an ecclesial book, see Avery Dulles, *Models of Revelation* (Dublin: Gill and Macmillan, 1983), esp. 193–210.

23. *DV,* 21. For the notion of Scripture being "received and reverenced" by the church, see the Council of Florence (DS 1334) and the Council of Trent (DS 1501).

INSPIRATION OF THE RECEPTION

Thirdly, the Spirit's inspiration, through the organon of the *sensus fidei,* continues to operate on the level of the Bible's reception. As "both a witness to divine revelation and an occasion for divine revelation,"[24] the Bible's potential as a revelatory text is realized in its reception. Here we can highlight at least two overlapping dimensions of that reception: spiritual reception and approbative reception.

Spiritual reception of the canonical texts is a dimension of the Spirit's inspiring activity in a fundamental sense: the interpretative dynamic at work in the text's production does not cease in its reception.[25] The history of reception of the Bible over two millennia has inspired a rich tapestry of spiritualities, theologies, saints, religious orders, reform movements, works of art, writings, traditions, identities, and styles of Christianity.[26] The history of theology and the history of doctrine could be narrated in terms of a history of diverse receptions of the Bible. Each reception brings to the fore elements that others may leave in the background; each reception, in its particular selection, is a distinctive configuration of the Christian tradition. No one reception exhausts the full meaning of what was originally given and originally received in revelation: the Christ event.

As a linguistic/symbolic mediator of that event, the scriptural text is only *potentially* revelatory; it requires the organon of the *sensus fidei* to "bring forth" the revelatory witness of the text.[27] The same hermeneuti-

---

24. Daniel J. Harrington, *How Do Catholics Read the Bible?* (Lanham, Md.: Rowman & Little-field Publishers, 2005), 36.

25. See Gabel, *Inspirationsverständnis im Wandel,* 332: "Scripture originated—as historical criticism has elaborated—in a long process, in the development of which traditioned material was over and over again placed in new contexts and interpreted anew. *Reading, understanding, and interpreting anew are inner moments of the formation process.* If that is so, there exists no reason to deny to later reading and interpreting of Scripture the inspiration of the Spirit. *Just as the Bible originated from living, Spirit-led proclamation, so it is intended for a living, Spirit-led proclamation. Therefore, the process of reading, hearing, understanding, interpreting and proclaiming belongs as an inner moment in the concept of inspiration.*" Italics are retained from the original German text.

26. For example, see Francis Schüssler Fiorenza, "The Jesus of Piety and the Historical Jesus," *Catholic Theological Society of America Proceedings* 49 (1994): 90–99.

27. As Dulles asserts: "As a human historical document, the Bible can be read by anyone with the requisite literary and historical skills, but as 'rendering God,' it requires skills of a religious order. To integrate the biblical clues in such a way as to find God in them, we must have skills of the same order, though not necessarily of the same degree, as the inspired authors." Dulles, *Models of Revelation,* 205.

cal capacity which produced the canon and its diverse receptions is required to engage with those texts here and now in order to make contemporary sense of them, by bridging story and significance. Scripture is a text that is to be read in faith; only faith can make revelatory sense of it; faith's capacity for making sense of it is the *sensus fidei*. A faith-reading is a reading "in the Spirit," hence our term "spiritual reception."[28] *Dei Verbum* 12c speaks of the need for an ecclesial reading of Scripture: "Sacred Scripture must be read and interpreted in the same Spirit in which it was written."[29] This receptive role of the *sensus fidei* has certain parallels to Calvin's notion of the "internal testimony of the Holy Spirit."[30]

As we have seen, contemporary hermeneutical theories such as that of Paul Ricoeur highlight the "productive imagination" *of the author* and *in the text,* a productive imagination which then requires engagement by the *reader's* productive imagination.[31] It is here that the application of the text to contemporary context is effected; it is here that the potentially revelatory text can become revelatory; it is here that, when the written Word is proclaimed in worship, the believer's "fully conscious and active participation"[32] through active hearing bridges spoken Word and received Word; it is here that individual Christians, in private *lectio divina* of the Word, appropriate that Word into the context of their lives.

28. Walter Vogels, in proposing a "linguistic text model of inspiration," writes of God not only as the author of Scripture but of God as also the *reader* of Scripture who "reads through human readers." Vogels, "Three Possible Models of Inspiration," 77.

29. Peter Schineller writes: "[T]here must be the ongoing attempt, under the inspiration of the Spirit, not only to understand the revelation in Scripture but also to interpret and proclaim that revelation in ever-new situations. There is therefore a history of revelation/faith that is itself creative. While there will be no new revelations to equal or overshadow the revelation of God's love in Jesus Christ, we can say that every time the gospel is heard and accepted in faith, there is a new revelation/faith event. The same God who spoke through the prophets and above all through Jesus, speaks today through the Holy Spirit." Schineller, "The Wisdom That Leads to Salvation," 92.

30. See John Calvin, *Institutes,* I. vii. 4–5. For a summary of the notion see chapter 2, entitled "The Testimony of the Spirit," in Berkouwer, *Holy Scripture,* esp. 55–57. Citing Calvin, Achtemeier writes: "Unless that same Spirit who inspired the process of the creation of Scripture also inspires its use, no witness occurs. . . . Some further act is necessary before the words of Scripture are able to convince the reader or hearer of their truth. It is that further act which is described as the inner testimony of the Holy Spirit. . . . Without the internal testimony of the Spirit, Scripture remains mute in its witness to the truth." Achtemeier, *Inspiration and Authority,* 123.

31. For representative works, see Ricoeur, "The Bible and the Imagination"; Paul Ricoeur, "Imagination in Discourse and in Action," in *From Text to Action: Essays in Hermeneutics, II* (Evanston, Ill.: Northwestern University Press, 1991), 168–87. For a survey of Ricoeur's theory of the productive imagination, see Jeanne Evans, *Paul Ricoeur's Hermeneutics of the Imagination: The Imagination as the Creative Element of Religious Literacy* (New York: Peter Lang, 1995).

32. *SC,* 14.

The capacity of *sensus fidei* is that ability which the Spirit gives to contemporary Christians, enabling them to engage with Scripture and to apply it to their daily lives.[33] *Lumen Gentium* 12 states that, with its *sensus fidei,* the People of God "receives" *(accipit)* the Word of God; with the help of its *sensus fidei,* "the people unfailingly adheres to this faith, penetrates it more deeply through right judgment, and applies it more fully in daily life." These four active verbs *(accipit, adhaeret, penetrat,* and *applicat)* highlight the necessarily active role of the *sensus fidei* in bridging the meaning of the written Word of God and its significance in the reality of contemporary life and its challenges. Elsewhere, in *Lumen Gentium* 35, the council speaks of the function of the *sensus fidei* in the lives of lay people as they employ it to help them apply the Gospel to the contexts of family, work, and society.[34] Through the operation of believers' *sensus fidei,* the Holy Spirit's work of inspiration brings to realization the living Word of God by making it alive in new contexts. The bridge between "story" and "significance," in whatever context, is the *sensus fidei.* In this way, the universal applicability of the written Word is manifested in its reception, as is its capacity to norm reception of "the faith" that can be salvific for all.

Does this mean we can speak then of "the inspiration of the reader" and of "inspired readings"? In a qualified sense, yes, but not necessarily. Just as it was only after the early church recognized certain works as canonical that a retrospective attribution of inspiration was made, so too it is only retrospectively that certain "readings" of Scripture *(sensus fidei)* could be said to be inspired interpretations, i.e., readings that bring to realization and application the Bible's living witness to salvific revelation. For such retrospective attribution, approbative reception is required.[35]

---

33. John McIntyre's theology of faith and imagination is suggestive at this point: "[T]he Holy Spirit is God's imagination let loose and working with all the freedom of God in the world, and in the lives, the words and actions, of the men and women of our time." McIntyre, *Faith, Theology and Imagination,* 64.

34. *LG,* 35: "Christ is the great prophet who proclaimed the kingdom of the Father both by the testimony of his life and the power of his word. Until the full manifestation of his glory, he fulfils this prophetic office, not only through the hierarchy who teach in his name and by his power, but also through the laity. He accordingly both establishes them as witnesses and provides them with a sense of the faith [*sensus fidei*] and the grace of the word so that the power of the Gospel may shine out in daily family and social life." See also John Paul II, *Christifideles Laici,* 14.

35. Within his own theological-epistemological schema, Congar does not name this activity of the Spirit in the reception of Scripture as strictly "inspiration": "The same Spirit who spoke by the prophets, who is the 'author' of Scripture, dwells in and gives life to the Church; this is the basis

Biblical scholarship in the last century has increasingly recognized the significance of perspective in the understanding, interpretation, and application of Scripture. Different horizons of reception enable faith's engagement with the text: economic, political, ecological, cultural, gendered, postcolonial, ethnic, linguistic. Acknowledging the Enlightenment's "prejudice against prejudice,"[36] we have come to realize how context not only shapes but indeed facilitates understanding, because it is the interpretative framework of the familiar that makes possible understanding of the new and unfamiliar. Understanding always takes place from a certain perspective, and it is that viewpoint which conditions and enables understanding.

However, such contexts and perspectives not only *enable* interpretation, they also *limit* interpretation. In spiritual receptions of the Bible, this limitation takes two forms. Firstly, there are many perspectives from which to view a particular object (in this case, a text). Just as the diverse *sensus fidei* in the canon are themselves individual and particular perspectives, so too one person's interpretation of those scriptural interpretations is only one way to understand them. An individual spiritual reception of Scripture is therefore a limited perspective (even though it may be for that reader illuminating and salvifically life-giving). Even though each interpretation may well be a legitimate one, such diversity can lead at times to a conflict of interpretations among believers, and even to such an extent that the unity of faith can be threatened. Some readings may go beyond legitimate diversity. How does the church distinguish "legitimate" and "illegitimate" interpretations? How are necessary diversity and necessary unity maintained?

Secondly, context and perspective are limiting because all those elements that make up the interpretative framework that enables understanding in the first place (e.g., linguistic, cultural worldview, and so on) are elements that are embedded in history. This is true for the scriptural writings themselves. Historically conditioned elements are embedded in the canonical text, and may, for future generations, impede the faithful mediation of salvific revelation witnessed to in the whole Bible. Further-

---

of the homogeneity of the ecclesial interpretation of Scripture. But whereas the Spirit *inspired* the writing of Scripture, it now *assists:* this makes for a qualitative difference between the two phases, and a corresponding obligation to make Scripture the norm, or at least the negative norm, of all interpretation and transmission." Congar, *Tradition and Traditions,* 313–14. Original italics.

36. Gadamer, *Truth and Method,* 271–77.

more, contemporary reception of the canon may perpetuate those elements and continue to "veil" the Bible's revelatory potential.[37] How can the faith community evaluate readings which attempt to liberate the text and the contemporary reader from those limitations?

Approbative reception is necessary. Contemporary spiritual receptions, as *sensus fidei,* need to be evaluated against certain criteria. The need for discerning "spirits" has always been part of the church's mission, as St Paul's first letter to the Corinthians reminds us. The community must discern which reception is a reception in the Spirit. Approbation by the wider community, we have seen, is a dynamic from the very earliest stages of the canonization process, when the perspective of individual transmitters is always under the judgment of a communal process of remembering. This dynamic of communal approbation continues to mark all stages of the traditioning process, as the canonical texts themselves enter into a reception-tradition process.

In other words, we here come up against the same problem which would have faced our forebears, as they sorted out the writings that would best maintain the integrity of Christian identity, with the difference being that we have the Scriptures which they have given us as our norm, and we have the ecclesial experience of centuries of reception of those Scriptures. According to the wisdom of that experience, and in the light of contemporary biblical scholarship, I now propose that ecclesial approbative reception of Scripture, in the same Spirit in which it was written, should proceed by keeping in equilibrium three sets of three enquiries: (1) examination of the three dimensions of production, text, and reception; (2) application of what will be called three ancillary "rules" for a genuinely ecclesial reception of Scripture; and (3) dialogic reception between what will be called three authoritative "voices" in the church. The dialogue among these nine together constitutes the *realization* of the Spirit's inspiring work of Scripture. Each, in varying ways, constitutes a test of the Spirit, and a test of a genuine "spiritual" reception of Scripture. Since the same Spirit is at work in all nine, each test must be seen in the light of the other eight.

Firstly, attention must be given in the interpretation of Scripture to the three dimensions of production, text, and reception. Since, as we have seen, it is the same Spirit who is at work in the Bible's production,

37. Cf. 2 Cor 3:12–18.

in its function as a normative text, and in its faithful reception, approbative reception of conflicting interpretations needs to give attention to the witness of the Spirit in all three "worlds": the world behind the text, the world of the text, and the world in front of the text.[38] An "inspired reading" is tested firstly by reconstructing the meaning of a text in the linguistic and cultural world in which the text was written. Historical-critical and social science approaches to the text aid the reader in reconstructing the text's intended meaning for the reader's context; liberationist approaches will highlight elements of domination and distortion in the world behind the text which can now be seen to cloud communication of the salvific revelation witnessed to in the Bible, taken as a whole.

In attending to the world *of* the text, approbation of a particular reading will give attention to the set text and all the linguistic elements that constitute its nature as a linguistic/symbolic mediator of meaning. Linguistic approaches to narrative and rhetoric aid a full reading of the text by highlighting the dynamic nature of written language, which can bring forth meanings beyond the intended meaning of the original producers, in a living web of allusion. These meanings too may be liberating or oppressing for contemporary readers, as liberationist approaches highlight.

A third level, the reader's own context, must be attended to in approbative reception. Readers bring to the act of reading their own worldview, which both enables and impedes a reading in the Spirit. As seen above, through the organon of the Holy Spirit, readers hopefully can bring their experience of salvific revelation in their own life as a framework for interpreting the working of the same God witnessed to in Scripture. In such cases, one could speak of the realization of Scripture's inspiration in its reception. However, if Scripture is read in such a way that it is not illuminating, nourishing, and indeed salvific and revelatory, then the inspiring work of the Spirit has not reached its desired end: salvation. Just as reconstruction of the worlds "behind the text" and "of the text" reveals ways in which the text may contain elements that impede communication of God's self-revelation, so too the text becomes revelatory when the *sensus fidei* inscribed in the canonical text is allowed to critique the limited historically conditioned horizons of understanding of contemporary readers. The alterity of the text here provokes a "differentiation of horizons" between the world which Scripture imagines and the limited

38. See the discussion in chapter 3 on the notion of three "worlds" in the work of Paul Ricoeur, and its appropriation into biblical hermeneutics by Sandra Schneiders.

worldview of the reader.[39] The biblical text may reveal how contemporary readers' own worldviews contain elements that may be impeding communication of the God of revelation. Through ecclesial approbative reception, the Spirit brings the light of faith to such blind spots. Thus, approbative reception, in giving attention to the Spirit at work in all three "worlds," seeks to discern those readings which are or are not made "in the same Spirit in which Scripture was written."[40]

Secondly, alongside attention to these three "worlds," approbative reception requires attention to three "rules." *Dei Verbum* 12c speaks of three overlapping faith contexts within which individual passages of Scripture are to be interpreted: (1) the context of the whole Bible, (2) the context of the living ecclesial tradition of the church's reception of Scripture, and (3) the context of the whole of Christian belief. These three contexts already shape the *sensus fidei* with which the reader interprets the text, but they must now become explicit "rules" guiding ecclesial judgment of any conflict of interpretations which may or may not threaten the unity of faith. After outlining in its previous paragraph the importance of a historical-critical study of scriptural texts, *Dei Verbum* 12 calls also for a Spirit-reading of Scripture:

> But since sacred Scripture must be read and interpreted in the same Spirit in which it was written [*sed, cum Sacra Scriptura eodem Spiritu quo scripta est etiam legenda et interpretanda sit*], no less attention must be devoted to (1) the content and unity of the whole of Scripture, taking into account (2) the living Tradition of the entire Church [*vivae totius ecclesiae traditionis*] and (3) the analogy of faith, if we are to derive their true meaning from the sacred texts.[41]

In a sense, these three rules are rules of intertextuality, naming dimensions of the ecclesial context within which approbative reception of Scripture's diverse interpretations is to proceed. Each of the three rules is an appeal to three factors that are themselves the products of the Spirit's interpretative activity through the epistemological organon of the Holy Spirit, the *sensus fidei*.

The first rule is "the content and unity of the whole of Scripture." Un-

---

39. See chapter 3 (p. 81) on the notion of "differentiation of horizons."

40. *DV*, 12.

41. Translation (corrected) from Ignace de la Potterie, "Interpretation of Holy Scripture in the Spirit in Which It Was Written (Dei Verbum 12c)," in *Vatican II: Assessment and Perspectives. Twenty-Five Years After (1962–1987)*, ed. René Latourelle (New York: Paulist Press, 1988), 220–66, at 221.

der the rubric of intertextuality, we have already noted the canonized interrelationship between each of the individual writings of the New Testament, and then, in a wider circle of intertextuality, between the New
Testament and Old Testament. It is only as part of the bipartite canon
that each writing is to be considered inspired. Each writing norms the
others. The whole norms interpretation of the part, and the part norms
interpretation of the whole. In that way unity constantly preserves the
diversity, and diversity is normed by the unity. We have already seen how
the inspiring activity of the Holy Spirit, through the organon of *sensus
fidei,* is the principle of continuity across the whole of the Bible. Now
that "whole" should test the present reader's reception of the text.

Secondly, attending to the "living Tradition of the entire Church" includes attention to the history of diachronic reception of Scripture in
church life throughout history, as the church transmits the faith in various ways within new contexts by applying it to those contexts. This need
to take into account the living tradition of the church is simply a reitera-
tion of an oft-repeated teaching of *Dei Verbum* that Scripture and tradition mutually interpret each other, a relationship we will discuss more
fully in the first section of chapter 7.

Dei Verbum's third rule is "the analogy of faith" *(analogia fidei).* According to the analogy of faith, "any passage of scripture or aspect of
faith should be interpreted in the context of the one, whole, and indivis-
ible faith of the church."[42] Although Scripture is the *norma normans* of
Christian faith, the church's beliefs provide a hermeneutical lens for the
interpretation of Scripture, in a hermeneutical circle of enquiry. The *fides
quae creditur,* the content of the faith, is the "pre-understanding" which
believers bring to the scriptural text, as their faith seeks deeper understanding in Scripture.[43] In a sense, this third rule (the whole of church

---

42. Gerald O'Collins and Edward G. Farrugia, *A Concise Dictionary of Theology,* rev. and expanded ed. (New York: Paulist Press, 2000), 8.

43. In reference to the hermeneutical "correspondence of relationships model" discussed above
in chapter 3, Boff writes: "It seems to me that the basic hermeneutical principle called 'the analogy
of faith,' or 'principle of totality,' or even 'canon within the canon,' functions and can only function along the lines of the correspondence of relationships model. We need not, then, look for
formulas to 'copy,' or techniques to 'apply,' from scripture. What scripture will offer us are rather
something like orientations, models, types, directives, principles, inspirations—elements permit-
ting us to acquire, on our own initiative, in our own right—'according to the mind of Christ,' or
'according to the Spirit,' the new, unpredictable situations with which we are continually con-
fronted. The Christian writings offer us not a *what,* but a *how*—a manner, a style, a spirit." Boff,
Theology and Praxis, 149.

belief) must operate in creative tension with the first rule (the whole of Scripture). Answers to particular contemporary questions should not be sought by applying isolated passages of Scripture, but in reconstructing the "spirit" of the whole Bible in the light of the question. Furthermore, we bring to any such reconstruction the whole history of the church's reception of the Bible in the light of other questions addressed to the tradition throughout history.

This rule of *analogia fidei* too is an intertextual rule, where here the wider context is the beliefs of the church. Not every belief of the faith has been formulated officially as doctrine. However, since the earliest decades of the church, as witnessed to in the New Testament, there has been a need to give finer credal formulation and theological coherence to the content of the faith.[44] From the fourth century on, this definition of the faith intensifies in the approbative reception by the *sensus fidelium* at general councils of bishops,[45] where there is a keen sense of the guidance of the Holy Spirit, with the term "inspiration" often used.

The texts that speak of the "inspiration" of the councils are without number. Even before Nicaea, and in reference to the information given by the New Testament itself, the councils had expressed their awareness that they were working with the Holy Spirit present and active among them.[46]

---

44. On creeds in the Old and New Testament, see Jaroslav Pelikan, *Credo: Historical and Theological Guide to Creeds and Confessions of Faith in the Christian Tradition* (New Haven, Conn.: Yale University Press, 2003), 130–36.

45. To note that councils are an element of the deliberative processes of approbative reception is not to affirm such approbation exclusively of councils or the magisterium. Bishops are among the *fideles* intended in the term *sensus fidelium,* but there are other "witnesses" or "voices" of the *universitas fidelium* involved in approbative reception, as we shall see.

46. Congar, *Tradition and Traditions,* 127. Congar goes on to note that it was this constant guidance by the Holy Spirit which was regarded as guaranteeing continuity with the past: "It follows that the work of manifestation or revelation of himself and his plan, which God initiated through the prophets, and then accomplished in Jesus Christ, to whom we have access through the witness of the apostles—this manifestation continues in the Church, through the action of the Holy Spirit. I have already briefly demonstrated how St. Thomas, for example, saw this continuity, while distinguishing within it different qualitative levels. I note here some more expressions of this awareness of continuity in the manifestation of the truth of salvation, as this is realized, according to the requirements of each particular age, during the course of the Church's history, under the action of the Holy Spirit 'revealing' the intention of God, and 'inspiring' for this the Fathers, councils, canons, and the major events of the life of the Church. . . . Between the time of the Church and the time of the prophets, of Christ and of the apostles, there exists a far-reaching continuity by reason of the fact that a single principle is active, working towards a single, unique term: the Holy Spirit." Ibid., 131, 137.

Such doctrinal formulations were more often needed because of conflicting interpretations of Scripture. These conciliar doctrines then become included among the "traditions" produced by the process of "living tradition," the previous rule.

In a hermeneutical circle of understanding, these doctrinal formulations by the *sensus fidelium* become a framework out of which Scripture is to be interpreted. Doctrine becomes *a* lens for interpreting Scripture; but Scripture remains the *norma normans* for the interpretation of doctrine. We have already noted, in our examination of the reasons/criteria of canonicity, a similar hermeneutical circle at play between the formation of the canon and the formation of a *regula fidei* (short summaries of the faith). Once the canon achieves a certain fixity, this same hermeneutical circle is at work between the interpretation of Scripture in the light of doctrine, and the interpretation of doctrines in the light of Scripture. In other words, the *analogia fidei* plays the same hermeneutical role that the *regula fidei* played during the formation of Scripture itself. Just as the *regula fidei* emerged out of a developing need to formulate and encapsulate the faith in creeds and statements of belief, so too, once Scripture was finalized, the need for such formulation did not diminish. Indeed, conflict in the interpretation of Scripture demanded finer linguistic formulation of belief. For example, in the Arian crisis, the Arians were maintaining that the term *homoousios* was non-scriptural; Athanasius replied that while it was non-scriptural, it was not *un*-scriptural. The credal term was seen to be in conformity with the content and unity of the whole of Scripture, and with the faith of the church, and indeed was deemed a necessary clarification of belief in order to avoid further misinterpretation of Scripture. Ecclesial interpretation of Scripture therefore proceeds through a hermeneutical circle of Scripture and doctrine. This third rule of the *analogia fidei* seeks to name one point in that hermeneutical circle of ecclesial enquiry.

But in discussion of the function of doctrines in the church, it is important to recall that doctrines do not draw attention to themselves, but rather to the salvific reality to which they point, ultimately the God of salvation.[47] Moreover, in the application of this rule of *analogia fidei*

---

47. *ST,* 2-2, q. 1, a. 2, ad 2: "for the act of the believer does not terminate in the proposition [*enuntiabile*] but in the reality [signified by the proposition]." For a discussion of Aquinas on this point, see Dulles, *The Assurance of Things Hoped For,* 33–36, 193. See also *ST,* 2-2, q. 1, a. 6: "Articulus [fidei] est perceptio divinae veritatis tendens in ipsam [veritatem]."

called for by *Dei Verbum,* attention must also be given to a correlative rule enunciated in the Decree on Ecumenism promulgated the previous year by Vatican II. "When comparing doctrines with one another, [Catholic theologians] should remember that in Catholic doctrine there exists an order or 'hierarchy' of truths, since they vary in their relation to the foundation of the Christian faith."[48] That foundation is salvific revelation itself, the *res* to which all articles of faith ultimately refer. That foundation can be summarized under the primary doctrines of the Trinity, the incarnation, and grace. Just as parts of the Bible are to be interpreted in the light of the whole Bible's witness to the God of Jesus Christ, so too that whole Bible and its parts are to be interpreted in the light of the whole of Christian belief, the *analogia fidei,* itself interpreted according to the hierarchy of truths.

We turn now to the three "voices" that are to be involved in the ecclesial dialogue required for arriving at an approbative reception of the rich and manifold spiritual receptions of Scripture. Who does the approving? The primary receiver of revelation is the whole church, and it is the whole church which has been given the capacity of the *sensus fidelium* to test receptions of revelation. Approbative reception therefore must involve all believers. Once again, the passage merits repeating in this context:

The whole body of the faithful [*universitas fidelium*] who have received an anointing which comes from the holy one (see 1 Jn 2:20 and 27) cannot be mistaken in belief. It shows this characteristic through the entire people's supernatural sense of the faith [*sensus fidei*], when, "from the bishops to the last of the faithful" (Augustine), it manifests a universal consensus in matters of faith and morals.[49]

The theological epistemology of Vatican II highlights three "voices" within the People of God that are necessarily involved in arriving at the entire church's approbative reception of revelation, as witnessed to in Scripture and tradition: (1) the *sensus fidelium,* (2) theological scholarship, and (3) the magisterium. Each of these three, the council teaches, is assisted by the Holy Spirit.[50] Part 3, "The Task," will now examine the neces-

48. *UR,* 11. Tanner translation, corrected.

49. *LG,* 12. *DV,* 10 also states: "Tradition and scripture make up a single sacred deposit of the word of God, which is *entrusted to the church.* By adhering to it *the entire holy people,* united to its pastors, remains always faithful."

50. *DV,* 8. Concerning the order of the authorities mentioned in *DV,* 8, Walter Kasper observes: "[I]t is no accident that the magisterium is only mentioned in third place. The ecclesiality

sary *conspiratio* and dialogue between these three voices. The Holy Spirit, at work in each of these three, is the Spirit of Dialogue between them. Therefore, the inspiration of the Holy Spirit within and through sacred Scripture is an ongoing event. Its origin we have seen is the organon of *sensus fidei/fidelium,* and its ongoing realization is likewise the activity of that organon of ecclesial knowing.

To conclude part 2: Three ecclesial realities have recurred in the above discussion—the *sensus fidei/fidelium,* tradition, and Scripture. Authoritative Christian Scripture was seen to be the product of the ecclesial organon of *sensus fidei/fidelium* and its hermeneutical reception of both the Jesus tradition and Jewish Scripture. The interpreting work of the *sensus fidelium* is a reality from the very origins of the church. Once the canon is adopted as the authoritative witness to revelation, the role of the *sensus fidelium* does not cease. It continues to function as the primary mode of the church's reception and traditioning of Scripture into the future. Throughout the history of the church's mission, it will be the *sensus fidelium* that makes possible effective inculturation and contextualization of the Gospel. Through it, the inspiration of Scripture is realized in its reception. The *sensus fidelium* is an ecclesiological reality because it enables the church to fulfill its mission of traditioning the Gospel, and therefore needs to be highlighted in any ecclesiology as the church's primary epistemological organon.

---

of faith is not exhausted by an attitude of obedience to the Church's teaching authority. That authority is situated within the community of believers and under the authority of the word of revelation. It is not a super-criterion ruling over the Church and its common search for truth in lonely Olympian majesty and issuing condemnations." Walter Kasper, *An Introduction to Christian Faith* (London: Burns & Oates, 1980), 146–47.

PART THREE

The Task

Sensus Fidelium, Theology,
and Magisterium

CHAPTER 7

The Threefold Teaching Office
of the Church

The mission of the church is to tradition faithfully the reality it has received: God's self-giving in Jesus Christ, made possible through the Holy Spirit, the principle of that gift's reception. In the church's fulfillment of that mission, the rubric of the "three offices of Christ" names three specific, albeit overlapping dimensions of church life. The specific "teaching office" is but one dimension. However, since it is in its treatment of the teaching office that *Lumen Gentium* locates discussion of the *sensus fidei totius populi*, part 3 of this volume, "The Task," will focus specifically on the task of the teaching office of the church and the function of the *sensus fidelium* within that office, without ignoring the overlap and interrelationship with the sanctifying and governing functions.

What is the specific "task" of the teaching office? The task of the *sanctifying* office is to lead believers to holiness; the task of the *governing* office is to order the life of believers though pastoral service. In this chapter we will begin to explore the task of the *teaching* office, the object of its responsibility, the question of who are the bearers of, and authorities within, that office, as well as the manner in which that office should be exercised if the faith is to be both preserved and handed on effectively. The task, we will see, necessarily involves a dialogic relationship between the *sensus fidelium,* theology, and the magisterium.

SCRIPTURE, TRADITION, AND MAGISTERIUM

In part 2, we reconstructed the early church's oral and written traditioning of the Gospel and the emergence from that traditioning process
of certain writings as canonical for the wider circle of church communities, and we proposed a way of understanding the inspiration of those
writings, a revelatory process which encompasses their ongoing reception
in the Spirit. In part 3 we now examine how the Spirit's way of working
in Scripture and tradition must be normatively applied to the way Scripture and tradition are to be received by the church's teaching office today.
At the heart of the reception of Scripture and tradition remains the work
of faith's organon for reception, the *sensus fidelium.*

The issue of the relationship between Scripture and tradition emerged
as especially problematic during the Reformation.[1] Today that ecumenical debate can be considered to be largely resolved. Perhaps the best in-
dicator of the shift in ecumenical understanding is the statement of the
1963 Faith and Order meeting of the World Council of Churches at
Montreal, which brings to the fore the notion of tradition as a living process of actualization of the Gospel.[2] Within Roman Catholicism too, the
1965 document *Dei Verbum* marks a significant shift away from a static
notion of tradition to a sense of a "living tradition," and a consequent
retrieval of a more dynamic understanding of the relationship between
Scripture and tradition.[3] Post-Tridentine scholastic theology's narrow de-

---

1. For a summary of the debate, see George H. Tavard, *Holy Writ or Holy Church: The Crisis of
the Protestant Reformation* (London: Burns & Oates, 1959).

2. "Our starting point is that we are all living in a tradition which goes back to our Lord and
has its roots in the Old Testament, and are all indebted to that tradition inasmuch as we have received the revealed truth, the Gospel, through its being transmitted from one generation to another. Thus we can say that we exist as Christians by the Tradition of the Gospel (the *paradosis* of
the *kerygma*) testified in Scripture, transmitted in and by the Church through the power of the
Holy Spirit. Tradition taken in this sense is actualized in the preaching of the Word, in the Sacraments and worship, in Christian teaching and theology, and in mission and witness to Christ by
the lives of the members of the Church." Fourth World Conference on Faith and Order, Montreal
1963, "Report of Section II: Scripture, Tradition and Traditions," in *The Ecumenical Movement: An
Anthology of Key Texts and Voices,* ed. Michael K. Kinnamon and Brian E. Cope (Grand Rapids,
Mich.: W. B. Eerdmans, 1997), 139–44, at 140 [para. 45].

3. On the notion of "living tradition," see Congar, *Tradition and Traditions,* 189–221. On the
parallels and differences between *Dei Verbum* and the Montreal agreement, see Joseph A. Burgess,
"Montreal (1963): A Case Study," in *The Quadrilog: Tradition and the Future of Ecumenism. Essays
in Honor of George H. Tavard,* ed. Kenneth Hagen (Collegeville, Minn.: Liturgical Press, 1994),
270–86.

piction of the two as "two sources" of revelation is reconceived in *Dei Verbum* in terms of a personalist and trinitarian notion of salvific revelation, and of this trinitarian event within human history as the ultimate source of revelation; Scripture and tradition flow from this divine revelatory well-spring. In part 1, we examined the nature of divine revelation as God's self-communication to humanity through Christ in the power of the Spirit, and saw that it is this living revelatory encounter that the church is empowered by the Spirit to tradition and mediate. Thus any consideration of the relationship between Scripture and tradition must be subsequent to consideration of the relationship between revelation and tradition.

The significance of these fundamental issues is highlighted in two articles by Joseph Ratzinger on revelation and tradition, in the light of the Council of Trent's document on Scripture and tradition.[4] Ratzinger addresses the influential studies on the Tridentine document by Josef Geiselmann, which trace the last-minute change in the Tridentine draft text from use of a *"partim . . . partim"* (partly . . . partly) formula, to the final version in which revelation is said to be *contineri in libris scriptis et sine scripto traditionibus* (contained in written books and in unwritten traditions).[5] At issue for Ratzinger is one of Geiselmann's conclusions: that Trent allows for a Catholic acceptance of the material sufficiency of Scripture. That conclusion, for Ratzinger, obscures a primary point intended by the Tridentine formulators: the living reality of revelation continues to be mediated in the church by the Holy Spirit.

Ratzinger highlights the influence on the Trent debates especially of the papal legate Cardinal Marcello Cervini on two points in particular. Firstly, the living Gospel is implanted into the hearts of believing Christians; this lived reality goes beyond any of its expressions, even in Scripture. Secondly, there is a pneumatological principle that enables the traditioning of that lived reality *in the present:* "the revealing activity of the

---

4. Ratzinger, "Revelation and Tradition"; Joseph Ratzinger, "On the Interpretation of the Tridentine Decree on Tradition," in *Revelation and Tradition,* ed. Karl Rahner and Joseph Ratzinger (New York: Herder and Herder, 1966), 50–66. The council's first decree, "Acceptance of the Sacred Books and Apostolic Traditions," was promulgated at the fourth session on April 8, 1546. See Tanner, *Decrees of the Ecumenical Councils,* 1:663–64.

5. For a summary of his position, see Josef Rupert Geiselmann, "Das Konzil von Trient über das Verhältnis der Heiligen Schrift und der nichtgeschriebenen Traditionen," in *Die mündliche Überlieferung: Beiträge zum Begriff der Tradition,* ed. Michael Schmaus (Munich: Max Hueber, 1957), 123–206.

Holy Spirit throughout the age of the Church."[6] In this way, the *institutio vitae christianae* (living of the Christian life), empowered by the Holy Spirit, constitutes tradition in the church. "Tradition refers to the *institutio vitae*, to the mode of realization of the word in actual Christian living. In other words, it is the form in which the word finds reality and without which the word would remain unreal."[7] According to Ratzinger, the living reality of revelation (the Gospel), while witnessed to by Scripture, is not exhausted by Scripture.[8] That living reality is realized by reception in faith of the Christ-reality, which is traditioned by the church.[9] Scripture therefore finds its rightful place within the lived faith of the church and its ongoing realization of the Christ-reality.[10]

However, Ratzinger then goes on to narrow the scope of the pneumatological principle he has taken over from Cervini. He equates the authority of the church exclusively with the magisterium, despite having highlighted that it is Christians' living of the Christ-reality in their daily lives which constitutes the traditioning of revelation. According to Ratzinger, rather than the whole church being seen as the organ of tradition, "the organ of tradition is the authority of the church, that is, those who have authority in it."[11] The authority of the church (read: of the magisterium) and the authority of Scripture are certainly seen to stand in a dialectical relationship in which the church stands under the authority of Scripture.[12]

6. Ratzinger, "On the Interpretation of the Tridentine Decree," 53.

7. Ibid., 59. Similarly, in the next chapter, we will be examining the narrative of an individual's life as "the primary mode of the *sensus fidei*."

8. "The fact that 'tradition' exists is primarily based on the non-identity of the two realities, 'revelation' and 'scripture.' Revelation means God's whole speech and action with man; it signifies a *reality* which scripture makes known but which is not itself simply identical with scripture. Revelation, therefore, is more than scripture to the extent that reality exceeds information about it. It might also be said that scripture is the material principle of revelation . . . but that it is not revelation itself. . . . This non-coincidence of scripture and revelation makes it clear that . . . there can never really, properly speaking, be a *sola scriptura* in regard to Christianity. . . . Scripture is not revelation but at most only a part of the latter's greater reality." Ratzinger, "Revelation and Tradition," 35, 37. Original italics.

9. "The actual reality which occurs in Christian revelation is nothing other than Christ himself. He is revelation in the proper sense. . . . This means that the reception of revelation is equivalent to entering into the Christ-reality. . . . It is only the Christ-*reality* which is 'sufficient.'" Ibid., 40. Original italics.

10. "The whole mystery of Christ's continuing presence is primarily the whole reality which is transmitted in tradition, the decisive fundamental reality which is antecedent to all particular explicit expressions of it, even those of scripture, and which represents what has in fact to be handed down." Ibid., 46.

11. Ibid.

12. "[T]here exists something like a certain independence of scripture as a separate, and in

Throughout this chapter we will explore the implications of the openings which Ratzinger provides to a richer understanding of authority in the reception of Scripture and tradition, without accepting, however, his virtual reduction of "the organ of tradition" to the authority of the magisterium.

Vatican II retrieves from the Council of Trent some of these insights highlighted by Ratzinger. In a cluster of statements which must be interpreted in the light of its teaching on "living tradition" in paragraph 8, *Dei Verbum* encapsulates the renewed Catholic understanding of the interrelationship between Scripture and tradition. "Sacred tradition and sacred scripture, then, are bound closely together, and communicate one with the other. Flowing from the same divine well-spring [God's self-communication], both of them merge, in a sense, and move towards the same goal. . . . Both scripture and tradition must be accepted and honoured with equal devotion and reverence."[13] In the next paragraph, the council states that "tradition and scripture make up a single sacred deposit of the word of God, which is entrusted to the church."[14] Indeed, "[the church] has always regarded and continues to regard the scriptures, taken together with sacred tradition, as the supreme rule of its faith."[15] Significantly, this interrelationship between Scripture and tradition is expressed in a more differentiated way by John Paul II in his encyclical on ecumenism, *Ut Unum Sint*, where, in identifying five "areas in need of fuller study before a true consensus of faith can be achieved," the pope lists first "the relationship between Sacred Scripture, as the highest authority in matters of faith, and Sacred Tradition, as indispensable to the interpretation of the Word of God."[16]

The relationship between Scripture and tradition is best understood in terms of the hermeneutical circle. The interpretation of Scripture and tradition constitutes two points in an ongoing circle of ecclesial self-understanding. Scripture and tradition mutually interpret each other. In this sense, Scripture is the *norma normans,* but it is not a *norma normans non normata.*[17] Tradition is normed by Scripture; but the interpre-

---

many respects perfectly unambiguous, criterion in the face of the Church's magisterium. That was undoubtedly a correct insight on Luther's part, and in the Catholic Church not enough place has been accorded to it on account of the claims of the magisterium, the intrinsic limits of which have not always been sufficiently clearly perceived." Ibid., 48.

13. *DV,* 9.   14. *DV,* 10.
15. *DV,* 21   16. *Ut Unum Sint,* 79.

17. On the circular relationship between Scripture and tradition in their production and ongoing reception, and the hermeneutical inadequacy of the axiom *norma normans non normata,* see Boff, *Theology and Praxis,* 140: "Scripture appears as a model interpretation, and thus as

tation of Scripture is to be, in turn, normed by the living tradition which formed Scripture. Together they witness to the "apostolic tradition" from which they both arise. It is therefore helpful to speak of Scripture as the *primary* norm of revelation, and of tradition as the *subordinate or secondary* norm, with the *supreme or ultimate* norm being the Christ-reality, the Word of God itself, i.e., God's self-giving through the Christ event revealed in the Spirit.[18] This supreme norm is not just some *past* event for contemporary Christians, but, as will be examined in the next two chapters, is a *present,* daily salvific reality which Christians are appropriating through the grace of the Holy Spirit and interpreting through the Spirit's organon of *sensus fidei.* This contemporary experience of revelation becomes the lens through which Christians can faithfully interpret Scripture and tradition (just as Scripture and tradition, in a hermeneutical circle of enquiry, provide a lens through which Christians make sense of their contemporary experiences of salvation).

Dei Verbum understands tradition, in its fundamental sense, as coterminous with the very life and mission of the church itself, as a living transmission process throughout history whereby the church, "in its doctrine, life and worship,"[19] makes sacramentally present in human history God's offer of salvific revelation through Christ in the Spirit, that ongoing revelatory event witnessed to in Scripture. Within this tradition process, it is the Spirit, as the principle of revelation's reception, who enables understanding of this offer and brings it to realization as a salvific reality:

By means of the same [living] tradition . . . the holy scriptures themselves are more thoroughly understood and constantly made effective in the church. Thus God, who spoke in the past, continues to converse with the spouse of his beloved Son. And *the holy Spirit, through whom the living voice of the Gospel rings out in the church*—and through it in the world—leads believers to the full truth and makes the word of Christ dwell in them in all its richness.[20]

---

an *interpreting interpretation,* a *norma normans ut normata.* The hermeneutic circle works from the inside out, in the sense that this hermeneutic paradigm grows richer as such through the interpretations that it permits. Its 'letter,' in its very unchangeability, is in some sense further determined by the significations that it has itself engendered. This is the very meaning of tradition. We see, then, that the 'circle' is inescapable. It reappears at every turn in the hermeneutic process. The concept of scripture as a *norma non normata,* then, must be transcended."

18. On the distinction between "supreme," "primary," and "secondary" norms, see Hermann J. Pottmeyer, "Tradition," in *Dictionary of Fundamental Theology,* ed. René Latourelle and Rino Fisichella (Middlegreen, Slough, England: St. Paul, 1994), 1119–26.

19. *DV,* 8a.

20. *DV,* 8c. Flannery translation.

It is in this sense that Yves Congar speaks of the Holy Spirit as "the transcendent subject of tradition."[21] In this sense, "the Holy Spirit is the Church's living memory."[22]

We have seen how this interpretative and applicative activity of the Holy Spirit is best explained through the organon of the *sensus fidei* given to all members of the church. Since the *sensus fidei* is the generator of the reception/tradition process, both Scripture and tradition are the product of the receptive activity of the *sensus fidei*. This reception is constitutive of the realization of divine revelation, as witnessed to in Scripture and tradition.[23] Therefore, the appropriate order when speaking of these three ecclesial realities is: *sensus fidei,* tradition, Scripture. The ecclesial reality of the *sensus fidei* is the prior and more fundamental reality, since it both generates the other two and enables their faithful interpretation.

We need now to examine briefly the origins of the Catholic Church's claims regarding the authoritative teaching role of the contemporary magisterium. They are claims that are best understood in terms of the process we have just outlined. We have already seen in chapter 5 how the apostolic tradition, encapsulating the apostolic hermeneutic, became normative for the early church, and we have seen how the "apostolic functions" of the earliest apostles were handed down in the early centuries through gradually emerging structures of leadership. By the end of the second century, the function of a mono-episcopate had emerged as commonplace throughout the Christian churches. By that time, whilst the eventual canon had not yet emerged, the central core of the New Testament canon (four Gospels and a corpus of Pauline letters) had also been widely received in the churches.

However, as we have seen, the final canon was not so much the re-

21. Congar, *Tradition and Traditions,* 338–46; Congar, *The Meaning of Tradition,* 51–58.

22. *Catechism of the Catholic Church,* para 1099.

23. As Sandra Schneiders asserts: "Revelation is not constituted uniquely by the divine initiative in self-giving. The reception of the gift by those to whom it is offered, empowering a reciprocal self-gift, is constitutive of revelation itself. Consequently, the revelation event that founded the Christian community was not constituted solely by the life, death, resurrection, and ascension of Jesus but also by the experience of that divine self-gift by Jesus' disciples. The experience, in turn, must be understood integrally as involving not only the disciples' interaction with the earthly and risen Jesus but their interpretation of that interaction by which they came to understand the Jesus-event as the Christ-event and their bringing of that understanding to expression in witness, all under the guiding influence of the Holy Spirit whom Jesus had 'handed over' to them. All of this, Jesus' self-manifestation to and in the disciples and their integral experience of and witness to the accepted self-gift, constitutes the revelation that founds the Christian community. In summary, what we mean by 'apostolic tradition' is this foundational revelation in its full integrity as uniquely accessible to us in the witness of those who participated in its original realization." Schneiders, *The Revelatory Text,* 76.

sult of decisions by a select group of church leaders, such as these *epis-copoi,* although it no doubt would have involved such leaders in some way. Rather, the selection and de-selection of works to be included in the canon was a much wider, diffuse, and prolonged process involving "the whole church." However, once the canon (canon 2, the normative list) does reach fixity in the following centuries, it quickly becomes the canon (canon 1, the norm of faith) employed by the *episcopoi* within the church in the exercise of their teaching authority.

Is there any correlation between the emergence of an authoritative norm of faith and an authoritative group for overseeing the application of the norm? Is there any correlation between affirmation of the inspiration of Scripture and the emergence of a teaching authority claiming assistance from the Holy Spirit? According to the Catholic position, the claim regarding the need for a group in the church to carry on the "apostolic functions" regarding transmission of revelation is correlative to the church's claims regarding the normativity of Scripture. As Francis Sullivan asserts,

> If our confidence that the Holy Spirit must have guided the second and third century Church in its discernment of the writings that were going to be normative for its faith, justifies our acceptance of the New Testament as inspired Scripture, it seems to me that we are justified in being equally confident that the Holy Spirit must have guided that second and third century Church in its recognition of its bishops as the rightful and authoritative teachers whose decisions about matters of Christian doctrine would be normative for its faith.[24]

But how should that episcopacy's teaching authority be exercised? In chapter 6, we examined the inspiration of Scripture. The question is now posed: should not the way the Spirit works in the inspiration of Scripture provide the *regula fidei* for understanding the way the Spirit assists the normative teaching authority, the magisterium?

Dei Verbum 10 teaches that there exists between Scripture, tradition, and the magisterium a necessary interrelationship:

> Thus it is clear that, by God's wise design, tradition, scripture and the church's teaching authority [*magisterium*] are so connected and associated that one does not stand without the others, but all together, and each in its own way, subject to the action of the one holy Spirit, contribute effectively to the salvation of souls.[25]

---

24. Sullivan, *Magisterium,* 51.

25. I have changed Tanner's translation of *magisterium* as "teaching function"; I follow Sullivan and others in translating *magisterium* here and elsewhere as "teaching authority."

However, in the previous section of the same paragraph, the text describes the reception and tradition process as one that involves the whole church:

Tradition and scripture together form a single sacred deposit of the word of God entrusted *to the church*. Holding fast to this, *the entire holy people,* united with its pastors, perseveres always faithful to the apostles' teaching and shared life, to the breaking of bread and prayer. Thus, as they hold, practise and witness to the heritage of the faith, bishops and faithful display a unique harmony [*conspiratio*].[26]

This *conspiratio* between the bishops and the faithful remains undeveloped in the juxtaposed theses of Vatican II regarding the teaching office, with some passages giving the impression of a passive relationship between bishops and faithful, and of an *ecclesia docens* and an *ecclesia discens*. A new synthesis is required that develops the council's juxtaposed and undeveloped teaching on the active *conspiratio* between bishops and the faithful.

Just as Sullivan sees the gradual development of the teaching magisterium within the church (as a normative authority for judging application of the biblical canon) as correlative to the gradual development of the canon as a norm for tradition, so too, as I have shown, the *sensus fidelium* came to be recognized as a wider communal authority in the traditioning of revelation. Just as Scripture, tradition, and the magisterium are the result of "God's wise design" through "the action of the one holy Spirit," so too the *sensus fidelium* is the result of "God's wise design," through "the action of the one holy Spirit." An intertextual reading of *Dei Verbum* 8 and *Lumen Gentium* 12 requires that, for a fuller exposition of the inchoate theological epistemology of Vatican II, the above passage from *Dei Verbum* 10 be expanded:

Thus it is clear that, by God's wise design, [the *sensus fidelium,*] tradition, scripture and the church's teaching authority [*magisterium*] are so connected and associated that one does not stand without the others, but all together, and each in its own way, subject to the action of the one holy Spirit, contribute effectively to the salvation of souls.

In the history of traditioning in the church, a fifth factor comes to be recognized, at least implicitly, as a necessary function or authority within the church, a function or authority that, according to *Dei Verbum* 8,

---

26. *DV,* 10. Tanner translation.

is also assisted by the Holy Spirit.[27] The ecclesial activity of theological scholarship also emerges as a charism deemed to be necessary in the ecclesial reception of revelation.[28] While the claim by Hans Küng that the origins of such a scholarly teaching function can be seen in the role of the *didaskaloi* in the early church is overstated,[29] the ecclesial affirmation of the importance of theologians in the exercise of the teaching office of the church is evident throughout history. Just as the emergence of the judgment of bishops as the final authority in matters of faith is not to be dismissed as illegitimate merely because it is a post–New Testament phenomenon, so too the emergence of theology as playing an important function within the teaching office of the church is not to be so dismissed. Just as the development of the role of bishops as "successors" of the "apostolic functions" is a continuation of a communal discernment evident within the churches of the New Testament, so too the task of theologians in the church is a continuation of the ecclesial interpretative functions likewise evident within that New Testament period. Theologians in every age attempt to re-engage the "apostolic hermeneutic" modeled in Scripture, by bridging "story" and "significance" for their time.

In conclusion: The exemplar and norm par excellence for how the Holy Spirit works in the reception and traditioning of revelation is the working of the Spirit within the formation, canonization, and inspiration of Scripture. Consequently, a pneumatology of Scripture is normative for a pneumatology of the exercise of the teaching office. How the

27. The paragraph merits repetition in this context: "This tradition which comes from the apostles progresses in the church under the assistance of the Holy Spirit. There is growth in understanding of what is handed on, both the words and the realities they signify. This comes about through contemplation and study by believers, who 'ponder these things in their hearts.'" Commentators interpret this contemplation and study as a reference to the discipline of theology. Two other factors are then cited: believers' "intimate understanding of spiritual things which they experience" (seen by most commentators as a reference to the *sensus fidelium*) and the preaching of the magisterium.

28. John Paul II, in speaking of the necessary process of reception of ecumenical dialogue statements by the church, notes the importance of the charism of theologians and their assistance by the Holy Spirit: "This process [of reception] which must be carried forward with prudence and in a spirit of faith, will be assisted by the Holy Spirit. If it is to be successful, its results must be made known in appropriate ways by competent persons. Significant in this regard is the contribution which theologians and faculties of theology are called to make by exercising their charism in the Church." John Paul II, *Ut Unum Sint*, 81.

29. For one critique, see Sullivan, *Magisterium*, 35–51. For Küng's position, see Küng, *Infallible?* 221–40.

Spirit's inspiration operates in Scripture is normative for the way the approbative reception of Scripture and tradition should proceed in the contemporary church through the interaction between the *sensus fidelium,* theology, and the magisterium. Through the dialogue between these three "voices," the inspiration of Scripture is brought to realization, and Scripture is actualized as the living Word of God.

JUXTAPOSITION IN *LUMEN GENTIUM*

In the history of the church, according to the historian Hubert Jedin, there can be distinguished five different models of exercising formal teaching authority, illustrating that no one model is characteristic or normative.[30] In the usage of the most recent model and period, the Latin word *magisterium* has come to denote the bearers of the teaching office, the bishops and the pope, as well as all the dimensions of their authoritative function.[31] In the documents of Vatican II, the two major texts directly treating the *magisterium* are *Dei Verbum* 10 and *Lumen Gentium* 25. However, interpretation of the conciliar teaching comes up against translation and terminological issues, and above all theological and canonical issues. In what follows, I propose a way forward in the debate, in the wake of what Vatican II has bequeathed to us in its documents.

30. Hubert Jedin, "Theologie und Lehramt," in *Lehramt und Theologie im 16. Jahrhundert,* ed. Remigius Bäumer (Münster: Aschendorff, 1976), 7–21. Cited and summarized in Schüssler Fiorenza, "Systematic Theology: Task and Methods," 82–84. The five different historical models are: (1) in the early church, most theologians were bishops, with the exercise of teaching authority by individual bishops, through regional synods, and general councils; (2) in the early Middle Ages, an expanding circle of authoritative decision making, according to need, existed: local synods, Roman synod, and general council called by the pope; (3) in the Renaissance period, university theological faculties assumed a greater role, with theologians given voting rights at general councils; (4) at the Council of Trent in the sixteenth century, theologians and laity were invited, and also many of the bishops were trained theologians; (5) in the last two centuries and at the two Vatican councils, theologians were invited and involved purely as advisors at the councils.

31. Congar writes: "In the sense of 'body of pastors' exercising authoritatively the function of teaching, *magisterium* or '*the* magisterium,' seems to us to be of recent usage. It appears first with Gregory XVI and Pius IX, and it is contemporary with the series of encyclicals generally considered to begin with *Mirari vos* (August 15, 1832). It has become common under Pius XII and, although with less constancy, with Paul VI." Yves Congar, "A Semantic History of the Term 'Magisterium,'" in *The Magisterium and Morality: Readings in Moral Theology, No. 3,* ed. Charles E. Curran and Richard A. McCormick (New York: Paulist Press, 1982), 297–313, at 309–10. Also on the nineteenth-century and twentieth-century stages of development of the modern sense of "magisterium," see Edmund Hill, *Ministry and Authority in the Catholic Church* (London: Chapman, 1988), 75–88.

In the words of Hermann Pottmeyer, "Here again, Vatican II has left us only with a building site."[32]

English translations of the documents of Vatican II translate *magisterium* variously and inconsistently. *Dei Verbum* 10 can be taken as an example. Tanner consistently translates the Latin *magisterium* as "teaching function," while Francis Sullivan and others translate *magisterium* here and elsewhere as "teaching authority."[33] Abbott in the same paragraph variously translates it as "teaching office" or "teaching authority." Flannery shifts between the transliteration "magisterium" and "teaching office." The official Vatican website translation uses both "teaching office" and "teaching authority."[34]

Likewise, as mentioned in chapter 2, the notion of "office" is used in the English-language theological and canonical literature in confusingly diverse ways. Part of that confusion relates to inconsistent translations of the Vatican II documents. The Latin *munus,* although translated as "office" when the reference to the *triplex munus* is clear through context, can elsewhere be found translated as "task." Likewise, the Latin *officium* is most times translated as "task" or "function," but also as "office." Confusion is added to the English-language discussion when canon law uses the phrase *officium ecclesiasticum* (ecclesiastical office) in a narrower sense.

But the issues are much deeper than matters of translation. In this chapter, I propose theological reasons for translating *magisterium* as the formal or hierarchical teaching authority, whose official authority is to be distinguished from, but interrelated with, the teaching authority of theologians and the teaching authority of the *sensus fidelium.* The dialogic interaction between all three I refer to as the church's "teaching office" *(munus docendi).* I believe such a usage can open the way to a new synthesis and a consistent theology of the teaching function in the church, in fidelity to *Lumen Gentium*'s affirmation that the *universitas fidelium* participates in the *munus propheticum,* the *munus docendi.*

Our investigation begins by continuing the discussion in chapter 2 regarding the use of the threefold office of Christ in *Lumen Gentium.*

32. Hermann J. Pottmeyer, *Towards a Papacy in Communion: Perspectives from Vatican Councils I & II* (New York: Crossroad, 1998), 128.

33. See Sullivan, *Magisterium.*

34. See http://www.vatican.va/archive/hist_councils/ii_vatican_council/documents/vat-ii_const_19651118_dei-verbum_en.html [accessed April 17, 2007].

The history of *Lumen Gentium*'s drafting is instructive.[35] The decision to place the chapter on the People of God (chapter 2) before the chapter on the hierarchy (chapter 3) marks a shift in Catholic teaching from depicting the laity in a derivative and passive relationship with the hierarchy in the mission of the church. Vatican II now presents a more unified notion in which all the baptized are depicted as participating, albeit in different ways, in that mission.

Initially in the drafting process, the principle that all the baptized faithful share fully in the mission of the church is expressed by means of the rubric which distinguishes the "common priesthood" from the "ministerial priesthood." With this rubric, the drafters are able to highlight the commonality and differences between the ordained and laity.[36] But, as the debate progresses, this focus on Christ the Priest and priesthood soon widens to include another, one could say more expansive, rubric, the *tria munera* (three offices) of Christ as priest, prophet, and king. Early in the drafting, this latter rubric is applied to the bishops alone as the ones who continue those offices, but later is applied to the whole church, and is used to call for a new way of conceiving the common participation by all the baptized in the priestly, prophetic, and kingly offices of Christ. It takes over two years for the council to fully adopt this threefold rubric, while still retaining, juxtaposed alongside it, the twofold theological rubric distinguishing the common and the ministerial priesthood. It is clear that the council therefore envisages an active role for all the baptized in appropriating and passing on the reality of salvific revelation.

The council is clearly and deliberately employing the *theological* rubric of the three offices as one way of breaking away from purely *juridical* notions of the church, such as the twelfth-century distinction between *potestas ordinis* (power of orders) and the *potestas jurisdictionis* (power of

---

35. For an exploration of the Calvinist origins of the *triplex munus* notion and of the conciliar debate and history of the drafting of *Lumen Gentium*, see Ormond Rush, "The Offices of Christ, *Lumen Gentium* and the People's Sense of the Faith," *Pacifica* 16 (2003): 137–52. Two important works in this discussion have been Ludwig Schick, *Das dreifache Amt Christi und der Kirche: Zur Entstehung und Entwicklung der Trilogien* (Frankfurt am Main: P. Lang, 1982); Peter J. Drilling, "The Priest, Prophet and King Trilogy: Elements of Its Meaning in *Lumen Gentium* and for Today," *Eglise et Théologie* 19 (1988): 179–206.

36. See Peter J. Drilling, "Common and Ministerial Priesthood: *Lumen Gentium,* Article Ten," *Irish Theological Quarterly* 53 (1987): 81–99. However, Drilling fails to address the interrelationship between the council's choice of this twofold rubric and that of the threefold office of Christ; even his further article on the latter rubric, mentioned above, fails to address the issue of the interrelationship between the two rubrics.

jurisdiction). The council, in the end, deliberately does not use the latter rubric, preferring to speak of the one *sacra potestas* (sacred power or authority). However, the three offices rubric is intended to cohere broadly with a juridical threefold distinction, that of *ministerium, regimen,* and *magisterium.* This nineteenth-century trio was an attempt to make a finer distinction within the notions of order (related to sanctification) and jurisdiction (related to governance) by separating out the teaching power of the bishops, as distinct from their sanctifying and governing powers.[37]

In the final version of *Lumen Gentium,* these twofold and threefold *juridical* notions, however, can still be found juxtaposed, if at times implicitly, alongside the *theological* notion of the *tria munera.* In the end, one does not find in *Lumen Gentium* a coherent theological and canonical synthesis in the light of the council's innovative shift to use of the *tria munera.* What one finds, as in many of the conciliar documents, is a juxtaposition of conflicting theological and juridical theses.[38] This lack of integration led Karl Rahner after the council to predict "that the council's teaching on sacred power [*sacra potestas*] 'will cause the canonists many headaches.'"[39]

In the face of such juxtaposition, particularly regarding our primary focus, the *munus docendi,* the interpreter of *Lumen Gentium* is presented with a twofold intra-textual difficulty: (1) the lack of integration of innovative and classical notions, and of theological and juridical notions, when chapter 2 on the whole People of God and chapter 3 on the hierarchy are read intra-textually, and (2) the lack of integration of theological and juridical rubrics within chapter 3 itself.[40]

37. On these distinctions, see Mörsdorf, "Ecclesiastical Authority."

38. On the juxtaposition of conflicting theological theses in the conciliar documents, see Ormond Rush, *Still Interpreting Vatican II: Some Hermeneutical Principles* (Mahwah, N.J.: Paulist Press, 2004), 27–30, 42, 49.

39. John Beal is quoting Rahner. John P. Beal, "The Exercise of the Power of Governance by Lay People: State of the Question," *The Jurist* 55 (1995): 1–92, at 27 n.83. Karl Rahner elsewhere states: "[T]his three-fold division is comparatively recent in the history of theology, and cannot be easily harmonized with the classical teaching of canonists on the two powers in the Church, the power of sanctification *(potestas ordinis)* and the power of government *(potestas iurisdictionis).* All three offices *(munera)* and powers *(potestates)* can be comprised within the one authority of the 'creative' word of God." See Karl Rahner, "Magisterium," in *Sacramentum Mundi: An Encyclopedia of Theology,* ed. Karl Rahner (New York: Herder and Herder, 1968), 3:351–58, at 352.

40. An *inter*-textual difficulty also arises with regard to the lack of integration across the documents between two other notions intrinsically related to the notion of teaching authority: revelation-faith and tradition-reception. Firstly, there is a lack of integration between *Dei Verbum*'s more personalist notion of revelation as primary to that of propositional revelation, and

Regarding the first difficulty, having taught that the whole body of the faithful participates in the prophetic office of Christ, when it comes to the participation of the hierarchy in that office, *Lumen Gentium* makes no attempt to integrate that previous teaching with its exposition of the specific role of the magisterium. In fact, as it stands alone, despite the inclusion from Vatican I of Bishop Vincent Gasser's qualification regarding the pope as sharing in "the charism of infallibility of the church itself,"[41] *Lumen Gentium* 25 could very well be interpreted as equating the *munus docendi* exclusively with the exercise of the magisterium, which could be falsely seen to be the primary receiver of divine revelation, a notion that chapter 2 was explicitly wanting to exclude.

Karl Rahner remarks that, apart from the notion of collegiality of the bishops, the magisterium is described in chapter 3 "without any notable advances by comparison with the First Vatican Council."[42] Therefore, when *Lumen Gentium* is read as a whole, one finds what Rahner calls "sporadic attempts," which "remained precisely at the level of initiatives and no more,"[43] to overcome the Vatican I model of teaching authority in the church.[44] The relationship between the participation of the *universitas fidelium* in the teaching office (in terms of the *tria munera* rubric) and the participation of the magisterium alone in teaching authority is not resolved.

Regarding the second intra-textual difficulty, there is a lack of integration of theological and juridical categories within chapter 3 itself, the chapter on the hierarchy.[45] We have seen above that one does not find a

---

Vatican I's primarily propositionalist notion of revelation, still clearly presupposed in *Lumen Gentium* 25's discussion of the magisterium. Secondly, there is lack of integration between *Dei Verbum*'s notion of a living tradition in which the *sensus fidelium,* theological scholarship, and the magisterium are said to be all assisted by the Holy Spirit. This "living" notion stands in tension with the static notion of tradition and teaching authority presupposed in *LG,* 25.

41. See footnote 43 of *Lumen Gentium,* chapter 3.

42. Karl Rahner, "The Teaching Office of the Church in the Present-Day Crisis of Authority," in *Theological Investigations,* vol. 12 (London: Darton, Longman & Todd, 1974), 12:3–30, at 4.

43. Ibid., 5.

44. Rahner notes: "In this connection chapters II and IV [of *Lumen Gentium*] are significant. Here an infallibility of faith is attributed to the people of God as a whole, as also to the people of the Church as the recipients of teaching in particular. The Council itself has not attempted to carry this further by relating what it says in these chapters to the statements in chapter III, where it is the hierarchical structure of the Church which is dealt with." Ibid., 5 n.4.

45. As the canonist John Beal states: "Instead of using the traditional categories of power of orders and power of jurisdiction, the council preferred to employ the tripartite distinction of the sanctifying, teaching, and governing functions of Christ and the Church, which had long been

coherent, systematic presentation of the teaching office of the church in the documents of Vatican II.[46] The council seemingly left for future scholarship an integration between the notions of (1) a single *sacra potestas,* (2) the implicit (but no longer explicitly cited) twofold classical notion of *potestas ordinis* and *potestas jurisdictionis,* (3) the threefold distinction of *ministerium, regimen,* and *magisterium,* and (4) the innovative theological notion of the *munus docendi* among the *tria munera* applied here exclusively to the pope and the bishops. The interpreter of Vatican II is left with the situation stated by Klaus Mörsdorf:

> In theology one speaks of office frequently in a sense that has nothing in common with the meaning of office in its legal usage, for example, when one speaks of the one office of the Church, or of the threefold office of the Church in teaching, sanctifying and governing, which has become the standard principle of division in the statements of Vatican II. The word most used at the council, *munus,* has many shades of meaning. In every statement made concerning "office," one must be conscious of the fluidity of the term.[47]

It was this situation and task that faced the formulators of the 1983 Code of Canon Law, described by the canonist John Beal as "the task of clarifying the ambiguities and answering the unresolved questions left by Vatican II."[48] However, in the end, the 1983 Code has not fully succeeded in achieving the desired integration, despite the statement of Pope John

---

held in disrepute in canonical circles. When the council did address issues of power, it usually spoke generically of *(sacra) potestas.* . . . [However] the consequent necessity of creating compromise language to insure consensus, and the absence of any explicit attempt to correlate conciliar teaching on *sacra potestas* and traditional doctrine on the distinct powers of orders and jurisdiction, all make efforts to educe from the conciliar documents a coherent doctrine on *sacra potestas* a problematic venture indeed. It is clear that the council sought to ground the role of bishops, both in the episcopal college and as heads of particular churches, in sacramental ordination rather than in papal concession alone. However, the meaning of the distinction between the three *munera* communicated in episcopal consecration and the episcopal *potestas* (or, perhaps, *potestates*) *ad actum expedita(e)* is not immediately apparent. Nor is it clear that the council intended its teaching on the *sacra potestas* of bishops as a radical break from the theologico-canonical doctrine on the powers of orders and jurisdiction that had evolved over nearly a millennium, rather than as a pragmatic, compromise solution to a long festering ecclesiological problem." Beal, "The Exercise of the Power of Governance," 16–17.

46. For example, regarding the office of governing, John Beal writes: "The council affirmed the participation of the faithful, lay and clerics alike, in the Church's three-fold mission of sanctifying, teaching and governing and encouraged an unprecedented active participation of lay people in the life of the Church. However, it was silent on the possibility of lay people exercising some share in the *sacra potestas.*" Ibid., 17.

47. Mörsdorf, "Ecclesiastical Office," 167–68.

48. Beal, "The Exercise of the Power of Governance," 17.

Paul II in his Apostolic Constitution *Sacrae Disciplinae Leges* promulgating the Code, in which he notes as "foremost among the elements" incorporated from *Lumen Gentium* into the Code:

the teaching by which all members of the People of God share, each in their own measure, in the threefold priestly, prophetic and kingly office of Christ, with which teaching is associated also that which looks to the duties and rights of Christ's faithful and specifically the laity.[49]

Many issues still require resolution within canon law studies regarding the relationship between the rubrics of *potestas ordinis* and *potestas jurisdictionis,* the relationship of those two *potestates* to the threefold distinction between *ministerium, regimen,* and *magisterium,* the function of "ecclesiastical office" *(officium ecclesiasticum)* within each of those, and the relationship of all of these to Vatican II's innovative use of the rubric of the *tria munera.*[50]

Despite the work that still needs to be done, what is clear is that the rubric of the three offices of Christ applied to the church was an attempt by Vatican II to break away from exclusively juridical notions of the church to a more expansive theological rubric based on three major dimensions of church life and ministry: (1) proclamation of the Gospel through witness, preaching, and teaching; (2) worship of God in daily life and especially through the sacraments; (3) governance for the sake of an ordered and faithful ecclesial life. To that end, chapter 2 of *Lumen Gentium* sets out to teach that all the faithful (bishops, priests, and laity), albeit in different juridical ways, participate in (1) the *munus sacerdotalis* (the priestly office), which is the *munus sanctificandi* (the office of sanctifying), (2) the *munus propheticum* (the prophetic office), which is the *munus docendi* (the office of teaching), and (3) the *munus regalis* (the kingly or pastoral office), which is the *munus regendi* (the office of governing).

There has been criticism of the *triplex munus* as unhelpful for contemporary ecclesiology. For example, Protestant theologians such as Wolfhart Pannenberg have given it a sustained critique, seeing in it a framework that has no foundation in Scripture.[51] It is problematic exegetically

49. *The Code of Canon Law,* (London: Collins, 1983), xiv.

50. For a proposal to do away with the notion of the twofold *potestas ordinis* and *potestas jurisdictionis,* see the doctoral thesis by Laurent Villemin (directed by Hervé Legrand), *Pouvoir d'ordre et pouvoir de juridiction: Histoire théologique de leur distinction* (Paris: Les Editions du Cerf, 2003).

51. See Wolfhart Pannenberg, *Jesus: God and Man,* 2nd ed. (Philadelphia: Westminster Press, 1968, 1977), 212–25.

to ground all three offices in the ministry of Christ, as portrayed in the Gospels; while Christ is interpreted as a prophet, and speaks in terms of the kingship of God, he is not interpreted as a priest. Walter Kasper, while acknowledging limitations of the *tria munera* notion, attempts a retrieval of the framework within his Spirit-Christology, because of its importance for Catholic ecclesiology through its prominence in *Lumen Gentium.*[52] Richard Gaillardetz has noted the lack of integration in Vatican II's vision and the constraints that inevitably come from employing such a narrowly Christomonist framework for structuring a systematic ecclesiology.[53]

My own approach attempts to address such concerns by my proposal above, in chapter 1, of a trinitarian theology and an ecclesiology in which the mission of the Word and the Spirit are intrinsically and consistently interrelated. The notion of the three offices of Christ, understood within such a trinitarian theology, can be reinterpreted in a way that is not Christomonist. Furthermore, I believe that, despite the limitations, the three "aspects" of the church's inner and outer life (sanctifying, teaching, and governing) do in fact provide a helpful, albeit limited, framework for discussing the nature and life of the church, one that no doubt requires other frameworks to complement the threefold rubric.[54] Moreover, the

52. Kasper, *Jesus the Christ,* 252–74. Kasper, while noting Karl Barth's reservations about the rubric, goes on, however, to state: "[O]ne should not expect too much from such historically established systematisations of Jesus' redemptive significance. Basically it is a matter of bringing out the one significance of Jesus' person and work under a three-fold aspect, and of affirming that for the world he is truth and light, the way to life, liberation and service under his rule, and that he is all this in the one Spirit." Kasper, *Jesus the Christ,* 254. Kasper goes on to align the three offices with the Johannine teaching that Jesus is the way (shepherd, pastor), the truth (teacher), and the life (sanctifier).

53. For his criticism of the "Christomonist approach to ministry," which he sees encapsulated in Vatican II's use of the *triplex munus,* and of the remaining juridical notion of *sacra potestas* in the conciliar documents, see Richard R. Gaillardetz, "Shifting Meanings in the Lay-Clergy Distinction," *Irish Theological Quarterly* 64 (1999): 115–39, at 127–30. Gaillardetz states: "The fact remains that, according to the Council, following a line of thought traditional through most of the second millennium, the unique exercise of the *tria munera* by the ordained who alone possess 'sacred power' means that the exercise within the Church of these *munera* by the non-ordained can only take the form of a 'cooperation in the apostolate of the hierarchy' (LG #33). . . . The Council clearly sought to address [acknowledgement of diversity of ministries and the distinctive role of the ordained] by extending the *tria munera* to all the baptized, and uniting the common priesthood and the ordained priesthood in the one priesthood of Christ. This advance was ultimately undermined, however, by an inability to integrate the Pneumatological foundations of the Church into this framework." Ibid., 129–30, 134.

54. "The doctrine of the *triplex munus* notably helps us towards a systematic idea of Christ's work and its continuation in the Church; but it must be observed that there are also other helps

fact that the bishops at Vatican II were employing this rubric to envision a more participative Catholic Church demands that any attempt at a new theological synthesis of Vatican II regarding the teaching *munus* of the church should at least begin with the conceptual opening which the threefold rubric was intended to offer.

Certainly the council has earlier in *Sacrosanctum Concilium* 14, without using the rubric of the sanctifying office, indeed called for "full, conscious and active participation" of all the faithful in the liturgy. I believe that it is this opening which lays the seed for the council's desire for fuller participation of all the faithful in other dimensions of the church's mission, and that their use of the *tria munera* later in *Lumen Gentium* is intended to achieve that purpose.[55] Despite that intention, the council left unresolved the implications of its affirmation of the participation of all the faithful in the governance of the church (the *munus regendi*).[56] Likewise, the council left unresolved the issue of the participation of the *universitas fidelium* in the teaching office of the church (the *munus docendi*). The next section proposes a way forward to a new synthesis regarding the office of teaching in the church, a new synthesis that I believe is faithful to both the "spirit" and "letter" of Vatican II.

THE ONE TEACHING OFFICE AND ITS AUTHORITIES

The teaching office of the church encompasses at least five overlapping activities and responsibilities: (1) to *proclaim* faithfully the truth of divine revelation through the witness of word and deed; (2) to *promote* the effective traditioning of revelation in new contexts; (3) to *formulate* officially, when necessary, the content of revelation as beliefs; (4) to *ex-*

---

to that end—medieval theologians recognized as many as ten offices—and that the three offices, as the conciliar documents make quite plain, cannot be sharply distinguished." Mörsdorf, "Ecclesiastical Authority," 134. For a five-part schema applied to ministry in the church (ministry as formation of community, ministry to God's word, service to the People of God, ministering to God's judgment, and ministry to the church's sacramentality), see the historical survey of Cooke, *Ministry to Word and Sacraments*.

55. See Rush, *Still Interpreting Vatican II*, 81–83.

56. Regarding the office of governing, John Beal writes: "The council affirmed the participation of the faithful, lay and clerics alike, in the Church's three-fold mission of sanctifying, teaching and governing and encouraged an unprecedented active participation of lay people in the life of the Church. However, it was silent on the possibility of lay people exercising some share in the *sacra potestas*." Beal, "The Exercise of the Power of Governance," 17.

plain, through teaching, the beliefs of the faith; (5) to safeguard and *preserve* the deposit of faith, by making official judgments with regard to its interpretations. These five activities and responsibilities are proclamation, promotion, formulation, explanation, and preservation.

Not all of those tasks are the exclusive prerogative of the magisterium. Most fall to all members of the church, and the fulfillment of those tasks is a vital dimension of the mission of the church and the traditioning of the Gospel throughout history. The tasks of formulation and preservation fall in a particular way to the hierarchical magisterium (although preservation of the deposit of faith is obviously the concern of all). *Dei Verbum* 10 on the magisterium, with its three verbs "listens" *(audit),* "guards" *(custodit),* and "expounds" *(exponit),* highlights that those latter two tasks presuppose a prior listening by the magisterium to the Word of God, the divine wellspring witnessed to in Scripture and tradition. It is that listening and receptive dimension which this and chapter 9 will explore. Such listening requires attention to both the past and the present. Attention to the present demands that the magisterium actively promote effective transmission of revelation in new contexts. The magisterium, then, constitutes more than a merely negative function in the church.

Vatican II's shift to speaking of the *munus docendi* in terms of the *munus propheticum* captures this broad notion of the teaching office of the church. In his commentary on *Lumen Gentium* 25, Rahner notes that it is significant that the dogmatic constitution chooses the more biblical notion of preaching when speaking of the primary role of the hierarchical magisterium. With its evocation of the biblical figure of the prophet it aligns the *munus docendi* to the *munus propheticum.*[57]

The prophetic office is more than oversight of interpretations and the formulation of doctrine; it is more than official witness, preaching, and teaching by bishops and the pope. It is as much concerned with effective transmission as with preservation and safeguarding of the faith. The whole People of God is to participate in this prophetic office, the teaching office, in different ways and with different kinds of authority. Lay

---

57. Rahner, in his commentary on *LG,* 25, remarks regarding the bishops' participation in the *munus propheticum—munus docendi:* "It is noteworthy (and important for an ecumenical theology) that the more doctrinal concept of teaching attributed to the bishops as *doctores* is subordinated to the biblical and more comprehensive or existential concept of preaching." Karl Rahner, "The Hierarchical Structure of the Church, with Special Reference to the Episcopate," in *Commentary on the Documents of Vatican II,* vol. 1, ed. Herbert Vorgrimler (London: Burns & Oates, 1967), 186–218, at 208.

people, within the *fideles,* participate most evidently by proclaiming the living Word of God through faithful witness as they apply and transmit and, indeed thereby, preserve the living Gospel in daily life in different historical contexts of family life, work, and society.

The lay faithful's sense of the faith as they do that must be allowed to contribute to, in some way, the formal judgment and the official formulation of church teaching. Discerning this application to daily life is vital for an effective and authoritative exercise of the teaching office, especially when it comes to formulate a matter of faith or morals. To speak of the teaching office of the church only in terms of the official proclamation, adjudication, and formulation by the hierarchical magisterium is, therefore, reductionistic.

In this section, prescinding from the as-yet-unresolved canonical issues arising from Vatican II's adoption of the three-offices-of-Christ rubric, it is proposed that some elements of the way forward to a new *theological* synthesis of *Lumen Gentium*'s juxtaposed theses is to speak of the one *munus* of teaching in the whole church, to cease translating *magisterium* into English as "the teaching office," and to cease equating the teaching office with the magisterium alone. I will therefore refer to the hierarchical magisterium as "the formal teaching authority" or "the hierarchical teaching authority," rather than simply "the teaching office."

Furthermore, if, following the second chapter of *Lumen Gentium,* there is more to the teaching office of the church than the functions of the magisterium, then a distinction should be made between *different authorities within the one teaching office.* Francis Sullivan, following the International Theological Commission, speaks of the magisterium, theology, and the *sensus fidelium* as "authorities that derive from the Word of God."[58] The way toward a new synthesis of Vatican II's teaching on this matter is to conceive the teaching office of the church in terms of a dialogic reception between the three authorities of the *sensus fidelium,* theology, and the magisterium.

Developing Sullivan's proposal, I wish to distinguish further between "ultimate," "primary," "secondary," and "derivative" authorities. The ultimate authority is revelation itself; the primary and secondary authorities

---

58. The phrase is taken from the 1975 document of the International Theological Commission, *Theses on the Relationship between the Ecclesiastical Magisterium and Theology,* Thesis 6, para 2. Text and commentary can be found in Sullivan, *Magisterium,* 174–218, at 194. For Sullivan's further delineation of those authorities, see Francis A. Sullivan, "Authority in an Ecclesiology of Communion," *New Theology Review* 10 (1997): 18–30, at 12–14.

are Scripture and tradition. Among the derived authorities, the church itself is the pre-eminent authority, with the magisterium, the *sensus fidelium,* and theology as further derived authorities within the church, each functioning in their own distinctive yet complementary way.

In any Christian understanding, the ultimate source or Author *(auctor)* of authority *(auctor-itas)* is God, the Author of creation and the Author of the economy of salvation. Therefore, the ultimate authority in determining the teaching of the church is "the Word of God,"[59] variously designated as "the integral and living Gospel,"[60] or simply "revelation."[61] This is both a past, definitive event and a continuously experienced reality down to the present. It is the foundation of Christian faith: God's living Word of revelatory salvation, God's self-communication embodied in word and event by Jesus Christ in the power of the Spirit and received in the power of the Spirit. Revelation is not only what God has revealed,

---

59. "The supreme norm *(norma suprema, norma non normata)* of Christian faith and its transmission is the word of God alone—which has become flesh in Jesus Christ and remains present in the Holy Spirit—and not any of its forms of attestation. For although the word of God is attested to in Holy Scripture, in the teaching, liturgy, and life of the church, and in the hearts of the faithful, it does not (owing to its eschatological character) exhaust itself in any of its forms of attestation. Rather, it generates, in great variety and fruitfulness, constantly new kinds of testifying." See Pottmeyer, "Tradition," 1124. See also Hermann J. Pottmeyer, "Normen, Kriterien und Strukturen der Überlieferung," in *Handbuch der Fundamentaltheologie,* ed. Walter Kern, Hermann J. Pottmeyer, and Max Seckler (Freiburg: Herder, 1988), 4:124–52; Walter Kasper, *Dogma unter dem Wort Gottes* (Mainz: Matthias-Grünewald, 1965). David Tracy likewise emphasizes the relationship between text and event in biblical texts: "Like Judaism but unlike Islam, Christianity considers the scriptures not the revelation itself but the original witness to the revelation. . . . It is the revelatory event and not the witnessing texts that must play the central role in Christian self-understanding." Robert M. Grant and David Tracy, *A Short History of the Interpretation of the Bible,* 2nd, rev. and enl. ed. (Philadelphia: Fortress Press, 1984), 176.

60. *DV,* 7b [*Evangelium integrum et vivum*]. Vatican II is here receiving and reconceiving the Council of Trent's reference to "the purity of the Gospel [*puritas ipsa Evangelii*]" (DS 1501). On "Gospel" as the most suitable category for speaking of the ultimate authority, see Thornhill, "The Gospel."

61. I take "revelation" and "the Word of God" (not here referring to Scripture, which is "the written Word of God") as parallel categories for the ultimate authority. On "the word of God" as the objective principle of theological epistemology, see Otto Hermann Pesch, "Das Wort Gottes als objektives Prinzip der theologischen Erkenntnis," in *Handbuch der Fundamentaltheologie,* ed. Walter Kern, Hermann J. Pottmeyer, and Max Seckler (Freiburg: Herder, 1988), 4:27–50. On "revelation" as the objective principle of theological epistemology, see Beinert, "Theologische Erkenntnislehre," 55–73. On the overcoming of the doctrinal-conceptual understanding of revelation as similar and parallel to the overcoming of the linguistic-objectivistic understanding of the Word of God, see Pottmeyer, "Theologische Erkenntnislehre als kritische Hermeneutik." In his treatment of the reception of revelation, Jean Marie Tillard employs the category of "the Word." See J. M. R. Tillard, *Church of Churches: The Ecclesiology of Communion* (Collegeville, Minn.: Liturgical Press, 1991), 105–44.

but revelation is more fundamentally "*God* revealing," the divine self-giving to humanity through Christ in the Spirit and the reception of that gift in the Spirit. The Christ event was witnessed and received by disciples who, enlightened by the Holy Spirit, appropriated and interpreted that event, and handed on their "apostolic faith" as a treasured "deposit," the authoritative reception of revelation thenceforth for the church. The witness of this apostolic faith is found above all in the writings of canonical Scripture and in its living transmission by the churches. Revelation is the Word of God; Scripture as its primary witness is the written Word of God. As we saw at the end of chapter 6, the scriptural witness functions as the primary authority, but it is an authority that is to be interpreted always in relationship with the secondary authority, tradition.

All ecclesial authority is "derivative" from this ultimate authority, and therefore derivative from its primary and secondary authoritative witnesses, Scripture and tradition. Foremost in the ecclesial authorities is that of the church itself. Since the whole church, and not any authoritative group within it, is the primary receiver of revelation, the believing church as a whole is the first of the authorities that derive from the Word of God. It is this whole church that is infallible in believing; it "cannot be mistaken in believing."[62] In this sense, *Lumen Gentium* 25, explicitly referencing Bishop Vincent Gasser's explanation of Vatican I's formulation, speaks of "the charism of infallibility of the church."[63]

From this primary authority of the church and its infallible reception of revelation is further derived all other ecclesiastical authorities regarding the teaching of belief. All these authorities are called to serve the faith of the church to which they are beholden. In addressing specifically the issue of teaching authority in the church, the three derived authorities which concern us are the *sensus fidelium,* theology, and the magisterium. All three are called to *sentire cum ecclesia* (to sense with the church). In terms of the reception hermeneutics employed here, these three authorities will be referred to alternatively as the *sensus fidelium,* the corporate *sensus theologiae* (the sense of theology), and the corporate *sensus magisterii* (the sense of the magisterium). Each is a reception of the faith from a particular ecclesial perspective. Each is authoritative in a distinctive way.[64]

The official teaching authority in the church is the magisterium. The

---

62. *LG*, 12.
63. See footnote 43 of *Lumen Gentium,* chapter 3.
64. Among other "authorities" in the church one could include creeds, conciliar decrees, doc-

magisterium is called to speak on behalf of the whole church and to speak the faith of the whole church. Only the magisterium can do that.[65] Any judgment of the magisterium on a matter of faith or morals is an approbative reception which expresses the *sensus magisterii,* the "sense of the magisterium." It includes a hermeneutical judgment of continuity regarding the judgments of the *sensus fidelium* and the *sensus theologiae.*

As we have seen, to state that the whole church is the primary recipient of the revelatory Word of God, and that the whole church is the recipient of the principle of revelation's reception, the Holy Spirit, is to exclude from the start any claim that the bearers of the magisterium are the sole receivers of a revelation which they then pass on to the rest of the faithful who have not received that revelation, and that they alone have the assistance of the Holy Spirit. That Christ chose "apostles" to hand on all that he had given them, as *Lumen Gentium* 25 teaches, is not to claim that Christ has given only the apostles "revelation," and that the bishops, their "successors," possess the faith of the church which other believers do not. The early church, in its struggles with Gnosticism, strenuously rejected any notion that the apostolic successors had access to secret knowledge of revelation beyond that which was publicly revealed.

The magisterium's authority is derivative because it is both servant of the living Word of God, and servant to the church, the People of God, who receive that living Word. "This teaching authority *(magisterium)* is not above the word of God but stands at its service."[66] In his commentary on *Dei Verbum* 10, Joseph Ratzinger makes two vital points, both excluding as inadequate the position of magisterial maximalism. Firstly, he states, the function of the magisterium as the formal authoritative interpreter of God's revelation is not to be conceived apart from the whole community of the faithful.[67] Secondly, according to Ratzinger, the ser-

---

trines, dogmas, the saints, the martyrs, the Patristic writings, and certain classic theological, spiritual, and liturgical texts. In the formulation of my proposal, such authorities are to be included under the umbrella category of "tradition," as previous concretizations of the living tradition at particular times in history.

65. As the moral theologian Richard McCormick remarks in relation to the limits of theology: "[T]heologians cannot speak for the whole church. Only the Pope and the bishops with the Pope can do that." Richard A. McCormick, "The Search for Truth in the Catholic Context," *America* 155 (1986): 276–81, at 279. As Komonchak notes: "The hierarchy is not the only instance of authority in the Church, but it is the one which has the chief and final responsibility of direction." Joseph A. Komonchak, "Authority and Magisterium," in *Vatican Authority and American Catholic Dissent: The Curran Case and its Consequences,* ed. William W. May (New York: Crossroad, 1987), 103–14, at 107.

66. *DV,* 10. Tanner translation.

67. "[*DV,* 10] first makes the point that the preservation and active realization of the word is the

vant function of the magisterium in relation to God's word (revelation) given to the whole community has often been obscured in practice.[68] Since "tradition and scripture together form a single sacred deposit of the word of God, entrusted to the church"[69] and not just to the magisterium, service to the Word implies service to the church and its mission of handing on that living Word.

The derivation of bishops' authority from Christ does not, therefore, constitute them, as an exclusive group within the church, as if they were the primary receivers of the faith. The magisterium too must *sentire cum ecclesia* (sense with the church). Its official hierarchical teaching authority comes from Christ, *through the church*. As Karl Rahner states, "the authority of the officially appointed teachers in the Church derives from the Church herself as a whole."[70] This broader ecclesial authority likewise derives from Christ. The dimensions of this twofold derivation, however, are interrelated, as Rahner points out:

[The] derivation of an authority from Christ need not from the outset be incompatible with a derivation of this same authority from the Church. Rather both kinds of derivation can constitute two sides of a single objective situation, because ultimately speaking the derivation of a specific office from Christ is nothing else than an element in the derivation of the Church as a whole from Christ.[71]

Although the authority of the magisterium is a derived authority, it is nevertheless a unique form of authority in the church. Vatican II uses the adjective *authenticum* and the adverb *authentice* to describe the quality

---

business of the whole people of God, not merely of the hierarchy. The ecclesial nature of the word, on which this idea is based, is therefore not simply a question which concerns the teaching office, but embraces the whole community of the faithful. If one compares the text with the corresponding section of the encyclical *Humani Generis* (DS 3886), the progress that has been made is clear. . . . This idea of *solo magisterio* is taken up here in the next paragraph, but the context makes it clear that the function of authentic interpretation which is restricted to the teaching office is a specific service that does not embrace the whole of the way in which the word is present, and in which it performs an irreplaceable function precisely for the whole Church, the bishops and laity together." Joseph Ratzinger, "Dogmatic Constitution of Divine Revelation: Origin and Background," in *Commentary on the Documents of Vatican II,* vol. 3, ed. H. Vorgrimler (New York: Herder, 1969), 196.

68. Once again, contrasting *DV,* 10 with *Humani Generis* (DS 3886), Ratzinger notes: "For the first time a text of the teaching office expressly points out the subordination of the teaching office to the word, e.g., its function as a servant. One can say, it is true, there could never have been any serious doubt that this was in fact the case. Nevertheless the actual procedure often tended somewhat to obscure this order of things, though it had always been acknowledged in principle." Ibid., 197.

69. *DV,* 10. Tanner translation.

70. Rahner, "The Teaching Office of the Church," 6.

71. Ibid., at 7.

of its teaching because of its origin in the commission of Christ. Bishops are "authoritative teachers *(doctores authentici),* that is, teachers endowed with the authority of Christ."[72] They teach "authoritatively *(authentice)*"[73] in matters of faith and morals (meaning matters related to the content of revelation). Theirs alone is "the task of authoritatively interpreting the word of God *(munus authentice interpretanda verbum Dei)*."[74] In commenting on the significance of translating *authenticum* and *authentice* as "authoritative" and "authoritatively," Sullivan remarks:

> If this meaning of *authentice* is not kept in mind, one could think that the Council was making the absurd claim that only bishops could give a genuine interpretation of the Word of God, or that they were the only ones who would interpret Scripture or Tradition with any kind of authority at all. The Council surely did not intend to deny that theologians and exegetes speak with the authority which their expertise confers on them. What the Council attributes exclusively to the "living magisterium" is authority to speak as pastors of the Church, endowed with the mandate to teach the Gospel in the name of Jesus Christ.[75]

The next authority under the Word of God is the *sensus fidelium.* In a sense, the *sensus fidelium* is pre-eminent among these derived authorities because it is here, in the lives of the faithful, that the Word of God is lived, and therefore, expressed. "Ordinary believers, when they articulate their faith, do have a real teaching authority, which comes from their dignity as recipients of God's prime revelation."[76] Scripture is nothing but the expression of the *sensus fidelium* of the apostolic era; tradition is nothing but the *sensus fidelium* bringing revelation to expression throughout history. Under the Word of God, the *sensus fidelium* of all generations beyond that apostolic era forever remains a *locus theologicus* in the church's search for truthful and meaningful expression of revelation, because the salvific revelation witnessed to in Scripture and tradi-

---

72. *LG,* 25. As Sullivan persuasively argues, *authenticum* is more appropriately translated as "authoritative" and *authentice* as "authoritatively." "In my opinion it is unfortunate that the translators of these documents have rendered the Latin *authenticum* and *authentice* by the English 'authentic' and 'authentically.' For the word 'authentic' in modern English means 'genuine.' It did once mean 'authoritative,' 'entitled to obedience,' but this meaning is now obsolete. And the fact is that what is now an obsolete meaning of the English 'authentic,' is the correct meaning of the Latin 'authenticum.' In other words, the correct translation would not be 'authentic' but 'authoritative.'" Sullivan, *Magisterium,* 27.

73. *LG,* 25.   74. *DV,* 10.

75. Sullivan, *Magisterium,* 28.

76. Vorgrimler, "From *Sensus Fidei* to *Consensus Fidelium,*" 8.

tion is to be found pre-eminently realized in the concrete experience of salvific revelation in human lives in diverse contexts. If Scripture and tradition encapsulate the faith as lived in a normative period in the past, the *sensus fidelium* encapsulates the faith as lived in the present.

The magisterium's reception of the *sensus fidelium,* in the exercise of its formal authority, is demanded primarily by the fundamental theological truth that the faith which the pope and his fellow bishops proclaim is the faith of the whole church. As has already been stated, any Gnostic notion of the apostles (and, therefore, their successors, the bishops) as the sole possessors of secret knowledge about God which the rest of the faithful do not possess has, since apostolic times, been fiercely resisted by the church. It is, however, a notion which can easily resurface in maximalist distortions of the magisterium's authority.

The predominant neo-scholastic model of the nineteenth century portrayed the laity (and therefore the *sensus laicorum*) as the *ecclesia discens* (the learning church) and of the magisterium (and therefore the *sensus magisterii*) as the *ecclesia docens* (the teaching church). Vatican II proposed a fundamental ecclesiological shift beyond that model. However, one could say that there is in the exercise of the teaching office an ecclesial rhythm in which, at some moments, the magisterium is the *ecclesia docens* and the *sensus fidelium* (now not simply the *sensus laicorum*) is the *ecclesia discens.* There are moments also when the magisterium is called to be a listening and learning body of teachers, a *magisterium discens.* Such a rhythm needs to be understood in terms of a *communio/receptio* ecclesiology. The previous division of the church between a passive laity and an active formal teaching authority is not to be reversed to the opposite extreme whereby the magisterium is seen to be a merely passive receiver of the *sensus fidelium,* even though it is the faith of the whole People of God which the bishops must teach. According to Wolfgang Beinert, a more subtle rhythm is needed.

To the extent that the magisterium does not establish the faith but preserves and communicates it as handed down by the community, it is subordinate to the *sensus fidelium;* to the extent, on the other hand, that the magisterium possesses its own apostolic commission to provide authentic interpretation and issue final decisions in matters of faith, it takes precedence over the *sensus fidelium* and ranks higher.[77]

77. Beinert, "Sensus Fidelium," 656–57.

The authorities of the *sensus fidelium* and the *sensus magisterii* both, under certain conditions, bring to expression the church's infallibility. This infallibility itself finds expression in two forms, an infallibility in believing and an infallibility in teaching. These two modalities *together* are expressions of the church's indefectibility.[78] On the interrelationship between both modalities of infallibility, Rahner states:

On any fully Catholic understanding of the Church the believing Church is not merely constituted as such by the factor of teaching authority [the magisterium]. On the contrary for authority of this sort to be able to exist at all a believing Church has already to be in existence as its necessary prior condition.[79]

This active believing, this active application of the faith to daily life, constitutes, Rahner goes on to assert, a vital dimension of the church's official teaching function:

The de facto bearers of the teaching office are, at least in respect of the content of their teaching, dependent upon a Church who is not constituted simply by the one-sided functions of the official authorities in the church. This faith, this history of faith, this development of dogma on which the teaching office depends in the concrete, are factors to which all the members of the Church contribute, each in his own way, by their lives, the confession of their faith, their prayers, their concrete decisions, the theology which they work out for themselves, and their activities in all this are very far from being confined merely to putting into practice truths and norms deriving from the teaching office itself.[80]

As we have seen, Vatican II teaches that the authority of the whole church derives directly from Christ; with regard to the authority to teach, it states that the *universitas fidelium* participates in the prophetic office of Christ. It is within this context that *Lumen Gentium* 12 discusses the *supernaturalis sensus fidei totius populi* [the *sensus fidei fidelium*]. The sense of the faith of the whole People of God, the primary receiver of "the faith," is an authority that likewise derives both from Christ and from the church as a whole.

However, the relationship between these two authorities in the church, the *sensus fidelium* and the magisterium, is left unresolved by Vatican II and still, after more than forty years since the close of the council, remains an issue requiring a new theological synthesis. The nature of these

78. On the church's indefectibility, see Sullivan, *Magisterium*, 4–11.
79. Rahner, "The Teaching Office of the Church," 7.
80. Ibid., 8.

two authorities becomes important in any explication of the infallibility that attaches to the discernment of these two authorities: an infallibility in believing when the *sensus fidelium* is seen to manifest a *consensus fidelium,* and an infallibility in teaching when the magisterium, under certain conditions, defines that *consensus* regarding a particular matter of faith or morals.

There is a third authority which derives from the Word of God, that of theology. Theology too, as an authority functioning within the prophetic (teaching) office of the church, is an authority which is constituted by virtue of its assistance by the Holy Spirit.

In order to exercise the prophetic function in the world, the People of God must continually reawaken or "rekindle" its own life of faith. It does this particularly by contemplating ever more deeply, under the guidance of the Holy Spirit, the contents of the faith itself and by dutifully presenting the reasonableness of the faith to those who ask for an account of it. For the sake of this mission, the Spirit of truth distributes among the faithful of every rank special graces "for the common good." Among the vocations awakened in this way by the Spirit in the Church is that of the theologian.[81]

Theology too, as the "contemplation and study by believers, who 'ponder these things in their hearts,'" is, according to *Dei Verbum* 8b, given "the assistance of the Holy Spirit."

In the exercise of its ecclesial function, theology has a special relationship with the hierarchical magisterium.[82] Although some have made a distinction between two *magisteria* in the church (the hierarchy and theologians), in a retrieval of Thomas Aquinas's distinction between the *magisterium cathedrae pastoralis* and the *magisterium cathedrae magistralis,*[83] I agree with scholars such as Sullivan and Gaillardetz who think that talk of theologians as "a second magisterium" blurs the distinction between

---

81. Congregation for the Doctrine of the Faith, *Instruction on the Ecclesial Vocation of the Theologian* (Vatican City: St. Paul Books and Media, 1990), para 5–6.

82. On different conceptions of the relationship between theology and the magisterium, see Anthony J. Figueiredo, *The Magisterium-Theology Relationship: Contemporary Theological Conceptions in the Light of Universal Church Teaching since 1835 and the Pronouncements of the Bishops of the United States* (Rome: Editrice Pontificia Università Gregoriana, 2001).

83. Aquinas's distinction can be found in IV *Sent.* D. 19, q. 2, a. 2, q² 2 ad 4 and *Quodlibet* III, 9 ad 3. On the two magisteria, see Avery Dulles, "The Two Magisteria: An Interim Reflection," *CTSA Proceedings* 35 (1980): 155–69. See also Congar, "A Semantic History of the Term 'Magisterium'"; Avery Dulles, "Doctrinal Authority for a Pilgrim Church," in Curran and McCormick, eds., *The Magisterium and Morality,* 247–70, at 259–61.

these two different kinds of authority in the church and sets up an alternative formal body for official adjudication and formulation of belief.[84] Just as the authority of the magisterium is a dimension of the one authority of the whole church deriving from the authority of the Word of God, so too is the specific authority of theologians. However, although I avoid *the term* magisterium in reference to theology and of two magisteria, I do believe it is helpful to speak of these as *two teaching authorities* within the *one teaching office (munus docendi)* of the church. Both are authorities which derive from the Word of God: the formal authority of the hierarchical magisterium and the scholarly authority of theologians and experts in associated disciplines, such as biblical studies and history. Sullivan refers to them as having two distinct "charisms of teaching."[85]

Theology as an academic discipline (with all its subdisciplines) provides a vital service to the magisterium. The history of theology and the history of doctrine demonstrate the close link between the theological scholarship of a particular period and the reception of that theological work by the official formulators of doctrine at that time. Although all theology is not official doctrine, all doctrine is necessarily expressed in the theological language of a particular period. The magisterium looks to theologians for language and concepts with which it can answer new questions addressed to the tradition or simply to express the ancient faith afresh for a new age.

Theology, for its part, is not the official voice for the faith of the whole church; that is the function of the magisterium. Theologians necessarily defer to the judgment of the magisterium, while at the same time continuing their work of *ressourcement* and *aggiornamento:* reinterpreting the sources of the faith, in order to express the faith more cogently within the theologian's own context.

84. See Sullivan, *Magisterium*, 29. Likewise, Richard Gaillardetz believes that "in practice this broader usage is likely to blur the distinctive teaching roles of theologians and the college of bishops." Gaillardetz, *Teaching with Authority,* 161. Richard McCormick similarly asserts: "*To acknowledge the public and critical role of theology is not to espouse two magisteria.* This statement is meant to meet head-on those who reject any pubic dissent as equivalent to espousing a second magisterium. That is, with all due respect, a red herring. Two different competences do not two magisteria make. Both competences—scholars and the magisterium—must relate healthily, even if not without tension, if the church's teaching office is to be credible and effective." McCormick, "The Search for Truth in the Catholic Context," 280. Original italics.

85. "I would say that there are at least two distinct charisms of teaching in the Church: the charism of scholarly teaching such as theologians exercise in the university lecture hall, and the charism of pastoral teaching, such as the bishops exercised at the Second Vatican Council. Indeed, the success of this council was due in large measure to the happy collaboration of these two charisms, each making its own distinctive contribution." Sullivan, *Magisterium*, 45–46.

Therefore, theology exists both in a dependent and in a somewhat autonomous relationship with the magisterium. Its dependence marks its nature as an ecclesial discipline; its autonomy marks its nature as an academic discipline. The tension that results from that special kind of relationship is necessary for effective evangelization and fulfillment of the mission of the church. In this way, theology has its own unique role to play in the transmission of revelation, and therefore speaks with a specific authority, yet in dialogic communion with the formal authority of the magisterium.[86]

Theology's function is not merely to explain and pass on to the faithful the decisions of the magisterium, although that is one aspect of its ecclesial role. The faithful are not only a target of theology's work; they are a primary source for theologizing. Contemporary positive experiences of salvation or negative experiences (what Edward Schillebeeckx calls "contrast experiences")[87] constitute fundamental sources and contexts for theological reflection. Theology's *ressourcement* of the sources of revelation is not restricted to the documents and practices of the past, although Scripture is "the soul of theology."[88] For the sake of *aggiornamento,* theology also engages in *ressourcement* of the present through reading the signs of the times. The God witnessed to in Scripture and tradition is known in the present. The present times and the present praxis of the Christian faith therefore should be a hermeneutical lens through which the God experienced in the past is interpreted. Theology's *loci* for enquiry include the salvific and revelatory work of God in the concrete lives

---

86. Ratzinger, again on *DV,* 10, comments: "To reduce the task of theology to the proof of the presence of the statements of the teaching office in the sources is to threaten the primacy of the sources which (were one to continue logically in this direction) would ultimately destroy the serving character of the teaching office. When seen against this background, the explicit emphasis on the ministerial function of the teaching office must be welcomed as warmly as the statement that its primary service is to listen, that it must constantly take up an attitude of openness towards the sources, which it has continually to consult and consider, in order to be able to interpret them truly and preserve them." Ratzinger, "Dogmatic Constitution of Divine Revelation," 197. On the magisterium and theology, Pope Paul VI teaches: "In the area of divine doctrine, there is but one primacy: the primacy of revealed truth, of faith, which both theology and the church's magisterium desire to support unanimously in their different ways." Quoted in Walter Principe, "Changing Church Teachings," *Grail: An Ecumenical Journal* 6 (1990): 13–40, at 25.

87. The notion of "contrast experience," adopted from Theodor Adorno, recurs throughout the later writings of Edward Schillebeeckx. For example, see Schillebeeckx, *Jesus,* 612–25.

88. *DV,* 24. See Joseph A. Fitzmyer, *Scripture: The Soul of Theology* (New York: Paulist Press, 1994); Gerald O'Collins and Daniel Kendall, *The Bible for Theology: Ten Principles for the Theological Use of Scripture* (New York: Paulist Press, 1997); William M. Thompson, *The Struggle for Theology's Soul: Contesting Scripture in Christology* (New York: Crossroad Herder, 1996).

of human beings in the present (or negatively, the ways in which God's reign is being impeded in the present). The *vitae fidelium* (the lives of the faithful), and "the joys and hopes, and the sorrows and anxieties of people today," "these are the concerns of the church," and therefore the concerns of theology.[89]

Theology thus has an intrinsic connection with the *sensus fidelium,* which, because it is expressive of salvific and revelatory experiences (or otherwise), is the starting point for theological reflection.[90] In searching to interpret the work of God in the present, theology's sourcing of the *vitae fidelium,* and the multifaceted context of those lives, is not a sourcing of "raw," "uninterpreted" data. God's salvific and revelatory presence is already being interpreted by individuals and communities. Through their *sensus fidei* they are making "theological sense" of their lives. Therefore, in tapping into the many senses of the faith within a community, a theologian's theologizing has already been started. As we will examine in the next chapter, through the interpretative activity of an individual's *sensus fidei,* the Gospel is being incarnated in particular ways in diverse contexts and cultures. Inculturation and contextualization are not the exclusive preserve of expert theologians. The necessary *aggiornamento* of the Gospel takes place daily in the lives of believing communities. It is theology's task to be attentive to that work of *aggiornamento,* to listen to it, to test it against the sources of the past (Scripture and tradition), to bring its diversity into a systematic whole, and to offer it back to the community of faith for the sake of its deeper understanding, interpretation, and application of the faith.

There exists, therefore, a dialogical relationship between the lived faith of the whole people, the work of theology, and the work of the magisterium.[91] The search for orthodoxy in the teaching of the church is necessarily a process of ecclesial dialogue.[92] For the sake of achieving a new theological synthesis of the inchoate theological epistemology and pneu-

---

89. *GS,* 1. Tanner translation.

90. On "praxis" as a starting point for theological reflection, see Juan Luis Segundo, *Liberation of Theology* (Maryknoll, N.Y.: Orbis Books, 1976). On retroductive warrants and praxis as a retroductive warrant in theological method, see Schüssler Fiorenza, *Foundational Theology,* esp. 306–10; Schüssler Fiorenza, "Systematic Theology: Task and Methods," esp. 77–80.

91. For a fuller discussion of this "triangular relationship," with a helpful graphic representation (244), see Gaillardetz, *Teaching with Authority,* 227–54.

92. On the need for "a new form of ecclesial authority" and a new understanding of "orthodoxy regarded as a process based on dialogue," see Kasper, *An Introduction to Christian Faith,* 149–50.

matology of Vatican II, the following further expansion of *Dei Verbum* 10, already expanded earlier to include the *sensus fidelium,* is legitimate, I propose, in light of the spirit and letter of the council and all its documents:

Thus it is clear that, by God's wise design, [the *sensus fidelium,*] tradition, scripture, [theology,] and the church's *magisterium* are so connected and associated that one does not stand without the others, but all together, and each in its own way, subject to the action of the one holy Spirit, contribute effectively to the salvation of souls.

In the one teaching office of the church, these three authorities must be interrelated if the formal teaching of the magisterium is to be "authoritative," and received as such. It is to an examination of such "effective authority" that we now turn.

TEACHING WITH AUTHORITY

Contemporary discussion of what constitutes the effective exercise of authority within any group generally includes the related aspects of legitimation, authorization, credibility, power, competence, consultation, participation, communication, subsidiarity, and leadership. These issues likewise arise when addressing the question of the effective exercise of the teaching office in the church. This section proposes that the teaching office will teach "with authority" if it fulfills at least two requirements: that all the three authorities under the Word of God participate and are seen to participate in the exercise of that office, and that all three authorities relate to one another according to the style of church called for by Vatican II.

Some have called for the incorporation of democratic processes into the life of the church as a legitimate way in which such participation can be practically realized.[93] Oftentimes such calls for democracy are reject-

---

93. The literature on democracy in the church is extensive. Only representative works can be cited here. Two volumes of the journal *Concilium,* entitled *Democratization of the Church* 3 (1971) and *The Tabu of Democracy in the Church* 5 (1992); Eugene C. Bianchi and Rosemary Radford Ruether, eds., *A Democratic Catholic Church: The Reconstruction of Roman Catholicism* (New York: Crossroad, 1992); Siegfried Wiedenhofer, "Sensus fidelium—Demokratisierung der Kirche?" in *Surrexit Dominus Vere: Die Gegenwart des Auferstandenen in seiner Kirche,* ed. J. Ernst and S. Leimgruber (Paderborn: 1995), 457–71; Siegfried Wiedenhofer; "Synodalität und Demokratisierung der Kirche aus dogmatische Perspektive," in *Demokratische Prozesse in dem Kirchen? Konzilien, Synoden, Räte, Theologie im kulturenllen Dialog* (Graz: Styria Verlag, 1998), 73–99; Siegfried

ed, generally invoking the maxim: "the church is not a democracy." To such rejections, Richard McCormick retorts:

> Yes, yes, of course the church is not a democracy. Left unsaid in that sweeping put-down is that the nondemocratic church would have inflicted far fewer self-wounds had it made use of some democratic procedures in its teaching-learning processes.[94]

The church is not a democracy. Nor is it an autocracy, a dictatorship (benevolent or otherwise), an oligarchy, a monarchy. The nature of the church, as the People of God, the Body of Christ, and the Temple of the Holy Spirit, is a unique divine and human community. The church in every age, however, has always assumed aspects of the human models of governance at work in the society around it. Christians in the twenty-first century, in their promotion of democracy within wider human society, might well have expectations that such processes could contribute to the betterment of governance within the church. Such expectations relate to the teaching office's ability to teach "with authority."

When discussion turns to the exercise of the teaching office, we encounter a certain overlap between the office of teaching and the office of governance. That overlap highlights the special authority of the magisterium in the teaching office of the church which distinguishes it from the other two authorities, i.e., its exercise of communal oversight and final judgment in interpreting and formulating matters of faith and morals. We have already seen that, theologically, the three authorities of the *sensus fidelium,* theology, and the magisterium are to be interrelated in the one teaching office. In this section, we will address the further issue of the style of governance of the magisterium in exercising its authority, and of the necessary interrelationship of the three authorities for the sake of both faithful and effective teaching.

A number of questions arise to guide our discussion: How does the church teach faithfully and effectively? How does it teach "with author-

Wiedenhofer, "Kritische Übernahme: Kann die Kirche demokratisiert werden?" *Herder Korrespondenz* 52 (1998): 347–51; Joseph Ratzinger and Hans Maier, *Demokratie in der Kirche: Möglichkeiten, Grenzen, Gefahren* (Limburg a.d. Lahn: 1970); Gottfried Leder, "Zum Verhältnis von Kirche und Demokratie: Anmerkungen zu einem notwendigen Dialog," *Stimmen der Zeit* 220 (2002): 37–50; Hervé Legrand, "Democrazia o sinodalità per la chiesa? Convergenze reali e divergenze profonde," *Ricerca* 12 (1996): 1–20; Karl Rahner, "Demokratie in der Kirche?" *Stimmen der Zeit* 182 (1968): 1–15; Heribert Heinemann, "Demokratisierung der Kirche oder Erneuerung synodaler Einrichtungen? Eine Anfrage an das Kirchenverständnis," in *Dialog als Selbstvollzug der Kirche,* ed. Gebhard Fürst (Freiburg: Herder, 1997), 270–83.

94. McCormick, "The Search for Truth in the Catholic Context," 280.

ity" such that official teaching is in fact perceived by the eyes of faith as legitimately authoritative? In order to warrant such authoritativeness, how is its competence on a particular matter best demonstrated? According to the Catholic vision, does the fact that special authority is given by Christ to the apostles and, through them, to the bishops and pope demand a particular style in which authority is exercised by the magisterium? Do claims to direct authorization from Christ and of a divinely instituted hierarchical structure justify both a "top-down" exercise of authority and indeed an authority tied to a use of power as domination? Is the exercise of authority and power in the church to be different from the ideal exercise of authority and power outside the church?

Two notions of teaching authority can be distinguished and related: *de jure* authority and *de facto* authority.[95] Each operates out of a particular understanding of power. And each operates out of a particular way of relating grace and nature. The first notion, *de jure* authority, is authority which is attached to an acknowledged position and position-holder within a community. In the governance of a group, particular persons have power over others; they exercise governance by virtue of their official position. Such juridical authority calls for juridical obedience. Here, an official statement is "authoritative" because it is promulgated by those "in authority."

The second notion of teaching authority, *de facto* authority, relates to a person's actual ability to teach competently, cogently, and effectively. In the articulation of a particular teaching, the official teachers and their statements are accepted, not only because of *de jure* authority, but because they and their teachings are actually *(de facto)* received and appropriated by those to whom the teaching is addressed. The exercise of authority is here understood to achieve its goal when official persons and their statements are perceived and received as "authoritative": because the persons teaching are deemed to be competent in the particular mat-

95. In what follows I am adapting the approaches of Bernard Hoose, "Introducing the Main Issues," in *Authority in the Roman Catholic Church: Theory and Practice,* ed. Bernard Hoose (Burlington, Vt.: Ashgate, 2002), 1–16; Gerard Mannion, "What Do We Mean by 'Authority'?" in Hoose, ed., *Authority in the Roman Catholic Church,* 19–36. On *de jure* and *de facto* authority, see David Tracy, "Freedom, Responsibility, Authority," in *Empowering Authority: The Charisms of Episcopacy and Primacy in the Church Today,* ed. Gary Chamberlain and Patrick J. Howell (Kansas City, Mo.: Sheed and Ward, 1990), 34–47; Richard P. McBrien, *Catholicism,* new ed. (San Francisco: HarperSanFrancisco, 1994), 739–40. For a similar distinction between "normative or legal authority" and "operative or relational authority," see George B. Wilson, "Authority with Credibility," *Human Development* 12 (1991): 38–41.

ter, because their statements are judged to have been made in fidelity to all the appropriate processes required for ensuring correct and comprehensive interpretation of the faith of the church on the subject matter, because what they teach "rings true" to "the ears of faith" and the way it is articulated is convincing.

The first notion of authority places the emphasis on the formal position of the one making a formal promulgation; the second notion places the emphasis on the effectiveness of the communication to elicit from the receiver of the formal teaching a positive reception. The two notions need to be interrelated and their interrelationship implies a communicative notion of authority. Exclusive emphasis on one without the other can lead to imbalance in exercise of the magisterium.

Seeing teaching authority exclusively in terms of *de jure* authority can lead to a model of formal teaching as simply "instruction from above."[96] This model presumes a vision of church as divided between an active teaching church *(ecclesia docens)* and a passive learning church *(ecclesia discens),* a church sharply divided between the teachers and the taught, the knowledgeable and the ignorant.[97] Also, such an instructional model of ecclesial teaching is oftentimes operating exclusively out of an instructional-propositional notion of revelation, with its consequent notion of faith seen exclusively as obedient assent to instructions from above. We have already discussed the intertextual difficulty that arises with regard to the lack of integration between Vatican I's propositionalist notion of revelation presupposed in *Lumen Gentium* 25's discussion of the magisterium, and *Dei Verbum's* more personalist notion of revelation as primary to that of propositional revelation. Furthermore, seeing teaching authority exclusively in terms of *de jure* authority can sometimes lead to an exercise of authority as a "power-over" others, what David McLoughlin calls "dominating power."[98]

But seeing formal teaching authority exclusively from the side of its effective reception (or non-reception) can lead to an equally unbalanced view. Such an unbalanced view might, for example, see public polling of opinions among Catholics as a legitimate access to the authoritative

96. Hoose, "Introducing the Main Issues," 10.

97. See Ladislas Örsy, *The Church Learning and Teaching* (Dublin: Dominican Publications, 1987).

98. David McLoughlin, "Tensions, Use and Abuse," *Priests and People* 11 (1997): 326–31, at 327–28.

voice of the *universitas fidelium*. It might also lead to exaggerated authority conceded to the judgment of an individual conscience or to the voice of an individual theologian as an independent authority, considered sure guides to the faith of the whole church. In this view, each individual believer is considered an authority unto themselves, without any acknowledgment of the teaching authority of the church as a whole.

The notions of *de jure* and *de facto* teaching authority give rise to different notions of the reception of formal teaching. According to the Roman Catholic understanding of *de jure* teaching authority, it is clear who are the official teachers, what are the official grades of authority to be attached to church pronouncements by the official magisterium, and what are the consequent responses required of all Catholics to each of those grades. Basically four grades have been used in official documents in recent decades: (1) definitive dogma, (2) definitive doctrine, (3) non-definitive but authoritative doctrine, and (4) prudential admonitions and provisional applications of church doctrine.[99] The required *de jure* response to each of those four grades is (1) theological faith, (2) firm acceptance, (3) *obsequium* of intellect and will, and (4) conscientious obedience.[100] However, determination of the precise grade of a particular pronouncement itself requires a careful process of weighing.[101]

According to the *de facto* notion of authority, the issue of reception of formal teaching is envisioned differently. A teaching is received as authoritative if it is seen to cohere with the recipient's own understanding, interpretation, and application of the matter of faith or morals being formally taught. In this view, approbative reception is understood to work both ways. The receiver too is required to make a judgment on what is true to the faith. Even if *de jure* assent is given to a teaching, the way in which the teaching is expressed may not be meaningful or relevant to the receiver. In this case, it could be said that the teaching has not been an effective communication of the faith. For the sake of authoritative and effective teaching, this two-way approbative reception calls for a further element of reception: the prior reception by the magisterium of the

99. See Congregation for the Doctrine of the Faith, "Profession of Faith and Oath of Fidelity," *Origins* 18 (March 16, 1989): 661, 663; Congregation for the Doctrine of the Faith, "The Ecclesial Vocation of the Theologian," *Origins* 20 (July 5, 1990): 118–26. For an analysis of these grades, see Gaillardetz, *Teaching with Authority*, 101–28.

100. On each of these responses, see Gaillardetz, *Teaching with Authority*, 258–71.

101. See Francis A. Sullivan, *Creative Fidelity: Weighing and Interpreting Documents of the Magisterium* (New York: Paulist Press, 1996).

faithful's sense of the faith within the magisterium's process of formulating a teaching in the first place. How that reception by the magisterium of the *sensus fidelium* might take place, and how the approbative reception by the *sensus fidelium* operates *de facto* will be explored in the next two chapters.

Related to *de facto* effective teaching and reception is the *style* of communication between the three authoritative voices in the teaching office of the church. We have already begun to examine a communicative and interactive exercise of authority that is necessary for effective teaching. Many elements make up a communicative model of authority. Joseph Komonchak notes:

> Authority is a social relationship, that is, a relationship between an A and a B. No one is an authority for one's self. . . . [A]uthority resides in the mutual knowledge and expectations of the two parties. . . . An A who can be intelligently, reasonably, and responsibly trusted is a genuine authority; an A who cannot be so trusted is not a genuine authority. Authority is trustworthy power.[102]

The elements of mutual knowledge, expectations, intelligence, reasonableness, trust, and trustworthiness are founded on the quality of the relationship between individuals. Indeed, authority, according to Francis Sullivan, is "the quality of leadership which elicits and justifies the willingness of others to be led by it."[103]

That willingness is best fostered when formal authority is exercised with a particular style. The history of the church presents ample example of *de jure* teaching authority that is exercised with dominating power, and with domination's instruments: indoctrination, coercion, control, force, and punishment.[104] The *Catechism of the Catholic Church,* in addressing the issue of the exercise of authority in civil society, states:

> Those who exercise authority should do so as a service. "Whoever would be great among you must be your servant." The exercise of authority is measured morally in terms of its divine origin, its reasonable nature and its specific object. No one can command or establish what is contrary to the dignity of persons and the natural law. The exercise of authority is meant to give outward expression to a just hierarchy of values in order to facilitate the exercise of freedom and responsibility by all.[105]

---

102. Komonchak, "Authority and Magisterium," 103, 105.
103. Sullivan, "Authority in an Ecclesiology of Communion," 18.
104. See McLoughlin, "Tensions, Use and Abuse," 327–28.
105. *Catechism of the Catholic Church,* para. 2235–36.

Not only outside the church in civil society, but also within the church, such an imperative should apply. *De jure* authority is to be exercised in the manner called for by the Gospel.[106]

It has been proposed that the fundamental intention of the bishops at Vatican II was to change the style in which contemporary Catholicism exercised its governance and communicated its message.[107] John O'Malley finds in Vatican II an intentional shift from "control" to "service" as the mode of church leadership, and a consequent desire for active participation and engagement by all in the church's mission. Furthermore, its vocabulary of inclusion and the use of words such as "dialogue," "collaboration," "partnership," "subsidiarity," and "collegiality" call for a decisive break with the style of leadership to be found in the preconciliar church.

To move toward a dialogic and communicative exercise of authority in the teaching office of the church demands a shift in style on the part of all three authorities. Not only the magisterium, but theologians and the faithful must relate in a particular way. However, because historically it has been seen for so long as the sole teaching authority in the church, it is the magisterium's mode of operating that firstly calls for conversion, before the climate of mutual respect can characterize the interaction of all.

Perhaps the way to describe that style of interaction is illustrated by the former Cardinal Joseph Ratzinger, as Prefect of the Congregation for the Doctrine of the Faith, on the occasion of the funeral of Cardinal Franz König, former Archbishop of Vienna, on March 28, 2004. König, a significant voice at Vatican II, had often been a critic of the Vatican's "inflated centralism" and the way it has exercised its authority.[108] At a press conference after the funeral, when asked about König's criticism, Cardinal Ratzinger stated in reply: "Perhaps we could sometimes be more gen-

---

106. The classic text is Mk 10:42–45 (parallels Mt 20:24–28 and Lk 22:24–27). See Edmund Hill, "What Does the New Testament Say?" *Priests and People* 11 (1997): 311–15.

107. This is the fundamental interpretation of Vatican II by the historian John O'Malley. See John W. O'Malley, "The Style of Vatican II: The 'How' of the Church Changed during the Council," *America* (February 24, 2003): 12–15; John W. O'Malley, *Vatican II: A Matter of Style. Weston Jesuit School of Theology 2003 President's Letter* (Cambridge, Mass.: Weston Jesuit School of Theology, 2003); John W. O'Malley, "Vatican II: Did Anything Happen?" *Theological Studies* 67 (2006): 3–33.

108. For a report of the funeral, König's criticisms, and Cardinal Ratzinger's comments, see Christa Pongratz-Lippitt, "Ratzinger regrets church centralism at König funeral," *The Tablet* (April 3, 2004): 29.

erous [*grosszügig*] in certain matters." *Grosszügig* can mean broad-minded, magnanimous, tolerant, as well as generous.

The way forward to a communicative exercise of teaching authority would be shown by *ein großzügiges Lehramt,* a broad-minded magisterium. Such a style of governance would be tolerant of wide-ranging diversity in expression of the one faith, broad-minded in allowing time for full dialogue in the church, magnanimous in relinquishing any dominating use of power, and generous in giving to local churches appropriate exercise of formal teaching power. Such a *grosszügig* exercise of formal teaching authority would be the model for the way theologians relate to both the *sensus fidelium* and to the magisterium itself, and for the way the faithful respectfully receive the formal teaching of the magisterium.

The formal teaching of the faith by the magisterium within the one-yet-threefold teaching office of the church will be received as authoritative to the extent that it attends to the *de facto* living of the faith by contemporary Christians, and the way they are attempting to best live and make sense of their faith in the concrete circumstances of their time, with all its difficulties. Before an examination of how the *sensus fidelium* is to be determined, therefore, we need to explore the way in which the *sensus fidei* aids the individual believer in living and making sense of the faith.

CHAPTER 8

Sensus Fidei and the Individual Believer

In part 3, we are examining the relationship between the *sensus fidelium,* theology, and the magisterium in the teaching office of the church. Determination of the *sensus fidei fidelium,* and its significance for theology and the magisterium, necessarily demands prior attention to the *sensus fidei fidelis,* the sense of the faith of the individual believer. Such an investigation includes both lay and ordained, bishops and theologians, since they are all individual *fideles* ("from the bishops to the last of the faithful").[1] Therefore, before we consider determination of the communal *sensus fidelium,* this chapter examines the locus, context, mode, norm, and form of the *sensus fidei* of an individual baptized Christian. The chapter concludes with an examination of eight characteristic ways in which that *sensus* functions in the life of the believer.

Who is the subject of the *sensus fidei?*[2] Who is the *fidelis* we are investigating at this stage? For the purposes of this chapter, I wish to restrict my enquiry: the subject of the *sensus fidei* is presumed to be a baptized and committed Christian who in an act of faith is responding to God's outreach through Christ in the power of the Spirit and is participating in the sacramental life of a community of faith and its mission in the world.

1. *LG,* 12, quoting Augustine, *De Praed. Sanct.* 14, 27 [PL 44, 980].
2. For a discussion of the object and subject of *sensus fidei,* see Dario Vitali, *Sensus fidelium: Una funzione ecclesiale di intelligenza della fede* (Brescia: Morcelliana, 1993), 157–78, 241–72.

My proposal applies, I believe, to both child and adult Christians, and to both Christians with little theological education and those with a sophisticated theological framework. In the next chapter, we will broaden the enquiry and explore the issue of a wider attribution of the capacity of *sensus fidei* in individuals, and the possibility that the scope of the determination of the *sensus fidelium* should be extended. But here we begin with a more particular focus.

What is the object toward which the individual's *sensus fidei* is oriented? Although we have already addressed this issue in chapter 1, it bears repeating here, in order to avoid any reductionistic notion of faith. *Sensus fidei* is a dimension of faith. In all theological knowing, revelation is the objective principle and faith is the subjective principle. Faith, understood in its meaning as *fides qua creditur* (the faith by which one believes), is the individual's reception of the divine word of revelation, i.e., God's address to humanity through Christ in the Spirit. This revelatory encounter is also a salvific encounter, since to be drawn into the trinitarian life of God is to know the fullness of human well-being. This divine self-communication requires reception by faith for its realization. It is this *fides qua,* Rahner claims, which is "a faith which leads [believers] to salvation and (given the further assumptions) justification, even though the contents of their faith, their *fides quae,* are of the most diverse and often contradictory kind."[3] The object of this *fides qua creditur,* and therefore of faith's organon for understanding, the *sensus fidei,* is ultimately the revelatory and salvific event of God's self-communication in history, i.e., revelation itself.

This also holds true for faith as *fides quae creditur* (the faith which one believes). The beliefs which the believer assents to, as formulated in the doctrines of the church, are not ultimately the object of the person's assent, which is, rather, the God who is revealing. Once again, it is important to remember with Thomas Aquinas that articles or propositions of faith are never the ultimate object of faith, "for the act of the believer does not terminate in the proposition [*enuntiabile*] but in the reality [signified by the proposition]."[4] Thus *fides qua creditur* and *fides quae creditur* are interrelated. Oftentimes the individual's interpretation of a belief

3. Rahner, "The Act of Faith and the Content of Faith," 152.
4. *ST,* 2-2, q. 1, a. 2, ad 2. For a discussion of Aquinas on this point, see Dulles, *The Assurance of Things Hoped For,* 33–36, 193. See also *ST,* 2-2, q. 1, a. 6: "Articulus [fidei] est perceptio divinae veritatis tendens in ipsam [veritatem]."

which that person has assented to can differ from the official interpretation of that belief. However, despite the possible discrepancy between what the church officially teaches and what the individual actually believes, to the baptized Christian who responds in the depths of their being to God's offer of revelatory salvation, the Holy Spirit grants a genuine "sense for the faith."[5]

THE PRIMARY LOCUS

The faith life of the individual finds its home within the church. Christian faith is an ecclesial faith. The church is primarily *a community* of faith. Christian faith, while finding concrete realization in the life of the individual *fidelis,* is primarily the faith of the whole church, the *universitas fidelium.* The church exists in order to offer that ecclesial faith, as both relationship and assent to beliefs, to individuals. The teaching office of the church, through the interplay of its three authorities of the *sensus fidelium,* theology, and the magisterium, plays a special role in the mediation of that faith.

The ecclesial locus of traditioning "the faith that was once for all delivered to the saints"[6] is most clearly modeled in the *Rite of Christian Initiation of Adults.* In this process, "the faith" is appropriated by catechumens through their coming to know and love those already Christians, through hearing of their experiences of salvation and listening to what the faith means to them. In other words, those Christians share their own unique *sensus fidei,* their own distinctive interpretation of the faith that has emerged from their own distinctive experience of salvation through Christ in the Spirit. A catechumen therefore is schooled and initiated into the way others have exercised their *sensus fidei,* their capacity to make sense of the faith for themselves. While the catechumens enrich their sense of the faith through study of Scripture, the creeds, doctrines,

---

5. "The faith of the average Christian is not just a pitiable sketch of the official faith. It is a salutary faith borne by God's self-communication. It is really the faith that God's grace wishes to bring forth and keep alive in the Church. . . . The *depositum fidei* is not first and foremost a sum of statements formulated in human language. It is God's Spirit, irrevocably communicated to humankind, activating in persons the salutary faith that they really possess. . . . [W]hat matters above all is the faith that really lives in the ordinary Christian. That is the faith that actually saves, in which God communicates himself to humanity, however pitiful and fragmentary its conceptualisation may be." Rahner, "What the Church Officially Teaches," 169–70.

6. Jude 3.

and practices of the church, and the guidance of the contemporary magisterium, at the same time the lives of the saints and "the believing" of those around them are proposed to them as living statements of what "the faith" means for daily life. They see how others have applied the faith to their lives. In formal ritual, those to be initiated have the Scriptures and the creed "handed over" to them and in turn they assent to "the faith which is to be believed" *(fides quae creditur)*. "This is our faith; this is the faith of the church." It will be the Holy Spirit's gift of the organon of *sensus fidei* which will enable the newly baptized to apply that faith in their own lives.

We have already examined the Spirit's role in the reception of the individual into the community through the three sacraments of initiation. During the Eucharist, the high point of Christian initiation, the *epiclesis* is a prayer for the sending and reception of the Holy Spirit upon the Eucharistic community. The newly baptized, because of the Holy Spirit, is now in communion with Christ, in communion with the others in the congregation, in communion with the worldwide community of believers, in communion with believers since the beginning of the church, and in communion with the saints in heaven.

After their ecclesial initiation, lest an inadequate sense of the faith, and indeed misunderstanding, cloud their perception of the truth, ongoing reflection on the meaning of the sacraments and constant study of "the faith" are necessary to deepen further their initiation into the triune Mystery. However, not only their sense of the faith requires ongoing education; likewise, their organon for understanding faith requires constant nurturing in order to ensure ever more faithful understanding, interpretation, and application of the faith. Since the early church, the Christian faith has been received and traditioned in this way from generation to generation. An individual Christian's faith finds its home in the faith of the church. The *sensus fidei fidelis* is nurtured out of the *sensus fidei fidelium* and in turn nurtures the community's faith.

The individual's reception of faith from the community calls forth credal assent to the community's beliefs and a willingness to be guided by the magisterium. The magisterium, as we have seen in the previous chapter, has a specific role in preserving the church's faith. In terms of the *de jure* authority attached to official church teaching, the *de jure* response demanded of individuals is clearly outlined according to the four levels of church teaching. In terms of the individual's *de facto* response to the magisterium's teaching regarding faith and morals, our enquiry now proceeds to explore the primary context, mode, norm, and form of the *sensus fidei* in the individual Christian.

THE PRIMARY CONTEXT

Lest talk of "faith" become too abstract, we need to ask: what is the context of such a faith, and its accompanying *sensus?* As a dimension of faith itself, the primary context of *sensus fidei* is an individual's faith relationship with God *(fides qua creditur)*, grounded in an individual Christian's experience of salvific revelation in everyday life, celebration of the sacraments, and participation in the mission of the church.[7]

Lumen Gentium 35 speaks of the laity's *sensus fidei,* which ensures that the power of the Gospel shines out in daily family and social life.[8] Furthermore, in a passage that refers to the three ways in which the apostolic tradition progresses with the help of the Holy Spirit, *Dei Verbum* 8 refers to, in addition to theology and the magisterium, "the intimate sense of spiritual realities which [believers] experience *(ex intima spiritualium rerum quam experiuntur intelligentia)."* Commentators agree that this sentence is intended as an alternative expression for *sensus fidei* referred to in *Lumen Gentium* 12.[9] As Dario Vitali points out, the correlation of *Lumen*

---

7. On Christian experience and the *sensus fidei,* see Harald Wagner, "Glaubenssinn, Glaubenszustimmung und Glaubenskonsensus," *Theologie und Glaube* 69 (1979): 263–71, esp. 265–67. See also Gaillardetz, *Teaching with Authority,* 271: "In the end, one's response to Church teaching can never be reduced to a simple matter of assent or dissent. To the extent that one's response to Church teaching is a truly personal response, *the definitive character of that response is ultimately disclosed only in the concrete shape of a believer's life.* Just as the true nature of Church doctrine is only discovered within the context of a rich Christian tradition that passes on God's word in innumerable forms, the true nature of the Christian's response to that doctrine is interwoven in the daily life of Christian discipleship. It is there, in the ongoing struggle to remain faithful as followers of Jesus, that we give our most profound answer to God's invitation to saving communion which is faithfully if imperfectly communicated to us in Christian doctrine." My italics.

8. *LG,* 35: "Christ is the great prophet who proclaimed the kingdom of the Father both by the testimony of his life and the power of his word. Until the full manifestation of his glory, he fulfils this prophetic office, not only through the hierarchy who teach in his name and by his power, but also through the laity. He accordingly both establishes them as witnesses and provides them with an appreciation of the faith [*sensus fidei*] and the grace of the word (see Acts 2:17–18; Apoc 19:10) so that the power of the Gospel may shine out in daily family and social life." See also John Paul II, *Christifideles Laici,* 14.

9. See Zoltán Alszeghy, "The *Sensus Fidei* and the Development of Dogma," in *Vatican II Assessment and Perspectives: Twenty-Five Years After (1962–1987),* vol. 1, ed. René Latourelle (New York: Paulist Press, 1988), 1:138–56; Vitali, *Sensus fidelium,* 263–66; Pié-Ninot, *"Sensus Fidei."* For

Gentium 12 and *Dei Verbum* 8 demands that we locate *sensus fidei* within Christians' personal experience of salvific revelation.[10]

According to Zoltán Alszeghy, *Dei Verbum*'s phrase "spiritual realities" is to be interpreted as referring to "intimate participation in the life of Christ," i.e., as referring to experience of the object of the *sensus fidei*, revelation itself, the Christ event.[11] Within such intimate participation, revelation attains its goal; here salvation is freely received and experienced as a transforming reality. In Christ through the Spirit, the believer experiences revelation and salvation. The Christian "knows" intimately the realities of which church doctrine speaks and which the sacraments celebrate. On this level, as Beinert states, the *sensus fidei* is more akin to the knowledge of a person one loves.[12] Believers possess, as Aquinas puts it, a connaturality with God as Mystery.[13] Newman would liken it to an "illative sense."[14] Tillard's definition highlights its gift for critical discernment in daily life:

> Being the consequence of the presence in the Church of the Spirit which inspired the prophets, Jesus, the apostles, [*sensus fidei*] is a kind of flair, a "spiritual sense," an *instinctus* which makes one living a life faithful to the Gospel grasp instinctively what is in harmony with the authentic meaning of the Word of God and what deviates from it. It is like a life of friendship in which one grasps instinctively what cheats it, the words which kill it, the falsehood of empty gestures. It is also like that by which the musical ear recognizes the right or wrong note. Often without really knowing why, or not being able to justify his reaction rationally, the Christian loyal to the faith and whose life is fully impregnated by the Gospel perceives that such and such a statement jars, is out of tune, that there is something amiss with such and such a decision.[15]

---

a minority view that does not interpret this sentence as a reference to the *sensus fidei*, see D. Sorrentino, "Esperienza spirituale e intelligenza della fede in *Dei Verbum* 8. Sul senso di 'intima spiritualium rerum quae experiuntur intelligentia,'" in *La terra e il seme*, ed. C. Sarnataro (Naples: M. D'Auria, 1998), 153–74.

10. See Vitali, *Sensus fidelium*, 241–72.

11. Alszeghy, "The *Sensus Fidei* and the Development of Dogma," 147.

12. Beinert, "Theologische Erkenntnislehre," 168.

13. See John W. Glaser, "Authority, Connatural Knowledge, and the Spontaneous Judgment of the Faithful," *Theological Studies* 29 (1968): 742–51. On the mystical connaturality of love in Aquinas's theological epistemology, see Thomas Ryan, "Revisiting Affective Knowledge and Connaturality in Aquinas," *Theological Studies* 66 (2005): 49–68.

14. Newman, *An Essay in Aid of a Grammar of Assent*, 270–99.

15. Jean M. R. Tillard, "Church and Apostolic Tradition," *Mid-Stream* 29 (1990): 247–56, at 248. Alszeghy similarly writes: "The *sensus fidei* is precisely this capacity to recognize the intimate experience of adherence to Christ and to judge everything on the basis of this knowledge." Alszeghy, "The *Sensus Fidei* and the Development of Dogma," 147.

However, there is perhaps no more problematic word in the philosophical and theological vocabulary than the word "experience." We have already discussed how the elements in the hermeneutical triad of understanding, interpretation, and application are to be distinguished but not separated. These hermeneutical insights are now helpful for understanding "Christian experience." Every experience of *understanding* is already an *interpretation* by means of a familiar framework, and already an *application* to present context. We bring a past into our present that enables us to experience it. Therefore there is a narrative quality to experience; we are always experiencing the present out of our past, the new out of the old. We may then move on to narrate the past out of the present, and to see the old in terms of the new. This pattern marks the course of a human being's life. "The formal quality of experience through time is inherently narrative."[16] The hermeneutical point I want to highlight here is that all experience is interpretative experience.[17] We are always seeing things from "somewhere," whether it be out of a particular past or from a particular perspective in the present. How we see things depends on where we have been and where we are now "standing." This means that our personal perspective is uniquely ours, but it is also limited. One cannot "see" things from every possible perspective. Both our interpreting framework and our perspective, therefore, are at the same time both enabling of understanding and limiting of understanding. We cannot escape the historical condition of human existence in time; our interpretations are always time-conditioned.

So too, at the deepest level of an individual's faith response to God's self-communication, experience of such an encounter is already an interpretation from a certain horizon. One's *understanding* of the faith is already an *interpretation* created out of one's past horizon or context, and such interpretative understanding is already an *application* to one's life context. The content of faith is understood in terms of one's unique life story. A Christian senses the faith only from a particular framework inherited from the past which conditions his or her perspective of the faith in the present and how to act on it in the future.

Two hermeneutical points can be made about *sensus fidei,* both as a

16. Stephen Crites, "The Narrative Quality of Experience," in *Why Narrative? Readings in Narrative Theology,* ed. Stanley Hauerwas, L. Gregory Jones, and Ronald F. Thiemann (Grand Rapids, Mich.: W. B. Eerdmans, 1989), 65–88, at 66.

17. On interpretative experience, see Schillebeeckx, *Christ,* 29–64.

capacity and as the resulting perception. Firstly, it is the organon of *sensus fidei* that bridges the hermeneutical gap between past and present. As a sense *for* the faith, it enables the expression of faith to be constantly rejuvenated. Secondly, *sensus fidei,* as the sense one has *of* the faith, can be defined as an individual's "interpretative experience" of revelatory salvation. That interpretative experience is constituted by the specific location, perspective, or context of the individual believer. We sense God from a particular place. Across a worldwide church, revelation (and the salvific encounter it mediates) is received from a great variety of horizons and applied in a vast plurality of ways. Whatever the particularity (social status, race, gender, culture, language, age, personal history, psychological type), how a person experiences revelatory salvation through Christ in the Spirit will be conditioned by who they are and what they personally need to be saved from in their individual and societal context. In a very concrete way, revelatory salvation is experienced differently by each individual. In this sense, God's loving salvation is "tailor-made" for each particular individual. Thus, the emergent *sensus fidei* will be unique to each individual. *Sensus fidei* is a concrete sense.

This is true not only at the level of *fides qua*. At the level of *fides quae,* as Rahner highlights, Christians may interpret the same doctrine in a plurality of ways.[18] Indeed, he says, every believer creates a concrete catechism, which is necessarily a selection of beliefs for this or that concrete situation in daily life. Each individual, he says, operates out of "an 'existentiell' hierarchy of truths which is not simply the equivalent of the objective hierarchy of truths."[19] This is not to say that any inadequate understanding of a doctrine doesn't need to be constantly addressed by the ecclesial community through catechesis and faith development pro-

18. Rahner writes: "The differences in the structures that form the concrete framework for faith are quite justifiable, and that applies to the *fides quae* as well as the *fides qua.* It is quite legitimate, since it is absolutely unavoidable, for the truths of faith to be present throughout the world in different ways in the consciousness of faith, sometimes moving to the foreground of this consciousness, sometimes receding to the background, since the persons possessing this faith are themselves different. There are age differences, differences in the times in which they lead their lives, sociological differences, personal differences, and so on." Rahner, "A Hierarchy of Truths," 165–66.

19. Ibid., 165. According to Leo O'Donovan, the German adjective *existentiell,* as used by Rahner, refers to "existence in the concrete and to the ways in which the structures of human existence are given concrete content. 'Existentiell Christology,' for example, is a person's lived faith relationship to Jesus Christ as distinguished from general concepts or doctrines about him." Leo J. O'Donovan, ed., *A World of Grace: An Introduction to the Themes and Foundations of Karl Rahner's Theology* (New York: Seabury Press, 1980), 191.

grams, in order that the doctrine may better illumine Christians' experience. But even given optimum education, diversity in interpretation will still remain, and indeed cannot be avoided. It is the concreteness and distinctiveness of both a person's *fides qua* and *fides quae* which give rise to a particular sense of the faith that is grounded in their Christian experience. An individual's capacity of *sensus fidei* applies Scripture and doctrine to life; the concrete meaning of Scripture and doctrine for one's unique life is the resultant *sensus fidei* of that individual.

THE PRIMARY MODE

The Spirit-activated organon of *sensus fidei* calls upon the heuristic and integrative resources of the "poietic" or "productive" imagination, its primary mode of operating.[20] According to Paul Ricoeur, "the imagination can be considered as the power of giving form to human experience."[21] Just as the imagination is not one "faculty" but rather "the whole mind working in certain ways,"[22] so too *sensus fidei* is the whole mind of the Christian working in certain ways. The exercise of the capacity of *sensus fidei* is an exercise of the creative Christian imagination.

There now falls across our discussion what William M. Thompson has called "the 'Bañez-Molina shadow' of the *sensus fidelium*."[23] In describing the interaction between God's grace and human response, where should the emphasis lie? On divine priority, freedom, and initiative (Bañez)? Or on human response, responsibility, and involvement (Molina)? Various models proposed throughout the history of theology have portrayed the sides of the divine-human polarity either actively or passively. How the encounter is modeled will condition one's theology of revelation, grace, creation, incarnation, sacraments, indeed every area of theology. Here we are concerned with the theology of revelation and faith. With regard to the cognitive aspect of revelation-faith, is God's re-

20. I prefer to use the transliteration "poietic" rather than "poetic" in order to highlight the primary sense of the Greek word *poiesis* as "creating," "making," or "doing."

21. Ricoeur, "The Bible and the Imagination," 144.

22. McIntyre, *Faith, Theology and Imagination,* 159.

23. Thompson, "Sensus Fidelium and Infallibility," 479. During the sixteenth-century "de auxiliis" controversy over "the helps" toward salvation, the Dominican Domingo Bañez placed emphasis on the efficacy of divine grace, while the Jesuit Luis de Molina emphasized the free and active participation of the human will. The controversy ended with papal approval for the legitimacy of both approaches.

velatory activity somehow outside the normal human processes of understanding? Or does divine revelation require human processes of understanding for its realization?

Noting the etymological similarity of the words "revelation" and "discovery" in their reference to "disclosure," Avery Dulles proposes "that
revelation can be brought within the category of discovery, and that it
may even be defined as a gifted discovery."[24] The reception of revelation,
he claims, is "a heuristic process," similar to a scientist's quest for discovery.[25] In Newman's discussion of apprehension, assent, certitude, infer-
ence, and the "illative sense," he refers to the art of a detective who suc-
cessfully recognizes and interprets the clues, and to the art of a lawyer
who sees in the evidence a pattern which others miss.[26] Jesus spoke of
those who "cannot interpret the signs of the times."[27] Revelation requires
the eyes of faith for divine manifestation to occur. It requires the eyes of

24. Avery Dulles, "Revelation and Discovery," in *Theology and Discovery: Essays in Honor of
Karl Rahner, S.J.,* ed. William J. Kelly (Milwaukee, Wis.: Marquette University Press, 1980), 1–29,
at 2. Dulles makes subtle distinctions between revelation, faith, and discovery: "Faith is not the
same as revelation. It is not even directly correlated with revelation, as I have been using the term.
For revelation, in the sense of discovery, is an insight in which the mind rests satisfied. Faith, however, is a stretching forth toward an insight not yet given. Faith animates the quest for revelation;
it sustains the process of discovery; but to the extent that discovery or revelation is given, faith is
supplanted. Faith, therefore, stands in dialectical tension with discovery, and hence also with revelation. The completeness of revelation, if it were ever given (as the asymptotic goal of revelation
within our pilgrim condition), would do away with the very possibility of faith." Dulles, "Revelation and Discovery," 25. Here I am indebted to Richard Gaillardetz for alerting me to the relevance of Dulles's discussion on discovery and revelation for explicating the heuristic function of
sensus fidei.

25. Dulles, "Revelation and Discovery," 3–10. Elsewhere, Dulles writes of discovery in terms of
Polanyi's "logic of discovery" and Newman's "illative sense," which discovers "patterns of intelligibility that point to a divinely given meaning. There is no way of strictly proving that the meaning
is really there. Either one recognizes it or one does not. As we contemplate the scene, there seem
to be moments when the pieces fall into a pattern. It is as though the meaning were given to us;
we perceive it as a gift, a grace. And yet we cannot say that reason is not at work. The illative sense
reasons in its own way." Dulles, *The Survival of Dogma,* 40.

26. "We often hear of the exploits of some great lawyer, judge or advocate, who is able in per-
plexed cases, when common minds see nothing but a hopeless heap of facts, foreign or contrary to
each other, to detect the principle which rightly interprets the riddle, and, to the admiration of all
hearers, converts a chaos into an orderly and luminous whole. This is what is meant by originality
in thinking: it is the discovery of an aspect of a subject-matter, simpler, it may be, and more intel-
ligible than any hitherto taken." Newman, *An Essay in Aid of a Grammar of Assent,* 291. On Newman and the illative sense, see John Coulson, *Religion and Imagination: "In Aid of a Grammar of
Assent"* (New York: Oxford University Press, 1981). See also Thomas K. Carr, *Newman and Gadamer: Toward a Hermeneutics of Religious Knowledge* (Atlanta, Ga.: Scholars Press, 1996).

27. Mt 16:3.

faith to disclose what remains unrecognized by eyes that do not see, by ears that do not hear.[28] It requires a sense for perceiving the Invisible.[29] *Sensus fidei* is such a heuristic and imaginative sense.

Discovery requires attentiveness; and attentiveness demands what Walter J. Burghardt calls "a long loving look at the real."[30] *Sensus fidei,* as a sense for the divine, engages in its search the five physical senses of touch, taste, smell, hearing, and sight as antennae alert to the divine presence. Through an active *sensus fidei,* the believer may "taste and see the goodness of the Lord."[31] *Sensus fidei,* as faith's capacity for discovery of revelation, pays attention to all things, expectant that anything (a tortured man on a cross?) can be a symbol mediating the divine. *Sensus fidei* then is an active sense forever on the lookout for God. Not only in liturgy, surely, but in the whole of human existence, *sensus fidei* engages the imagination, with "full, conscious and active participation," in God's process of symbolically mediated self-communication.[32] Paying attention leads to noticing; noticing leads to recognition; recognition leads to disclosure.

In the individual's discovery and reception of divine revelation, there is an active, human element that is co-constitutive of the sense or meaning of revelation as experienced. God not only reveals but also enables us to interpret; "everything he does, he gives us to do."[33] The revealing God is at work in the activity of human interpretation, through the principle of reception, the Holy Spirit. In the disclosive and communicative process of revelation, God's Holy Spirit is the "go-between" who lures the receiver to make sense of what is communicated.[34] In this way, the human receiver is creatively and fully involved in the actualization of the communication. Revelation is not achieved until it is received.

---

28. Mk 8:18.

29. Heb 11:27 speaks of Moses' faith, which radiated forth from him "like someone who could see the Invisible." New Jerusalem Bible translation.

30. Walter J. Burghardt, "Contemplation: A Long Loving Look at the Real," *Church* (Winter 1989): 14–18.

31. Ps 34:8.

32. *SC,* 14. On the sacramental imagination and participation in liturgy, see Ormond Rush, "Full, Conscious and Active Participation: Formation in the Sacramental Imagination," *Liturgy News* 33 (2003): 3–4.

33. Thompson, "Sensus Fidelium and Infallibility," 479.

34. See John V. Taylor, *The Go-Between God: The Holy Spirit and the Christian Mission* (London: SCM Press, 1972). On St. Paul's pneumatology, Dulles writes: "In modern terminology we might say that the Holy Spirit functions for Paul as constituting a new horizon whereby reason is enabled to transcend itself and achieve a discovery beyond its normal capacity." Dulles, "Revelation and Discovery," 17.

To understand this dynamic of communication, it may be helpful to conceive of faith experience as analogous to aesthetic experience, and to conceive of the activity of faith's organon of *sensus fidei* as analogous to an individual's "aesthetic taste" for and appreciation of a work of art.[35] Following that analogy, the Latin word *sensus* is best translated into Greek as *aisthesis* (perception), from which comes the word "aesthetics."[36] Thus the *sensus fidei* or *aisthesis tès pisteos* construed by the recipient of revelation is analogous to the constructive *aisthesis* or perception by the recipient of a work of art.

If the analogy is appropriate, then a reception aesthetics can here provide a relevant background theory for our exploration of the nature and function of *sensus fidei*. For an aesthetics from the perspective of reception, the reader, viewer, or listener of a work of art is a "co-creator" of the work's meaning as art, along with the original creator of the work.[37] The *poiesis* ("creating" or "making") on the part of the original producer requires a corresponding *poiesis* on the part of the receiver, if the work is to achieve its effect. The receiver is needed to actively "make sense" of the work. Music demands an active listener. A novel is dead until it is read. A sculpture comes alive as a viewer moves around it and engages with it. Each recipient brings to the encounter a horizon of expectation, which enables it to be an aesthetic experience through which meaningful communication takes place. Such a making-meaning-of-the-work is achieved by those interlocking processes of the mind which together we call "the imagination." This imagining is poietic (i.e., involves a *poiesis*) since it makes sense of and gives meaning to the work by "putting the pieces together" into a coherent whole.

In faith's making-sense of revelation, this integrative poietic imagination is no less at work. In the felicitous expression of Michael Paul Gallagher, "ultimately it is through imagination that we cope with the difficult docking manoeuvre between a hidden God and a fallen humanity."[38]

---

35. Beinert, for example, uses the analogies of aesthetic experience and human love. See Beinert, "Theologische Erkenntnislehre," 167–68. For a discussion from the field of cognitive psychology on the analogous relationship between aesthetic and religious experience, see Fraser N. Watts and J. Mark G. Williams, *The Psychology of Religious Knowing* (New York: Cambridge University Press, 1988), 59–62.

36. On *aisthesis* as a translation of *sensus*, see Benjamin Hederico, ed., *Lexicon Graeco-Latinum et Latino-Graecum* (Rome: Congregatio de Propaganda Fide, 1832), 29.

37. For a theological appropriation of reception aesthetics as a fruitful background theory for this issue, see Rush, *The Reception of Doctrine*, 65–98, 187–275.

38. Michael Paul Gallagher, "Imagination and Faith," *The Way* 24 (1984): 122.

Much recent work has been done on the role of imagination in faith, especially by writers such as William Lynch, Ray Hart, David Tracy, John McIntyre, Garrett Green, Sandra Schneiders, David Bryant, Michael Cook, Catherine Mary Hilkert, Paul Avis, Richard Viladesau, and Richard Côté.[39] There has emerged from this literature a litany of expressions: the ironic imagination, the parabolic imagination, the dialogic imagination, the analogical imagination, the sacramental imagination, the moral imagination, the scriptural imagination, the paschal imagination. If revelation, as Dulles and others claim, is best understood as being symbolically mediated,[40] then God's self-communication through the mediation of symbol finds its point of contact in the human imagination. For Garrett Green, human imagination is the *Anknüpfungspunkt* (point of contact) between symbolically mediated revelation and human reception in faith.[41]

Sensus fidei, as faith's organon for understanding, interpreting, and applying revelation, has as its primary mode the poietic imagination, which weaves together the disconnected threads of a life into a meaningful tapestry where God is now portrayed as the significant redeeming figure. A *sensus fidei,* as the product of that imagining, is the "sense of the faith"

39. For the major works of Lynch, see William F. Lynch, *Christ and Apollo: The Dimensions of the Literary Imagination* (New York: Sheed and Ward, 1960); *Images of Hope: Imagination as Healer of the Hopeless* (Baltimore: Helicon, 1965); *Christ and Prometheus: A New Image of the Secular* (Notre Dame, Ind.: University of Notre Dame Press, 1970); *Images of Faith: An Exploration of the Ironic Imagination* (Notre Dame, Ind.: University of Notre Dame Press, 1973). For a full bibliography and analysis of Lynch's work, see Gerald J. Bednar, *Faith as Imagination: The Contribution of William F. Lynch, S.J.* (Kansas City, Mo.: Sheed and Ward, 1996). See also Ray L. Hart, *Unfinished Man and the Imagination: Toward an Ontology and a Rhetoric of Revelation* (Atlanta, Ga.: Scholars Press, 1985); Tracy, *The Analogical Imagination;* McIntyre, *Faith, Theology and Imagination;* Garrett Green, *Imagining God: Theology and the Religious Imagination* (San Francisco: Harper & Row, 1989); Schneiders, *The Revelatory Text;* David J. Bryant, *Faith and the Play of Imagination: On the Role of Imagination in Religion* (Macon, Ga.: Mercer University Press, 1989); Michael L. Cook, *Christology as Narrative Quest* (Collegeville, Minn.: Liturgical Press, 1997); Mary Catherine Hilkert, *Naming Grace: Preaching and the Sacramental Imagination* (New York: Continuum, 1997); Paul D. L. Avis, *God and the Creative Imagination: Metaphor, Symbol, and Myth in Religion and Theology* (New York: Routledge, 1999); Richard Viladesau, *Theological Aesthetics: God in Imagination, Beauty, and Art* (New York: Oxford University Press, 1999); Richard Côté, *Lazarus! Come out! Why Faith Needs Imagination* (Toronto: Novalis, 2003).

40. See Dulles, *Models of Revelation,* 131–54. See also Justin J. Kelly, "Knowing by Heart: The Symbolic Structure of Revelation and Faith," in *Faithful Witness: Foundations of Theology for Today's Church,* ed. Leo J. O'Donovan and T. Howland Sanks (New York: Crossroad, 1989), 63–84; Ross A. Shecterle, *The Theology of Revelation of Avery Dulles, 1980–1994: Symbolic Mediation* (Lewiston, N.Y.: Edwin Mellen Press, 1996).

41. Green, *Imagining God,* 5.

that is woven. This weaving takes place either consciously or unconsciously. The imaginative work of construing an integrated *sensus fidei* is a making-sense of one's past, present, and future life, in the light of faith and with the eyes of faith. It is a work of discovery and integration that begins with one's experienced need for salvation and experience of God's grace within a concrete context. As such, the very work of imagination through the organon of *sensus fidei* is an expression of one's believing. The faith it expresses is salvific and revelatory because it relates intimately to that person's actual experience and reception of salvation through Jesus Christ in the Spirit. In this way, the imaginative construal of a *sensus fidei* involves the explicit or implicit creation of a concrete catechism and an *existentiell* (or concrete) hierarchy of truths formed in the interplay between personal experience of revelation and Scripture, the official teachings of the church, and the objective hierarchy of truths. This ongoing process is integral to the development in the individual of a specific form of spirituality which is found to be meaningful from the perspective of one's social status, race, gender, culture, language, age, personal history, psychological type. Above all in this way is the Gospel inculturated, contextualized, and traditioned throughout history.

Within the moral sphere, the imaginative work of *sensus fidei* requires, first of all, the complementary judgment of conscience.[42] Conscience is the organon of *sensus fidei* functioning in its critical and practical mode. For St. Paul, conscience or *syneidesis* ("knowledge shared with oneself"), as "the organ for the reception of the kerygma,"[43] is founded on a capac-

---

42. John Paul II, in *Veritatis Splendor,* 59, states: "The judgment of conscience is a *practical judgment,* a judgment which makes known what man must do or not do, or which assesses an act already performed by him. It is a judgment which applies to a concrete situation the rational conviction that one must love and do good and avoid evil." Here the work of Paul Ricoeur on imagination and conscience can be helpful as a background theory for this present discussion. A comprehensive theology of conscience is not here attempted. Mark I. Wallace writes of the shift in Ricoeur's thought concerning the role of imagination in the reception of revelation. "Without conscience, the voice that summons the self to its responsibilities falls on deaf ears. In Ricoeur's earlier writings the imagination played the role of a sort of *preaeparatio evangelica* for the reception of the divine word. While not denying this previous emphasis, the focus is now on the subject's *moral* capacity to select which figures of the imagination best enable the subject's care and concern for the other. The work of imagination and the testimony of conscience together empower the subject to appropriate the command to take responsibility for the other's welfare." See Mark I. Wallace, "Introduction," in *Figuring the Sacred: Religion, Narrative, and Imagination,* ed. Paul Ricoeur (Minneapolis: Fortress Press, 1995), 1–32, at 29. On the "moral imagination," see Philip S. Keane, *Christian Ethics and Imagination* (New York: Paulist Press, 1984); Mark Johnson, *Moral Imagination: Implications of Cognitive Science for Ethics* (Chicago: University of Chicago, 1993).

43. Ricoeur writes: "Conscience is thus the anthropological presupposition with which 'justifi-

ity all Christians possess. Not all possibilities presented by the imagination for action are necessarily true to the faith. In the conflicts of concrete situations the moral capacity of conscience chooses the way of truth and wisdom in the light of particular circumstances. Conscience, in Ricoeur's precise sense of "personal conviction in a concrete situation,"[44] has a close connection with *phronesis,* practical wisdom. *Sensus fidei* is this practical, sapiential, and critical sense; it is faith knowledge applied in the concrete every day, bridging faith and reason, theory and praxis, story and significance, Gospel and context, the teaching of the magisterium and one's life.

But, within the ecclesial locus of faith, an individual's sense of the faith is not an authoritative perspective; an individual's conscience is not an independent authority. Conscience must make its practical judgments in the light of reception of the church's formal teaching authority, the magisterium, which speaks for the whole church. However, here, in the interface between the operation of an individual's *sensus fidei* (here as "conscience") and the teaching authority of the magisterium, we encounter once again the relationship between *de jure* authority and *de facto* authority in the church's teaching office. Presuming respectful openness to the magisterium, what is the primary norm for testing the fidelity of an individual's *sensus fidei* against the faith of the church as taught by the magisterium? What norm informs the judgment of conscience? What practical wisdom? Whose practical wisdom?

THE PRIMARY NORM

Fundamental to this imaginative construal of a *sensus fidei,* if it is to be *Christian* faith, is the role of Scripture and tradition in fashioning the Christian imagination. Together they function as the norm of faith and of any sense of the faith, through their witness to the God revealed through Jesus Christ in the Spirit.

We have seen in the previous chapter how Scripture and tradition, as the primary and secondary witnesses to revelation, the Word of God,

---

cation by faith' would remain an event marked by a radical extrinsicness. In this sense, conscience becomes *the organ of the reception of the kerygma,* in a perspective that remains profoundly Pauline." Paul Ricoeur, "The Summoned Subject in the School of the Narratives of the Prophetic Vocation," in *Figuring the Sacred: Religion, Narrative, and Imagination* (Minneapolis: Fortress Press, 1995), 262–75, at 272. My italics.

44. Paul Ricoeur, David Pellauer, and John McCarthy, "Conversation," in *The Whole and Divided Self,* ed. David E. Aune and John McCarthy (New York: Crossroad, 1997), 221–43, at 235.

constitute the primary and secondary authorities to which the church and all derived ecclesial authorities are beholden. Together Scripture and tradition function as a norm for the faith through a hermeneutical circle of ecclesial self-understanding. Tradition, in its inclusive sense, is the transmission process by which the church hands on not only what it has received in faith, but also the diverse modes of that communication, including the content of revelation, both implicitly held and officially formulated in doctrine. Ultimately, what the church is transmitting is God's offer of salvific revelation through Christ in the power of the Spirit. "In its doctrine, life and worship, [the church] perpetuates and transmits to every generation all that it itself is, all that it believes."[45]

The diverse media of tradition fashion the Christian imagination of each generation. Through the language and images of Scripture itself, through liturgy with its manifold imaginative forms, through creeds and doctrines, through public prayer and private prayer, through rosary beads and prayer books, through music and poetry, through novels and film, through incense and stained-glass windows, through exemplary lives of canonized saints and of contemporary heroes in the faith, through paintings and statues, through family life and formal catechesis, through commitment to justice and political engagement, the faith is revealed, handed on, and experienced.

Although to be included among the media and contents of tradition, Scripture above all "norms" the ecclesial traditioning process. It is a norm, however, that requires constant reception and reinterpretation throughout history and within diverse contexts. As we saw in chapter 6, the inspiring work of the Spirit in the production and text of Scripture finds its realization in receptions of Scripture which bear fruit in concrete living of the Gospel. Here I wish to focus more narrowly on only two aspects concerning Scripture's normative function which are significant for its ongoing reception: (1) the role of imagination and (2) the role of narrative, both in Scripture's normative witness to Christ and in the church's reception of that witness.

Scripture itself is a work of the poietic imagination. As Alonso Schökel reminds us, "what was written with imagination, must be read with imagination."[46] *Sensus fidei,* as faith in its imaginative and interpretative

---

45. *DV,* 8.

46. Luis Alonso Schökel and José María Bravo, *A Manual of Hermeneutics,* trans. Brook W. R. Pearson (Sheffield, England: Sheffield Academic Press, 1998), 170.

mode, is the bridge between story and significance, between the world that Scripture imagines ("the world of the text") and the individual's imagining of real possibilities within "the world before the text."[47] A dialectical relationship exists between Scripture, which forms the imagination of the reader, and the human imagination, which gives form to the scriptural text through the work of interpretation. Scripture both forms within the reader what Sandra Schneiders calls a "paschal imagination,"[48] and yet requires engagement of the paschal imagination for the refiguring of its own meaning. The reader brings to the act of reading the imagination of one who has experienced the paschal mystery in daily life.

The world that Scripture imagines is a narrative world, stretching from God's rule over creation at the genesis of human time, into the open future when God will rule over all at the end of human time. This narrative world Jesus called "the reign of God." Jesus' configuration of this world is the product of what John McIntyre calls his "parabolic imagination."[49] His parables, as witnessed to in Scripture, are invitational forms of discourse, invitations to a different way of seeing things—seeing with the eyes of faith. Jesus invites his hearers (as does the evangelist invite his readers) to enter into God's way of seeing by entering into the world configured by his parables. Upon entering that world, they are invited to see things from a different perspective, from God's perspective, from the perspective of divine, not human, wisdom. From within that world, they are invited to see themselves as possibly different, by identification with characters in the narrative who live under the reign of God. Identification with characters in the narrative who do not live under the reign of God is equally revelatory of the hearer's true perspective. Upon leaving that "imaginary world" and re-entering the so-called "real world," they are invited to imagine themselves as transformed, changed, according to the reign of God.[50] Jesus invites conversion of their imagination. His parables "would have us think the unthinkable, conceive the incon-

47. On the "scriptural imagination" and "the world of the text," see Johnson, "Imagining the World Scripture Imagines."

48. Schneiders, *The Revelatory Text*, 102–8.

49. McIntyre, *Faith, Theology and Imagination*, 19–39. Further, Ricoeur speaks of the narrative-parable as paradigmatic of the Bible as a whole: "Here we may have, it seems to me, the most complete illustration of the biblical form of imagination, the process of parabolization working in the text and engendering in the reader a similar dynamic of interpretation through thought and action." Ricoeur, "The Bible and the Imagination," 147.

50. On the notion of *catharsis* and the reader's aesthetic experience, see Rush, *The Reception of Doctrine*, 76–79.

ceivable, and imagine the unimaginable, namely, the real possibility of 'a new heaven and a new earth.'"[51] Through this process of conversion, the reign of God can become a reality in its reception. As Ricoeur puts it, "the kingdom of God is not what the parables tell about, but what happens in parables."[52]

In moving from Scripture to the meaning of Scripture for Christian living, we pass from "the work of imagination in the text" to "the work of imagination about the text,"[53] from the notion of the Bible as forming the believer's "paschal imagination" to the complementary notion of the reader's paschal imagination needing to give living form to the biblical text. This bridge from story to significance is the constructive work of the organon of *sensus fidei.*

But the normativity of Scripture for a faithful *sensus fidei* requires care in its application. The world configured by Scripture and the world refigured by the reader might both contain elements which in fact work against a faithful fashioning of the imagination. In some of its symbols and metaphors, the world imagined by Scripture may perpetuate the very opposite of a world where God reigns. Furthermore, the imagination of the contemporary reader also may be blinded to its own shadows and sinfulness. The reader's always-inchoate paschal imagination must constantly come under the norm of the paschal mystery itself.

It is here that the capacity of *sensus fidei* for discernment emerges as a highly significant element in the individual's reception of revelation.[54] *Sensus fidei* is that critical capacity which senses intuitively what is "of God" and what is "not of God." As Martin Luther would put it, it seeks to discern what interpretation "brings forth Christ" and what does not.[55] Tillard's definition quoted above (see page 220) captures this critical capacity of *sensus fidei:* it not only grasps instinctively what is in harmony

---

51. Richard G. Côté, "Christology and the Paschal Imagination," in *Concilium. Who Do You Say That I Am?* ed. Werner Jeanrond and Christoph Theobald (London: SCM Press, 1997), 80–88, at 84.

52. Ricoeur, "The Bible and the Imagination," 165.

53. Ibid., 166.

54. On notions of "discernment" in Scripture and in the history of spirituality, see Luke Timothy Johnson, *Scripture and Discernment: Decision Making in the Church* (Nashville, Tenn.: Abingdon Press, 1996); Mark A. McIntosh, *Discernment and Truth: The Spirituality and Theology of Knowledge* (New York: Crossroad, 2004).

55. Martin Luther, *Werke: Kritische Gesamtausgabe Deutsche Bibel,* vol. 7 (Weimar: 1906), 7:384. See the allusion to Luther's maxim in International Theological Commission, "On the Interpretation of Dogmas," *Origins* 20 (May 17, 1990): 1–14, at 10 [Section C, I, 4].

with the authentic meaning of the Word of God, but also what deviates from it, what cheats it, the words which kill it, the falsehood of empty gestures, what jars, is out of tune, what is amiss with such and such a decision, with such and such a faith-formulation.[56]

The second aspect of Scripture's normativity for faith which concerns us here, alongside the role of imagination, is the narrative nature of confessing the Christian faith. The Christian Gospel has an inherently narrative structure. Certainly narrative is only one form of revelatory discourse to be found in the Bible, alongside prophetic, prescriptive, wisdom, and hymnic discourse.[57] However, the world which the whole Bible evokes is a narrative of a God who intervenes to reveal and to save.[58] On scholarly attention to this narrative structure of biblical faith, Agustín del Agua writes:

The narrative form of confessing faith throughout the New Testament does not simply follow a generalized trend in religious phenomenology but is a result of the narrative nature of the Christian message. An event is being confessed and communicated. Therefore, Christian faith can be truly understood only by telling a story, just as happens in any individual process of Christian faith: it is the intervention of God in their lives (experienced as foundational) that allows believers to narrate themselves (narrative identity) in the key of salvation.[59]

The story of salvation is precisely that, a story, stretching from the beginning of cosmic time to the open future of the eschaton when God will truly reign and God will be all in all. The story of salvation reaches its most succinct formulation in the doctrine of the Trinity: the threeness of the one God we have experienced in the history of salvation, as God reaching out to humanity through Christ in the Spirit, truly reveals the

56. Tillard, "Church and Apostolic Tradition," 248.

57. See Paul Ricoeur, "Toward a Hermeneutic of the Idea of Revelation," in *Essays on Biblical Interpretation* (Philadelphia: Fortress Press, 1980), 73–118.

58. See the range of articles in Das and Matera, *The Forgotten God.*

59. Agustín del Agua, "The Narrative Identity of Christians According to the New Testament," in *Concilium. Creating Identity,* ed. Hermann Häring, Maureen Junker-Kenny, and Dietmar Mieth (London: SCM Press, 2000), 91–99, at 91. Likewise, Johann Baptist Metz writes: "Theology is above all concerned with direct experiences expressed in narrative language. This is clear throughout Scripture, from the beginning, the story of creation, to the end, where a vision of the new heaven and the new earth is revealed. All this is disclosed in narrative. The world created from nothing, man made from the dust, the new kingdom proclaimed by Jesus, himself the new man, resurrection as a passage through death to life, the end as a new beginning, the life of future glory—all these show that reasoning is not the original form of theological expression, which is above all that of narrative." Johann Baptist Metz, "A Short Apology of Narrative," in *Why Narrative? Readings in Narrative Theology,* ed. Stanley Hauerwas, L. Gregory Jones, and Ronald F. Thiemann (Grand Rapids, Mich.: W. B. Eerdmans, 1989), 251–62, at 252.

inner life of God. As Michael Root writes: "Narrative is not merely orna-
mental in soteriology but constitutive."[60]

THE PRIMARY FORM

If the norm of a faithful *sensus fidei* is the God of Jesus Christ as witnessed to in Scripture and tradition, then the primary form of a *sensus
fidei* is a life lived out in fidelity to the God of Jesus Christ within the
community of his disciples, the church.[61] *Sensus fidei fidelis,* as an understanding, interpretation, and application of the faith, ultimately takes
the form, not so much of verbal formulation of personal belief (though
it includes that), but of an individual's whole life and his or her ongoing
conversion to Christ through the power of the Spirit.

Already I have spoken of the narrative structure of the faith as witnessed to in Scripture and of the narrative quality of experience, especially in terms of the hermeneutical triad of understanding, interpretation,
and application. The implications of employing the category of narrative
for understanding a sense of the faith now needs to be made more explicit by articulating a particular notion of the human person and of personal identity. What anthropological background theory best correlates
with the poietic imaginative capacity of *sensus fidei* as we have outlined
it? Who is this "self" who believes and has a sense of the faith? What anthropological vision of human identity can help ground our theological
vision of the identity of a Christian believer? Does a Christian's sense of
self impact on his or her sense of the faith, and vice versa?

Just as the doctrines of the faith are not timeless faith propositions requiring no interpretation, so too the believing self who makes sense of
the faith is not some fixed unchanging substance. I propose (1) that, if
the contents of the faith presuppose a narrative, and if personal identity
is narrative in form, then the identity of the Christian is best understood
in terms of narrative; and (2) that the narrative identity of a Christian
and his or her *sensus fidei* are mutually formative.

60. Michael Root, "The Narrative Structure of Soteriology," in *Why Narrative? Readings in
Narrative Theology,* ed. Stanley Hauerwas, L. Gregory Jones, and Ronald F. Thiemann (Grand
Rapids, Mich.: W. B. Eerdmans, 1989), 263–78, at 263.

61. As Jean Tillard has remarked, "[*sensus fidei's*] importance comes from its essential link with
a Christian life lived in evangelical authenticity, of which it is an expression. This is an aspect too
little noticed by theologians who deal with *sensus fidei.* . . . What gives the seal of truth is the evangelical authenticity of life." Tillard, "Church and Apostolic Tradition," 249.

Among the many interpretative theories of identity, Paul Ricoeur's hermeneutics of the self is a useful background theory for our purposes.[62] In his philosophical writings, Ricoeur plays with the two Latin words *idem* (the same) and *ipse* (self) and distinguishes the "who" which endures through time, and the "who" which changes through time. Rejecting any reductionistic notion of "self" and personal identity, he distinguishes *idem* identity (identity of "the same") and *ipse* identity (identity of "the self"). Across time the self remains constant and yet is always changing. For Ricoeur, only a recounted narrative of a life story can capture this dialectic of sameness and newness. Retrospectively, the self's life story is given unity through a narrative in which the self is at once the narrator and a character in the plot. Paradoxically the element drawing the self forth into newness is the persistent presence of "others," whether the other be a friend or stranger, or one's own self encountered in conscience. Constantly the self is summoned by otherness, summoned outward and forward through time into the open future.[63]

For Ricoeur, in his more theological writings, the primary literary paradigm of "the summoned subject" is that of the Old Testament prophet responding to the call of God.[64] The dialectic of call and response in the prophetic literature displays a dialogic structure at work in all receptions of the faith, and for our purposes, at work in the construction of a sense

62. For comment on the shift to interpretative theories of identity in theology, see the comment of Fortin-Melkevik, "The Identity of the Christian Following Jesus Christ," 91–92: "Theologies of identity now touch on all sectors of theological reflection and raise the question of encounter with the figure of Jesus Christ. . . . The human subjects who take up the story of their lives, who re-read the course of their existence in the light of their encounter with Jesus Christ, are thus put at the centre of a number of theologies. In so doing one gives priority to the way which retraces the Bible stories that address the stories of contemporaries. . . . The move from a problematic of Christian identity to the identity of the Christian is more than a bit of flirting; the paradigm of pluralism within the community is at stake. That is why this transition from Christian identity to the identity of the Christian is increasingly important in the local churches."

63. See Paul Ricoeur, *Oneself as Another* (Chicago: University of Chicago Press, 1992). For a succinct summary of the main theses of the book, see Paul Ricoeur, "Approaching the Human Person," *Ethical Perspectives* 6 (1999): 45–54. See also Henry Isaac Venema, *Identifying Selfhood: Imagination, Narrative, and Hermeneutics in the Thought of Paul Ricoeur* (Albany: State University of New York Press, 2000); Richard A. Cohen and James L. Marsh, *Ricoeur as Another: The Ethics of Subjectivity* (Albany: State University of New York Press, 2002).

64. Two of Ricoeur's 1986 Gifford Lectures are not included in *Oneself as Another* because of their specifically theological focus. The eleventh lecture is published in English as Paul Ricoeur, "The Self in the Mirror of the Scriptures," in *The Whole and Divided Self*, ed. David E. Aune and John McCarthy (New York: Crossroad, 1997), 201–20. The final, twelfth lecture is published as Ricoeur, "The Summoned Subject."

of the faith. For Ricoeur, the counterpart in the New Testament of the responding prophet is found in the Pauline notion of conformity to the Christ figure. Paul speaks of identification with Christ, of incorporation into Christ, of a dialectic between the old self and the new self. Baptized Christians are summoned to have "the mind of Christ": "for to me, living is Christ and dying is gain"; "let the same mind be in you that was in Christ Jesus"; "I want to know Christ and the power of his resurrection and the sharing of his sufferings by becoming like him in his death."[65]

In tracing the history of literary and theological reception of this figure of the prophetic and the christomorphic subject, Ricoeur highlights two paradigms in particular: Augustine's figure of the "inner teacher" and the notion of conscience. First, Augustine in his work *The Teacher,* written from the horizon of a Neo-Platonic notion of illumination, internalizes the role of teacher into a process of "inward learning," recalling the Johannine assurance "you do not need anyone to teach you . . . his anointing teaches you about all things."[66] Ricoeur's second figure is that of conscience, "surely the most internalized expressions of the responding self."[67] For the summoned subject, the call of conscience becomes "a call of the self to itself."[68] Here, for the theologian, one arrives at the deepest sense of Ricoeur's title *Oneself as Another:* from the perspective of the risk of Christian faith and rejection of the false dichotomy between autonomy and heteronomy, response to the call of conscience is a free risk where the self discovers oneself as Another, Christ.

The constant refashioning of one's life through conversion of the poietic imagination is a taking on of "the same mind that was in Christ Jesus."[69] It is an imitation or representation of Christ (in Latin, *imitatio christi;* in Greek, *mimesis christou*). Once again, the work of Ricoeur can provide a helpful background theory in our discussion of the imaginative role of *sensus fidei* and the interpretation of Scripture. Literary *mimesis* (imitation or representation) for Ricoeur relates to three worlds: *mimesis I* (the world behind the text), *mimesis II* (the world of the text), and *mimesis III* (the world in front of the text). The work of imagination in each of these worlds he calls prefiguration, configuration, and refiguration.[70] Imitation of Christ *(mimesis christou)* can also be conceived in terms of these three worlds. Sandra Schneiders in particular has related

65. 1 Cor 2:16; Phil 1:21; Phil 2:5; Phil 3:10.   66. 1 Jn 2:27.
67. Ricoeur, "The Summoned Subject," 271.   68. Ibid., 273.
69. Phil 2:5.   70. See Ricoeur, "Threefold Mimesis."

Ricoeur's work to the prefiguring, configuring, and refiguring of Christ taking place in the world behind the scriptural text, in the world of the text and in the world in front of the text.[71]

Our discussion here has thus returned to the issue of Scripture's inspiration and the role of the Spirit in the reception of Scripture. Since the Spirit is the principle of reception of revelation, the potentially revelatory text becomes revelatory in its reception. For the reader in the world in front of the text, life in Christ is life in the Spirit. Living the Christ life configured in Scripture is only possible in the Spirit. In this way, the inspiration of Scripture reaches its end in the witness of a life of committed discipleship to Jesus Christ in the here and now. In the world in front of the text, the reader refigures Christ within the flow of his or her own life story. This work of refiguration is the function of *sensus fidei* and the realization of the inspiration of Scripture. Furthermore, the refiguration of the identity of the Christian as a lived sense of the faith is a *mimesis christou* in the world. This new imagining of oneself as a Christian in particular concrete situations of life is the primary form of one's *sensus fidei*. It is a sense of how the reign of God that Jesus imagined in parable could be refigured and made real in one's everyday world. It is a new imagining of what it means for me to be a disciple of this Jesus. It is a conceiving of my life as a life in Christ, of my life's story as a narrative of my emerging unique identity as a Christian in a new context. Thus one's "sense of the faith" is determined by "the narrative quality" of Christian experience.

To reimagine the world which Scripture imagines, and to reimagine myself within that world, is to imagine myself as another, as new, as different, as Christ. The self-identity of the Christian is an ongoing project of conversion.[72] It is an imaginative projection of oneself into one's *past* and a reconstruction of the narrative thread of one's life history up to the *present*. It is situating oneself in relationship to God in a narrative of sin and salvation. It is also an imaginative projection of oneself into a possible new *future* as a "new creation," in Pauline terms. It is imagining "the old self" as past and "the new self" as a transformed identity, the same yet different. In the tension between experience and expectation, a new space opens out into a different, redeemed self. Sameness and difference,

---

71. See Schneiders, *The Revelatory Text.*

72. Deal W. Hudson, "The Catholic View of Conversion," in *Handbook of Religious Conversion,* ed. H. Newton Malony and Samuel Southard (Birmingham, Ala.: Religious Education Press, 1992), 108–22.

continuity and discontinuity mark the narrative journey of the self along the journey of the disciple. The faithful imagining of *sensus fidei* thus functions to preserve continuity with the self's past and it functions to disrupt that continuity by opening up new possibilities in the future.

THE EIGHT CHARACTERISTICS

I have suggested that *sensus fidei* is both an imaginative capacity to interpret revelation, and the particular interpretation of revelation constructed by the individual believer in the Christian community. On the level of *fides qua,* this imaginative activity enables the believing self to discover and make sense of revelation within the narrative of one's life. On the level of *fides quae,* each individual necessarily constructs, consciously or unconsciously, their own concrete catechism according to the norm of the God of Jesus Christ as witnessed to in Scripture and tradition. From our investigation of the primary locus, context, mode, norm, and form of the *sensus fidei,* various characteristics have emerged. I now propose a framework which highlights eight such overlapping characteristics of the imaginative organon of *sensus fidei* as it functions in the life of the individual: the personal, the heuristic, the cognitive, the practical, the soteriological, the integrative, the critical, and the ecclesial. These eight characteristics of *sensus fidei's* activity go to the heart of an individual's ongoing conversion and the changing shape of their sense of the faith. Through this imaginative activity, the faith is received and traditioned in different cultures and contexts down through history and throughout the world church today.

Firstly, *sensus fidei* has a *personal* dimension. It is the fruit of faith, faith understood as one's personal relationship with God, encountered through Christ in the power of the Spirit *(fides qua creditur).* This *sensus* which faith possesses constitutes an interior affinity with the God who is reaching out in a movement of self-giving and saving love. Faith is personal communion with the Triune God. One's sense for the faith is ultimately grounded in this personal relationship of love.

Secondly, *sensus fidei* is a *heuristic* sense. It discovers and uncovers. With an imagination formed by ecclesial faith, it perceives a revelatory presence mediated through symbol. Indeed, in its recognition, symbol becomes mediatory only when imagination "sees the Invisible." The ordinary is recognized as extraordinary, the human as divine.

Thirdly, *sensus fidei* has a *cognitive* dimension. From the hermeneutical circle between *fides qua* and *fides quae,* there comes a "knowing" which is grounded in this personal and loving affinity with God as Mystery. St. Paul could say, "I *know* [*oida*] the one in whom I have put my trust."[73] Because of the believer's communion with God there exists a "connatural knowledge" of the loved one. This knowledge is often more intuitive, tacit, rather than capable of being clearly articulated in concepts. The narrative of a life tells it best. On this level, symbol, metaphor, and story, rather than idea or concept, constitute the first language of articulation. This connatural knowing (*fides qua*) is more instinctual and intuitive. It enables and conditions the believer's reception (understanding, interpretation, and application) of the formal teachings of the magisterium (*fides quae),* a personal reception which finds its expression in an individual's "concrete catechism."

Fourthly, *sensus fidei* is a *practical* sense. Closely related to the cognitive dimension, this aspect highlights the close relationship between knowing and doing/acting. The faithful one sets out to show the truth by doing the good. Through personally knowing the revealing God on an intuitive level and through receiving the church's explicit proclamation of the Gospel, the believer acquires *phronesis,* practical wisdom, for applying "the faith" within the challenges of a particular context. Knowing the implications of faith for daily life comes intuitively, albeit within the tension between sinfulness and liberation. Oftentimes reasons cannot be given for this sense of the faith. Love knows what love must do. In being a practical sense, *sensus fidei* is thus too a moral sense, as conscience brings judgment and decision to bear on consequent action.

Fifthly, *sensus fidei* is a *soteriological* sense. It is a sense for the faith that emerges out of an experience of salvation in one's own life. It senses salvation, and names it; it senses the Savior, and sees new possibilities for conversion. Its object of interpretation is revelatory salvation as real for me, for us, for our world. My experience of salvation gives meaning to the knowledge of revelation; the knowledge of revelation enables the experience of salvation to be named. I live out that salvation in a life of faithful discipleship to Jesus Christ in the power of the Spirit, within the community of faith, the sacrament of salvation.

Sixthly, *sensus fidei* is an *integrative* sense. This dimension is evident in all the previous five characteristics. This integration bridges past and

73. 2 Tm 1:12.

present, story and significance, faith and personal identity, doctrine and life, belief and practice, communal faith and individual faith. The threads of one's life of sin and salvation are drawn into a meaningful whole, as a story in which God is redeeming and revealing.

Seventhly, *sensus fidei* is a *critical* sense. This salvific and revelatory knowledge gives the capacity for perceptive judgment. The faithful believer develops an intuitive sense of what does or does not "bring forth Christ." This critical dimension is present in the engagement of conscience, wherein judgment and choice are made after imagination presents possibilities for action. This suspicious dimension of *sensus fidei* is like the critical eye of the prophet. It is always attentive in the reading of Scripture and tradition to any false interpretation that would not be true to the faith. The faithful Christian knows how easily the Gospel can become the plaything of ideologies. This critical dimension, however, also turns self-critical, always placing one's own developing *sensus fidei* under the criterion of the Gospel and its constant call to conversion.

Finally, *sensus fidei* is an *ecclesial* sense. It prompts individuals to "sense with the church" *(sentire cum ecclesia)*. To test further their own sense of the faith, beyond their own interpretation of the faith of the church, individuals turn to the criterion of other Christian believers' *sensus fidei* and the whole church's sense of the faith. Here the critical dimension above is extended to include an openness on the part of the individual to be critiqued by the wider Christian community (the *sensus fidei fidelium*) and by those entrusted with formal authoritative oversight of faithful transmission of the Gospel (the magisterium). In the tension between individual perception of the faith and the magisterium's perception on behalf of the whole church, the Spirit is always prompting individuals to ask: is their sense of the faith in accord with that of the entire church, "the faith once delivered to all the saints"?[74] If not, how might they come to see things differently, through a "differentiation of horizons"? If their unique sense of the faith might very well be judged to be in harmony with the faith of the entire church, how can their innovative *sensus fidei,* likewise in a differentiation of horizons, contribute to an enrichment and perhaps conversion of the *sensus fidelium,* the *sensus theologiae,* and the *sensus magisterii?* How the fresh perspective of individuals might play a constructive role in the teaching office of the church is the focus of the next chapter.

74. Jude 3.

CHAPTER 9

Sensus Fidelium and Teaching the Faith of the Church

Having explored the *sensus fidei fidelis,* we can now move to an exploration of the *sensus fidei fidelium,* or, more succinctly, the *sensus fidelium.* The twofold definition of *sensus fidei fidelis* likewise applies when speaking of the *sensus fidei fidelium.* The term can refer both to (1) a *sensus* or organon for the understanding, interpretation, and application of revelation, but here referring to a *sensus* or organon that is possessed by the whole people and is thus a corporate or ecclesial capacity, and (2) the interpretations that are the result of the interpretative activity of that organon, but here referring to the totality of diverse interpretations by individuals that are the result of the exercise of that corporate interpretative *sensus.*

Firstly, the *sensus fidelium* is a corporate organon at work in the church, enabling the one church throughout the world to receive revelation faithfully and meaningfully, and then to tradition it effectively. This corporate organon is the church's "eyes of faith" throughout the centuries. Since the primary mode of the *sensus fidei* is imagination, as we saw in the previous chapter, the organon of *sensus fidelium* is what we could call the ecclesial imagination. It is the means by which the church bridges story and significance as it moves through history, into new and diverse contexts. We have seen its role in the formation of the canon of Scripture.

Because it is one and the same Holy Spirit working at the individual and communal level, there is a *conspiratio* at work in the maintenance of the unity of faith and the diverse senses made of the one faith. Because the church is a *communio fidelium,* the *sensus fidei* is not only an organon that is at work in individual *fideles;* in a real sense, the church as a *communio fidelium* possesses this capacity or organon. Just as the universal church, as a *communio ecclesiarum,* is the one church found in the many, so too the corporate organon of the *sensus fidelium* is a single ecclesial capacity, but which works through the individuals of the church (as the *sensus fidei fidelis*). The same Holy Spirit is given both to the whole church and to individuals within the church. It is to the whole church that the "ministry of memory" is given, not just to the magisterium (which nevertheless has a distinctive role in the preservation of that memory).[1] If "the Holy Spirit is the living memory of the church,"[2] then the Spirit's communal organon of *sensus fidelium* is the means by which the Spirit weaves a continuity of ecclesial memory throughout the history of the church.

The eight characteristics of the organon of *sensus fidei* operating in the individual, explored in the previous chapter, likewise apply as characteristics of the corporate imaginative organon of the *sensus fidelium.* Those eight characteristics, we saw, were the personal, the heuristic, the cognitive, the practical, the soteriological, the integrative, the critical, and the ecclesial. The corporate imaginative capacity functions in these eight ways in both the local and the universal church, constantly drawing the church toward conversion of the ecclesial imagination.

Here, in focusing specifically on the *sensus fidelium,* we are focusing on the Holy Spirit's gift to the whole church of an imaginative organon for the understanding, interpretation, and application of revelation, i.e.,

---

1. "The great Tradition has always been unanimous that one of the chief functions of the Spirit is not only to assure the faithful transmission of the *acta et dicta* of the Lord Jesus but also to make understood the meaning and implications of his words and his *semeia,* to reveal how the Scriptures are fulfilled in him and hence how his Pasch was the 'once for all' (the *epaphax*) of his divine design. The Spirit thus gives the Church its 'memory.'" J. M. R. Tillard, "Ministry and Apostolic Tradition," *Mid-Stream* 29 (1990): 199–207, at 199. While Tillard, in using the phrases "service of memory" and "ministry of memory," is no doubt employing the word "ministry" in its technical sense as applied to ordained bishops, the phrase can be somewhat misleading, as if the memory of the church resides in the magisterium alone (which of course Tillard is not advocating). In my proposal, it is the organon of *sensus fidelium* which is the ecclesial organon for faithful remembering.

2. *Catechism of the Catholic Church,* no. 1099.

the reception of revelation. At a communal level, the corporate organon operates through the Spirit's "normal" process of working throughout history: conciliarity or synodality, and its mode of operation through reception of "the other" in dialogue. It is the Spirit's communal organon of *sensus fidelium* that grounds the interrelationship and dialogic mode of operation among the three authorities of the church's teaching office: the *sensus fidelium* (here seen as that organon's diversity of interpretations), theology, and the magisterium. Furthermore, it is this organon that enables the church's infallibility in believing, manifested when it leads to "a universal *consensus* in matters of faith and morals" (*LG,* 12). Likewise, it is this organon that enables infallibility in teaching by the magisterium under certain conditions (*LG,* 25).

Secondly, the *sensus fidelium* is the diverse interpretations of the one faith throughout the world. It is the totality of the spiritual receptions of the faith by all members of the church, as they each apply the faith in their own lives. At one level, this variety of expression can be spoken of in the singular, as "the collective faith-consciousness."[3] However, the one "faith once delivered to the saints"[4] is understood, interpreted, and applied in a wide variety of ways. This diversity is not a breach of the unity of faith, but is the expression of the very universality of salvation in Christ which is experienced in many ways throughout the world in different cultures and contexts, and in different times throughout history. The issue of "determining the *sensus fidelium*" necessarily involves attention to this diversity of expression of the faith. Many times in our discussion, therefore, it is this meaning of the term (as various "senses" of the faith) that is intended when speaking of the interaction between the *sensus fidelium,* theology, and the magisterium. But, as we shall see, the corporate organon of the *sensus fidelium* is not only at work in the diversity of interpretations through the world-church, but is an organon at work also in the work of theology and in the operation of the magisterium, as well as in the interaction of all three.

Later, we will discuss another term which is defined variously in the literature, the *consensus fidelium.* It will be proposed that the *consensus fidelium* is best understood as the end product of a process of determining the church's unified diversity of faith regarding a particular matter. A

---

3. Vorgrimler, "From *Sensus Fidei* to *Consensus Fidelium,*" 3.
4. Jude 3.

consensus fidelium is a single expression of the faith, and it is the function of the magisterium alone to make such an authoritative statement on behalf of and for the whole church. However, because that single statement must express the faith of the whole church, any determination of a *consensus fidelium* must begin with a determination of the diverse *sensus fidelium* through the world-church. In what follows we will examine the sources, the agents and instruments, and the dialogue which should constitute the proper determination of the *sensus fidelium*. We will then address the issue of a *consensus fidelium*.

THE VARYING SOURCES

Seven times in the Book of Revelation the call resounds: "Let anyone who has an ear listen to what the Spirit is saying to the churches."[5] Where, and through whom, is the Holy Spirit speaking to the church today? What are the *loci receptionis* (places of reception) for listening to and determining the *sensus fidelium* and for beginning the ecclesial process of approbative reception? Within the Roman Catholic Church, who is to be regarded as "in" the church? Is the Holy Spirit to be discerned only from voices within the Catholic Church, or also from voices in other Christian churches?[6]

In expanding concentric rings of dialogue, paralleling the expanding search for dialogue imaged in *Gaudium et Spes* 92, I propose to distinguish primary, secondary, and ancillary sources for accessing and determining the *sensus fidelium*. My perspective and my starting point are Roman Catholic, but also ecumenical. The primary source for a Catholic determination of the *sensus fidelium*, I propose, comes from the diverse

---

5. Rv 2:7, 11, 17, 29; 3:6, 13, 22.

6. The issue of whether the Holy Spirit could be speaking through "believers" of other religions or even non-believers is not strictly an issue directly related to the theme of the *sensus fidelium*, which is an organon given through Christian baptism and a dimension of Christian faith. It is a theme, however, that relates to the mission of the church in the world, and in that sense is relevant to the proclamation of the Good News to the world. Consequently, the religious "sense" *(sensus religiosus)* of adherents of other religions could be called an "exogenous source" for all three authorities within the church's teaching office, aiding it in a more effective and relevant interpretation of revelation in the light of the signs of the times. The botanical term "exogenous" literally means "growing by additions on the outside." I use the term in the analogous sense in which Yves Congar speaks of "exogenous reception." Congar, however, is referring to the way a local church appropriates some ecclesial value from another local church, but within the communion of churches. See Congar, "Reception as an Ecclesiological Reality."

sensus fidei of individual believers who are attempting to live a committed and sacramental life in the Catholic Church. The secondary source comes from baptized Catholics on a scale of lessening involvement in Catholic ecclesial life, from those who are "inactive," to the "lapsed," and to those "disaffected" with the church, but who might or might not still regard themselves as Catholics in some way. The ancillary source is the sense of the faith by baptized believers within other Christian churches or ecclesial communities (with a corresponding scale of ecclesial involvement).

The *primary source,* from within the Catholic Church, is the multitude of individual baptized Catholics who are attempting to live the Christ life in power of the Spirit, and to participate regularly in the sacramental life and mission of the church. This primary source includes lay people, religious, deacons, priests, bishops, the pope, all here considered in their fundamental identity as baptized and committed Catholic Christians. In the previous chapter it was to this group that we restricted our enquiry as we examined the way in which the organon of *sensus fidei* functions in the life of each baptized and committed believer. Wolfgang Beinert, in addressing the "rules" for the determination of the *sensus fidelium,* believes that such determination should be restricted to this group; he highlights the importance of active discipleship as a surer sign of an authentic sense of the faith.[7] There is, he asserts, a close link between a living of the faith and an authentic sense of the faith. The personal, cognitive, and soteriological dimensions of the *sensus fidei* are here especially pertinent: "I *know* the one in whom I have put my trust."[8]

Any theology of the *sensus fidei* and the *sensus fidelium* must certainly give priority to a perception of the faith by one seeking constant conversion to the Gospel, who regularly avails himself or herself of the sacraments, who is constantly being nourished by the reading of Scripture and personal prayer, and who is attempting to apply the Gospel in his or her life by promoting the reign of God in the world. Such living faith commitment gives insider knowledge through intimacy with Christ made possible through openness to the grace of the Holy Spirit. This insider knowledge gives rise to a consequent sense of the faith, as we ex-

---

7. See Wolfgang Beinert, "Der Glaubenssinn der Gläubigen in der systematischen Theologie," in *Mitsprache im Glauben? Vom Glaubenssinn der Gläubigen,* ed. Günther Koch (Würzburg: Echter, 1993), 51–78, at 72.

8. 2 Tm 1:12.

plored in chapter 8. Certainly sinfulness in the life of all believers can cloud interpretation of the faith in such committed believers, but just as importantly, experience of forgiveness and salvation within a life marked by sinfulness is fundamental to experience of the God of Jesus Christ; it is out of an experience of grace, forgiveness, and salvation that one senses the heart of faith. The Christian Gospel is fundamentally about the possibility of such salvation; that is the Good News. In highlighting the importance of the narrative of a life, we have seen how faith and faith's perception has its stages, and that in the life of the believer there is constant need for ongoing conversion to Christ through the grace of the Holy Spirit.

Giving priority to this primary source is not to exclude critical, prophetic voices in the church in the determination of the *sensus fidelium.* The tension, for example, between Paul and Peter was highly significant in the ongoing conversion of the early church's ecclesial imagination, as it articulated its faith in the light of new questions. It seems that, according to Paul, "Peter was in danger of betraying the Gospel of his master."[9] Beinert's rule, therefore, of giving priority to the perception of committed, sacramental Catholics does not deny the importance of listening to voices that challenge the church from within to a more prophetic following of Christ. Such voices are a challenge to constant conversion to Christ for all the *fideles,* in order that there might be a conversion of the corporate ecclesial imagination.

Within this category of the primary source of the *sensus fidelium,* there are three groups within the *fideles* that can be distinguished for the purposes of our study: the laity, theologians, and bishops. There are others, of course, besides these who are to be included, e.g., religious, deacons, and priests. The instruments for reception examined later in this chapter will highlight their particular contribution. But it is helpful at this stage to distinguish these three groups for two reasons. Firstly, the *sensus laicorum* (the sense of the laity) is often restrictively understood to be synonymous with the *sensus fidelium.* The sense of the faithful encompasses more than the laity's sense of the faith, even though they constitute the vast majority of the body of the faithful. Secondly, theologians and bishops, while they also constitute two of the authorities in the teaching office, are also to be included in the determination of the *sensus fidelium*

9. Beinert, "Der Glaubenssinn der Gläubigen in der systematischen Theologie," 72.

because of their primary identity as individual baptized *fideles*. *Lumen Gentium* 12, as we have seen, speaks of the *sensus fidei totius populi*, the sense of all the *fideles*, "from the bishops to the last of the faithful."[10] Therefore, the significance of an individual bishop's or theologian's *sensus fidei* needs to be made explicit in any theology of the *sensus fidelium*, and it is important both to relate that individual *sensus fidei* to, and to distinguish it from, that individual's participation in "theology" or "magisterium," as authorities in the teaching office of the church. In the next section, therefore, we will discuss in greater detail these three groups within the *fideles* whose individual perspectives on the faith contribute to the *sensus fidelium* within the primary source: the *sensus laicorum*, the *sensus theologorum* (the sense of theologians), and the *sensus episcoporum* (the sense of bishops). Later, we will distinguish these notions from the three teaching *authorities*, defined as the *sensus fidelium*, the *sensus theologiae* (the sense of theology), and the *sensus magisterii* (the sense of the magisterium). A *consensus fidelium*, we shall see, is the result of the dialogic interaction between the three teaching authorities, but formulated and promulgated officially by the magisterium.

However, there is another source within the Catholic Church that should be attended to in a full determination of the *sensus fidelium*, beyond that of committed, sacramental Catholics. This *secondary source* consists of those baptized Catholics who in a wide variety of ways are not fully "faithful" to their baptismal commitment through ongoing participation in the sacramental life and mission of the church, a vibrant prayer life, the reading of Scripture—all dimensions necessary for availing oneself fully of the power of the Spirit for living the new life in Christ. This lack of openness to the Spirit surely diminishes the effectiveness of the Spirit's "eyes of faith" for interpreting things aright. But does it render its perspective totally unimportant and of no concern to the church's teaching office in its task of listening to all voices of the Spirit and indeed of thereby effectively proclaiming the Gospel to this very group of Catholics? This secondary source includes that diverse group of Catholics who could be variously and somewhat vaguely described as "inactive," "lapsed," "disaffected," or "marginalized." Some within this vastly varying group might indeed have a strong sense of identity with the Catholic Church; others might not.

10. *LG*, 12, quoting Augustine, *De Praed. Sanct.* 14, 27 [PL 44, 980].

In disagreeing with the position of Bernard Sesboüé, who, like Beinert, believes that determination of the *sensus fidelium* should be restricted to those Catholics who "practice" the faith and should exclude those
who do not, John Burkhard rightly states that Vatican II does not make
such a distinction.[11] There are grounds, I believe, for not restricting the
determination of the *sensus fidelium* exclusively to so-called "practicing
Catholics." For example, the question necessarily arises: how does one
determine faithful adherence to Christ? Sinfulness marks the lives of all
members of the church. Furthermore, even those who faithfully participate in the sacraments may not be open to all aspects of the message
of Christ, and therefore are in need of ongoing conversion. Oftentimes,
inactive, lapsed, marginalized, and disaffected Catholics raise questions
that may be a genuine call to greater fidelity to the Christ life. Rosemary Haughton, in her book *The Catholic Thing,* calls for retaining fuzzy
boundaries in describing Catholic membership and highlights the evangelical witness of people on the margins of the Catholic Church.[12]

The questions therefore arise: Is the Spirit's organon for faith rendered
inactive or null and void should one stop attending Sunday Eucharist?
In speaking of "faith" and degrees of faith, is it not theologically legitimate to see faith in more developmental and dynamic terms, in which
individuals are seen to go through "stages of faith," with their transi-
tional and indeed necessary crises of faith, with the Spirit's organon of
sensus fidei active in some way at all stages and crisis points?[13] Such a dif-

11. "The teaching of Vatican II on the [*sensus fidelium*] refers to all believers and makes no such
distinction among the faithful. Obviously, there are real differences of engagement in the faith
and in the Church on the part of Christians. However, to insist too much on the differences results in diminishing our appreciation of the real bonds of baptism. . . . [The] Spirit can also be addressing the wider Church precisely through the radical questioning, rejection, or indifference toward the Church of the marginally involved—or even by the Church's hostile critics. The [*sensus
fidelium*] also calls for making room for a forum in which all the baptised can be involved. It is salutary and startling to recall just how appreciative Jesus was of the religiously alienated persons of
his day and their conflicts with their religious leaders." Burkhard, "*Sensus Fidei:* Recent Theological Reflection (1990–2001). Part I," 463–64. Burkhard is referring to Bernard Sesboüé, "Le 'sensus
fidelium' en morale à la lumière de Vatican II," *Le Supplément* 181 (1992): 153–66. In a later article,
Burkhard also questions the limitation of my enquiry to committed, sacramental Catholics in Ormond Rush, "*Sensus Fidei:* Faith 'Making Sense' of Revelation," *Theological Studies* 62 (2001): 231–
61. See Burkhard, "*Sensus Fidei:* Recent Theological Reflection (1990–2001). Part II," 46–48. My
intention in that article was to begin my research into the *sensus fidei fidelis* and the *sensus fidelium*
with an investigation into an "ideal type." In continuing that investigation in this present work, I
now move on to broaden the scope of my enquiry.

12. See Rosemary Haughton, *The Catholic Thing* (Springfield, Ill.: Templegate, 1979).

13. On stages of faith, see James W. Fowler, *Stages of Faith: The Psychology of Human Develop-*

fuse and wide-ranging group of baptized Catholics must, in some way, be included among those whose sense of the faith is to be determined and discerned by the church. They may well provide perspectives on the challenges of living the faith in contemporary society which may aid the church in responding to new questions never before posed to the tradition. Furthermore, their sense of the faith may indeed aid the church in finding new language to express new answers to old questions in a culture where the old answers, while still true answers, no longer meaningfully animate the faith life of Christians in the way they have been expressed in the past.

The *ancillary source* is the sense of the faith perceived by baptized Christians from other churches. Several scholars have proposed that the determination of the *sensus fidelium* by the Catholic Church should now include the ecclesial experience of Christian salvation that has been outside the Catholic Church since the division between the East and West, and since the Reformation division in the West.[14] Certainly it is true, as John Burkhard remarks, that the intended reference of the bishops when formulating the teaching on the *sensus fidei totius populi* in *Lumen Gentium* 12 was to the *universitas fidelium* within the Catholic Church.[15] However, historical reconstruction of "authorial intention" (through a hermeneutics of the authors) is but one moment in a comprehensive hermeneutic for interpreting the council; there must also be incorporated a hermeneutics of the texts themselves and a hermeneutics of reception.[16] The possibility of a new synthesis on this matter emerges when we move beyond an exclusive hermeneutics of the authors (a reconstruction of authorial intention) and an exclusive focus on this particular passage (*LG,* 12), to include both an intra-textual reading (of *Lumen Gentium* as a whole) and an inter-textual reading of all the council documents, in the light of new questions addressed to the texts which emerge in the process of reception.

Intra-textually (reading within *Lumen Gentium*), the restriction in *Lu-*

---

ment and the Quest for Meaning (San Francisco: Harper & Row, 1981). For a summary and critique of Fowler, see H. Newton Malony, "The Concept of Faith in Psychology," in *Handbook of Faith,* ed. James Michael Lee (Birmingham, Ala.: Religious Education Press, 1990), 71–95.

14. See, for example, Patrick J. Hartin, "*Sensus Fidelium:* A Roman Catholic Reflection on Its Significance for Ecumenical Thought," *Journal of Ecumenical Studies* 28 (1991): 74–87, esp. 82–84. Heft, "'Sensus Fidelium' and the Marian Dogmas."

15. See Burkhard, "*Sensus Fidei:* Recent Theological Reflection (1990–2001). Part I," 462.

16. See Rush, *Still Interpreting Vatican II.*

men Gentium 12 of the *sensus fidei* to the Catholic Church stands in tension with the notion in *Lumen Gentium* 8 that the church of Christ "subsists in" the Catholic Church; "many elements of sanctification and of truth" are to be found outside the confines of the Catholic Church.[17] *Lumen Gentium* 12 implicitly teaches that the anointing of the Spirit comes through baptism. Furthermore, an inter-textual reading of all the documents highlights that *Unitatis Redintegratio* 3 explicitly recognizes the baptism of other churches.[18] The Catholic Church's recognition of the baptism of other churches raises the question of whether the *sensus fidei* which accompanies the gift of the Spirit in baptism demands theological recognition of the *sensus fidei* of the baptized from other churches. Therefore, an inter-textual reading requires that the council's document *Unitatis Redintegratio,* promulgated on the same day as *Lumen Gentium,* be used to interpret the meaning of the vision outlined in the latter, and in particular paragraph 12 regarding the *sensus fidelium.*

A comprehensive interpretation of the council on this matter must include attention to the reception of both the "spirit" of the conciliar event and the "letter" of its documents. Reception over the last forty years of the council's call for ecumenical dialogue has been grounded implicitly in the above intra-textual and inter-textual readings. Moreover, in those ecumenical dialogues the Catholic Church has discovered a way toward a new synthesis from the openings created by the council and its documents. This new synthesis has meant the emergence of a new self-understanding of the Roman Catholic Church. Through participation in these ecumenical dialogues, the Catholic Church is implicitly recognizing, or is at least willing to explore the recognition of, the legitimacy of the different ecclesial ways of being Christian and senses of the faith which have developed since the division between the Eastern and Western wings of Christianity, and since the Reformation divisions in the West. If this is the case, then significant theological weight is to be given to these parallel spiritual and theological receptions of the Gospel.

The term "receptive ecumenism" has come to designate the learning

17. On the significance of the verb *"subsistit,"* see Francis A. Sullivan, "The Significance of the Vatican II Declaration That the Church of Christ 'Subsists in' the Roman Catholic Church," in *Vatican II Assessment and Perspectives: Twenty-Five Years After (1962–1987),* vol. 2, ed. René Latourelle (New York: Paulist Press, 1989), 2:272–87.

18. "[A]ll who have been justified by faith in baptism are members of Christ's body, and have a right to be called Christians, and so are deservedly recognised as sisters and brothers in the Lord by the children of the Catholic Church." Tanner translation, corrected.

process that emerges in ecumenical dialogues; the Catholic Church can learn from other churches and ecclesial communities.[19] Such receptive ecumenism calls each of the churches participating in dialogue to renewed conversion to the Gospel.[20] The spiritual and theological receptions of other Christians beyond the Catholic Church may come, through dialogue, to be recognized by Catholics as receptions of revelation which are genuine senses of the faith, and which should be included in a Catholic determination of the *sensus fidelium.*

THREE GROUPS IN THE PRIMARY SOURCE

Particular attention needs to be given to a special triad of voices within the primary source of the *sensus fidelium.* Those three groups of voices are the sense of the faith coming from the laity (the *sensus laicorum*), the sense of the faith of theologians (the *sensus theologorum*), and the sense of the faith of bishops (the *sensus episcoporum*). Described in this way, these groups are here examined as groups within the *sensus fidelium,* and not as the three formal authorities in the teaching office. These authorities will be later examined as the *sensus fidelium,* the *sensus theologiae,* and the *sensus magisterii.*

Some approaches to the *sensus fidelium* simplistically equate it with the *sensus laicorum.* Certainly, since the vast majority of the *fideles* are lay people, and since the individual *sensus fidei* of theologians and bishops is already adequately accessed and determined in the processes of their formal functions, the determination of the *sensus fidelium* will need to give much more attention to the *sensus laicorum* than is currently the case. However, highlighting the distinction between, and commonality of, these three groups is important for three reasons.

Firstly, I wish to bring to the fore, following *Lumen Gentium,* that

19. For example, see Paul Murray, ed., *Receptive Ecumenism and the Call to Catholic Learning: Exploring a Way for Contemporary Ecumenism* (Oxford: Oxford University Press, 2008). This book publishes the proceedings of the landmark conference in Durham, England, January 12–17, 2006, entitled "Catholic Learning: Explorations in Receptive Ecumenism, An International Colloquium in Honour of Walter Cardinal Kasper." The colloquium was sponsored by the Department of Theology and Religion, Durham University and St. Cuthbert's Seminary, Ushaw College, Durham.

20. On ecclesial conversion in ecumenical dialogue, see Groupe des Dombes, *For the Conversion of the Churches* (Geneva: WCC Publications, 1993). For a history and analysis of the work of the Groupe des Dombes, see Catherine E. Clifford, *The Groupe des Dombes: A Dialogue of Conversion* (New York: Peter Lang, 2005).

theologians and bishops are to be included in the *fideles* when the *sensus fidelium* is being determined. Secondly, I wish to highlight that an individual's *sensus fidei* is not insignificant when that person comes to exercise his or her function formally either as a theologian among the community of theologians, or as a bishop among the college of bishops. Theologians and bishops are *fideles,* who live out their lives seeking, like all believers, to be ever more faithful disciples of Jesus. However, it is still legitimate and important to distinguish them among the *fideles* as two distinct groups. This is not to make them "special" among the *fideles* at the level of baptismal identity. Rather it highlights how, in their official role as theologian or bishop, their own distinctive *sensus fidei* needs to be acknowledged, since it directly affects their contribution at that official level. Thirdly, I wish to highlight the pervasive function of the *sensus fidei* (both as interpretative organon and as emerging interpretations) in the exercise of all three authorities within the teaching office of the church. It constitutes the continuum of faith within and between each of the three authorities, since it constitutes the Spirit's *conspiratio* with the church's teaching office.

The *Sensus Laicorum*

Lay people constitute the vast majority of individuals active in the church's mission in the world. Accessing their sense of the faith as they go about that mission is vital for a teaching office that is to be relevant and effective in its service of that mission. All that was said in the previous chapter of the *sensus fidei* in the life of the individual believer of course applies to the lay person. In this section, we will examine further aspects of the contribution of the *sensus fidei* of lay people to the *sensus fidelium,* in particular by looking at what, according to Vatican II, is the "secular" context of the lives of lay people, and by examining, with the four categories of witness, charism, signs of the times, and prophecy, the unique contribution that is the *sensus laicorum.*

"At Vatican II the Roman Catholic Church for the first time in history took up the question of the status and role of the laity, and provided a theological perspective on a Christian spirituality that takes seriously lay experiences, vocations, and ministries."[21] We have already seen how *Lumen Gentium,* after discussing in its second chapter the participation of

---

21. Edward C. Sellner, "Lay Spirituality," in *The New Dictionary of Catholic Spirituality,* ed. Michael Downey (Collegeville, Minn.: Liturgical Press, 1993), 589–96, at 592.

the whole People of God (pope, bishops, lay people) in the prophetic office and the gift of *sensus fidei* given to all, goes on in chapter 3 to speak of the particular way the pope and bishops participate in that office, and then in chapter 4, the particular way the laity participate.[22] This is reiterated in the Decree on the Apostolate of the Laity, *Apostolicam Actuositatem.*[23]

Lumen Gentium's classic passage regarding the laity's participation particularly in the prophetic office, and the function of God's gift of the *sensus fidei* in that participation, highlights how the Spirit, through that gift, enables lay people to apply the Gospel to their Christian lives, above all through witness:

> Christ, the great prophet, who by the witness of his life and the power of his word, proclaimed the Father's kingdom, continues to carry out his prophetic office [*munus propheticum*], until the full manifestation of his glory, not only through the hierarchy who teach in his name and by his power, but also through the laity whom he constitutes his witnesses and equips with an understanding of the faith [*sensus fidei*] and a grace of speech precisely so that the power of the gospel may shine forth in the daily life of family and society.[24]

It is this application of the Gospel to daily life, in new contexts and cultures, that constitutes the fundamental role of the laity in the traditioning of revelation and the particular contribution to the teaching office of their sense of the faith as lay people. Vatican II admittedly makes tentative moves beyond giving a passive role to lay people in the matter of church teaching. It highlights the importance of the intuitions of lay people with regard to an effective fulfillment of the church's mission. For example, *Lumen Gentium* 37 states: "In accordance with the knowl-

---

22. In clarifying what it means by "laity," *LG,* 31 states: "Under the title laity are here understood all Christ's faithful, except those who are in sacred orders or are members of a religious state that is recognised by the church; that is to say, the faithful who, since they have been incorporated into Christ by baptism, constitute the people of God and, in their own way made sharers in Christ's priestly, prophetic and royal office, play their own part in the mission of the whole christian people in the church and in the world." Tanner translation.

23. "In the church, there is diversity in ministry but unity in mission. The office and power of teaching in the name of Christ, of sanctifying and ruling, were conferred by him on the apostles and their successors. Laypeople, sharing in the priestly, prophetic and kingly offices of Christ, play their part in the mission of the whole people of God in the church and in the world." *AA,* 2. Tanner translation. This is further elaborated by John Paul II in his *Christifideles Laici,* where he mentions the importance of the *sensus fidei* in lay people's living of the Gospel in the world. John Paul II, *Christifideles Laici,* 14.

24. *LG,* 35a. Tanner translation, corrected.

edge, competence or authority that they possess, [the laity] have the right and indeed sometimes the duty to make known their opinion on matters which concern the good of the church."[25] The paragraph refers in a footnote to a statement repeated by Pius XII: "In decisive battles it happens at times that the best initiatives come from the front line."[26]

In the previous chapter we spoke of "the primary context" of the *sensus fidei,* the everyday life of Christians. Vatican II sees the particular participation of the laity in the mission of the church in terms of their secular context:

The laity have their own special character which is secular. . . . They live in the world, that is to say, in each and all of the world's occupations and affairs, and in the ordinary circumstances of family and social life; these are the things that form the context of their life.[27]

Dolores Leckey speaks of "the baptized who are at work in the banks and studios, the offices and classrooms and homes. These people are the church in the world, and they are stirring the old order with the powerful existential questions that have been shaped in the cauldrons of their own lives."[28]

To categorize the context of the lives of lay people as "secular" is not necessarily to dichotomize "secular" and "sacred" or "nature" and "grace." In his discussion of the secular context of lay people, Paul Lakeland speaks of "secularity" in a way that is not dualistic:

To speak . . . of the secular is not to speak of a godless reality which requires some special divine act to open it up to an awareness of the holy. Just as we can speak of a graced nature, so we can also talk of a secular that is always already sacred. Nature is graced, even for those with no knowledge of God, and the world is always already sacred, whether or not we know it to be so.[29]

---

25. Tanner translation.

26. Tanner translation. The footnote cites two sources: Pius XII, Allocution, *De quelle consolation,* October 14, 1951: *AAS* 43 (1951), 789; idem, Allocution, *L'importance de la presse catholique,* February 17, 1950: *AAS* 42 (1950), 256.

27. *LG,* 31. Tanner translation.

28. Dolores R. Leckey, *Laity Stirring the Church: Prophetic Questions* (Philadelphia: Fortress Press, 1987), 13. For her commentary on the Decree on the Apostolate of the Laity, see Dolores R. Leckey, *The Laity and Christian Education: Apostolicam Actuositatem, Gravissimum Educationis, Rediscovering Vatican II* (New York: Paulist Press, 2006).

29. Paul Lakeland, *The Liberation of the Laity: In Search of an Accountable Church* (New York: Continuum, 2003), 151.

The official title of *Gaudium et Spes* appropriately captures the reality of the church, not "over against" the world, but "the church *in* the world." Although the ordained and the religious too live embedded in the world,[30] lay people in a particular way are engaged in the affairs of the world to an extent that makes their perspective on living the faith in the world a particularly pertinent one.

Within the broader context of the secular world, the particular contexts of individual lay people are richly diverse.[31] No list of the possibilities adequately covers all secular contexts of lay people and the consequent senses of the faith that emerge from the perspectives of each context. Among that diversity, the worlds of marriage and family life, the workplace, and civic life could be called "the three principal arenas of lay life."[32] Other factors marking those contexts range from location in a particular local culture and society to participation in a globalized environment with all its intertwining cultural, economic, and political forces. The particular context of individual lay people can be further differentiated by the categories of gender, level of education or economic prosperity, race, language, culture, health, security, personal history, and so on. Not only do these locations and categories name the diverse ways in which lay people are present in the world as agents for the mission of the church, they also name the factors which come to bear on the way lay people make sense of their faith within those historical determining factors.

The organon of the *sensus fidei* enables lay people to interpret their experience and context in the light of the Gospel, and to interpret the Gospel in the light of their experience and context. In chapter 8 we highlighted this integrative characteristic of the *sensus fidei*. *Gaudium et Spes*

---

30. Lakeland writes: "It is probably not helpful, in the end, to suggest that the ordained minister does not find the things of this world real and interesting in themselves, any more than it is correct to think of the layperson as living outside the Christian story, within the world. Rather, the Christian story must be seen as one that lets the world be the world. The clergy may perhaps be the keepers of the story in a way that laypersons are not, but all—lay and ordained alike—live within the story, as they live within the world." Ibid., 150.

31. In reference to what she calls "the laity's parable" (Jesus' parable about yeast, flour, and dough), Dolores Leckey says of the laity's presence in the world: "We are everywhere: in offices, in schools, in scientific laboratories, in the military, in hospitals, in theatres and orchestras, in public transportation, in the media—scattered throughout the dough of the world. But . . . the laity are not passively being kneaded, but are themselves agents of change, the stirrers and the mixers." Leckey, *Laity Stirring the Church,* 119.

32. Ibid., 69.

speaks of how Christians make "a living synthesis" of their secular activities and their religious values: "[Christians] should bring their human,
domestic, professional, scientific, and technical activities into a living
synthesis [*unam synthesim vitalem*] with religious values which orientate
and coordinate everything to the glory of God."[33] This ability for synthesis is the integrative capacity of the *sensus fidei,* a capacity for bridging
past and present, story and significance, faith and personal identity, doctrine and life, belief and practice, communal faith and individual faith—
from the horizon of contemporary life.

The traditioning of the faith by lay people in diverse contexts is not a
passive transmission, but presupposes an active, positive hermeneutical
contribution, that of reception in particular contexts. Lay people bring
"a lay hermeneutic" to their interpretation of revelation.[34] The particularity of an individual's synthesis of the faith has already been discussed in
terms of that person's "spirituality." The shaping of a lay spirituality, or
more concretely, the spirituality of a particular lay person, operates according to the eight characteristics of the *sensus fidei.* Lay people, in expressing the way they make sense of their lives through a particular spirituality, are bringing to expression their sense of the faith. These multiple
expressions are primary sources for the academic discipline of spirituality, and the study of lay spirituality in particular, which functions as a
subdiscipline within theology, and which constitutes an important instrument for bringing to articulation the *sensus laicorum.*[35]

Jean Marie Tillard has highlighted the need to recognize the problematic nature of uneducated faith when considering the role that lay people
play in the determination of the faith.[36] The *sensus laicorum,* therefore,
is not sought for its scholarly perspective; that is the contribution to the
teaching office of theologians. The *sensus laicorum,* rather, is sought for
its expression of lived faith. Deeper than a sophisticated or unsophisticated *fides quae* is a knowing which is of the mystical kind. Among the

33. *GS,* 43.

34. On "a lay hermeneutic," see Bernard J. Lee, *The Future Church of 140 BCE: A Hidden Revolution* (New York: Crossroad, 1995). Lee calls for "the emergence of a lay hermeneutic into a real
voice" (ibid., 144).

35. On lay spirituality, see Michael Downey, "Lay People and Spirituality," in *The New Westminster Dictionary of Christian Spirituality,* ed. Philip Sheldrake (Louisville, Ky.: Westminster John
Knox Press, 2005), 400–402; Sellner, "Lay Spirituality." On diverse approaches to the academic
discipline of spirituality, see Elizabeth Dreyer and Mark S. Burrows, eds., *Minding the Spirit: The
Study of Christian Spirituality* (Baltimore: Johns Hopkins University Press, 2005).

36. J. M. R. Tillard, "Sensus Fidelium," *One in Christ* 11 (1987): 2–29.

eight characteristics of the *sensus fidei,* the personal and the cognitive are here significant. It is in the ordinariness of the everyday that the depths of personal salvific encounter with the Triune God are to be found. It is from this mystical, ordinary, lived knowing that the activity of God's salvific revelation in the present is to be located. Lay people's sense of the faith at this level is a primary source that must necessarily be accessed by the teaching office of the church.

Four rubrics are helpful for investigating the positive contribution of the *sensus laicorum* to the life and mission of the church, and in particular its necessary contribution to the teaching office of the church: witness, charism, the signs of the times, and prophecy. All four are interrelated. All four involve in some way the imaginative capacity of the organon of *sensus fidei* and its eight characteristics. Through these four rubrics we can examine not only how the principle of reception, the Holy Spirit, enables effective application of the Gospel within new contexts by lay people, but also how the Holy Spirit enables the teaching office to fulfill its task effectively.

Firstly, the most credible and effective proclamation of the Gospel takes the form of witness, a recurring word throughout the documents of Vatican II. But credible and effective proclamation by lay people is not just a category for understanding the church's mission *ad extra;* it is a necessary source to be tapped for the sake of rejuvenation of official teachings of the church in its life *ad intra.* Witness provides credible testimony through word and active involvement. *Lumen Gentium* 31 speaks of lay people's presence in the world in terms of "sanctification" and "witness," without specifically relating the first to the *munus sanctificandi* and the latter to the *munus propheticum,* as it does elsewhere.

It is [in the context of their life] that God calls [the laity] to work for the sanctification of the world as it were from the inside, like leaven, through carrying out their own task in the spirit of the gospel, and in this way revealing Christ to others principally through the witness of their lives, resplendent in faith, hope and charity. It is, therefore, their special task to shed light upon and order all temporal matters, in which they are closely involved, in such a way that these are always carried out and developed in Christ's way and to the praise of the creator and redeemer.[37]

If it is "their special task to shed light upon and order all temporal matters, in which they are closely involved," then the light of faith, which

---

37. *LG,* 31. Tanner translation.

enables them to shed such light, is perceived with the eyes of faith, which in turn gives them a special sense of the faith as it is to be lived in the contemporary world.

> Christ . . . continues to carry out his prophetic office . . . through the laity whom he constitutes his witnesses and equips with an understanding of the faith [*sensus fidei*] and a grace of speech precisely so that the power of the gospel may shine forth in the daily life of family and society.[38]

In the previous chapter, we examined the primary form of the *sensus fidei*, that of the narrative of a life of witness. Effective witness involves a hermeneutical process in which an individual applies the Gospel to a particular situation. With the Gospel written on their hearts, and with the eyes of faith, lay people manifest the effectiveness and credibility of the faith.

Secondly, Vatican II particularly highlights the importance of the Spirit's charisms, distributed diversely, for effective witness to the Gospel.[39] The notion of *sensus fidei* and that of charism need to be both distinguished and interrelated. The *sensus fidei* is a gift given to all by virtue of their baptismal anointing by the Spirit. It is to be distinguished from the special charisms given by the Spirit to select individuals for the sake of all. Both are given by the one Spirit, and are to be seen operating together in a *conspiratio* toward the one goal: effective exercise of the prophetic office of Christ. This link between them is clear from the structure of *Lumen Gentium* 12 with its two sections, the first on the *sensus fidei totius populi* and the second on charisms in the church. The particular charism given by the Spirit to a lay person, whatever that charism may be, not only contributes in a special way to the mission of the church, but also gives to that individual special insight into the application of the faith, from the perspective of their particular charism. Thus, the individual charism contributes to the distinctiveness of the individual's *sensus fidei*. It is this distinctive perspective, arising from their charisms, that the *sensus laicorum* contributes to the teaching office of the church.

Thirdly, given the laity's close involvement in secular life, the ability to

---

38. *LG,* 35. Tanner translation.

39. On charisms, see Karl Rahner, *The Dynamic Element in the Church* (London: Burns and Oates, 1964); Albert Vanhoye, "The Biblical Question of 'Charisms' After Vatican II," in *Vatican II Assessment and Perspectives: Twenty-Five Years After (1962–1987),* vol. 1, ed. René Latourelle (New York: Paulist Press, 1988), 1:439–68; Doris Donnelly, ed., *Retrieving Charisms for the Twenty-first Century* (Collegeville, Minn.: Liturgical Press, 1999).

read the signs of the times is of particular importance for the church.[40] In a section entitled "Responding to the Promptings of the Spirit," *Gaudium et Spes* states:

Impelled by its belief that it is being led by the spirit of the Lord who fills the whole earth, God's people works to discern the true signs of God's presence and purposes in the events, needs and desires which it shares with the rest of modern humanity. It is faith which shows everything in a new light and clarifies God's purpose in his complete calling of the human race, thus pointing the mind towards solutions which are fully human.[41]

With the eyes of faith, lay people attempt to discern in contemporary life what is of God and what is not. Whether it be parents coping with the impact of societal changes on their children, artists sensing and naming the challenges of shifts in societal norms and conventions, or scientists and medical personnel facing new ethical possibilities, lay people are constantly facing issues which require interpretation, evaluation, and response. Forces such as globalization and consumerism directly affect the lives of lay Christians; challenges such as the ecological crisis, global poverty, and injustice of many kinds cry out for response from individuals. Official church teaching regarding appropriate responses to such changes, forces, and challenges are often published after a lengthy period of ecclesial reflection. In the meantime, laity are intuitively sensing the faith and its application to this or that sign of the times, and responding to those signs either individually or in groups. Their intuitive responses should be resourced in the process of official ecclesial reflection.

Fourthly, prophecy that is "true" is a reading of the signs of the times from the perspective of God. In the prophetic office, this prophetic element is essential for ongoing teaching that is relevant and responsive to

---

40. *GS*, 4 states: "[T]he church has the duty in every age of examining the signs of the times and interpreting them in the light of the gospel, so that it can offer in a manner appropriate to each generation replies to the continual human questionings on the meaning of this life and the life to come and on how they are related." Tanner translation. On the signs of the times, see Rino Fisichella, "Signs of the Times," in *Dictionary of Fundamental Theology*, ed. René Latourelle and Rino Fisichella (Middlegreen, Slough, England: St. Paul, 1994), 995–1001; Juan Luis Segundo, "Revelation, Faith, Signs of the Times," in *Signs of the Times: Theological Reflections* (Maryknoll, N.Y.: Orbis Books, 1993), 128–48; Juan Luis Segundo, "The Signs of the Times," in *Vatican II: A Forgotten Future?* ed. Alberto Melloni and Christoph Theobald (London: SCM Press, 2005), 73–85; Peter Hünermann, ed., *Das zweite vatikanische Konzil und die Zeichen der Zeit heute* (Freiburg im Breisgau: Verlag Herder, 2006).

41. *GS*, 11. Tanner translation.

the situation of the contemporary world.[42] Prophets, true or false, claim to feel and see as God feels and sees regarding a particular situation.[43] In the history of the church it is the saints who prophetically call the church back to the Gospel. In every age, there are prophets among the laity who challenge by their ability to read faithfully the signs of the times when others in the church are blind. The *sensus laicorum* can be an expression of such prophetic critique. This critique can come not only from those who are actively involved in the sacramental life of the church. If their perspective is sought, the inactive, the lapsed, the disaffected, and the marginalized may bring to the discourse of faith questions from the margins which are for the good of the church and provide a prophetic "utterance" which speaks God's word in the present.[44] Oftentimes those questions bring the perspective of the subversive wisdom of Jesus the prophet to the prophetic office of the church and unsettle the conventional wisdom of ecclesial life. In this way, lay people, according to Dolores Leckey, are "stirring the church" with "prophetic questions," "energetic questions, questions which press the institutional church to be engaged in these issues to seek deeper understanding, and to be open to new levels of consciousness."[45]

In their witness in the world, lay people therefore have a special sense of how to bridge "story" and "significance." Through the exercise of their particular charisms, they are able to see things with the eyes of faith that others, not given that charism, cannot see. Within the daily challenges of family life, work, and civic life, they attempt to sense what signs of the times are in harmony with the Gospel, and those which impede it. In the light of those signs of the times, they can intuitively and prophetically raise the consciousness of the church to address new questions in order that the church might be a more effective sacrament of salvation in the world. The contribution of the *sensus laicorum* is thus indispensable for the teaching office of the church as it attempts to preach the Gospel.

42. See Victor Dunne, *Prophecy in the Church: The Vision of Yves Congar* (New York: Peter Lang, 2000).

43. "[T]he fundamental experience of the prophet is a fellowship with the feelings of God, a *sympathy with the divine pathos,* a communion with the divine consciousness which comes about through the prophet's reflection of, or participation in, the divine pathos. . . . The prophet hears God's voice and feels his heart." Abraham J. Heschel, *The Prophets* (New York: Harper & Row, 1969), 1:26. Original italics.

44. See Terry A. Veling, *Living in the Margins: Intentional Communities and the Art of Interpretation* (New York: Crossroad, 1996).

45. Leckey, *Laity Stirring the Church,* 15.

The *Sensus Theologorum*

The dynamics of believing we examined in the previous chapter on the individual believer are no less applicable to the faith life of an individual theologian, lay or ordained, seen as a baptized believer, a *fidelis* among the *fideles*. All of the eight dimensions characterizing the function of the *sensus fidei* mark the life and work of the theologian. Likewise, the four rubrics of witness, charism, the signs of the times, and prophecy are relevant for understanding the role of the *sensus fidei* in a theologian's life and work. I would like to highlight the importance of just some of those characteristics and categories.

The discipline of "theology" is here understood to encompass a broad range of interrelated disciplines, such as biblical, patristic, historical, liturgical, moral, canonical, pastoral, and the various areas of systematic theology. The major difference between a theologian's identity as an individual believer and his or her membership in the community of theological scholars lies in an informal or formal ecclesial recognition that this particular believer has been given by the Holy Spirit a specific gift for academic, theological scholarship. Pope John Paul calls this gift a charism.[46] Being a theologian is an ecclesial vocation aroused by the Holy Spirit: "Among the vocations awakened by the Spirit [in the Church] is that of the theologian."[47] Already we have seen how *Dei Verbum* 8 speaks of the assistance of the Holy Spirit at work in theological reflection. The specific charism of theology is a charism given to some for the sake of all.[48] It is an ability for critical and faithful scholarship in aid of the church's mission of effectively traditioning the faith. The work of theologians is an ecclesial activity rooted in individual and communal faith.

As within the lives of lay people, so in the faith of the theologian, there is a *conspiratio* between the Spirit's organon of *sensus fidei* and the special charism for theology the Spirit gives to different individuals. However,

---

46. "This process [of reception] which must be carried forward with prudence and in a spirit of faith, will be assisted by the Holy Spirit. If it is to be successful, its results must be made known in appropriate ways by competent persons. Significant in this regard is the contribution which theologians and faculties of theology are called to make by exercising their charism in the Church." John Paul II, *Ut Unum Sint,* 81.

47. Congregation for the Doctrine of the Faith, *Instruction on the Ecclesial Vocation of the Theologian,* 6.

48. As already noted, the organon of *sensus fidei* is not a charism in the strict sense. A charism is an ability gifted by the Spirit to certain individuals for the spiritual good of the whole community; the *sensus fidei* is given to all, for the sake of all.

the Spirit's bringing together of the *sensus fidei* of a theologian and his or her charism of theological skill is a *conspiratio* of particular significance for the church. The result of this *conspiratio* is a *sensus theologi,* the sense of the faith of a theologian, with its sophisticated frameworks marking it out from the sense of the faith of others lacking scholarly articulation of the faith.

The work of theologizing, while grounded in the church's communal faith, is at the same time grounded in the theologian's individual faith seeking understanding, interpretation, and application. The organon of *sensus fidei* is the engine of that theological work. The productive imagination of the theologian, his or her organon of the *sensus fidei,* is therefore the source of that theologian's particular vision. With it, theologians attempt imaginative integration of the faith by constructing a coherent, systematic vision. This synthesis is their sense of the faith. They do not make exclusive claims on the fidelity of their own synthesis, but offer their personal *sensus fidei* to the wider community of theologians, and ultimately to the wider church. An individual's theological synthesis always awaits ecclesial approbation.

A theologian aims to express the Christian community's hopes, to name and prophetically challenge its sinfulness and challenge its myopic vision, and to produce a new prophetic vision of the salvific and revelatory meaning of the Gospel for a particular time and place. In this way, the great theologians and spiritual writers of Christian history have produced works which continue to be received as "classics" of the tradition. They are classics because of two factors. The first is the imaginative scope of the writer's vision. Whether it be Basil the Great or Augustine, Bonaventure or Aquinas, Teresa of Avila or Edith Stein, Congar or Rahner, their contribution, as theologians, to the life of the church in their time is the power of their comprehensive theological vision to illumine the faith of their contemporaries. The other factor marking them out as classics is that they continue to be received by later generations. The imaginative scope of the original writer's vision continues to illumine faith in new contexts. At the heart of that continuing reception is the creative imagination of those who can reinterpret those works for a new generation. Tradition requires ongoing reception. Such diachronic reception of previous theological work is at the heart of the task of theologians, as they find in the classics resources for addressing new questions that arise in history.

The elements which engage the productive imagination of the theologian are many and varied. As we will soon examine, essential and primary is the theologian's attention to the salvific experience of contemporary Christians and the ways in which they have made sense of the faith in their daily lives. Thus the *sensus laicorum* of a theologian's community is an important starting point of enquiry. Other elements include the particular chosen theological method. They also include foundational texts and practices emerging from the tradition process of the church's life through history: Scripture, creeds and magisterial definitions, theological, liturgical, and spiritual classics. But the theologian not only engages with works from the past; he or she searches for resonances of the Gospel in relevant background theories from related non-theological disciplines such as philosophy, psychology, cosmology, sociology, culture studies, gender studies, literary studies, the natural sciences. This engagement with the past and present proceeds in constant dialogue with the assessment of other contemporary theologians and the oversight of the magisterium.

An important element in a theologian's imaginative engagement with these resources is that of selection. His or her reception of the faith always involves selection. This selective aspect of reception (i.e., of a *sensus fidei*) means that certain elements of the tradition are brought to the fore and others painted into the background. From Scripture, the theologian might bring to the fore particular elements of the scriptural narrative for his or her particular purposes (e.g., the Exodus, or Jesus' hospitality) or might emphasize the *sensus fidei* of a particular biblical author (e.g., a Johannine vision rather than a Pauline vision). From the innumerable resources and background theories available, the creative theologian selects ones which resonate with his or her own experience of the Christian Gospel and which enable him or her to synthesize that Gospel in the fresh categories of those selected background theories.

But hermeneutical reception of these resources for theological construction is selective in a second sense: it takes place from the horizon of a particular context.

Theology is done from a certain place and in a certain time. Whether it is done in the catacombs or the desert, in the monastery or the medieval university, in the chapter house or the seminary, in the small basic community or the modern research university, no theology has a "God's eye-view," a "view from nowhere." Even if theology's hands reach for the Infinite, theology's feet are firmly planted in the theologian's specific social location. Theology may be done *for* the whole People of God, but it originates *from* specific local incarnations of that multi-generational community.[49]

The dogmatic basis of the necessary particularity of theology is the particularity of salvation. Here the soteriological function of the *sensus fidei* plays a vital role in the construction of a meaningful and transformative theology. Salvation, salvific revelation, is offered to particular human beings, not to "humanity" as some disincarnate, generic abstraction. Divine salvation, through Christ in the Spirit, is not an abstract event from the past but a present reality for those who, in faith, receive it. Salvific revelation is a present reality experienced in the context of the individual receiver.[50] A fundamental resource, therefore, for the theologian, is the present salvific, redemptive work of God, through Christ in the Spirit, within the lives of human beings of today. Discernment of the signs of the times, which might point to that redemptive work, is therefore needed. If the subject of theology, God, is to be spoken of as a living God, then theology must begin with the *here* and the *now.* The contemporary recipients of salvation are daily attempting to make sense of that experience through their *sensus fidei.* It is the task of theology to tap into those senses of the faith and to bring them to synthetic expression.

Attention to and determination of the local *sensus fidelium,* a local community's diverse senses of the faith, is therefore a primary task of that community's theologians. Theology's starting point is necessarily "local," in the sense of grounded in a particular *locus,* whether that "location" be context, culture, place.[51] The theologian too must be increasingly aware of the forces of globalization which impact directly on the lives of local

49. Terrence W. Tilley, "Catholic Theology: Contextual, Historical, Inventive," in *Catholic Theology Facing the Future: Historical Perspectives,* ed. Dermot A. Lane (New York: Paulist Press, 2003), 131–36, at 131–32. Original italics.

50. See Gerald O'Collins, "Revelation Past and Present," in *Vatican II: Assessment and Perspectives. Twenty-Five Years After (1962–1987),* vol. 1, ed. René Latourelle (New York: Paulist Press, 1988), 1:125–37.

51. On the recognition of "local theologies" and "contextual theologies," see Stephen B. Bevans, *Models of Contextual Theology,* rev. and expanded ed. (Maryknoll, N.Y.: Orbis Books, 2002); John Reader, *Local Theology: Church and Community in Dialogue* (London: SPCK, 1994); Robert J. Schreiter, *Constructing Local Theologies* (Maryknoll, N.Y.: Orbis Books, 1985); Clemens Sedmak, *Doing Local Theology: A Guide for Artisans of a New Humanity* (Maryknoll, N.Y.: Orbis Books, 2002). For a summary of such approaches, and his three imperatives for a genuinely Catholic theology ("always contextualize," "always historicize," "always invent"), see Tilley, "Catholic Theology."

communities.[52] In turning to these local senses of the faith, a theologian listens to the discernment of God's salvific and revelatory activity by other Christians in this time and place. Thus, listening to the varied *sensus laicorum* within a local community is an essential task for a theologian. This fundamental source, capturing contemporary experiences of salvation, constitutes the lens through which the theologian, in a hermeneutical circle of enquiry, can interpret Scripture and the tradition's interpretations of God's salvific work through Jesus Christ. It is both a work of approbative reception and synthesis into a new theological reception. From this local diversity, read in the light of Scripture and tradition, the theologian attempts a synthesis of *this* community's sense of the faith.

In this way, the discipline of theology becomes one of the essential ecclesial "instruments" for the determination of the *sensus fidelium* worldwide. We will be later examining other such ecclesial instruments, but theology, at the local level, is a vital activity for beginning the vast ecclesial task of listening to and discerning the "results" of the Spirit's enabling of Christians to understand, interpret, and apply the faith in new ways. These "results" of the Spirit's work are resources for the church to freshly reformulate the faith, in aid of a more persuasive proclamation of the salvific truth of the Gospel. When the Gospel is proclaimed in this rejuvenated way, those who then, in turn, receive it back will recognize it as *the lived faith* of the church: "This is *our* faith; this is the faith of the church."

A theologian's synthesis of the local community's senses of the faith takes place alongside an ongoing synthesis of the theologian's own sense of the faith. Here the category of "witness" comes to the fore. An individual theologian's discernment of God's present salvific and revelatory activity by determining the *sensus fidelium* of a local community takes place in parallel with their discernment of God's salvific activity in their own lives. Their own individual experience comes to expression in their own *sensus fidei*. Through it, they give cogent witness to the faith by the persuasiveness of their vision. A theologian's systematic theology is his or her "personal catechism," in Rahner's sense of the term, as examined in the previous chapter. As with all Christians' sense of the faith, the theolo-

---

52. See Schreiter, *The New Catholicity;* Robert J. Schreiter, "Mediating the Global and the Local in Conversation: Challenges to the Church in the Twenty-First Century," in *Theology and Conversation: Towards a Relational Theology,* ed. Jacques Haers and P. De Mey (Leuven; Dudley, Mass.: Peeters, 2003), 439–55.

gian's too has its own history in the flow of the theologian's own life. The primary form of the *sensus fidei* is the narrative of an individual's lifelong journey of faith in which the individual is constantly being called to closer conversion to Christ. Any theological work that a theologian produces is ultimately, therefore, only a secondary form which his or her sense of the faith takes. A theologian's work expresses implicitly the primary witness of his or her life of conversion to the Gospel.

According to Bernard Lonergan, personal conversion is foundational for the theologian's task.[53] This narrative dimension of the individual's theologizing means that the theologian's *sensus fidei* is always a work in progress. As his or her *fides qua creditur* develops through constant conversion, so too the theologian's *fides quae creditur,* his or her personal catechism, undergoes further reconfiguration. Conversion is at work in each of the eight dimensions of the organon of *sensus fidei:* the personal, the heuristic, the cognitive, the practical, the soteriological, the integrative, the critical, and the ecclesial. The personal dimension, however, underpins all the others. Conversion in the theologian's personal faith-relationship informs and is formed by his or her ongoing engagement with Scripture, tradition, the oversight of the magisterium, and with the *sensus fidelium* within their own local community and the universal community of faith.

Since the primary form of the *sensus fidei* is the narrative of a life, this ongoing hermeneutical circle between the theologian's *fides qua creditur* and *fides quae creditur* has its own narrative quality, as William Reiser notes:

Ideally, something happens to men and women who spend most of their waking hours thinking about what the community believes and who share fully the com-

---

53. Lonergan speaks of three dimensions of conversion: the intellectual, the religious, and the moral. See Bernard Lonergan, "'Theology in Its New Context' and 'The Dimensions of Conversion,'" in *Conversion: Perspectives on Personal and Social Transformation,* ed. Walter E. Conn (New York: Alba House, 1978), 3–21; Bernard Lonergan, *Method in Theology* (Minneapolis: The Seabury Press, 1972), esp. 267–93. "Conversion is a matter of moving from one set of roots to another. It is a process that does not occur in the market place. It is a process that may be occasioned by scientific inquiry. But it occurs only inasmuch as a man discovers what is unauthentic in himself and turns away from it, inasmuch as he discovers what the fullness of human authenticity can be and embraces it with his whole being. It is something very cognate to the Christian gospel, which cries out: Repent! The kingdom of God is at hand." Lonergan, *Method in Theology,* 271. Further on conversion and the theologian, see also Avery Dulles, "Fundamental Theology and the Dynamics of Conversion," in *The Craft of Theology: From Symbol to System* (New York: Crossroad, 1992). Others have extended Lonergan's framework; for example, on religious, Christic, ecclesial, moral, intellectual, psychological, and bodily conversion, see Anthony Kelly, *Eschatology and Hope* (Maryknoll, N.Y.: Orbis Books, 2006), 209–18.

munity's experience of the mystery that has taken up its dwelling among them. Deepening understanding of the mystery one has been contemplating for many years does not lead to displacing or relativizing one's religious tradition, or even to going beyond it in some Gnostic fashion. Rather, one's religiousness shifts to a new key. One increasingly apprehends Christian faith with the nondiscursive insight of the mystic. . . . Indeed, the difference between where a theologian "is," spiritually speaking, at the outset of his or her vocation and where the theologian winds up after many years of reflection on the whole Christian mystery may be roughly analogous to the difference between the discursive and unitive ways.[54]

Just as one can speak of stages of faith, so too one may speak of stages in the theologian's own sense of the faith. In the terms of Ricoeur, examined in chapter 8, the *idem* and *ipse* of the theologian's faith journey is marked by conversion in which his or her sense of the faith is constantly refashioned in relationship to his or her sense of identity as a disciple of Jesus Christ within the church.

Beyond offering his or her work to the local community, a theologian offers it to the church in two further ways. First, his or her *sensus fidei* is offered to the local, regional, and international theological community of scholars, seeking scholarly approbative reception from his or her peers. Secondly, his or her *sensus fidei* is offered at the same time to the wider official church, seeking the approbative reception finally of the magisterium, likewise operating locally and universally. These levels of theological and magisterial reception are an evaluation which involves the corporate organon of *sensus fidelium;* the particular mode of that organon's approbation, we have seen, should proceed through conciliarity-synodality, dialogue and reception. These classic ways of discerning the Spirit of Dialogue, the Spirit of Reception, always involve the organon of *sensus fidelium* which, through dialogue and reception, safeguards the one faith of the whole Body of Christ found in diverse expressions throughout the world-church.

The procedures of approbation are ecclesial and grounded in the Spirit to the degree that they are dialogic and marked by certain virtues. On all levels, especially within the church, dialogue is to be characterized by clearness, meekness, trust, and pedagogical prudence.[55] These vir-

---

54. William Reiser, "'Knowing' Jesus: Do Theologians Have a Special Way?" in *The Convergence of Theology: A Festschrift Honoring Gerald O'Collins, S.J.,* ed. Daniel Kendall and Stephen T. Davis (New York: Paulist Press, 2001), 159–75, at 162.

55. Paul VI, *Ecclesiam Suam,* 81.

tues firstly should mark the approbation process within the theological community itself. The individual *sensus theologi* (sense of faith of a theologian) oftentimes stands in tension with the plural *sensus theologorum* (senses of the faith of other theologians). A theologian who is not open to the critique of his or her peers is guilty of theological hubris. A theologian open to that critique and open to his or her own further conversion creates within the discipline of theology the opportunity for consensus.

When such openness characterizes the international community of scholars, there can emerge from the diversity of theological visions a unity or collective understanding on a particular matter of faith or morals. In a manner akin to a paradigm shift in science,[56] there might then emerge from those diverse *sensus theologorum* (the senses of theologians) a *sensus theologiae* (the sense of theology). Among the international community of theological scholars, it is on this level of international consensus that we can begin to speak of the *sensus theologiae* as an authority within the teaching office of the church. With the ecclesial organon of the *sensus fidelium* as its instrument of discernment, this dynamic of reception among theologians, always a work in progress, constitutes the formal function of theology as an ecclesial authority under the Word of God in the church's wider reception of revelation. No individual theologian's construct is an independent authority derived from the Word of God; only the ecclesial activity of theological scholarship and a possible emerging consensus among theologians has that authority.

The *Sensus Episcoporum*

The dynamics of believing and conversion we examined in the previous chapter on the individual believer are no less applicable to the faith life of an individual bishop or pope, seen as a baptized believer, a *fidelis* among the *fideles*. Their *sensus fidei* operates with the same eight characteristics. Similarly, the four rubrics of witness, charism, the signs of the times, and prophecy are applicable when examining the *sensus fidei* of bishops and popes.

In church order, of course, there is a significant difference between a *fidelis* who is a lay person and one who is a bishop. The difference

---

56. On the notion of paradigm shift in science applied to theology, particularly in regard to theological method, see Hans Küng and David Tracy, eds., *Paradigm Change in Theology: A Symposium for the Future* (New York: Crossroad, 1989).

lies, firstly, in the ecclesial recognition that this particular believer has been given by the Holy Spirit a personal charism for episcopal ministry, and, secondly, in the fact that this particular believer has been ordained a bishop, made a member of the college of bishops, and, as a consequence, received "the sure charism of truth."[57] This charism is ultimately given to the college of bishops *as a whole,* in their capacity as the magisterium, the official teaching authority in the church. The charism of truth, however, possessed by the magisterium in virtue of special assistance to bishops by the Holy Spirit in the exercise of their teaching authority, is always to be related to the same Spirit's organon of *sensus fidelium.* Faith's organon for discernment which brought forth the canon of Scripture is not replaced or cancelled out by the later historical development of the magisterium, as it is currently understood. The Spirit's special assistance to the magisterium in matters of truth is necessarily related to the magisterium's dialogic relationship with the *sensus fidelium* and theology, in a *conspiratio* of the one Spirit of Truth.[58]

However, including a bishop among the *fideles* in the term *sensus fidelium* is an important way of highlighting the fact that no bishop exercises his official role in the magisterium without his own *sensus fidei fidelis* coming into play in some way. A bishop's particular spirituality and theological vision is not cancelled out at episcopal ordination. Furthermore, the "charism of truth" is not to be understood in terms of an automatic or supernatural infusion at episcopal ordination of special additional knowledge concerning revelation. Nor is the episcopal charism of truth to be seen even in terms of acquiring the collective wisdom of the college of bishops by virtue of sacramental ordination and sheer membership in the college. Just as baptismal anointing by the Spirit does not give the one being initiated into the church infused knowledge and sophisticated theological articulation of the full depth and breadth of the beliefs of faith, neither does episcopal ordination give the individual bishop comprehensive knowledge and sophisticated theological articulation of faith and morals. It may be, in some cases, that the "uneducated faith" that Tillard attributes to many lay people[59] applies also to some bishops

---

57. *DV,* 8.

58. See Margaret O'Gara and Michael Vertin, "The Holy Spirit's Assistance to the Magisterium in Teaching: Theological and Philosophical Issues," *Catholic Theological Society of America Proceedings* 51 (1996): 125–42.

59. See Tillard, "Sensus Fidelium."

whose theological education has not developed beyond that of their seminary years, as the event of Vatican II so often revealed. It is not insignificant for a theology of the magisterium that not every individual bishop has a finely articulated theological framework out of which he structures his understanding, interpretation, and application of the faith. Although some bishops, who have been lecturers in seminaries or theological colleges, are selected for their theological charism, the primary criterion in the selection of a bishop is not possession of the charism for theological scholarship, but rather the charism for pastoral leadership.

What is the relationship between the individual perception of each bishop throughout a worldwide church and the magisterium's perception of orthodoxy? I propose that the relationship is best explored by making distinctions between (1) the *sensus fidei* of each individual bishop, (2) the collective reality of plural and diverse perspectives of all bishops as a *sensus episcoporum* (the varying senses of the faith of the bishops), and (3) the official and single mind of the magisterium, understood here as the *sensus magisterii,* the "sense of the magisterium."

Like all Christians, individual bishops necessarily operate out of their own personal attempt to make sense of the faith and so to witness to the faith with personal conviction. A bishop's personal sense of the faith cannot be said to express the fullness of the faith; it has no independent "authority" over against the faith of the whole church. Bishops' senses of the faith reflect their unique individual experience of salvation in the God of Jesus Christ and their sense of what constitutes fidelity to revelation. It is only through such individual appropriation that the faith is meaningful. What is true for all Christians, however, is no less true for bishops: the necessary particularity of that *sensus fidei* is also its limitation. Awareness of that limitation should lead to a willingness to seek and accept from other bishops a broadening of their own perspectives. The danger to the whole church of "theological hubris" can come from an individual lay person, theologian, or bishop. Just as the individual lay person must consider their own *sensus fidei* to be subject to the approbative reception of the whole church, and just as the individual academic theologian must consider his or her own *sensus fidei* to be subject to the approbative reception of the wider community of scholars and ultimately the whole church, so too an individual bishop must consider his own *sensus fidei* to be subject to the approbative reception of other bishops and of the whole church.

Consequently, like all Christians, an individual bishop is constantly called to conversion of his sense of the faith. Impulses to conversion can come at the local and wider level. Within his diocese the bishop's own *sensus fidei* can be challenged, enriched, and constantly renewed, in his listening both to his people and to his theologians. In his pastoral leadership, a bishop comes to know the problems people encounter in living the faith and comes to learn the ways in which they creatively and faithfully respond to those challenges. The words of Jesus the Good Shepherd, proffered as the exemplar for the bishop in his participation in Christ's office of king/shepherd/pastor ("I am the good shepherd. I know my own and my own know me"),[60] challenge each bishop as pastor to know his flock and "the joys and hopes and the sorrows and anxieties"[61] within which the people in his diocese struggle to make sense of their faith. It is at this level of "local listening" that the dialogic reception process between the *sensus fidelium* (albeit in one local place) and the official magisterium has its beginnings; likewise, it is at this level, as theologians and bishop together evaluate their particular interpretations of the local *sensus fidelium,* especially the *sensus laicorum,* that the authoritative dialogic process between theology and the magisterium has its beginnings.

Similarly, on a wider level, in his collegial exchange with his brother bishops, a bishop's own *sensus fidei* is challenged, enriched, and constantly renewed with exposure to the *sensus fidei* of other bishops. Local groupings of bishops, as well as national and regional episcopal conferences provide vital exchange points in which local perspectives inform and challenge the whole group, and wider perspectives inform and challenge local perspectives. This dynamic of personal learning and conversion is also operative when the college of bishops comes together formally at the highest level at which bishops exercise their magisterium: an ecumenical council.

The theological status of the *sensus fidei* of staff members within the departments of the Roman Curia, particularly the Congregation of the Doctrine of the Faith, is somewhat ambiguous when considering the authority of the magisterium. The Roman Curia is the administrative arm

---

60. Jn 10:14. See *LG,* 27, where discussion of the bishops' participation in the kingly office of Christ proceeds in terms of "shepherd" and "pastor," rather than "king." Through chapter 3 of *Lumen Gentium* (18–29), in fact, the notion of the bishop as "pastor" is loosely used as the overarching category for discussion of all three offices.

61. *GS,* 1.

of the bishop of Rome in his function as the pope of the universal church. Not all members of the staff in the Curia are bishops, and few of the bishops within the Curia and their committees are the primary sanctifiers, teachers, and pastors of local churches within the *communio ecclesiarum.* Nonetheless, their personal *sensus fidei* is brought to bear on the judgments they make in service of the pope's role in the magisterium of the church. However, their curial function does provide opportunities for listening and conversion, as bishops from local dioceses come to Rome for *ad limina* visits and there is direct interaction with the dicasteries of the Curia.

A paradigmatic case for examining the dynamic of learning and conversion in the formation of a *sensus magisterii* from diverse *sensus episcoporum* was Vatican II. It was an event for which we have unprecedented documentation, including detailed diaries of many of the major protagonists—popes, bishops, theologians, and observers. The four years of Vatican II provide many examples of "the learning bishop," as bishops conversed formally and informally, learning from one another. Likewise, the learning took place as the bishops regularly attended talks by *periti* or theological experts who afforded them opportunities for intellectual conversion concerning the issues being debated on the council floor.[62] Examples could be given which would highlight the clash of differing *sensus fidei* among the bishops. The college of bishops at Vatican II did not automatically have a common mind; that collective sense, as a *sensus magisterii,* emerged only through long and tortuous debate. Indeed, "the mind of the council" came to expression in consensus documents which managed to achieve that corporate sense by deftly juxtaposing diverse theological frameworks and diverse *sensus episcoporum.*[63]

For example, the equal fervor and sincerity of the *fides qua creditur* of

62. "Almost all the bishops came to the Council in some trepidation . . . they soon enough found the debates boringly repetitive—particularly those who were not very agile in distinguishing among various points of view. . . . The numerous diaries kept bear witness, especially at the beginning, to a passive, 'student' attitude. . . . With all this, Vatican II turned out to be the greatest achievement of the Catholic episcopate and the Holy Spirit. In the end there is no denying that only the conversion of the bishops, under the guidance of the Holy Spirit, made possible the progress (or, perhaps one should say, the 'overturning') from the inert and timid passivity of the replies sent to Rome by so many hundreds of bishops in 1960 to the body of decisions approved by the Council." Giuseppe Alberigo, "Vatican II and Its History," in *Vatican II: A Forgotten Future?* ed. Alberto Melloni and Christoph Theobald, *Concilium 2005/4* (London: SCM Press, 2005), 9–20, at 9–10.

63. See Rush, *Still Interpreting Vatican II,* 27–30, 42, 49.

cardinals such as Ernesto Ruffini and Giuseppe Siri, or Leo Josef Suenens and Julius Döpfner, could not be questioned. However, their own individual *fides quae creditur* or *sensus fidei* were quite different. Some like
Suenens or Döpfner were calling for an ecclesial *intellectual* conversion
from what they saw as the constraints of the neo-scholasticism which
shaped the *sensus fidei* of cardinals such as Ruffini or Siri. Over the four
years of the council, as the bishops engaged informally with theologians
inside and outside the council hall, formally with theologians in commission meetings, and in their formal and informal debates with one another, the individual *sensus fidei* of each bishop was being challenged and
refashioned, and thus the *sensus fidei episcoporum* was being refashioned,
to give rise ultimately to a new expression of the *sensus magisterii* itself. In
that refashioning, what was achieved over four years was a conversion of
the ecclesial imagination of the Catholic Church.

   This conversion of the ecclesial imagination is demanded of each individual bishop by virtue of his participation in the charism of truth and
in the magisterium of the church. His own personal reception of God's
loving outreach (his *fides qua creditur*) demands a constant conversion
on all levels of the imaginative organon of *sensus fidei:* the personal, the
heuristic, the cognitive, the practical, the soteriological, the integrative,
the critical, and the ecclesial. A bishop's own personal interpretation of
revelation and the doctrines of the church (his concrete *fides quae creditur*) requires a constant intellectual conversion. That requires ongoing
engagement with contemporary theology and its proposals for fresh perspectives in the church's evangelizing mission. With such openness to
conversion, bishops, as individual Christians, become credible witnesses
to the faith, exercise their special charism effectively and authoritatively,
are attentive to the signs of the times shaping their people's lives, and are
prophets of the Word of God challenging all that impedes the reign of
God.

   The charism of truth which bishops possess as a college requires reception of theological scholarship and the *sensus fidelium* for its realization.
The limitations of a single bishop's *sensus fidei* and indeed the potential
limitations of the *sensus episcoporum* are reduced to the degree that the
magisterium is exercised in dialogic reception of the *sensus fidelium* of the
whole People of God and of the scholarship of theologians. Of course,
it is also the richness of an individual bishop's *sensus fidei* that brings co-
gency to his witness, preaching, and pastoral leadership. And likewise, it

is through dialogue at all the levels discussed above that the richness of that personal vision contributes to the deliberations of the magisterium, the reflections of theologians, and the wider *sensus fidelium.*

AGENTS AND INSTRUMENTS OF RECEPTION

By receptive "agents" and "instruments," I mean persons, functions, processes, procedures, ecclesial bodies, or institutional structures which facilitate ecclesial reception of the *sensus fidelium.* Two important aspects of these receptors need to be distinguished; they can be either or both (1) means by which the *sensus fidelium* is intentionally sought out and listened to, and (2) means by which the *sensus fidelium* is given opportunity to express itself in an ongoing way. Together these elements highlight the active seeking out of the *sensus fidelium* by the church, and the need for concrete structures facilitating participation within the church.

Two most important and potentially effective agents for listening to, receiving, and determining the *sensus fidelium* are "the listening theologian" and "the listening bishop." With these two receptors, the process begins for reception of the *sensus fidelium* which culminates in more formal dialogue between the two authorities of theology and the magisterium regarding their respective receptions of the *sensus fidelium.* We have already seen how theology must begin its quest by attending to the way in which the faith is being lived. The most potent resource for the rejuvenation of the Gospel, the goal to which theology aspires, is the lived application of the Gospel by Christians themselves. For the listening theologian, the theological task has already been started, by both uneducated Christians lacking any sophisticated theological framework for articulating their faith, and educated Catholics with such a framework. Here, too, the listening bishop seeks out the lived faith of the church which he is called to safeguard and promote. His safeguarding looks not only to the past, but to the present, where, before his very eyes, the Gospel is being interpreted and applied in ways that can only but be resources for reinvigoration of the church's evangelizing mission. Within a local diocese, a diocesan pastoral council provides a more formal opportunity for listening by the bishop. Likewise since presbyters, themselves agents of reception for the *sensus fidelium* within their parishes, can provide the bishop with further avenues of insight into the *sensus fidelium* of their diocese, the formal structure of the council of priests provides a similar opportunity.

In these two agents, the listening theologian and the listening bishop, a process begins for seeking out, clarifying, evaluating, and determining the *sensus fidelium*. The focus on these two agents emphasizes that even formal, institutional structures are not enough; there must be a "culture of dialogue" *(Dialogkultur)*.[64] Reception can occur only if there is openness and listening on both sides.

However, such a culture of dialogue demands more formal processes and institutions. In its desire for the full participation of the laity in the threefold office of Christ, Vatican II teaches:

> In accordance with the knowledge, competence or authority that they possess, [the laity] have the right and indeed sometimes the duty to make known their opinion on matters which concern the good of the church. If possible this should be done through *the institutions set up for this purpose by the church*.[65]

In his encyclical *Novo Millennio Ineunte,* John Paul II writes of "structures of participation" through which the church is able "to listen more widely to the entire People of God."[66] In the ecclesial dialogue between the three authorities of the teaching office, what structures of participation and dialogue do theology and the magisterium have for reception of the *sensus fidelium?* If, as Francis Sullivan asserts, authority is "the quality of leadership which elicits and justifies the willingness of others to be led by it,"[67] then the authoritativeness of the church's teaching office is directly proportional to the existence of effective dialogue between "structures of participation," whether formal or informal. Such structures of participation are receptive instruments for attending to the *sensus fidelium* and bringing it to expression.

Calls for a "culture of dialogue" in the church are sometimes dismissed as inappropriate calls for more democracy in the church. A culture of dialogue, however, finds its theological grounding, not in the democratic tradition, but in the fundamental dogma of Christianity, the Trinity:

---

64. Hermann J. Pottmeyer, "Die Mitsprache der Gläubigen in Glaubenssachen: Eine alte Praxis und ihre Wiederentdeckung," *Internationale katholische Zeitschrift "Communio"* 25 (1996): 135–47, at 146–47. See also Hermann J. Pottmeyer, "Auf dem Weg zu einer dialogischen Kirche: Wie Kirche sich ihrer selbst bewußt wird," in *Dialog als Selbstvollzug der Kirche,* ed. Gebhard Fürst (Freiburg: Herder, 1997), 117–32. See further Michael Putney, "A Church in Dialogue with Itself and with Others," *Compass* 34 (2000): 3–16.

65. *LG,* 37.

66. John Paul II, *Novo Millennio Ineunte. Apostolic Letter of John Paul II* (Strathfield, Australia: St. Pauls Publications, 2001), 58.

67. Sullivan, "Authority in an Ecclesiology of Communion," 18.

God's image is in Godself a threefold dialogue, and reveals and gives itself to us in a threefold dialogue; the church then will only be fully the true church of God, if it comes to pass as a dialogical community.[68]

Within that inner-trinitarian life, the Holy Spirit is the Dialogue between Father and Son; in God's outreach to humanity, it is the Spirit of Dialogue who facilitates the reception of the Word of God in human history. To foster a culture of dialogue is to foster the work of the Holy Spirit for the sake of a more faithful reception of God's Word.[69]

However, the democratic tradition can provide models for the way in which a culture of dialogue can be institutionalized. In chapter 7 we began addressing the issue of democracy in the church, and claimed that although the church is not a democracy, since it is both a divine and human institution, the use of democratic structures of participation within church life are not inimical to the nature of the church as a divine institution.[70] Throughout the history of the church, a form of consultation and deliberation has existed which has many similarities to forms of democratic consultation and governance: the "synod" or "council."[71] The synodal life of the church on all levels exists in order to receive the *sensus fidelium.*

[M]anifestations of the Church's synodal life are the privileged way of reception. This is because it is only in councils and synods that one finds the most explicit *conspiratio* among the churches as well as between pastors and the faithful in the midst of the local churches.[72]

---

68. Pottmeyer, "Die Mitsprache der Gläubigen in Glaubenssachen," 145.

69. On the Holy Spirit and dialogue, see Bernd Jochen Hilberath, "Vom Heiligen Geist des Dialogs: Das Dialogische Prinzip in Gotteslehre und Heilsgeschehen," in *Dialog als Selbstvollzug der Kirche,* ed. Gebhard Fürst (Freiburg: Herder, 1997), 93–116.

70. See Steinruck, "Was die Gläubigen in der Geschichte der Kirche," 47.

71. See Winfried Aymans, *Das synodale Element in der Kirchenverfassung* (Munich: 1970); Wolfgang Beinert, "Konziliarität der Kirche: Ein Beitrag zur ökumenischen Epistemologie," in *Vom Finden und Verkünden der Wahrheit in der Kirche: Beiträge zur theologischen Erkenntnislehre* (Freiburg: Herder, 1993), 325–50; Congar, "The Conciliar Structure or Regime of the Church"; Congar, "The Council as an Assembly and the Church as Essentially Conciliar"; Heinemann, "Demokratisierung der Kirche"; Richard Puza, "Das synodale Prinzip in historischer, rechtstheologischer und kanonistischer Bedeutung," in *Dialog als Selbstvollzug der Kirche,* ed. Gebhard Fürst (Freiburg: Herder, 1997), 242–69; Wiedenhofer, "Synodalität und Demokratisierung der Kirche aus dogmatische Perspektive"; John Zizioulas, "The Development of Conciliar Structures to the Time of the First Ecumenical Council," in *Councils and the Ecumenical Movement* (Geneva: World Council of Churches, 1968), 34–51.

72. Legrand, "Reception, *Sensus Fidelium,* and Synodal Life," 421.

If the principle of synodality names the ancient way of discerning the Spirit in the church, what dialogic structures constitute institutional instruments for listening to or allowing participation of the voices of the primary, secondary, and ancillary sources of the *sensus fidelium?*

The primary source of the *sensus fidelium,* as we have seen, is Catholics who regularly avail themselves of the sacraments and are committed to the mission of the church. How can the church, through institutional structures, access their sense of the faith? Here any synodal structure that gets people together and facilitates exchange is to be included among the instruments of reception. Bradford Hinze has examined some practices of dialogue in the contemporary Roman Catholic Church and noted their strengths and weaknesses, successes and failures, and their promotion or their devaluation by the Roman Curia.[73] He notes the structures of the parish and diocesan pastoral council as local instruments for facilitating dialogue. He goes on to study other examples: the initiative of the U.S. bishops for a national consultation process leading up to the 1976 national assembly Call to Action, the dialogic process involved in the preparation of certain pastoral letters of the U.S. bishops' conference, the Common Ground initiative, the processes of the chapters of women religious congregations, the international Synod of Bishops, and finally ecumenical and interreligious dialogues.

Therefore, many opportunities exist already for exchange among the faithful. For example, on the informal level of parish life there are prayer and study groups where faith sharing can take place. On the formal level, dialogic opportunities are to be found in the parish pastoral council, the council of priests, diocesan pastoral council, various diocesan committees, and, most formally, the diocesan synod. On the local, national, and regional level, lay and religious organizations provide forums in which individuals can express themselves. Formal structures include the national and regional episcopal conferences and their agencies. Among the non-official sources for hearing what committed Catholics have to say are groups in Europe such as *Kirchenvolksbegehren* (Petition of the People of the Church),[74] *Wir Sind Kirche* (We Are the Church),[75] and in the United States, the Voice of

73. Hinze, *Practices of Dialogue.*

74. See Norbert Mette, "'Kein geeigneter Beitrag zum innerkirchlichen Dialog'? Das 'Kirchenvolksbegehren' als Testfall einer dialogischen Kirche," in *Dialog als Selbstvollzug der Kirche,* ed. Gebhard Fürst (Freiburg: Herder, 1997), 329–43.

75. See E. Leuninger, *Wir sind das Volk Gottes: Demokratisierung in der Kirche* (Frankfurt am Main, 1992).

the Faithful.[76] These latter groups can be instruments for accessing both the primary and the secondary sources of the *sensus fidelium*.

Two instruments not necessarily set up by the church are often mentioned as possible "receptors" or "sensors" for also accessing both the primary and secondary sources: public opinion polls and professional surveys. Clearly the *sensus fidelium* is not to be determined through opinion polls.[77] Majority thinking does not necessarily reflect the Gospel. Oftentimes in the history of the church, it is only a minority who raise a prophetic voice to challenge the majority who have fallen away from the truth of the Gospel. Opinion polls may simply reveal the spiritual blindness of the majority. What is to be discerned in seeking out the *sensus fidelium* is "the faith of the church," which more often brings to bear the subversive wisdom of the Gospel, thus challenging the sense of the faith of a local church caught up in the conventional wisdom of the society in which it is immersed.

However, majority thinking often does need to play a role. Voting to determine the thinking of the majority is the procedure employed in both the election of popes and the determination of the mind of an ecumenical council. That voting in both cases is always preceded by prayer for the enlightenment of the Holy Spirit highlights once again that, since earliest times, the church has acknowledged that the Holy Spirit does not enlighten the eyes of faith magically, but proceeds by the normal processes of human thinking, judgment, and decision-making, in this case, by voting. However, voting as a means of determining the worldwide *sensus fidelium* on particular matters of faith and morals would be not only impractical but also inappropriate. The mode and form of the *sensus fidelium* (imagination and the narrative of a life) are not so easily converted to the surety of a vote. Oftentimes the holiest of people have an uneducated faith, as Tillard notes,[78] which does not hold up to theological scrutiny and the requirements of a finely articulated faith. The genuine elements of such uneducated faith are best discerned, not through voting, but in a local theology's reception of the *sensus fidelium*.

76. See James E. Post, "The Emerging Role of the Catholic Laity: Lessons from Voice of the Faithful," in *Common Calling: The Laity and Governance of the Catholic Church*, ed. Stephen J. Pope (Washington, D.C.: Georgetown University Press, 2004), 209–28. For a summary, see Donald B. Cozzens, *Faith That Dares to Speak* (Collegeville, Minn.: Liturgical Press, 2004), 95–108.

77. See Dario Vitali, "Sensus fidelium e opinione pubblica nella Chiesa," *Gregorianum* 82 (2001): 689–717.

78. See throughout Tillard, "Sensus Fidelium."

Nevertheless, majority thinking revealed in public opinion and public polls can play a certain role for another reason. That oftentimes in the history of the church only a minority has held to the faith does not mean that at other times the majority does not intuit genuine ways in which formulations of faith and morals no longer ring true to their faith. Calls for change indicated in opinion polls or information on the actual beliefs of people in the pews (or not in the pews) cannot but be helpful to theologians and bishops, if only to indicate areas where a more persuasive proclamation of the truth of the Gospel is called for. Significant dissent among the faithful regarding a particular church teaching may or may not be indicative of a genuine *sensus fidelium,* but such statistical information is best not ignored. It needs to be discerned within the dialogue between the authorities of the teaching office.

Polling can play a role within the ecclesial process of reception. As John Burkhard suggests, polling by the church itself might avoid some of the inadequacies of non-church polling:

If public opinion can serve a useful function *within* the process of determining the *sensus fidelium,* then perhaps the official Church needs to take more seriously the consulting of its pastors, theologians, and the faithful by conducting its own polls and gathering the necessary information for making important decisions on urgent matters, e.g., the dangerous decline in the numbers of ordained priests, etc. If there is reason to be suspicious of the methods and motives of some of the secular groups who conduct polls or interpret their results, that very fact does not absolve the official Church itself from arranging for the conducting of sound polls under its direction.[79]

While the results of such professional surveys undertaken by church authorities are not per se expressions of the *sensus fidelium,* they can, however, play a certain role in the reception of the *sensus fidelium.* The church has availed itself of this form of enquiry. For example, surveys such as the National Church Life Survey in Australia do give information of value for ongoing reflection by theology and the magisterium.[80]

Two institutional structures that are of specific importance are, as already noted, and as will be further explained in the next section, the "institutions" of theology and the magisterium. Reception of the *sensus fidelium* is at the heart of their function. Faculties of theology, at one

79. Burkhard, "*Sensus Fidei:* Recent Theological Reflection (1990–2001). Part II," 50.
80. See www.ncls.org.au [accessed April 25, 2007].

time included in the deliberation of general councils, are important institutional means for promoting critical interpretation of the faith. Beyond the dialogue and mutual critique initiated by published theological works, local and international colloquia among theologians extend such opportunities among theologians, as do professional associations of theologians. The official international structure through which the magisterium calls upon the expertise of theologians is the International Theological Commission, as well as the use of theologians within the office of the Congregation for the Doctrine of the Faith.

The secondary source for determining the *sensus fidelium,* Catholics who are inactive, lapsed, disaffected, or marginalized in the church, can provide voices through whom the Holy Spirit is genuinely challenging the church. With the dramatic downturn in the number of Catholics participating in the sacramental life of the church in many countries, this secondary source constitutes the majority of Catholics in such countries. To ignore the perspective of this group is to miss the opportunity for ecclesial learning not only with regard to how to reach out more effectively to such individuals, but also with regard to prophetic intuitions which may well indicate inchoate development in doctrine. Many of the instruments for discerning this secondary source parallel those mentioned earlier with regard to the primary source.

A fundamental instrument for attending to the ancillary source of the *sensus fidelium,* i.e., the sense of the faith of other Christians, is the bilateral and multilateral dialogues formally entered into by the Roman Catholic Church. Among the greatest fruits of Vatican II, formal dialogues between Christian churches and ecclesial communities have produced tangible results.[81] Key to the achievements of formal ecumenical dialogue has been, firstly, the shift to employing what is called an "ecumenical methodology" and, secondly, the recognition of "receptive ecumenism" as a process of mutual learning between churches. Through an ecumeni-

---

81. The website of the Pontifical Council for Promoting Christian Unity provides documentation related to ecumenical dialogues. See http://www.vatican.va/roman_curia/pontifical_councils/chrstuni/index.htm [accessed April 25, 2007]. The website for the Centro Pro Unione in Rome likewise provides a comprehensive resource for the history and documents produced by official international dialogues involving the Roman Catholic Church. See http://www.prounione.urbe.it/dia-int/e_dialogues.html [accessed April 25, 2007]. For the official dialogues in the United States involving the Roman Catholic Church, see the extensive listing on the website of the Bishops' Committee for Ecumenical and Interreligious Affairs http://www.usccb.org/seia/officialdialogues.shtml#10 [accessed April 25, 2007].

cal methodology both parties in dialogue together re-receive Scripture and tradition on a particular matter.[82] Re-reception enables perspectives not previously envisaged or even rejected in the past to be accepted as a legitimate interpretation of revelation.[83] Receptive ecumenism, a parallel notion to that of ecumenical methodology, highlights that such re-reception of the past entails a reception of the perspective of the other in the dialogue, which in turn is received as a challenge to one's own self-perception and perception of the faith.

For the Roman Catholic Church, this has opened up opportunities for learning from other churches. In other words, "Catholic learning" is a reception by the Catholic Church of the sense of the faith of sister churches. An ecumenical methodology reveals legitimate diversity in the way Scripture and tradition can be interpreted; receptive ecumenism is an acknowledgment that it is legitimate for one church to take on and learn from the reception of the other in a way that brings new perspectives on the receiving church's own doctrines, church order, and practices. For the Catholic Church, these perspectives or senses of the faith of other churches are an ancillary source that cannot be ignored in the determination of the *sensus fidelium* of the whole People of God. Official Catholic involvement in bilateral and multilateral dialogues is, therefore, a *de facto* instrument for consulting the *sensus fidelium* of other Christian churches of the East and West.

Perhaps one of the greatest learnings that the Catholic Church can appropriate from its dialogue with other churches is the very practice and spirit of dialogue itself. The culture of dialogue that produces honest and robust exchange between churches is a model which the Catholic Church can well apply for discernment of the *sensus fidelium* within the

---

82. "The appearance of the problematic of reception is certainly one of the elements which has contributed to the evolution of the method implemented in the ecumenical dialogues. For the partners engaged in the dialogue, it is a question not of comparing term by term the propositions advanced during the discussions with their respective confessional statements, but of elaborating formulations apt to express the faith received from the apostles. The abandoning of the comparative method at Lund (1952) called for new in-depth approaches regarding the method to be followed in the ecumenical dialogues. The problematic of reception situated differently the different partners in the discussion: not one group facing the other but all submitted to the one Word of God, which they receive in the linguistic and cultural conditioning of their respective traditions." Routhier, "Reception in Current Theological Debate," 51–52.

83. I am here using the term "re-reception" in the restricted sense intended in documents such as the Anglican–Roman Catholic International Commission, *Mary: Grace and Hope in Christ* (Harrisburg: Morehouse, 2005).

Roman Catholic communion itself. It is through such a culture of dialogue among the three authorities of the teaching office that a *consensus fidelium* genuinely emerges.

CONSENSUS FIDELIUM

Ongoing reception of the *sensus fidelium* by theology and the magisterium regarding a certain matter of faith or morals cannot be an endless circle of enquiry without a firm determination at some point. The church from its earliest decades has sought clear statement of its beliefs. The desire for clarity in authoritative teaching is in service not only of the preservation of the truth of revelation, but also of the unity of faith. The church requires formulation of its beliefs in a form that can be professed by all. Such formulation of the church's faith on a particular matter is a *consensus fidelium*. The phrase *consensus fidelium* does not designate an organon of the faith; the ecclesial organon of the faith remains always the *sensus fidelium*. Nor is a *consensus fidelium* the variety of interpretations which individuals and local communities make of the faith; such a variety of faith expressions are the diverse *sensus fidelium* throughout the world church.

The history of the church illustrates both the need for and examples of *consensus fidelium*.[84] Although arrived at during a period of the church which did not have the current explicit structures of the teaching office, the final determination of the canon (as canon 1 and canon 2) is the premier exemplar of a formulation of a *consensus fidelium,* even though its form is not that of a "definition." In part 2, "The Norm," we saw how the canon's development was a lengthy process, which involved the *sensus fidei* of many individual writers and the approbative reception by the organon of *sensus fidelium* within and between many local churches over time. The creeds and definitions of the councils of the early church are other such exemplars of a *consensus fidelium* arrived at through dialogue and reception. In recent history, the process for promulgating the Marian dogmas in 1854 and 1950 involved a discernment of the *sensus fidelium,* in order that a *consensus fidelium* could be stated; from the diversity of expressions of the *sensus fidelium,* a single expression of the faith was formulated as a dogma expressing that *consensus fidelium*.[85] Vatican II, as

---

84. The Latin nominative plural of *consensus* is *consensus*.
85. See J. Robert Dionne, *The Papacy and the Church: A Study of Praxis and Reception in*

we have seen, is a recent exemplar of how the teaching office can arrive at a *sensus magisterii*, and promulgate in its documents a *consensus fidelium* regarding a plethora of matters related to the living of faith in the contemporary world.

A *consensus fidelium* is a judgment by the magisterium, in dialogue with the *sensus fidelium* and theologians, on a particular matter of faith or morals and formulated into a statement of belief. The final stage of formulation of a *consensus fidelium* is the process of achieving a *sensus magisterii*, since the magisterium alone is the official teaching authority within the church's teaching office. Only the magisterium can speak for the whole church. However, the magisterium can only speak the faith of the whole church. Although the final judgment and formulation is that of the magisterium, the process of approbative reception regarding that particular matter of faith involves all three authorities in the teaching office. The organon for judgment at all levels of approbation, including the final *sensus magisterii*, is the organon of *sensus fidelium* given to the whole church. Consequently, broad ecclesial dialogue among the three authorities of the teaching office is the necessary presupposition of a genuine *consensus fidelium*, including an infallible *consensus fidelium*.

Expression of a *consensus fidelium* aims toward a single formulation of a particular element of the faith that intends to be universally understandable, interpretable, and applicable. It aims to express the sense that the whole body of the faithful have regarding a particular matter of faith or morals. It is what the Council of Trent called the *universus ecclesiae sensus* (the universal sense of the church).[86] It differs from the multifarious *sensus fidelium* in that the particular matter of faith or morals that is being "sensed" is here expressed in one formulation, in one interpretation intended to be meaningfully understood and applicable across cultures and contexts by all in the local churches of the world-church.

In the process of approbative reception, achievement of a *sensus magisterii* is arrived at, not only in dialogic interaction with the other two authorities, but also through dialogue and mutual reception among the diverse *sensus episcoporum*, with and under the pope. The pope, in teaching *ex cathedra*, likewise always does so in relation to the faith of the whole church, and in *communio/receptio* with the whole college of bishops. Vat-

---

Ecumenical Perspective (New York: Philosophical Library, 1987); Heft, "'Sensus Fidelium' and the Marian Dogmas."

86. DS 1637. Quoted in Pié-Ninot, *"Sensus Fidei,"* 993.

ican II's teaching on collegiality demands such dialogue in the achievement of a *sensus magisterii*. Exercise of the "charism of truth" presupposes dialogue in search of the truth. Consensus within the *communio hierarchicum*, intimately linked through episcopal ordination to a *communio ecclesiarum*, seeks to determine consensus among the *communio fidelium*. To that end, open collegial conversation within the college of bishops and its diverse *sensus episcoporum* goes on *de facto* at various levels, informally and formally: small, provincial meetings of bishops, national and regional episcopal conferences, international synods of bishops, consistories of cardinals, dialogue between bishops and the pope either directly or through his curial intermediary the Congregation for the Doctrine of the Faith, and finally ecumenical councils.

The modes of promulgation of such determinations by the magisterium range from papal or conciliar documents to documents from Roman curial dicasteries. Likewise the level of *de jure* authority of these promulgations varies.[87] Because there are different authoritative levels of a *sensus magisterii,* the resulting magisterial judgments stating a *consensus fidelium* have different levels of authority. That not all *sensus magisterii* are to be considered infallible *sensus* regarding the faith is indicated in current teaching of the magisterium by the assigning of different levels of authority to statements of the magisterium. To revisit these levels, there are four grades of authority: (1) definitive dogma, (2) definitive doctrine, (3) non-definitive but authoritative doctrine, and finally (4) prudential admonitions and provisional applications of church doctrine. The response required *de jure* of Catholics to each of those four grades is, respectively: (1) theological faith, (2) firm acceptance, (3) *obsequium* of intellect and will, and (4) conscientious obedience. A magisterial teaching of whatever level of authority, as an expression of the *sensus magisterii*, is to be received *de jure* by the faithful as an expression of the *consensus fidelium*, with the presumption that it has been arrived at through dialogue and reception between the three teaching authorities.

Only the first grade of church teaching, definitive dogma, which requires the response of theological faith, includes *consensus fidelium* which

---

87. For an examination of the variety of modes of promulgation and their differing canonical authority, see Francis G. Morrisey, *Papal and Curial Pronouncements: Their Canonical Significance in Light of the 1983 Code of Canon Law,* 2nd ed. rev. and updated by Michel Thériault (Ottawa: Faculty of Canon Law, Saint Paul University, 1995). For a theological assessment of the different levels of authority of these papal and curial documents, as well as the varying authority of conciliar documents, see Sullivan, *Creative Fidelity.*

have been arrived at by an infallible exercise of the church's magisterium. The subject matter of such infallible definitions is restricted by *Lumen Gentium* 25 to the content of revelation only, the deposit of faith. According to Salvador Pié-Ninot, for the content of such statements to be regarded as infallible, they must fulfill four conditions: "when it is a matter of universal consent, when it refers to revelation, when it is the work of the Holy Spirit, and when it is recognized by the magisterium."[88] However, the majority of the determinations and promulgations of the *sensus magisterii* are on the level of grades 2, 3, and 4.

Arriving at a *sensus magisterii,* within the magisterium and through ongoing reception between the three authorities, takes time. We have already seen the lengthy process involved in the achievement of the *consensus fidelium* that is the canon of Scripture. As Cardinal Newman asserts, truth is "the daughter of time."[89] Through time, the church undergoes a continuous *paideia* (education) under God's Spirit with regard to the significance of revelation for new times.[90] The teaching church is forever learning; "true teaching follows true learning, and true learning is a process that takes time."[91] In referring to the interaction between the magisterium, theology, and the *sensus fidelium,* and the reception of Scripture and tradition by all three, Beinert remarks: "With that [interaction] is brought into play the factor of time. Dialogue and exchange of ideas are processes which can drag on for a long time: consensus can never and in no way be forced."[92] Likewise, in asserting the "complementarity and necessary interaction" between the cautious pastoral sensitivity

88. See Pié-Ninot, *"Sensus Fidei,"* 993. He cites *DV,* 8, 10; *LG,* 12, 25.

89. John Henry Newman, *An Essay on the Development of Christian Doctrine,* 6th ed. (Notre Dame, Ind.: University of Notre Dame Press, 1989), 47. Newman cites *Crabbe's Tales* as the source of the phrase. It is quoted in the context of Newman's discussion of the particular class of development he calls "historical development," which he says is "the gradual formation of opinion concerning persons, facts, and events. Judgments, which were at one time confined to a few, at length spread through a community, and attain general reception by the accumulation and concurrence of testimony. Thus some authoritative accounts die away; others gain a footing, and are ultimately received as truths. . . . Thus by development the Canon of the New Testament has been formed." Ibid., 46–47.

90. On this process in terms of *paideia,* see Juan Luis Segundo, *The Liberation of Dogma: Faith, Revelation, and Dogmatic Teaching Authority* (Maryknoll, N.Y.: Orbis Books, 1992).

91. O'Gara and Vertin, "The Holy Spirit's Assistance to the Magisterium in Teaching," 140. See also Frederick E. Crowe, "The Church as Learner: Two Crises, One Kairos," in *Appropriating the Lonergan Idea,* ed. Michael Vertin (Washington, D.C.: The Catholic University of America Press, 1989), 370–84; Örsy, *The Church Learning and Teaching.*

92. Beinert, "Der Glaubenssinn der Gläubigen in der systematischen Theologie," 74.

of the magisterium (the *cathedra pastoralis*) and the academic rigor and innovative speculation of theologians (the *cathedra magistralis*), Tillard highlights the virtue of patience as a necessary factor in the teaching of the truth in the church:

> This [complementarity and necessary interaction] needs patience and forbids rapid decisions or short-cuts. But in God's design, time is an essential factor. The Catholic Church knows by experience how difficult it is to correct a too hasty decision. This is why it is its tradition to teach a truth slowly articulated through a *consensus* of which the *cathedra magistralis* (exegetes, dogmaticians, canonists, moralists) as well as the *sensus fidei* of the whole People of God including "people in the pews" are the builders, together with the *cathedra pastoralis*.[93]

In addition to the classic case of the canon's formation, the history of the church bears witness to this factor of time for ensuring meaningful and truthful formulation of belief. For example, the fifty-six-year reception of the creed of the Council of Nicaea (A.D. 325) leading up to the Council of Constantinople (381) reveals that a further question had not been answered by the first Nicene Creed: what is the status of the Holy Spirit? The most illuminating contemporary example of the factor of time is Vatican II itself. It provides a model for both the importance of the factor of time for arriving at consensus, and of that slow process as an ongoing conversion of the ecclesial imagination. The council is the fruit of an ecclesial dialogue that was going on long before the council was called and, through the four years of debate and drafting, the fruit of a long and multilayered process of clarification and firming of conviction.[94]

The element of time necessarily at work in the process leading to a *consensus fidelium* is likewise necessarily at work in the juridical, spiri-

---

93. J. M. R. Tillard, "How Is Christian Truth Taught in the Roman Catholic Church?" *One in Christ* 34 (1998): 293–306, at 300.

94. Tillard remarks: "Vatican II itself is the result of a very long quest for *consensus*. It started with the birth of biblical, liturgical, ecumenical, patristic movements, often accompanied by negative reactions, provoking theological confrontations and discussions followed by an increasingly more positive 'reception' from the hierarchy after consultation with scholars and local pastors. The encyclical letters of Pius XII [on biblical studies and liturgy] opened up the way to Vatican II. During this council, an incessant two-way dynamism from local bishops to conciliar commissions, with a complicated interplay of *consultatio* and *vota, schema* and *modi, observationes* and *relatio, expensio modorum* and *interventiones in aula* made possible the *consensus* expressed in the final *suffragium* (voting). It is obvious that it is a mistake to describe this whole process as a mere 'democratic poll,' a way to 'canvass opinion in view of a final decision.' It is a mutual learning." Ibid., 297–98.

tual, and theological reception of a *consensus fidelium* after its promulgation. The end point of formulating a *consensus fidelium* marks a beginning point when the element of time once again becomes a factor. Once a church teaching is promulgated, the hermeneutical process of interpretation by individual believers and theologians, examined in the previous chapter, comes into play. No matter what the grade of authority attached to a teaching and the corresponding juridical response required, once a *consensus fidelium* has been arrived at, that single formulation by the magisterium necessarily initiates a process of spiritual and theological reception throughout the worldwide church. The effectiveness of the magisterium's intention to produce a single formulation that will be understandable, interpretable, and applicable in all cultures and contexts is now tested. So continues the ongoing dialogue and reception between the magisterium, the *sensus fidelium,* and theology.

However, is this to downplay the ability of the magisterium to state infallibly the content of revelation on behalf of the whole church? Vatican II reiterated the teaching of Vatican I that "definitions of the Roman Pontiff are *of themselves, and not by the consent of the church,* irreformable" *(ex sese, non autem ex consensu ecclesiae irreformabiles).*[95] However, Vatican I's formulation was not intended to separate papal teaching from the *consensus ecclesiae;* rather, the formula was specifically intended as an answer to the question posed by the Gallican Articles of 1682, which called for juridical ratification of papal teachings by the bishops for them to be binding. Vatican I's teaching regarding the exercise of "the infallible teaching authority of the Roman Pontiff" is an exercise of "that infallibility which the divine Redeemer willed his church to enjoy."[96] *Pastor Aeternus* presupposes that the pope will always be drawing on the faith of the whole church and, with that presumption, any teaching claim-

---

95. *LG,* 25. In what follows, I use the translation of chapter 4 of Vatican I's *Pastor Aeternus* in Tanner, *Decrees of the Ecumenical Councils,* 815–16. On the background to the Vatican I debate on this matter, see Richard F. Costigan, *The Consensus of the Church and Papal Infallibility: A Study in the Background of Vatican I* (Washington, D.C.: The Catholic University of America Press, 2005). On the conciliar debate and the *juridical* intention of the *"ex sese"* formulation, see also Georges Dejaifve, "'Ex sese, non autem ex consensu ecclesiae,'" *Salesianum* 24 (1962): 283–97; Heinrich Fries, "'Ex sese, non ex consensu ecclesiae,'" in *Volk Gottes: Zum Kirchenverständnis der katholischen, evangelischen und anglikanischen Theologie,* ed. Remigius Bäumer and Heimo Dolch (Freiburg: Herder, 1967), 481–500; Margaret O'Gara, *Triumph in Defeat: Infallibility, Vatican I, and the French Minority Bishops* (Washington, D.C.: The Catholic University of America Press, 1988).

96. "The infallible teaching authority of the Roman Pontiff" is the title of chapter 4 of *Pastor Aeternus.* See Tanner, *Decrees of the Ecumenical Councils,* 2:815, 816.

ing to be taught infallibly will therefore find resonance with the whole church.[97] The irreformability of infallibly taught papal definitions, understood in Vatican I's strictly juridical sense, does not exclude the need for such teachings to be understood, interpreted, and applied. According to Catholic belief, an infallibly taught dogma is a true statement of the content of revelation. To highlight the role of *hermeneutical* reception in making meaning of such a statement is not to deny the truth of the statement. Truth is not exhausted by meaning. A truthful statement of belief can be found to be meaningful in different ways.[98]

The nature of the true formulation of a *consensus fidelium* is best understood according to "the logic of question and answer."[99] Dogmatic and doctrinal statements are true answers to a particular question posed to the tradition of the church in a particular way. As the church moves through history, old answers that have been given to questions previously posed sometimes might no longer be understood and even misunderstood, and thus need to be reinterpreted, in order to communicate the truth of the original answer in a meaningful way. Moreover, new questions arise for which answers have not been formulated by the tradition.[100]

97. "Vatican I taught that definitions enunciated under infallibility are 'irreformable' in the juridical sense that they are not subject to further appeal. However, from an ecclesiological viewpoint, infallibility in teaching *(in docendo)* must always be accompanied by an infallibility in believing *(in credendo)*; thus, the actual acceptance of an irreformable papal decision by the church's members confirms that a definition really has been made under infallibility; if such acceptance or 'reception' were not given, it would suggest that a particular papal pronouncement lacked some condition essential for it really to be a genuine exercise of infallibility." John T. Ford, "Infallibility," in *The New Dictionary of Theology,* ed. Joseph A. Komonchak, Mary Collins, and Dermot A. Lane (Dublin: Gill and Macmillan, 1987), 517–21, at 519.

98. John Paul II, *Ut Unum Sint,* 19: "Because by its nature the content of faith is meant for all humanity, it must be translated into all cultures. Indeed, the element which determines communion in truth is *the meaning of truth.* The expression of truth can take different forms."

99. On "the logic of question and answer," see chapter 3. The phrase comes from Collingwood, *An Autobiography,* 29–43.

100. Timothy Radcliffe writes: "Indeed there are questions to which I believe that the Church does not as yet know the answers. If we are to seek the truth, then sometimes we must confess our perplexity. We must live through moments when we are faced with apparently contradictory truths. . . . We formulate tentative hypotheses and submit them to the judgement of the Church, hoping that even if they are not accepted at least they may be helpful. . . . So there is no short cut to the truth. Being truthful takes time. The role of the Magisterium is, or ought to be, to ensure that the Church takes the necessary time. It needs to pose tough questions when new views are articulated, not because of a fear of change or as 'doctrinal enforcers,' though that may sometimes be necessary, but to ensure that in the search for truth we do not take lazy short cuts and grab at premature and inadequate answers. The role of the Magisterium is to keep us talking,

The search for new answers to those new and old questions is an essential quest of the organon of *sensus fidelium*. It is in the daily lives of individuals, as they seek to apply the Gospel in their specific context, that lived answers to both new and old questions are formulated. Accessing these spiritual receptions of believers is an essential task of the church's teaching office, if it is to teach the faith as believed by the whole church past and present. From those "lived answers" to new and old questions it finds the essential elements of new formulations of *consensus fidelium*. This is an enquiry that is ongoing and one that takes time before a firm determination of the faith regarding a new question can be officially formulated. Theological reception of Scripture and tradition in the light of these questions provides the church with scholarly enquiry into the ways in which the riches of the past can indeed provide answers to questions that believers in the past could never have envisaged.

This learning process through the logic of question and answer highlights the circular relationship between *infallibilitas in credendo* (infallibility in believing) and *infallibilitas in docendo* (infallibility in teaching). The circle of believing and teaching involves reception before and after official promulgation. As we have seen earlier, an intra-textual reading of *Lumen Gentium* highlights that paragraph 25 discussing infallibility in teaching stands in tension with paragraph 12 on infallibility in believing. The council leaves to theological scholarship the explanation of that tension through a new synthesis. Any such synthesis of the council's teaching must maintain the necessary interplay between infallibility in believing and infallibility in teaching. Infallibility in believing operates on the level of *fides qua creditur*; infallibility in teaching operates on the level of *fides quae creditur*. Infallibility in believing involves the sure sense of the organon of *sensus fidelium*; infallibility in teaching involves a *consensus fidelium*. Infallibility in believing attaches to the believing of all the baptized; infallibility in teaching attaches to exercise of the magisterium under certain conditions. In the *conspiratio* between both modes of infallibility, it is the organon of *sensus fidelium* which constitutes "the church's own charism of infallibility."[101]

Individual expressions of the faith, as *sensus fidei* of a lay person, bish-

---

thinking and praying about what is central to our faith, as we journey towards the one who is beyond all words." Timothy Radcliffe, "How to Discover What We Believe," *The Tablet* (January 26, 2006): 12–13, at 13.

101. *LG,* 25c.

op, or pope, cannot be said to be arrived at through an infallible judgment, although the content of what is believed may indeed cohere with infallible church teaching. That is, the diverse concrete catechisms of individuals and multiple communal expressions of the faith (as *fides quae creditur*) cannot be spoken of as infallible senses of the faith. While one could speak of the organon of *sensus fidei* in an individual and the church as a whole as an infallible *sensus* for the faith, the consequent *sensus fidei* (interpretations of the faith that emerge for individuals diversely throughout the world-church), if expressed in statements or propositions, cannot be so described.

However, any baptized individual's participation in the church's infallibility in believing is significant for our discussion of the *consensus fidelium* because that infallibility is at work in the *reception* of all grades of church teaching. All teachings ultimately point to God and invite faith in God.[102] The organon of *sensus fidei* (whether individual or communal) is infallible *in credendo* because it is faith in its activity as *fides qua creditur*. That loving faith relationship between God and individuals or between God and a whole community of faith is true and sure because it is God who is the object of believing.

It is on this level of reception that *Lumen Gentium* 12 speaks of an infallibility in believing, as a consequence of the supernatural sense of the faith—*in credendo falli nequit* (cannot err in matters of believing).

The universal body of the faithful who have received the anointing of the holy one, cannot be mistaken in believing [*in credendo falli nequit*]. It displays this particular quality through a supernatural sense of the faith in the whole people when, "from the bishops to the last of the faithful laity", it expresses the consent of all [*universalem consensum*] in matters of faith and morals.[103]

On matters directly related to the content of revelation, a final *consensus fidelium* is a "display" or "manifestation" of this infallibility of believing, in the form of an infallible teaching. Here infallibility in believing and infallibility in teaching come together under the classic conditions required for an infallible teaching. The next part of the paragraph from

---

102. As we examined in the previous chapter, according to Aquinas, articles or propositions of faith are never the ultimate object of faith, "for the act of the believer does not terminate in the proposition [*enuntiabile*] but in the reality [signified by the proposition]." *ST*, 2-2, q. 1, a. 2, ad 2. See also *ST*, 2-2, q. 1, a. 6: "Articulus [fidei] est perceptio divinae veritatis tendens in ipsam [veritatem]."

103. *LG*, 12. Tanner translation corrected.

Lumen Gentium 12, however, sets out further conditions, conditions that relate to the ongoing reception of revelation before and after an official formulation of the faith.

Through this sense of the faith which is aroused and sustained by the Spirit of truth, the People of God, under the guidance of the sacred magisterium to which it is faithfully obedient, receives no longer the words of human beings but truly the word of God; [the People of God] adheres indefectibly [*indefectibiliter*] to "the faith which was once for all delivered to the saints"; *it penetrates more deeply into that same faith through right judgment and applies it more fully to life.*

The way the People of God "penetrates more deeply into that same faith through right judgment and applies it more fully to life" is through the mutual reception of the three authorities of the teaching office, both before and after the promulgatPO ion of a teaching, of whatever authority. The four Latin verbs used here are *accipit* (most often translated as "receives"), *adhaeret, penetrat,* and *applicat.* Such ecclesial reception, penetration, judgment, and application describe the hermeneutical triad of understanding, interpretation, and application always at work in the reception of revelation by the organon of *sensus fidelium.*

The living faith of the whole church is to be found expressed in the commitment, witness, and worship of Christian individuals and communities as they daily attempt to incarnate the Gospel of Jesus Christ through the power of the Spirit. An authoritative teaching office will find in that lived faith, expressed through the *sensus fidelium,* an indispensable source for fulfilling its task of constantly revitalizing its doctrinal and moral teaching. If it is to teach the faith of the whole church, the teaching office itself must be a process of dialogue for receiving the faith of the church in order to teach the church's faith meaningfully and truthfully.

Epilogue

Ongoing Conversion of the Ecclesial Imagination

The primary *task* of the teaching office is to teach the meaning and truth of what God has achieved and revealed through Jesus Christ in the Spirit for the sake of humanity's salvation. The *norm* for inspiring and regulating that task is the foundational apostolic reception of that salvific and revelatory event, as witnessed to in Scripture and traditioned by the church. The *principle* for understanding, interpreting, and applying salvific revelation is the Holy Spirit. The Spirit's organon for that task is the *sensus fidelium.*

Jesus spoke of eyes that do not see.[1] He healed physical blindness, but was as much concerned with spiritual blindness. The eyes of faith are in constant need of Christ's healing. "In its pilgrimage on earth Christ summons the church to continual reformation [*perennem reformationem*], of which it is always in need, in so far as it is an institution of human beings here on earth."[2] That *perennis reformatio* demands *perennis conversio,* continual conversion to Christ. "Each one therefore ought to be more radically converted to the Gospel and, without ever losing sight of God's plan, change his or her way of looking at things."[3] Continual ecclesial conversion involves continual conversion of the teaching office's "way of looking at" Scripture and tradition, as well as its "way of looking at"

1. Mk 8:18: "Do you have eyes, and fail to see? Do you have ears, and fail to hear? And do you not remember?"
2. *UR,* 6. Tanner translation.
3. John Paul II, *Ut Unum Sint,* 15.

the signs of the times, those signs of God working in new ways here and now, or being impeded from working.

The *sensus fidelium,* we have seen, is the imaginative organon for looking at past and present reality with "the eyes of faith." Continual conversion includes ongoing conversion of the eyes of faith, the ecclesial imagination. With the eyes of faith, the church and individuals within the church as it moves through history strive to perceive the meaning of Scripture and tradition as it applies to new situations. With the eyes of faith, the church imagines the direction and shape of a renewed church for the sake of more effective realization of its mission in the present. The imaginative organon of *sensus fidelium* enables the church to rejuvenate the tradition with creative fidelity. Continuity with the past is preserved through creative innovation; sameness is maintained through faithful rejuvenation; unity is preserved through legitimate diversity.

However, innovation, rejuvenation, and diversity are not just the result of ongoing understanding, interpretation, and application from the perspective of new times and of new contexts. Within that very process generated by the *sensus fidelium,* the imaginative organon of *sensus fidelium* is itself constantly being "attuned" and "calibrated" by the Holy Spirit, so that the church may more acutely recognize in the signs of the times the new things that God is doing. This constant calibration or attunement of the imaginative organon of the *sensus fidelium* constitutes an ongoing conversion of the ecclesial imagination by the Spirit. This ongoing healing of the eyes of faith involves the church's *perennis reformatio* and *perennis conversio.*

Ongoing conversion of the ecclesial imagination, of the organon of *sensus fidelium,* is first of all effected by constant relearning on the part of the church through fresh reception of Scripture and tradition. Each of the three authorities in the teaching office are authoritative witnesses, to the degree that they are learners from each other as they each receive and apply Scripture and tradition in their own distinctive way. Only a dialogue of mutual learning between these three authorities assures the church that it is being faithful to the treasure once given, the apostolic tradition, as expressed through the apostolic imagination in Scripture. That interaction should be what John Paul II called an ongoing "dialogue of conversion."[4] The dialogue of conversion needed between sepa-

---

4. Ibid., 35.

rated churches must likewise characterize vital dialogue "in the church itself."[5] Cultivating "a culture of dialogue" within the church between these authorities therefore means cultivating a culture of conversion.

But that dialogue of conversion within the teaching office is facilitated not only by the church's dialogue with Scripture and tradition, but also by the church's dialogue with God in the present. God has indeed spoken definitively in the past; witness to that divine Word is sought in the written Word of God as traditioned by the church. But the same God witnessed to in Scripture and tradition continues to speak to humanity in the present. That contemporary divine-human dialogue must be discerned by listening to the salvific experience of contemporary Christians and attending to the signs of the times which are shaping their lives. Listening to God speaking in the present enables the church to recognize and to faithfully interpret what the same God has spoken in the past—and vice versa.

When contemporary Christians attempt to make sense of their saving and revelatory encounter with God, God's living Word in the present is to be found. Hence, the faithful's sense of the faith emerging from those contemporary encounters of salvation is a privileged ecclesial *locus* for hearing the voice of the living God, the same God who once "long ago . . . spoke to our ancestors in many and various ways by the prophets, [and] has spoken to us by a Son."[6] Only the Holy Spirit enables the church to recognize and interpret the living voice of the Son in the present.

This divine-human dialogue, with the witnesses of the past and within the present activity of God, takes place via the interpretative organon of the *sensus fidelium*. This organon is the *Anknüpfungspunkt* (point of contact) between God and humanity in the present. "In this way, the God who spoke of old still maintains an uninterrupted conversation with the bride of his beloved Son."[7] That divine-human conversation can proceed because the principle of reception in that divine-human dialogue, the Holy Spirit, "is active, making the living voice of the gospel ring out in the church, and through it in the world, leading those who believe into the whole truth, and making the message of Christ dwell in them in all its richness."[8]

---

5. *GS*, 92. The paragraph speaks of four concentric circles of dialogue: within the Catholic Church, between separated churches, with other religions, and with all humanity.

6. Heb 1:1–2.   7. *DV*, 8. Tanner translation.

8. Ibid.

Thus, the same Spirit at work in the inspiration of Scripture on all three levels of production, text, and reception is at work refashioning the perceptive skills of the organon of *sensus fidelium,* enabling the eyes of faith to re-read the past in the light of the present and to interpret the present in the light of the past. The same ecclesial organon for understanding, interpreting, and applying the Gospel which produced the writings and the canon of Scripture remains at work in the church making Scripture, through its reception, God's inspired Word speaking in the present.

The God who is fully revealed in Jesus Christ through the Spirit paradoxically forever remains Mystery and is forever new. The otherness of God's Mystery is not diminished by God's self-revelation. Hence, encounter with God's otherness in human history engenders a continual "differentiation of horizons" between God and the understanding of human beings. Therefore, interpretation of revelation demands a "hermeneutics of alterity." In the ongoing divine-human dialogue facilitated by the Spirit's organon, new questions arise in human history for which former divine-human dialogue has not given answers. Jesus did not give his disciples answers to every question that would arise throughout the history of the church; the Jesus Christ proclaimed in the Gospels does not give the church of today detailed solutions to every pastoral question that arises or will arise. The whole people of God, through dialogue between the authorities of the teaching office, discerns answers, with the help of the Spirit. It is the Spirit, the principle of reception, who enables the church to find new answers and new solutions to new questions and new challenges, but all in the light of the God revealed through what Jesus Christ, the Crucified and Risen One, has taught and done and is. The answers to new questions *can* be found in the witness of Scripture and tradition—but those sources must be interpreted in the light of what God is doing *now.*

This ongoing dialogue, between God and humanity and between the three authorities in the teaching office, is a process of discovery and learning; it is to be a dialogue of conversion to the Gospel. From new perspectives throughout history, the church comes to understand, interpret, and apply the Gospel in new ways. This fact of ongoing discovery in church history has often been called "the development of doctrine." Such an organic model is not fully adequate for naming the process of ecclesial discovery, learning, and conversion throughout history.

This book has proposed a more appropriate way of understanding that process, as one of ongoing hermeneutical reception of revelation enabled by the Holy Spirit. In this way, the inspiration of Scripture requires constant realization throughout the history of the church. The Spirit's work in the production of the canon needs to be brought to fruition with a Spirit-inspired reception of the texts. By enabling this reception within the church, the Spirit continues to mark the church with unity, catholicity, apostolicity, and holiness: a unity that finds expression in diverse catholicity; a catholic unity that perpetuates the apostolic ecclesial imagination by faithfully bridging "story" and "significance" in every age; and an apostolicity that comes to expression in the holiness of Christians by their commitment, witness, and worship of the God who continues to save them through Christ in the power of the Spirit.

In this way, the church is *semper ipse sed nunquam idem* (always itself but never the same), as it is carried through history on the wings of the Spirit of Reception. God's Word and Spirit, who are the co-instituting principles of the church, continually co-constitute the church in its mission. The Holy Spirit, the principle of reception, enables the church to receive the Word of salvation and revelation, and leads it to the fullness of truth. It is the task of the ever-converting teaching office to receive that Word so that its witness may be faithfully rejuvenated in every age. As St Irenaeus wrote:

The preaching of the Church presents in every respect an unshakeable stability, remains identical to itself and benefits, as we have shown, from the witness of the prophets, apostles and all their disciples, a witness which embraces "the beginning, the middle and the end," in brief, the totality of the "economy" of God and his operation infallibly ordained for the salvation of man and establishing our faith. From then on, this faith, which we have received from the Church, we preserve it with care, for unceasingly, through the action of the Spirit of God, such a deposit of great price enclosed in an excellent vessel, rejuvenates and causes a rejuvenation of the very vessel which contains it.[9]

Such is the ongoing conversion of the ecclesial imagination, the eyes of faith.

9. *Adv. Haer.* III, 24, 1. Quoted in Tillard, *Church of Churches,* 144.

Bibliography

Achtemeier, Paul J. *Inspiration and Authority: Nature and Function of Christian Scripture.* Peabody, Mass.: Hendrickson Publishers, 1999.

Alberigo, Giuseppe. "The Christian Situation after Vatican II." In *The Reception of Vatican II,* edited by Giuseppe Alberigo, Jean Pierre Jossua, and Joseph A. Komonchak, 1–24. Washington, D.C.: The Catholic University of America Press, 1987.

———. "Vatican II and Its History." In *Vatican II: A Forgotten Future?* edited by Alberto Melloni and Christoph Theobald, 9–20. *Concilium 2005/4.* London: SCM Press, 2005.

Allen, Graham. *Intertextuality.* New York: Routledge, 2000.

Alonso Schökel, Luis. *The Inspired Word: Scripture in the Light of Language and Literature.* New York: Herder and Herder, 1965.

Alonso Schökel, Luis, and José María Bravo. *A Manual of Hermeneutics.* Translated by Brook W. R. Pearson. Sheffield, England: Sheffield Academic Press, 1998.

Alszeghy, Zoltán. "The *Sensus Fidei* and the Development of Dogma." In *Vatican II Assessment and Perspectives: Twenty-Five Years After (1962–1987),* vol. 1, edited by René Latourelle, 1:138–56. New York: Paulist Press, 1988.

Anglican–Roman Catholic International Commission. *Mary: Grace and Hope in Christ.* Harrisburg, Pa.: Morehouse, 2005.

Avis, Paul D. L. *God and the Creative Imagination: Metaphor, Symbol, and Myth in Religion and Theology.* New York: Routledge, 1999.

Aymans, Winfried. *Das synodale Element in der Kirchenverfassung.* Munich, 1970.

Bailey, Kenneth E. "Informal Controlled Oral Tradition and the Synoptic Gospels." *Asia Journal of Theology* 5 (1991): 34–54.

———. "Middle Eastern Oral Tradition and the Synoptic Tradition." *Expository Times* (1995): 363–67.

———. *Jacob and the Prodigal: How Jesus Retold Israel's Story.* Downers Grove, Ill.: InterVarsity Press, 2003.

Barth, Karl. *Church Dogmatics. Volume 1: The Doctrine of the Word of God. Part 1.* Edited by G. W. Bromiley and T. F. Torrance. 2d ed. New York: T&T Clark International, 2004.

Barton, John. "Marcion Revisited." In *The Canon Debate,* edited by Lee Martin Mc-Donald and James A. Sanders, 341–54. Peabody, Mass.: Hendrickson Publishers, 2002.

Bauckham, Richard. "For Whom Were the Gospels Written?" In *The Gospels for All Christians: Rethinking the Gospel Audience,* edited by Richard Bauckham, 9–48. Edinburgh: T&T Clark, 1998.

———. *Jesus and the Eyewitnesses: The Gospels as Eyewitness Testimony.* Grand Rapids, Mich.: William B. Eerdmans, 2006.

Bauer, Walter. *Orthodoxy and Heresy in Earliest Christianity.* Edited by Robert A. Kraft and Gerhard Krodel. Philadelphia: Fortress Press, 1971.

Beal, John P. "The Exercise of the Power of Governance by Lay People: State of the Question." *The Jurist* 55 (1995): 1–92.

Bednar, Gerald J. *Faith as Imagination: The Contribution of William F. Lynch, S.J.* Kansas City, Mo.: Sheed & Ward, 1996.

Beinert, Wolfgang. "Der Glaubenssinn der Gläubigen in der systematischen Theologie." In *Mitsprache im Glauben? Vom Glaubenssinn der Gläubigen,* edited by Günther Koch, 51–78. Würzburg: Echter, 1993.

———. "Konziliarität der Kirche: Ein Beitrag zur ökumenischen Epistemologie." In *Vom Finden und Verkünden der Wahrheit in der Kirche: Beiträge zur theologischen Erkenntnislehre,* 325–50. Freiburg: Herder, 1993.

———. "Der Glaubenssinn der Gläubigen in Theologie- und Dogmengeschichte: Ein Überblick." In *Der Glaubenssinn des Gottesvolkes: Konkurrent oder Partner des Lehramts?* edited by Dietrich Wiederkehr, 66–131. Questiones Disputatae 151. Freiburg: Herder, 1994.

———. "Ecclesial Magisterium." In *Handbook of Catholic Theology,* edited by Wolfgang Beinert and Francis Schüssler Fiorenza, 194–99. New York: Crossroad, 1995.

———. "Sensus Fidelium." In *Handbook of Catholic Theology,* edited by Wolfgang Beinert and Francis Schüssler Fiorenza, 655–57. New York: Crossroad, 1995.

———. "Theologische Erkenntnislehre." In *Glaubenszugänge: Lehrbuch der Katholischen Dogmatik,* vol. 1, edited by Wolfgang Beinert, 1:47–197. Paderborn: Ferdinand Schöningh, 1995.

———. "The Subjects of Reception." In *Reception and Communion Among Churches,* edited by Hervé Legrand, Julio Manzanares, and Antonio García y García, 324–46. Washington, D.C.: The Catholic University of America Press, 1997.

———. *Kann man dem Glauben trauen? Grundlagen theologischer Erkenntnis.* Regensburg: Verlag Friedrich Pustet, 2004.

Berkouwer, G. C. *Holy Scripture.* Grand Rapids, Mich.: W. B. Eerdmans, 1975.

Bevans, Stephen B. *Models of Contextual Theology.* Rev. and expanded ed. Maryknoll, N.Y.: Orbis Books, 2002.

Bianchi, Eugene C., and Rosemary Radford Ruether, eds. *A Democratic Catholic Church: The Reconstruction of Roman Catholicism.* New York: Crossroad, 1992.

Blondel, Maurice. "History and Dogma." In *The Letter on Apologetics and History and Dogma,* 219–87. New York: Holt, 1965.

Bock, Darrell L. *The Missing Gospels: Unearthing the Truth Behind Alternative Christianities.* Nashville, Tenn.: Nelson Books, 2006.

Boff, Clodovis. *Theology and Praxis: Epistemological Foundations.* Maryknoll, N.Y.: Orbis Books, 1987.

Boring, M. Eugene. "Excursus: Matthew as Interpreter of Scripture." In *The New In-*

terpreter's Bible, vol. 8, 151–54. Nashville, Tenn.: Abingdon Press, 1994.

Bovon, François. "The Interpretation of the Scriptures of Israel." In *Luke the Theologian: Fifty-five Years of Research (1950–2005),* 87–121. Waco, Tex.: Baylor University Press, 2006.

Brown, Raymond E. "The Paraclete in the Fourth Gospel." *New Testament Studies* 13 (1966–67): 113–32.

———. *Priest and Bishop: Biblical Reflections.* London: G. Chapman, 1971.

———. *The Churches the Apostles Left Behind.* New York: Paulist Press, 1984.

———. "Diverse Views of the Spirit in the New Testament: A Preliminary Contribution of Exegesis to Doctrinal Reflection." In *Biblical Exegesis and Church Doctrine,* 101–13. New York: Paulist Press, 1985.

———. "The Christologies of New Testament Christians." In *An Introduction to New Testament Christology,* 103–52. New York: Paulist Press, 1994.

———. *An Introduction to the New Testament.* New York: Doubleday, 1997.

Brown, Raymond E., Carolyn Osiek, and Pheme Perkins. "Early Church." In *The New Jerome Biblical Commentary,* edited by Raymond E. Brown, Joseph A. Fitzmyer, and Roland E. Murphy, 1338–53. Englewood Cliffs, N.J.: Prentice-Hall, 1990.

Brown, Schuyler. "Apostleship in the New Testament as an Historical and Theological Problem." *New Testament Studies* 30 (1984): 474–80.

Brown, Tricia Gates. *Spirit in the Writings of John: Johannine Pneumatology in Social-Scientific Perspective.* New York: T&T Clark International, 2003.

Brueggemann, Walter. *An Introduction to the Old Testament: The Canon and Christian Imagination.* Louisville, Ky.: Westminster John Knox Press, 2003.

Bryant, David J. *Faith and the Play of Imagination: On the Role of Imagination in Religion.* Macon, Ga.: Mercer University Press, 1989.

Burge, Gary M. *The Anointed Community: The Holy Spirit in the Johannine Tradition.* Grand Rapids, Mich.: W. B. Eerdmans, 1986.

Burgess, Joseph A. "Montreal (1963): A Case Study." In *The Quadrilog: Tradition and the Future of Ecumenism. Essays in Honor of George H. Tavard,* edited by Kenneth Hagen, 270–86. Collegeville, Minn.: Liturgical Press, 1994.

Burghardt, Walter J. "Contemplation: A Long Loving Look at the Real." *Church* (Winter 1989): 14–18.

Burkhard, John J. "*Sensus fidei:* Meaning, Role and Future of a Teaching of Vatican II." *Louvain Studies* 17 (1992): 18–34.

———. "*Sensus Fidei:* Theological Reflection Since Vatican II. Part I: 1965–1984." *Heythrop Journal* 34 (1993): 41–59.

———. "*Sensus Fidei:* Theological Reflection Since Vatican II. Part II: 1985–1989." *Heythrop Journal* 34 (1993): 123–36.

———. *Apostolicity Then and Now: An Ecumenical Church in a Postmodern World.* Collegeville, Minn.: Liturgical Press, 2004.

———. "*Sensus Fidei:* Recent Theological Reflection (1990–2001). Part I." *Heythrop Journal* 46 (2005): 450–75.

———. "*Sensus Fidei:* Recent Theological Reflection (1990–2001). Part II." *Heythrop Journal* 47 (2006): 38–54.

Byrne, Brendan. *Romans.* Collegeville, Minn.: Liturgical Press, 1996.

Byrskog, Samuel. "A New Perspective on the Jesus Tradition: Reflections on James Dunn's *Jesus Remembered.*" *Journal for the Study of the New Testament* 26 (2004): 459–71.

Calvin, John. *The Institutes of Christian Religion.* Translated by A. N. S. Lane and Hilary Osborne. Grand Rapids, Mich.: Baker Book House, 1987.

Campenhausen, Hans. *The Formation of the Christian Bible.* Philadelphia: Fortress Press, 1972.

Carr, Thomas K. *Newman and Gadamer: Toward a Hermeneutics of Religious Knowledge.* Atlanta, Ga.: Scholars Press, 1996.

Carson, D. A., and H. G. M. Williamson, eds. *It Is Written: Scripture Citing Scripture: Essays in Honour of Barnabas Lindars, SSF.* New York: Cambridge University Press, 1988.

Catechism of the Catholic Church. London: Geoffrey Chapman, 1994.

Childs, Brevard S. *The New Testament as Canon: An Introduction.* Philadelphia: Fortress Press, 1985.

Clifford, Catherine E. *The Groupe des Dombes: A Dialogue of Conversion.* New York: Peter Lang, 2005.

The Code of Canon Law. London: Collins, 1983.

Cohen, Richard A., and James L. Marsh. *Ricoeur as Another: The Ethics of Subjectivity.* Albany: State University of New York Press, 2002.

Collingwood, R. G. *An Autobiography.* New York: Oxford University Press, 1939.

Collins, Raymond F. "Inspiration." In *The New Jerome Biblical Commentary,* edited by Raymond E. Brown, Joseph A. Fitzmyer, and Roland E. Murphy, 1023–33. Englewood Cliffs, N.J.: Prentice-Hall, 1990.

Congar, Yves. *The Meaning of Tradition.* New York: Hawthorn Books, 1964.

———. *Tradition and Traditions: An Historical and a Theological Essay.* London: Burns & Oates, 1966.

———. "The Council as an Assembly and the Church as Essentially Conciliar." In *One, Holy, Catholic, and Apostolic: Studies in the Nature and Role of the Church in the Modern World,* edited by Herbert Vorgrimler, 44–88. London: Sheed and Ward, 1968.

———. "Indefectibility and Infallibility." *Compass* 5 (1971): 43–45.

———. "La 'Réception' comme réalité ecclésiologique." *Revue des Sciences Philosophiques et Théologiques* 56 (1972): 369–402.

———. "Reception as an Ecclesiological Reality." *Concilium* 77 (1972): 43–68.

———. "A Semantic History of the Term 'Magisterium.'" In *The Magisterium and Morality: Readings in Moral Theology, No. 3,* edited by Charles E. Curran and Richard A. McCormick, 297–313. New York: Paulist Press, 1982.

———. "The Conciliar Structure or Regime of the Church." *Concilium* 167 (1983): 3–9.

———. *The Word and the Spirit.* Translated by David Smith. London: Geoffrey Chapman, 1986.

———. *I Believe in the Holy Spirit.* New York: Crossroad, 1997.

Congregation for the Doctrine of the Faith. "Profession of Faith and Oath of Fidelity." *Origins* 18 (March 16, 1989): 661, 663.

———. "The Ecclesial Vocation of the Theologian." *Origins* 20 (July 5, 1990): 118–26.

———. *Instruction on the Ecclesial Vocation of the Theologian.* Vatican City: St. Paul Books and Media, 1990.

Cook, Michael L. *Christology as Narrative Quest.* Collegeville, Minn.: Liturgical Press, 1997.

Cooke, Bernard J. *Ministry to Word and Sacraments: History and Theology.* Philadelphia: Fortress Press, 1976.

Coriden, James A. "The Holy Spirit and Church Governance." *The Jurist* 66 (2006): 339–73.

Costigan, Richard F. *The Consensus of the Church and Papal Infallibility: A Study in the Background of Vatican I.* Washington, D.C.: The Catholic University of America Press, 2005.

Côté, Richard G. "Christology and the Paschal Imagination." In *Concilium. Who Do You Say That I Am?* edited by Werner Jeanrond and Christoph Theobald, 80–88. London: SCM Press, 1997.

———. *Lazarus! Come Out! Why Faith Needs Imagination.* Toronto: Novalis, 2003.

Coulson, John. *Religion and Imagination: "In Aid of a Grammar of Assent."* New York: Oxford University Press, 1981.

Countryman, L. W. "Tertullian and the Regula Fidei." *Second Century* 2 (1982): 208–27.

Court, John M. *New Testament Writers and the Old Testament: An Introduction.* London: SPCK, 2002.

Cozzens, Donald B. *Faith That Dares to Speak.* Collegeville, Minn.: Liturgical Press, 2004.

Crites, Stephen. "The Narrative Quality of Experience." In *Why Narrative? Readings in Narrative Theology,* edited by Stanley Hauerwas, L. Gregory Jones, and Ronald F. Thiemann, 65–88. Grand Rapids, Mich.: W. B. Eerdmans, 1989.

Crowe, Frederick E. "The Church as Learner: Two Crises, One Kairos." In *Appropriating the Lonergan Idea,* edited by Michael Vertin, 370–84. Washington, D.C.: The Catholic University of America Press, 1989.

Cullmann, Oscar. *The Early Church: Studies in Early Christian History and Theology.* Philadelphia: Westminister Press, 1956.

Das, A. Andrew, and Frank J. Matera. *The Forgotten God: Perspectives in Biblical Theology. Essays in Honor of Paul J. Achtemeier on the Occasion of his Seventy-fifth Birthday.* Louisville, Ky.: Westminster John Knox Press, 2002.

de la Potterie, Ignace. "Interpretation of Holy Scripture in the Spirit in Which It Was Written (Dei Verbum 12c)." In *Vatican II: Assessment and Perspectives. Twenty-Five Years After (1962–1987),* edited by René Latourelle, 220–66. New York: Paulist Press, 1988.

Dejaifve, Georges. "'Ex sese, non autem ex consensu ecclesiae.'" *Salesianum* 24 (1962): 283–97.

del Agua, Agustín. "The Narrative Identity of Christians According to the New Testament." In *Concilium. Creating Identity,* edited by Hermann Häring, Maureen Junker-Kenny, and Dietmar Mieth, 91–99. London: SCM Press, 2000.

Dines, Jennifer M. *The Septuagint.* New York: T&T Clark, 2004.

Dionne, J. Robert. *The Papacy and the Church: A Study of Praxis and Reception in Ecumenical Perspective.* New York: Philosophical Library, 1987.

Donahue, John R. "Scripture: A Roman Catholic Perspective." *Review & Expositor* 79 (1982): 231–44.

Donahue, John R., and Daniel J. Harrington. *The Gospel of Mark, Sacra Pagina Series; v. 2.* Collegeville, Minn.: Liturgical Press, 2002.

Donnelly, Doris, ed. *Retrieving Charisms for the Twenty-first Century.* Collegeville, Minn.: Liturgical Press, 1999.

Downey, Michael. "Lay People and Spirituality." In *The New Westminster Dictionary of Christian Spirituality,* edited by Philip Sheldrake, 400–402. Louisville, Ky.: Westminster John Knox Press, 2005.

Downs, David J. "'Early Catholicism' and Apocalypticism in the Pastoral Epistles." *Catholic Biblical Quarterly* 67 (2005): 641–61.

Dreyer, Elizabeth, and Mark S. Burrows, eds. *Minding the Spirit: The Study of Christian Spirituality.* Baltimore, Md.: Johns Hopkins University Press, 2005.

Drilling, Peter J. "Common and Ministerial Priesthood: *Lumen Gentium,* Article Ten." *Irish Theological Quarterly* 53 (1987): 81–99.

———. "The Priest, Prophet and King Trilogy: Elements of Its Meaning in *Lumen Gentium* and for Today." *Eglise et Théologie* 19 (1988): 179–206.

Dulles, Avery. "Revelation and Discovery." In *Theology and Discovery: Essays in Honor of Karl Rahner, S.J.,* edited by William J. Kelly, 1–29. Milwaukee, Wis.: Marquette University Press, 1980.

———. "The Two Magisteria: An Interim Reflection." *CTSA Proceedings* 35 (1980): 155–69.

———. "Doctrinal Authority for a Pilgrim Church." In *The Magisterium and Morality. Readings in Moral Theology, No. 3,* edited by Charles E. Curran and Richard A. McCormick, 247–70. New York: Paulist Press, 1982.

———. *Models of Revelation.* Dublin: Gill and Macmillan, 1983.

———. *The Catholicity of the Church.* Oxford: Clarendon Press, 1985.

———. *The Survival of Dogma: Faith, Authority and Dogma in a Changing World.* New York: Crossroad, 1987.

———. "Fundamental Theology and the Dynamics of Conversion." In *The Craft of Theology: From Symbol to System.* New York: Crossroad, 1992.

———. *The Assurance of Things Hoped For: A Theology of Christian Faith.* New York: Oxford University Press, 1994.

Dungan, David L. *Constantine's Bible: Politics and the Making of the New Testament.* Minneapolis: Fortress Press, 2006.

Dunn, James D. G. *Jesus and the Spirit: A Study of the Religious and Charismatic Experience of Jesus and the First Christians as Reflected in the New Testament.* London: SCM Press, 1975.

———. *Unity and Diversity in the New Testament: An Inquiry into the Character of Earliest Christianity.* 2nd ed. London: SCM Press, 1990.

———. *The Theology of Paul the Apostle.* Grand Rapids, Mich.: W. B. Eerdmans, 1998.

———. "Jesus in Oral Memory: The Initial Stages of the Jesus Tradition." In *Jesus: A Colloquium in the Holy Land,* edited by Doris Donnelly, 84–145. New York: Continuum, 2001.

———. "Has the Canon a Continuing Function?" In *The Canon Debate,* edited by Lee Martin McDonald and James A. Sanders, 558–79. Peabody, Mass.: Hendrickson Publishers, 2002.

———. "Altering the Default Setting: Re-envisaging the Early Transmission of the Jesus Tradition." *New Testament Studies* 49 (2003): 139–75.

———. *Jesus Remembered.* Grand Rapids, Mich.: W. B. Eerdmans, 2003.

———. "On History, Memory and Eyewitnesses: In Response to Bengt Holmberg and Samuel Byrskog." *Journal for the Study of the New Testament* 26 (2004): 473–87.

———. *A New Perspective on Jesus: What the Quest for the Historical Jesus Missed.* Grand Rapids, Mich.: Baker Academic, 2005.

Dunne, Victor. *Prophecy in the Church: The Vision of Yves Congar.* New York: Peter Lang, 2000.

Dupuis, Jacques, and Josef Neuner. *The Christian Faith in the Doctrinal Documents of the Catholic Church.* 7th rev. and enl. ed. New York: Alba House, 2001.

Edwards, Denis. *Breath of Life: A Theology of the Creator Spirit.* Maryknoll, N.Y.: Orbis Books, 2004.

Ehrman, Bart D. *The Orthodox Corruption of Scripture: The Effect of Early Christological Controversies on the Text of the New Testament.* New York: Oxford University Press, 1993.

————. *Lost Christianities: The Battle for Scripture and the Faiths We Never Knew.* New York: Oxford University Press, 2003.

Espín, Orlando O. "Traditioning: Culture, Daily Life and Popular Religion and Their Impact on Christian Tradition." In *Futuring Our Past: Explorations in the Theology of Tradition,* edited by Orlando O. Espín and Gary Macy, 1–22. Maryknoll, N.Y.: Orbis Books, 2006.

Evans, Craig A., and James A. Sanders, eds. *Luke and Scripture: The Function of Sacred Tradition in Luke-Acts.* Minneapolis: Fortress Press, 1993.

————, eds. *Paul and the Scriptures of Israel.* Sheffield, England: JSOT Press, 1993.

Evans, Jeanne. *Paul Ricoeur's Hermeneutics of the Imagination: The Imagination as the Creative Element of Religious Literacy.* New York: Peter Lang, 1995.

Fagan, Seán. "Conscience." In *The New Dictionary of Theology,* edited by Joseph A. Komonchak, Mary Collins, and Dermot A. Lane, 226–30. Dublin: Gill and Macmillan, 1987.

Fee, Gordon D. *God's Empowering Presence: The Holy Spirit in the Letters of Paul.* Peabody, Mass.: Hendrickson Publishers, 1994.

————. *Paul, the Spirit, and the People of God.* Peabody, Mass.: Hendrickson Publishers, 1996.

Figueiredo, Anthony J. *The Magisterium-Theology Relationship: Contemporary Theological Conceptions in the Light of Universal Church Teaching since 1835 and the Pronouncements of the Bishops of the United States.* Rome: Editrice Pontificia Università Gregoriana, 2001.

Finucane, Daniel J. *Sensus Fidelium: The Use of a Concept in the Post–Vatican II Era.* San Francisco: International Scholars Publications, 1996.

Fisichella, Rino. "Signs of the Times." In *Dictionary of Fundamental Theology,* edited by René Latourelle and Rino Fisichella, 995–1001. Middlegreen, Slough, England: St. Paul, 1994.

Fitzmyer, Joseph A. "The Office of Teaching in the Christian Church according to the New Testament." In *Teaching Authority and Infallibility in the Church: Lutherans and Catholics in Dialogue VI,* edited by Paul C. Empie et al., 186–212. Minneapolis: Augsburg Publishing House, 1980.

————. *Scripture: The Soul of Theology.* New York: Paulist Press, 1994.

Ford, John T. "Infallibility." In *The New Dictionary of Theology,* edited by Joseph A. Komonchak, Mary Collins, and Dermot A. Lane, 517–21. Dublin: Gill and Macmillan, 1987.

Forte, Bruno. *The Church: Icon of the Trinity. A Brief Study.* Boston: St. Paul Books and Media, 1991.

Fortin-Melkevik, Anne. "The Identity of the Christian Following Jesus Christ." In *Concilium. Who Do You Say That I Am?* edited by Werner Jeanrond and Christoph Theobald, 91–101. London: SCM Press, 1997.

Fourth World Conference on Faith and Order, Montreal 1963. "Report of Section II:

Scripture, Tradition and Traditions." In *The Ecumenical Movement: An Anthology of Key Texts and Voices,* edited by Michael K. Kinnamon and Brian E. Cope, 139–44. Grand Rapids, Mich.: W. B. Eerdmans, 1997.

Fowler, James W. *Stages of Faith: The Psychology of Human Development and the Quest for Meaning.* San Francisco: Harper & Row, 1981.

Fransen, Piet F. *The New Life of Grace.* London: Geoffrey Chapman, 1971.

Fries, Heinrich. "'Ex sese, non ex consensu ecclesiae.'" In *Volk Gottes: Zum Kirchenverständnis der katholischen, evangelischen und anglikanischen Theologie,* edited by Remigius Bäumer and Heimo Dolch, 481–500. Freiburg: Herder, 1967.

———. *Fundamental Theology.* Washington, D.C.: The Catholic University of America Press, 1996.

Gabel, Helmut. *Inspirationsverständnis im Wandel: Theologische Neuorientierung im Umfeld des Zweiten Vatikanischen Konzils.* Mainz: Matthias-Grünewald-Verlag, 1991.

Gadamer, Hans Georg. *Truth and Method.* 2nd rev. ed. New York: Crossroad, 1989.

Gaillardetz, Richard R. *Teaching with Authority: A Theology of the Magisterium in the Church.* Collegeville, Minn.: Liturgical Press, 1997.

———. "Shifting Meanings in the Lay-Clergy Distinction." *Irish Theological Quarterly* 64 (1999): 115–39.

Gallagher, Michael Paul. "Imagination and Faith." *The Way* 24 (1984): 122.

Gamble, Harry Y. "The New Testament Canon: Recent Research and the Status Questionis." In *The Canon Debate,* edited by Lee Martin McDonald and James A. Sanders, 267–94. Peabody, Mass.: Hendrickson Publishers, 2002.

Geiselmann, Josef Rupert. "Das Konzil von Trient über das Verhältnis der Heiligen Schrift und der nichtgeschriebenen Traditionen." In *Die mündliche Überlieferung: Beiträge zum Begriff der Tradition,* edited by Michael Schmaus, 123–206. Munich: Max Hueber, 1957.

Glaser, John W. "Authority, Connatural Knowledge, and the Spontaneous Judgment of the Faithful." *Theological Studies* 29 (1968): 742–51.

Graham, William A. "Scripture." In *The Encyclopedia of Religion,* edited by Mircea Eliade, 13: 133–45. New York: Macmillan, 1987.

Grant, Robert M., and David Tracy. *A Short History of the Interpretation of the Bible.* 2nd, rev. and enl. ed. Philadelphia: Fortress Press, 1984.

Green, Garrett. *Imagining God: Theology and the Religious Imagination.* San Francisco: Harper & Row, 1989.

Grelot, Pierre. "Relations between the Old and New Testaments in Jesus Christ." In *Problems and Perspectives of Fundamental Theology,* edited by René Latourelle and Gerald O'Collins, 186–205. New York: Paulist Press, 1982.

Grillmeier, Alois. "The Reception of Chalcedon in the Roman Catholic Church." *Ecumenical Review* 22 (1970): 383–411.

———. "The Reception of Church Councils." In *Foundations of Theology,* edited by Philip McShane, 102–14. Dublin: Gill and Macmillan, 1971.

———. *Christ in Christian Tradition. Volume Two: From the Council of Chalcedon (451) to Gregory the Great (590–604). Part One: Reception and Contradiction: The Development of the Discussion about Chalcedon from 451 to the Beginning of the Reign of Justinian.* Atlanta: John Knox Press, 1987.

Groupe des Dombes. *For the Conversion of the Churches.* Geneva: WCC Publications, 1993.

Hanson, R. P. C. *Tradition in the Early Church.* London: SCM Press, 1962.

Harrington, Daniel J. *The Gospel of Matthew, Sacra Pagina Series; v. 1.* Collegeville, Minn.: Liturgical Press, 1991.

———. *How Do Catholics Read the Bible?* Lanham, Md.: Rowman & Littlefield Publishers, 2005.

Hart, Ray L. *Unfinished Man and the Imagination: Toward an Ontology and a Rhetoric of Revelation.* Atlanta, Ga.: Scholars Press, 1985.

Hartin, Patrick J. "*Sensus Fidelium:* A Roman Catholic Reflection on Its Significance for Ecumenical Thought." *Journal of Ecumenical Studies* 28 (1991): 74–87.

Haughton, Rosemary. *The Catholic Thing.* Springfield, Ill.: Templegate, 1979.

Hays, Richard B. *Echoes of Scripture in the Letters of Paul.* New Haven, Conn.: Yale University Press, 1989.

———. "The Conversion of the Imagination: Scripture and Eschatology in 1 Corinthians." *New Testament Studies* 45 (1999): 391–412.

———. "The Canonical Matrix of the Gospels." In *The Cambridge Companion to the Gospels,* edited by Stephen C. Barton, 53–75. New York: Cambridge University Press, 2006.

Healey, Joseph P. "Faith: Old Testament." In *The Anchor Bible Dictionary,* vol. 2, edited by David Noel Freedman, 2:744–49. New York: Doubleday, 1992.

Hederico, Benjamin, ed. *Lexicon Graeco-Latinum et Latino-Graecum.* Rome: Congregatio de Propaganda Fide, 1832.

Heft, James L. "'Sensus Fidelium' and the Marian Dogmas." *One in Christ* 28 (1992): 106–25.

Heinemann, Heribert. "Demokratisierung der Kirche oder Erneuerung synodaler Einrichtungen?: Eine Anfrage an das Kirchenverständnis." In *Dialog als Selbstvollzug der Kirche,* edited by Gebhard Fürst, 270–83. Freiburg: Herder, 1997.

Hengel, Martin. "The Titles of the Gospels and the Gospel of Mark." In *Studies in the Gospel of Mark,* 64–84. Philadelphia: Fortress Press, 1985.

———. *The Four Gospels and the One Gospel of Jesus Christ: An Investigation of the Collection and Origin of the Canonical Gospels.* Harrisburg, Pa.: Trinity Press International, 2000.

———. "The Four Gospels and the One Gospel of Jesus Christ." In *The Earliest Gospels: The Origins and Transmission of the Earliest Christian Gospels. The Contribution of the Chester Beatty Gospel Codex P[45],* edited by Charles Horton, 13–26. New York: T&T Clark International, 2004.

Henn, William. *One Faith: Biblical and Patristic Contributions Toward Understanding Unity in Faith.* New York: Paulist Press, 1995.

Heschel, Abraham J. *The Prophets.* New York: Harper & Row, 1969.

Hilberath, Bernd Jochen. "Vom Heiligen Geist des Dialogs: Das Dialogische Prinzip in Gotteslehre und Heilsgeschehen." In *Dialog als Selbstvollzug der Kirche,* edited by Gebhard Fürst, 93–116. Freiburg: Herder, 1997.

Hilkert, Mary Catherine. *Naming Grace: Preaching and the Sacramental Imagination.* New York: Continuum, 1997.

Hill, Edmund. *Ministry and Authority in the Catholic Church.* London: Chapman, 1988.

———. "What Does the New Testament Say?" *Priests and People* 11 (1997): 311–15.

Hinze, Bradford E. *Practices of Dialogue in the Roman Catholic Church: Aims and Obstacles, Lessons and Laments.* New York: Continuum, 2006.

Hoffman, Thomas A. "Inspiration, Normativeness, Canonicity, and the Unique Sacred Character of the Bible." *Catholic Biblical Quarterly* 44 (1982): 447–69.

Holmberg, Bengt. *Paul and Power: The Structure of Authority in the Primitive Church as Reflected in the Pauline Epistles.* Philadelphia: Fortress Press, 1978.

———. "Questions of Method in James Dunn's *Jesus Remembered.*" *Journal for the Study of the New Testament* 26 (2004): 445–57.

Holmgren, Fredrick Carlson. *The Old Testament and the Significance of Jesus: Embracing Change—Maintaining Christian Identity. The Emerging Center in Biblical Scholarship.* Grand Rapids, Mich.: W. B. Eerdmans, 1999.

Hoose, Bernard. "Introducing the Main Issues." In *Authority in the Roman Catholic Church: Theory and Practice,* edited by Bernard Hoose, 1–16. Burlington, Vt.: Ashgate, 2002.

Horsley, Richard A. *Hearing the Whole Story: The Politics of Plot in Mark's Gospel.* Louisville, Ky.: Westminster John Knox Press, 2001.

Horsley, Richard A., Jonathan A. Draper, and John Miles Foley, eds. *Performing the Gospel: Orality, Memory, and Mark.* Minneapolis: Fortress Press, 2006.

Hübner, Hans. *Biblische Theologie des Neuen Testaments.* Göttingen: Vandenhoeck & Ruprecht, 1990.

———. "New Testament Interpretation of the Old Testament." In *Hebrew Bible, Old Testament: The History of Its Interpretation. Volume 1: From the Beginnings to the Middle Ages (Until 1300). Part 1: Antiquity,* edited by Magne Sæbø, 332–72. Göttingen: Vandenhoeck & Ruprecht, 1996.

Hudson, Deal W. "The Catholic View of Conversion." In *Handbook of Religious Conversion,* edited by H. Newton Malony and Samuel Southard, 108–22. Birmingham, Ala.: Religious Education Press, 1992.

Hultgren, Arland J. *The Rise of Normative Christianity.* Minneapolis: Fortress Press, 1994.

Hünermann, Peter, ed. *Das zweite vatikanische Konzil und die Zeichen der Zeit heute.* Freiburg im Breisgau: Verlag Herder, 2006.

Hur, Ju. *A Dynamic Reading of the Holy Spirit in Luke–Acts.* Sheffield, England: Sheffield Academic Press, 2001.

Hurtado, Larry W. *Lord Jesus Christ: Devotion to Jesus in Earliest Christianity.* Grand Rapids, Mich.: W. B. Eerdmans, 2003.

International Committee on English in the Liturgy. *Rite of Christian Initiation of Adults.* Study ed. Washington, D.C.: United States Catholic Conference, 1988.

International Theological Commission. "On the Interpretation of Dogmas." *Origins* 20 (May 17, 1990): 1–14.

Jauss, Hans Robert. "Limits and Tasks of Literary Hermeneutics." *Diogenes* 109 (1980): 92–119.

———. *Question and Answer: Forms of Dialogic Understanding.* Minneapolis: University of Minnesota Press, 1989.

———. "Rückschau auf die Begriffsgeschichte von Verstehen." In *Wege des Verstehens,* 11–29. Munich: Wilhelm Fink, 1994.

Jedin, Hubert. "Theologie und Lehramt." In *Lehramt und Theologie im 16. Jahrhundert,* edited by Remigius Bäumer, 7–21. Münster: Aschendorff, 1976.

John Paul II. *Ut Unum Sint.* Vatican City: Libreria Editrice Vaticana, 1995.

———. *Novo Millennio Ineunte. Apostolic Letter of John Paul II.* Strathfield, Australia: St. Pauls Publications, 2001.

Johnson, Luke Timothy. *Scripture and Discernment: Decision Making in the Church.* Nashville, Tenn.: Abingdon Press, 1996.

———. "Imagining the World Scripture Imagines." *Modern Theology* 14 (1998): 165–80.

————. *The Creed: What Christians Believe and Why It Matters.* New York: Doubleday, 2003.

Johnson, Mark. *Moral Imagination: Implications of Cognitive Science for Ethics.* Chicago: University of Chicago Press, 1993.

Juel, Donald. *Messianic Exegesis: Christological Interpretation of the Old Testament in Early Christianity.* Philadelphia: Fortress Press, 1988.

Kasper, Walter. *Dogma unter dem Wort Gottes.* Mainz: Matthias-Grünewald, 1965.

————. *Jesus the Christ.* New York: Paulist Press, 1976.

————. *An Introduction to Christian Faith.* London: Burns & Oates, 1980.

————. *The God of Jesus Christ.* London: SCM Press, 1983.

————. "The Apostolic Succession: An Ecumenical Problem." In *Leadership in the Church: How Traditional Roles Can Serve the Christian Community Today,* 114–43. New York: Crossroad, 2003.

————. "The Renewal of Pneumatology in Contemporary Catholic Life and Theology: Towards a Rapprochement between East and West." In *That They May All Be One: The Call to Unity,* 96–121. New York: Burns & Oates, 2004.

Keane, Philip S. *Christian Ethics and Imagination.* New York: Paulist Press, 1984.

Kearney, Richard. *The Wake of Imagination: Toward a Postmodern Culture.* London: Routledge, 1994.

Keck, Leander E. *A Future for the Historical Jesus: The Place of Jesus in Preaching and Theology.* Philadelphia: Fortress Press, 1981.

Keesmaat, Sylvia C. *Paul and His Story: (Re)-interpreting the Exodus Tradition.* Sheffield, England: Sheffield Academic Press, 1999.

Kelber, Werner H. "Jesus and Tradition: Words in Time, Words in Space." *Semeia* 65 (1994): 139–67.

Kelly, Anthony. *Eschatology and Hope.* Maryknoll, N.Y.: Orbis Books, 2006.

Kelly, J. N. D. *Early Christian Creeds.* 3rd ed. London: Longman, 1972.

Kelly, Justin J. "Knowing by Heart: The Symbolic Structure of Revelation and Faith." In *Faithful Witness: Foundations of Theology for Today's Church,* edited by Leo J. O'Donovan and T. Howland Sanks, 63–84. New York: Crossroad, 1989.

Kirchschläger, Walter. "Was das Neue Testament über den Glaubenssinn der Gläubigen sagt." In *Mitsprache im Glauben? Vom Glaubenssinn der Gläubigen,* edited by Günther Koch, 7–24. Würzburg: Echter, 1993.

Komonchak, Joseph A. "Authority and Magisterium." In *Vatican Authority and American Catholic Dissent: The Curran Case and Its Consequences,* edited by William W. May, 103–14. New York: Crossroad, 1987.

————. "Defending Our Hope: On the Fundamental Tasks of Theology." In *Faithful Witness: Foundations of Theology for Today's Church,* edited by Leo J. O'Donovan and T. Howland Sanks, 14–26. New York: Crossroad, 1989.

————. "The Epistemology of Reception." In *Reception and Communion Among Churches,* edited by Hervé Legrand, Julio Manzanares, and Antonio García y García, 180–203. Washington, D.C.: The Catholic University of America Press, 1997.

Küng, Hans. *Infallible? An Inquiry.* Garden City, N.Y.: Doubleday, 1971.

Küng, Hans, and David Tracy, eds. *Paradigm Change in Theology: A Symposium for the Future.* New York: Crossroad, 1989.

Lakeland, Paul. *The Liberation of the Laity: In Search of an Accountable Church.* New York: Continuum, 2003.

Lakoff, George, and Mark Johnson. *Philosophy in the Flesh: The Embodied Mind and Its Challenge to Western Thought.* New York: Basic Books, 1999.

Law, David R. *Inspiration.* London: Continuum, 2001.

Leckey, Dolores R. *Laity Stirring the Church: Prophetic Questions.* Philadelphia: Fortress Press, 1987.

———. *The Laity and Christian Education: Apostolicam Actuositatem, Gravissimum Educationis, Rediscovering Vatican II.* New York: Paulist Press, 2006.

Leder, Gottfried. "Zum Verhältnis von Kirche und Demokratie: Anmerkungen zu einem notwendigen Dialog." *Stimmen der Zeit* 220 (2002): 37–50.

Lee, Bernard J. *The Future Church of 140 BCE: A Hidden Revolution.* New York: Crossroad, 1995.

Legrand, Hervé. "Democrazia o sinodalità per la chiesa? Convergenze reali e divergenze profonde." *Ricerca* 12 (1996): 1–20.

———. "Reception, *Sensus Fidelium,* and Synodal Life: An Effort at Articulation." In *Reception and Communion Among Churches,* edited by Hervé Legrand, Julio Manzanares, and Antonio García y García, 405–31. Washington, D.C.: The Catholic University of America Press, 1997.

Lennan, Richard. *Risking the Church: The Challenges of Catholic Faith.* New York: Oxford University Press, 2004.

Leuninger, E. *Wir sind das Volk Gottes: Demokratisierung in der Kirche.* Frankfurt am Main, 1992.

Lips, Hermann von. *Der neutestamentliche Kanon: Seine Geschichte und Bedeutung, Zürcher Grundrisse zur Bibel.* Zürich: Theologischer Verlag, 2004.

Lonergan, Bernard. *Method in Theology.* Minneapolis: The Seabury Press, 1972.

———. "'Theology in Its New Context' and 'The Dimensions of Conversion.'" In *Conversion: Perspectives on Personal and Social Transformation,* edited by Walter E. Conn, 3–21. New York: Alba House, 1978.

———. "The Origins of Christian Realism." In *A Second Collection: Papers,* edited by William F. Ryan and Bernard Tyrrell, 239–61. Toronto: University of Toronto Press, 1996.

Loveday, Alexander. "What Is a Gospel?" In *The Cambridge Companion to the Gospels,* edited by Stephen C. Barton, 13–33. New York: Cambridge University Press, 2006.

Ludlow, Morwenna. "'Criteria of Canonicity' and the Early Church." In *Die Einheit der Schrift und die Vielfalt des Kanons = The Unity of Scripture and the Diversity of the Canon,* edited by John Barton and Michael Wolter, 69–93. New York: Walter de Gruyter, 2003.

Lührmann, Dieter. "Faith: New Testament." In *The Anchor Bible Dictionary,* vol. 2, edited by David Noel Freedman, 749–58. New York: Doubleday, 1992.

Luther, Martin. *Werke: Kritische Gesamtausgabe Deutsche Bibel.* Vol. 7. Weimar, 1906.

Lynch, William F. *Christ and Apollo: The Dimensions of the Literary Imagination.* New York: Sheed and Ward, 1960.

———. *Images of Hope: Imagination as Healer of the Hopeless.* Baltimore: Helicon, 1965.

———. *Christ and Prometheus: A New Image of the Secular.* Notre Dame, Ind.: University of Notre Dame Press, 1970.

———. *Images of Faith: An Exploration of the Ironic Imagination.* Notre Dame, Ind.: University of Notre Dame Press, 1973.

Madges, William, and Michael J. Daley, eds. *The Many Marks of the Church.* New London, Conn.: Twenty-Third Publications, 2006.

Malony, H. Newton. "The Concept of Faith in Psychology." In *Handbook of Faith,* edited by James Michael Lee, 71–95. Birmingham, Ala.: Religious Education Press, 1990.

Mannion, Gerard. "What Do We Mean by 'Authority'?" In *Authority in the Roman Catholic Church: Theory and Practice,* edited by Bernard Hoose, 19–36. Burlington, Vt.: Ashgate, 2002.

Marrow, Stanley B. "*Parrhesia* and the New Testament." *Catholic Biblical Quarterly* 44 (1982): 431–46.

———. *Speaking the Word Fearlessly: Boldness in the New Testament.* New York: Paulist Press, 1982.

Matera, Frank J. *New Testament Christology.* Louisville, Ky.: Westminster John Knox Press, 1999.

McBrien, Richard P. *Catholicism.* New ed. San Francisco: HarperSanFrancisco, 1994.

McCormick, Richard A. "The Search for Truth in the Catholic Context." *America* 155 (1986): 276–81.

McDonald, Lee Martin. *The Formation of the Christian Biblical Canon.* Rev. & expanded ed. Peabody, Mass.: Hendrickson Publishers, 1995.

———. "Identifying Scripture and Canon in the Early Church: The Criteria Question." In *The Canon Debate,* edited by Lee Martin McDonald and James A. Sanders, 416–39. Peabody, Mass.: Hendrickson Publishers, 2002.

McDonnell, Kilian. *The Other Hand of God: The Holy Spirit as the Universal Touch and Goal.* Collegeville, Minn.: Liturgical Press, 2003.

McIntosh, Mark A. *Discernment and Truth: The Spirituality and Theology of Knowledge.* New York: Crossroad, 2004.

McIntyre, John. *Faith, Theology and Imagination.* Edinburgh: The Handsel Press, 1987.

McKenzie, John L. "The Social Character of Inspiration." *Catholic Biblical Quarterly* 24 (1962): 115–24.

McLoughlin, David. "Tensions, Use and Abuse." *Priests and People* 11 (1997): 326–31.

Meier, John P. *A Marginal Jew: Rethinking the Historical Jesus.* Vol. 3: *Companions and Competitors.* New York: Doubleday, 2001.

Melbourne, Bertram L. *Slow to Understand: The Disciples in Synoptic Perspective.* Lanham, Md.: University Press of America, 1988.

Menken, Maarten F. F. *Old Testament Quotations in the Fourth Gospel: Studies in Textual Form.* Kampen: Kok Pharos Publishing House, 1996.

Mette, Norbert. "'Kein geeigneter Beitrag zum innerkirchlichen Dialog'? Das 'Kirchenvolksbegehren' als Testfall einer dialogischen Kirche." In *Dialog als Selbstvollzug der Kirche,* edited by Gebhard Fürst, 329–43. Freiburg: Herder, 1997.

Metz, Johann Baptist. "A Short Apology of Narrative." In *Why Narrative? Readings in Narrative Theology,* edited by Stanley Hauerwas, L. Gregory Jones, and Ronald F. Thiemann, 251–62. Grand Rapids, Mich.: W. B. Eerdmans, 1989.

Metzger, Bruce M. *The Canon of the New Testament: Its Origin, Development, and Significance.* New York: Oxford University Press, 1987.

Miserda, Marko. *Subjektivität im Glauben: Eine theologisch-methodologische Untersuchung zur Diskussion über den "Glaubens-Sinn" in der katholischen Theologie des 19. Jahrhunderts.* Frankfurt am Main: P. Lang, 1996.

Moessner, David P. *Jesus and the Heritage of Israel: Luke's Narrative Claim upon Israel's Legacy.* Harrisburg, Pa.: Trinity Press International, 1999.

Moloney, Francis J. *The Gospel of John, Sacra Pagina Series; v. 4.* Collegeville, Minn.: Liturgical Press, 1998.

———. "John 18:15–27: A Johannine View of the Church." In *A Hard Saying: The Gospel and Culture,* 131–47. Collegeville, Minn.: Liturgical Press, 2001.

———. *Mark: Storyteller, Interpreter, Evangelist.* Peabody, Mass.: Hendrickson Publishers, 2004.

———. "The Gospel of John as Scripture." In *The Gospel of John: Text and Context,* 333–47. Boston: Brill, 2005.

Mondin, Battista. "Legitimacy and Limits of Theological Pluralism." *L'Osservatore Romano* (April 6, 1978): 6.

Montague, George T. "The Fire in the Word: The Holy Spirit in Scripture." In *Advents of the Spirit: An Introduction to the Current Study of Pneumatology,* edited by Bradford E. Hinze and D. Lyle Dabney, 35–65. Milwaukee, Wis.: Marquette University Press, 2001.

Moody Smith, D. "When Did the Gospels Become Scripture?" *Journal of Biblical Literature* 119 (2000): 3–20.

Morrisey, Francis G. *Papal and Curial Pronouncements: Their Canonical Significance in Light of the 1983 Code of Canon Law.* 2nd ed. rev. and updated by Michel Thériault. Ottawa: Faculty of Canon Law, Saint Paul University, 1995.

Mörsdorf, Klaus. "Ecclesiastical Authority." In *Sacramentum Mundi: An Encyclopedia of Theology,* edited by Karl Rahner, 2: 133–39. New York: Herder and Herder, 1968.

———. "Ecclesiastical Office: I. In Canon Law." In *Sacramentum Mundi: An Encyclopedia of Theology,* edited by Karl Rahner, 2: 167–70. New York: Herder and Herder, 1968.

Moyise, Steve. "Intertextuality and the Study of the Old Testament in the New Testament." In *The Old Testament in the New Testament: Essays in Honour of J. L. North,* edited by Steve Moyise, 14–41. Sheffield, England: Sheffield Academic Press, 2000.

———, ed. *The Old Testament in the New Testament: Essays in Honour of J. L. North.* Sheffield, England: Sheffield Academic Press, 2000.

———. *The Old Testament in the New: An Introduction.* New York: Continuum, 2001.

Müller, Mogens. "The Theological Interpretation of the Figure of Jesus in the Gospel of Matthew: Some Principal Features in Matthean Christology." *New Testament Studies* 45 (1999): 157–73.

———. "The New Testament Reception of the Old Testament." In *The New Testament as Reception,* edited by Mogens Müller and Henrik Tronier, 1–14. New York: Sheffield Academic Press, 2002.

Murray, Paul, ed. *Receptive Ecumenism and the Call to Catholic Learning: Exploring a Way for Contemporary Ecumenism.* Oxford: Oxford University Press, 2008.

Newman, John Henry. *An Essay in Aid of a Grammar of Assent.* Notre Dame, Ind.: University of Notre Dame Press, 1979.

———. *An Essay on the Development of Christian Doctrine.* 6th ed. Notre Dame, Ind.: University of Notre Dame Press, 1989.

O'Collins, Gerald. *Foundations of Theology.* Chicago: Loyola University Press, 1971.

———. "Revelation Past and Present." In *Vatican II: Assessment and Perspectives. Twenty-Five Years After (1962–1987),* vol. 1, edited by René Latourelle, 125–37. New York: Paulist Press, 1988.

O'Collins, Gerald, and Edward G. Farrugia. *A Concise Dictionary of Theology.* Rev. and expanded ed. New York: Paulist Press, 2000.

O'Collins, Gerald, and Daniel Kendall. *The Bible for Theology: Ten Principles for the Theological Use of Scripture.* New York: Paulist Press, 1997.

O'Donovan, Leo J., ed. *A World of Grace: An Introduction to the Themes and Foundations of Karl Rahner's Theology.* New York: Seabury Press, 1980.

O'Gara, Margaret. *Triumph in Defeat: Infallibility, Vatican I, and the French Minority Bishops.* Washington, D.C.: The Catholic University of America Press, 1988.

O'Gara, Margaret, and Michael Vertin. "The Holy Spirit's Assistance to the Magisterium in Teaching: Theological and Philosophical Issues." *Catholic Theological Society of America Proceedings* 51 (1996): 125–42.

O'Malley, John W. "The Style of Vatican II: The 'How' of the Church Changed during the Council." *America* (February 24, 2003): 12–15.

———. *Vatican II: A Matter of Style.* Weston Jesuit School of Theology 2003 President's Letter. Cambridge, Mass.: Weston Jesuit School of Theology, 2003.

———. "Vatican II: Did Anything Happen?" *Theological Studies* 67 (2006): 3–33.

Ohly, Christoph. *Sensus Fidei Fidelium: Zur Einordung des Glaubenssinnes aller Gläubigen in die Communio-struktur der Kirche im geschichtlichen Spiegel dogmatisch-kanonistischer Erkenntnisse und der Aussagen des II. Vaticanum.* St. Ottilien: EOS Verlag, 1999.

Ong, Walter J. *Orality and Literacy: The Technologizing of the Word.* London: Routledge, 1982, 2002.

"Organon." In *The Oxford English Dictionary,* edited by J. A. Simpson and E. S. C. Weiner, 10:925. New York: Clarendon Press, 1989.

Örsy, Ladislas. *The Church Learning and Teaching.* Dublin: Dominican Publications, 1987.

Pannenberg, Wolfhart. *Jesus: God of Man.* 2nd ed. Philadelphia: Westminster Press, 1968, 1977.

Pelikan, Jaroslav. *Credo: Historical and Theological Guide to Creeds and Confessions of Faith in the Christian Tradition.* New Haven, Conn.: Yale University Press, 2003.

Pelikan, Jaroslav, and Valerie R. Hotchkiss, eds. *Creeds and Confessions of Faith in the Christian Tradition.* 4 vols. New Haven, Conn.: Yale University Press, 2003.

Pesch, Otto Hermann. "Das Wort Gottes als objektives Prinzip der theologischen Erkenntnis." In *Handbuch der Fundamentaltheologie,* edited by Walter Kern, Hermann J. Pottmeyer, and Max Seckler, 4:27–50. Freiburg: Herder, 1988.

Phan, Peter C. "Method in Liberation Theologies." *Theological Studies* 61 (2000): 40–63.

Pié-Ninot, Salvador. *"Sensus Fidei."* In *Dictionary of Fundamental Theology,* edited by René Latourelle and Rino Fisichella, 992–95. Middlegreen, Slough, England: St. Paul, 1994.

Pongratz-Lippitt, Christa. "Ratzinger regrets church centralism at König funeral." *The Tablet* (April 3, 2004): 29.

Pontifical Biblical Commission. *The Interpretation of the Bible in the Church.* Rome: Libreria Editrice Vaticana, 1993.

———. *The Jewish People and Their Sacred Scriptures in the Christian Bible.* Vatican City: Libreria Editrice Vaticana, 2002.

Porsch, Felix. *Pneuma und Wort: Ein exegetischer Beitrag zur Pneumatologie des Johannesevangeliums.* Frankfurt: Knecht, 1974.

Porter, Stanley E. "The Use of the Old Testament in the New Testament: A Brief Comment on Method and Terminology." In *Early Christian Interpretation of the*

Scriptures of Israel: Investigations and Proposals, edited by Craig A. Evans and James A. Sanders, 79–96. Sheffield, England: Sheffield Academic Press, 1997.

———. "When and How Was the Pauline Canon Compiled? An Assessment of Theories." In *The Pauline Canon,* edited by Stanley E. Porter, 95–127. Boston: Brill, 2004.

Post, James E. "The Emerging Role of the Catholic Laity: Lessons from Voice of the Faithful." In *Common Calling: The Laity and Governance of the Catholic Church,* edited by Stephen J. Pope, 209–28. Washington, D.C.: Georgetown University Press, 2004.

Pottmeyer, Hermann J. "Theologische Erkenntnislehre als kritische Hermeneutik." In *Philosophisch-theologische Grenzfragen,* edited by Julie Kirchberg and Johannes Müther, 205–10. Essen: Ludgerus, 1986.

———. "Normen, Kriterien und Strukturen der Überlieferung." In *Handbuch der Fundamentaltheologie,* edited by Walter Kern, Hermann J. Pottmeyer, and Max Seckler, 4:124–52. Freiburg: Herder, 1988.

———. "Tradition." In *Dictionary of Fundamental Theology,* edited by René Latourelle and Rino Fisichella, 1119–26. Middlegreen, Slough, England: St. Paul, 1994.

———. "Die Mitsprache der Gläubigen in Glaubenssachen: Eine alte Praxis und ihre Wiederentdeckung." *Internationale katholische Zeitschrift "Communio"* 25 (1996): 135–47.

———. "Auf dem Weg zu einer dialogischen Kirche: Wie Kirche sich ihrer selbst bewußt wird." In *Dialog als Selbstvollzug der Kirche,* edited by Gebhard Fürst, 117–32. Freiburg: Herder, 1997.

———. *Towards a Papacy in Communion: Perspectives from Vatican Councils I & II.* New York: Crossroad, 1998.

Principe, Walter. "Changing Church Teachings." *Grail: An Ecumenical Journal* 6 (1990): 13–40.

Putney, Michael. "A Church in Dialogue with Itself and with Others." *Compass* 34 (2000): 3–16.

Puza, Richard. "Das synodale Prinzip in historischer, rechtstheologischer und kanonistischer Bedeutung." In *Dialog als Selbstvollzug der Kirche,* edited by Gebhard Fürst, 242–69. Freiburg: Herder, 1997.

Radcliffe, Timothy. "How to Discover What We Believe." *The Tablet* (January 26, 2006): 12–13.

Rahner, Karl. "Some Implications of the Scholastic Concept of Uncreated Grace." In *Theological Investigations,* vol. 1, 1:319–46. New York: Seabury, 1961.

———. *The Dynamic Element in the Church.* London: Burns and Oates, 1964.

———. *Inspiration in the Bible.* 2nd rev. ed. London: Burns & Oates, 1964.

———. "The Hierarchical Structure of the Church, with Special Reference to the Episcopate." In *Commentary on the Documents of Vatican II,* vol. 1, edited by Herbert Vorgrimler, 186–218. London: Burns & Oates, 1967.

———. "Demokratie in der Kirche?" *Stimmen der Zeit* 182 (1968): 1–15.

———. "Magisterium." In *Sacramentum Mundi: An Encyclopedia of Theology,* edited by Karl Rahner, 3:351–58. New York: Herder and Herder, 1968.

———. *The Trinity.* New York: Herder and Herder, 1970.

———. "Heresies in the Church Today?" In *Theological Investigations,* vol. 12, 117–41. London: Darton, Longman & Todd, 1974.

———. "Pluralism in Theology and the Unity of the Creed in the Church." In *Theological Investigations,* vol. 11, 3–23. London: Darton, Longman & Todd, 1974.

————. "The Teaching Office of the Church in the Present-Day Crisis of Authority." In *Theological Investigations,* vol. 12, 3–30. London: Darton, Longman & Todd, 1974.

————. "What Is a Dogmatic Statement?" In *Theological Investigations,* vol. 5, 42–66. New York: Seabury, 1975.

————. "The Faith of the Christian and the Doctrine of the Church." In *Theological Investigations,* vol. 14, 24–46. London: Darton, Longman & Todd, 1976.

————. "Basic Theological Interpretation of the Second Vatican Council." In *Theological Investigations,* vol. 20, 77–89. London: Darton, Longman & Todd, 1981.

————. "Reflections on the Adult Christian." *Theology Digest* 31 (1984): 123–26.

————. "The Act of Faith and the Content of Faith." In *Theological Investigations,* vol. 21, 151–61. London: Darton, Longman & Todd, 1988.

————. "A Hierarchy of Truths." In *Theological Investigations,* vol. 21, 162–67. London: Darton, Longman & Todd, 1988.

————. "The Relation Between Theology and Popular Religion." In *Theological Investigations,* vol. 22, 140–47. London: Darton, Longman & Todd, 1991.

————. "What the Church Officially Teaches and What the People Actually Believe." In *Theological Investigations,* vol. 22, 165–75. London: Darton, Longman & Todd, 1991.

Ratzinger, Joseph. "On the Interpretation of the Tridentine Decree on Tradition." In *Revelation and Tradition,* edited by Karl Rahner and Joseph Ratzinger, 50–66. New York: Herder and Herder, 1966.

————. "Revelation and Tradition." In *Revelation and Tradition,* edited by Karl Rahner and Joseph Ratzinger, 26–49. New York: Herder and Herder, 1966.

————. "Dogmatic Constitution of Divine Revelation: Origin and Background." In *Commentary on the Documents of Vatican II,* vol. 3, edited by H. Vorgrimler. New York: Herder, 1969.

Ratzinger, Joseph, and Hans Maier. *Demokratie in der Kirche: Möglichkeiten, Grenzen, Gefahren.* Limburg a.d. Lahn, 1970.

Reader, John. *Local Theology: Church and Community in Dialogue.* London: SPCK, 1994.

Reiser, William. "'Knowing' Jesus: Do Theologians Have a Special Way?" In *The Convergence of Theology: A Festschrift Honoring Gerald O'Collins, S.J.,* edited by Daniel Kendall and Stephen T. Davis, 159–75. New York: Paulist Press, 2001.

Reumann, John Henry Paul. *Variety and Unity in New Testament Thought.* New York: Oxford University Press, 1991.

Rhoads, David. "Performance Criticism: An Emerging Methodology in Second Testament Studies. Part I." *Biblical Theology Bulletin* 36 (2006): 118–33.

————. "Performance Criticism: An Emerging Methodology in Second Testament Studies. Part II." *Biblical Theology Bulletin* 36 (2006): 164–84.

Ricoeur, Paul. "Toward a Hermeneutic of the Idea of Revelation." In *Essays on Biblical Interpretation.* Philadelphia: Fortress Press, 1980.

————. "Time and Narrative: Threefold Mimesis." In *Time and Narrative,* vol. 1, 52–87. Chicago: University of Chicago Press, 1984.

————. "Response to Josef Blank." In *Paradigm Change in Theology: A Symposium for the Future,* edited by Hans Küng and David Tracy, 283–86. Edinburgh: T&T Clark, 1989.

————. "Imagination in Discourse and in Action." In *From Text to Action: Essays in Hermeneutics, II,* 168–87. Evanston, Ill.: Northwestern University Press, 1991.

————. *Oneself as Another.* Chicago: University of Chicago Press, 1992.

————. "The Bible and the Imagination." In *Figuring the Sacred: Religion, Narrative, and Imagination,* 144–66. Minneapolis: Fortress Press, 1995.

————. "The Summoned Subject in the School of the Narratives of the Prophetic Vocation." In *Figuring the Sacred: Religion, Narrative, and Imagination,* 262–75. Minneapolis: Fortress Press, 1995.

————. "The Self in the Mirror of the Scriptures." In *The Whole and Divided Self,* edited by David E. Aune and John McCarthy, 201–20. New York: Crossroad, 1997.

————. "Approaching the Human Person." *Ethical Perspectives* 6 (1999): 45–54.

Ricoeur, Paul, David Pellauer, and John McCarthy. "Conversation." In *The Whole and Divided Self,* edited by David E. Aune and John McCarthy, 221–43. New York: Crossroad, 1997.

Root, Michael. "The Narrative Structure of Soteriology." In *Why Narrative? Readings in Narrative Theology,* edited by Stanley Hauerwas, L. Gregory Jones, and Ronald F. Thiemann, 263–78. Grand Rapids, Mich.: W. B. Eerdmans, 1989.

Rousselot, Pierre. *The Eyes of Faith.* Edited by John M. McDermott and Avery Dulles. New York: Fordham University Press, 1990.

Routhier, Gilles. "Reception in Current Theological Debate." In *Reception and Communion Among Churches,* edited by Hervé Legrand, Julio Manzanares, and Antonio García y García, 17–52. Washington, D.C.: The Catholic University of America Press, 1997.

Rush, Ormond. "Reception Hermeneutics and the 'Development' of Doctrine." *Pacifica* 6 (1993): 125–40.

————. *The Reception of Doctrine: An Appropriation of Hans Robert Jauss' Reception Aesthetics and Literary Hermeneutics.* Rome: Gregorian University Press, 1997.

————. "*Sensus Fidei:* Faith 'Making Sense' of Revelation." *Theological Studies* 62 (2001): 231–61.

————. "Full, Conscious and Active Participation: Formation in the Sacramental Imagination." *Liturgy News* 33 (2003): 3–4.

————. "The Offices of Christ, *Lumen Gentium* and the People's Sense of the Faith." *Pacifica* 16 (2003): 137–52.

————. *Still Interpreting Vatican II: Some Hermeneutical Principles.* Mahwah, N.J.: Paulist Press, 2004.

Ryan, Thomas. "Revisiting Affective Knowledge and Connaturality in Aquinas." *Theological Studies* 66 (2005): 49–68.

Sanders, James A. *Canon and Community: A Guide to Canonical Criticism.* Philadelphia: Fortress Press, 1984.

————. *From Sacred Story to Sacred Text: Canon as Paradigm.* Philadelphia: Fortress Press, 1987.

————. "Isaiah in Luke." In *Luke and Scripture: The Function of Sacred Tradition in Luke-Acts,* edited by Craig A. Evans, 14–25. Minneapolis: Fortress Press, 1993.

————. "The Issue of Closure in the Canonical Process." In *The Canon Debate,* edited by Lee Martin McDonald and James A. Sanders, 252–63. Peabody, Mass.: Hendrickson Publishers, 2002.

Scanlon, Michael J. "Catholicism and Living Tradition: The Church as a Community of Reception." In *Empowering Authority: The Charisms of Episcopacy and Primacy in the Church Today,* edited by Patrick J. Howell and Gary Chamberlain, 1–16. Kansas City: Sheed and Ward, 1990.

Schick, Ludwig. *Das dreifache Amt Christi und der Kirche: Zur Entstehung und Entwicklung der Trilogien.* Frankfurt am Main: P. Lang, 1982.

Schillebeeckx, Edward. "The Problem of the Infallibility of the Church's Teaching Office: A Theological Reflection." *Concilium* 3 (1977): 77–94.

———. *Jesus: An Experiment in Christology.* London: Collins, 1979.

———. *Christ: The Christian Experience in the Modern World.* London: SCM Press, 1980.

———. *Interim Report on the Books "Jesus" & "Christ."* New York: Crossroad, 1981.

———. "The Role of History in What Is Called the New Paradigm." In *Paradigm Change in Theology: A Symposium for the Future,* edited by Hans Küng and David Tracy, 307–19. Edinburgh: T&T Clark, 1989.

Schineller, Peter. "The Wisdom That Leads to Salvation: Revelation and Scripture." In *Faithful Witness: Foundations of Theology for Today's Church,* edited by Leo J. O'Donovan and T. Howland Sanks, 85–98. New York: Crossroad, 1989.

Schmucker, Robert W. *Sensus Fidei: Der Glaubenssinn in seiner vorkonziliaren Entwicklungsgeschichte und in den Dokumenten des Zweiten Vatikanischen Konzils.* Regensburg: Roderer Verlag, 1998.

Schneemelcher, Wilhelm, and R. McL. Wilson, eds. *New Testament Apocrypha.* Vol. 1, *Gospels and Related Writings.* Rev. ed. Louisville, Ky.: Westminster John Knox Press, 1991.

Schneiders, Sandra M. *The Revelatory Text: Interpreting the New Testament as Sacred Scripture.* 2nd ed. Collegeville, Minn.: Liturgical Press, 1999.

Schreiter, Robert J. *Constructing Local Theologies.* Maryknoll, N.Y.: Orbis Books, 1985.

———. *The New Catholicity: Theology between the Global and the Local.* Maryknoll, N.Y.: Orbis Books, 1997.

———. "Mediating the Global and the Local in Conversation: Challenges to the Church in the Twenty-First Century." In *Theology and Conversation: Towards a Relational Theology,* edited by Jacques Haers and P. De Mey, 439–55. Dudley, Mass.: Peeters, 2003.

Schröter, Jens. "Jesus and the Canon: The Early Jesus Traditions in the Context of the Origins of the New Testament Canon." In *Performing the Gospel: Orality, Memory, and Mark,* edited by Richard A. Horsley, Jonathan A. Draper, and John Miles Foley, 104–22. Minneapolis: Fortress Press, 2006.

Schüssler Fiorenza, Francis. *Foundational Theology: Jesus and the Church.* New York: Crossroad, 1984.

———. "The Crisis of Scriptural Authority: Interpretation and Reception." *Interpretation* 44 (1990): 353–68.

———. "Systematic Theology: Task and Methods." In *Systematic Theology: Roman Catholic Perspectives,* edited by Francis Schüssler Fiorenza and John P. Galvin, 3–87. Minneapolis: Fortress Press, 1991.

———. "The Jesus of Piety and the Historical Jesus." *Catholic Theological Society of America Proceedings* 49 (1994): 90–99.

Sedmak, Clemens. *Doing Local Theology: A Guide for Artisans of a New Humanity.* Maryknoll, N.Y.: Orbis Books, 2002.

Segundo, Juan Luis. *Liberation of Theology.* Maryknoll, N.Y.: Orbis Books, 1976.

———. *The Liberation of Dogma: Faith, Revelation, and Dogmatic Teaching Authority.* Maryknoll, N.Y.: Orbis Books, 1992.

———. "Revelation, Faith, Signs of the Times." In *Signs of the Times: Theological Reflections*, 128–48. Maryknoll, N.Y.: Orbis Books, 1993.

———. "The Signs of the Times." In *Vatican II: A Forgotten Future?* edited by Alberto Melloni and Christoph Theobald, 73–85. London: SCM Press, 2005.

Sellner, Edward C. "Lay Spirituality." In *The New Dictionary of Catholic Spirituality*, edited by Michael Downey, 589–96. Collegeville, Minn.: Liturgical Press, 1993.

"Sensus." In *Oxford Latin Dictionary*, edited by P. G. W. Glare, 7:1735–36. Oxford: Clarendon, 1980.

Sesboüé, Bernard. "Le 'sensus fidelium' en morale à la lumière de Vatican II." *Le Supplément* 181 (1992): 153–66.

Shecterle, Ross A. *The Theology of Revelation of Avery Dulles, 1980–1994: Symbolic Mediation*. Lewiston, N.Y.: Edwin Mellen Press, 1996.

Shepherd, William H. *The Narrative Function of the Holy Spirit as a Character in Luke-Acts*. Atlanta, Ga.: Scholars Press, 1994.

Sheppard, Gerald T. "Canonization: Hearing the Voice of the Same God through Historically Dissimilar Traditions." *Interpretation* 36 (1982): 21–33.

———. "Canon." In *The Encyclopedia of Religion*, edited by Mircea Eliade, 3:62–69. New York: Macmillan, 1987.

Smith, John E. *Experience and God*. New York: Fordham University Press, 1995.

Sorrentino, D. "Esperienza spirituale e intelligenza della fede in *Dei Verbum* 8. Sul senso di 'intima spiritualium rerum quae experiuntur intelligentia.'" In *La terra e il seme*, edited by C. Sarnataro, 153–74. Naples: M. D'Auria, 1998.

Soskice, Janet Martin. "The Truth Looks Different from Here: On Seeking the Unity of Truth from a Diversity of Perspectives." In *Christ and Context: The Confrontation between Gospel and Culture*, edited by Hilary D. Regan and Allan J. Torrance, 43–62. Edinburgh: T&T Clark, 1993.

Stanton, Graham. "The Fourfold Gospel." In *Norms of Faith and Life*, edited by Everett Ferguson, 1–30. New York: Garland, 1999.

———. *The Gospels and Jesus*. 2nd ed. New York: Oxford University Press, 2002.

———. "Jesus and Gospel." In *Jesus and Gospel*, 9–62. New York: Cambridge University Press, 2004.

Stanton, Graham, Bruce W. Longenecker, and Stephen C. Barton, eds. *The Holy Spirit and Christian Origins: Essays in Honor of James D. G. Dunn*. Grand Rapids, Mich.: W. B. Eerdmans, 2004.

Steinruck, Josef. "Was die Gläubigen in der Geschichte der Kirche zu vermelden hatten." In *Mitsprache im Glauben? Vom Glaubenssinn der Gläubigen*, edited by Günther Koch, 25–50. Würzburg: Echter, 1993.

Stronstad, Roger. *The Prophethood of All Believers: A Study in Luke's Charismatic Theology*. Sheffield, England: Sheffield Academic Press, 1999.

Stuhlmueller, Carroll. "The Biblical View of Faith: A Catholic Perspective." In *Handbook of Faith*, edited by James Michael Lee, 99–122. Birmingham, Ala.: Religious Education Press, 1990.

Sullivan, Francis A. *Magisterium: Teaching Authority in the Catholic Church*. New York: Paulist Press, 1983.

———. *The Church We Believe In: One, Holy, Catholic, and Apostolic*. New York: Paulist Press, 1988.

———. "The Significance of the Vatican II Declaration That the Church of Christ 'Subsists in' the Roman Catholic Church." In *Vatican II Assessment and Perspectives:*

Twenty-Five Years After (1962–1987), vol. 2, edited by René Latourelle, 272–87. New York: Paulist Press, 1989.

———. *Creative Fidelity: Weighing and Interpreting Documents of the Magisterium.* New York: Paulist Press, 1996.

———. "Authority in an Ecclesiology of Communion." *New Theology Review* 10 (1997): 18–30.

———. *From Apostles to Bishops: The Development of the Episcopacy in the Early Church.* New York: Newman Press, 2001.

Sundberg, Albert C. "Toward a Revised History of the New Testament Canon." In *Studia Evangelica IV, Texte and Untersuchungen 89,* 452–61. Berlin: Akademie-Verlag, 1964.

———. "The Bible Canon and the Christian Doctrine of Inspiration." *Interpretation* 29 (1975): 352–71.

Tanner, Norman P. *Decrees of the Ecumenical Councils.* 2 vols. Washington, D.C.: Georgetown University Press, 1990.

Tavard, George H. *Holy Writ or Holy Church: The Crisis of the Protestant Reformation.* London: Burns & Oates, 1959.

Taylor, John V. *The Go-Between God: The Holy Spirit and the Christian Mission.* London: SCM Press, 1972.

Thompson, Michael B. "The Holy Internet: Communication Between Churches in the First Christian Generation." In *The Gospels for All Christians: Rethinking the Gospel Audience,* edited by Richard Bauckham, 49–70. Edinburgh: T&T Clark, 1998.

Thompson, William M. "Sensus Fidelium and Infallibility." *American Ecclesiastical Review* 167 (1973): 450–86.

———. *The Struggle for Theology's Soul: Contesting Scripture in Christology.* New York: Crossroad Herder, 1996.

Thornhill, John. *Christian Mystery in the Secular Age: The Foundation and Task of Theology.* Westminster, Md.: Christian Classics, 1991.

———. "The Gospel: The Ultimate Authority in the Life of the Church." *The Australasian Catholic Record* 72 (1995): 131–42.

Tillard, J. M. R. "Sensus Fidelium." *One in Christ* 11 (1987): 2–29.

———. "Church and Apostolic Tradition." *Mid-Stream* 29 (1990): 247–56.

———. "Ministry and Apostolic Tradition." *Mid-Stream* 29 (1990): 199–207.

———. *Church of Churches: The Ecclesiology of Communion.* Collegeville, Minn.: Liturgical Press, 1991.

———. "How Is Christian Truth Taught in the Roman Catholic Church?" *One in Christ* 34 (1998): 293–306.

Tilley, Terrence W. "Catholic Theology: Contextual, Historical, Inventive." In *Catholic Theology Facing the Future: Historical Perspectives,* edited by Dermot A. Lane, 131–36. New York: Paulist Press, 2003.

———. "Remembering the Historic Jesus: A New Research Program?" *Theological Studies* 68 (2007): 3–35.

Tillich, Paul. *Systematic Theology.* Vol. 1, *Reason and Revelation; Being and God.* Chicago: University of Chicago Press, 1951.

———. *Frühe Hauptwerke.* Stuttgart, 1959.

Tracy, David. *The Analogical Imagination: Christian Theology and the Culture of Pluralism.* New York: Crossroad, 1981.

———. "Freedom, Responsibility, Authority." In *Empowering Authority: The Charisms of Episcopacy and Primacy in the Church Today,* edited by Gary Chamberlain and Patrick J. Howell, 34–47. Kansas City, Mo.: Sheed & Ward, 1990.

Trites, Allison A. *The New Testament Concept of Witness.* New York: Cambridge University Press, 1977.

Ulrich, Eugene Charles. *The Dead Sea Scrolls and the Origins of the Bible.* Grand Rapids, Mich.: W. B. Eerdmans, 1999.

Vanhoye, Albert. "The Biblical Question of 'Charisms' After Vatican II." In *Vatican II Assessment and Perspectives: Twenty-Five Years After (1962–1987),* vol. 1, edited by René Latourelle, 439–68. New York: Paulist Press, 1988.

Vawter, Bruce. *Biblical Inspiration.* Philadelphia: Westminster Press, 1972.

Veling, Terry A. *Living in the Margins: Intentional Communities and the Art of Interpretation.* New York: Crossroad, 1996.

Venema, Henry Isaac. *Identifying Selfhood: Imagination, Narrative, and Hermeneutics in the Thought of Paul Ricoeur.* Albany: State University of New York Press, 2000.

Viladesau, Richard. *Theological Aesthetics: God in Imagination, Beauty, and Art.* New York: Oxford University Press, 1999.

Villemin, Laurent. *Pouvoir d'ordre et pouvoir de juridiction: Histoire théologique de leur distinction.* Paris: Les Editions du Cerf, 2003.

Vitali, Dario. *Sensus fidelium: Una funzione ecclesiale di intelligenza della fede.* Brescia: Morcelliana, 1993.

———. "Sensus fidelium e opinione pubblica nella Chiesa." *Gregorianum* 82 (2001): 689–717.

Vogels, Walter. "Three Possible Models of Inspiration." In *Scrittura ispirata: Atti del Simposio internazionale sull'ispirazione promosso dall'Ateneo pontificio Regina Apostolorum,* edited by Antonio Izquierdo, 61–79. Vatican City: Libreria editrice vaticana, 2002.

Vorgrimler, Herbert. "From *Sensus Fidei* to *Consensus Fidelium.*" *Concilium* 180 (1985): 3–11.

Wagner, Harald. "Glaubenssinn, Glaubenszustimmung und Glaubenskonsensus." *Theologie und Glaube* 69 (1979): 263–71.

Wall, R. W. "Biblical Intertextuality." In *Dictionary of New Testament Background,* edited by Craig A. Evans and Stanley E. Porter, 541–51. Downers Grove, Ill.: InterVarsity Press, 2000.

Wallace, Mark I. "Introduction." In *Figuring the Sacred: Religion, Narrative, and Imagination,* edited by Paul Ricoeur, 1–32. Minneapolis: Fortress Press, 1995.

Watson, Francis. *Paul and the Hermeneutics of Faith.* New York: T&T Clark International, 2004.

———. "The Fourfold Gospel." In *The Cambridge Companion to the Gospels,* edited by Stephen C. Barton, 34–52. New York: Cambridge University Press, 2006.

Watts, Fraser N., and J. Mark G. Williams. *The Psychology of Religious Knowing.* New York: Cambridge University Press, 1988.

Wenk, Matthias. *Community-Forming Power: The Socio-Ethical Role of the Spirit in Luke-Acts.* Sheffield, England: Sheffield Academic Press, 2000.

Wicks, Jared. "Canon of Scripture." In *Dictionary of Fundamental Theology,* edited by René Latourelle and Rino Fisichella, 94–101. Middlegreen, Slough, England: St. Paul, 1994.

———. "Deposit of Faith." In *Dictionary of Fundamental Theology,* edited by René Latourelle and Rino Fisichella, 229–39. Middlegreen, Slough, England: St. Paul, 1994.

————. "Rule of Faith." In *Dictionary of Fundamental Theology,* edited by René Latourelle and Rino Fisichella, 959–61. Middlegreen, Slough, England: St. Paul, 1994.

Wiedenhofer, Siegfried. "Sensus fidelium—Demokratisierung der Kirche?" In *Surrexit Dominus Vere: Die Gegenwart des Auferstandenen in seiner Kirche,* edited by J. Ernst and S. Leimgruber, 457–71. Paderborn, 1995.

————. "Kritische Übernahme: Kann die Kirche demokratisiert werden?" *Herder Korrespondenz* 52 (1998): 347–51.

————. "Synodalität und Demokratisierung der Kirche aus dogmatische Perspektive." In *Demokratische Prozesse in dem Kirchen? Konzilien, Synoden, Räte, Theologie im kulturenllen Dialog,* 73–99. Graz: Styria Verlag, 1998.

Wilson, George B. "Authority with Credibility." *Human Development* 12 (1991): 38–41.

Wolterstorff, Nicholas. "The Unity Behind the Canon." In *One Scripture or Many? Canon from Biblical, Theological, and Philosophical Perspectives,* edited by Christine Helmer and Christof Landmesser, 217–32. New York: Oxford University Press, 2004.

Wright, N. T. *Jesus and the Victory of God.* London: SPCK, 1996.

————. *Judas and the Gospel of Jesus: Understanding a Newly Discovered Ancient Text and Its Contemporary Significance.* London: SPCK, 2006.

Young, Frances. *The Art of Performance: Towards a Theology of Holy Scripture.* London: Darton, Longman and Todd, 1990.

Zizioulas, John. "The Development of Conciliar Structures to the Time of the First Ecumenical Council." In *Councils and the Ecumenical Movement,* 34–51. Geneva: World Council of Churches, 1968.

————. "The Theological Problem of 'Reception.'" *Centro Pro Unione Bulletin* 26 (1984): 3–6.

Index

Agua, Agustín del, 233
Alszeghy, Zoltán, 220
analogia fidei. See analogy of faith
analogy of faith, 167, 168–71
apostles, 23, 47, 51–52, 58, 116–29, 134, 141,
    147, 148, 156, 157, 181, 183, 198, 201, 209,
    220, 297
apostolic age, 52, 117, 119, 123, 147, 150
apostolic functions, 123–24, 125, 128, 181, 182,
    184
apostolic hermeneutic, 127, 140, 181, 184
apostolic imagination, 127, 140, 294. *See also*
    ecclesial imagination; imagination
apostolicity, 46, 56, 59, 61, 62, 132, 133, 134,
    297; as mark of the Spirit, 51–53
apostolic tradition, 10, 52, 53, 60, 65, 117, 118,
    123, 125–28, 129, 138, 141, 147, 180, 181, 219,
    294
approbative reception. *See* reception
Aquinas, 2, 3, 203, 262, 290n102
Augustine, 2, 65n7, 154n2, 171, 236, 262
authority, 18, 22, 23, 52, 57, 62, 95, 98, 115,
    116–52; apostolic, 116–29; and canon of
    Scripture, 116–152; *de facto,* 209, 211–14; *de
    jure,* 209–13, 218, 229, 284; diverse historical
    models of teaching, 185; effective, 207–14,
    275; the Gospel as the ultimate, 195, 196–
    97; grades of in church teachings, 211, 284,
    287; on individual, 18, 62, 95, 211, 218–19,
    229, 254, 268, 270; of the magisterium, 9,
    178, 179, 182, 183, 186, 189, 194, 197–200;
    the magisterium as a derived, 196, 197;

magisterium as the formal teaching, 195,
    208, 269, 283; of the Roman Curia, 271–72;
    of Scripture, 178–79; Scripture as the
    primary, 195–96, 197; of *sensus fidelium,* 183,
    186, 200–203; *sensus fidelium* as a derived,
    196, 197; of theology, 183–84, 186, 203–6,
    268; theology as a derived, 196, 197; three
    authorities in the one teaching office,
    193–207; tradition as the secondary, 195–96,
    197; Vatican I model of teaching, 189; the
    whole church as a preeminent yet derived,
    196, 197, 202
Avis, Paul, 227

Bailey, Kenneth, 97–98
Barth, Karl, 28, 54, 70
Basil the Great, St., 262
Bauckham, Richard, 97–98, 114–15
Bauer, Walter, 134
Beal, John, 190
Beinert, Wolfgang, 5, 201, 220, 226n35, 245,
    246, 248, 285
Bishop of Rome. *See* pope
bishops: 39, 47–48, 50, 59, 125, 128–129,
    148, 149, 160, 169, 171, 182, 183, 184, 185,
    187, 188, 189, 190, 191, 194, 198, 199, 200,
    201, 209, 215, 245, 246, 247, 251, 252, 253,
    268–74, 274–75, 279, 283–84, 287, 290;
    the individual as subject to faith of whole
    church, 270–71; individual *sensus fidei* of,
    215, 268–74; listening bishop and reception
    of *sensus fidelium,* 274–75. *See also*

The Eyes of Faith: The Sense of the Faithful & the Church's Reception of Revelation was designed and typeset in Adobe Garamond by Kachergis Book Design of Pittsboro, North Carolina. It was printed on 60-pound House Natural Smooth and bound by Sheridan Books of Ann Arbor, Michigan.